The Scottish Diaspora

Tanja Bueltmann, Andrew Hinson and Graeme Morton

EDINBURGH
University Press

For
Stewart the Goldfish (1992–)
Wish You Were Here

Edinburgh University Press Ltd
22 George Square, Edinburgh EH8 9LF
www.euppublishing.com

Typeset in 11/13 Ehrhardt by
Servis Filmsetting Ltd, Stockport, Cheshire,
printed and bound in Great Britain by
CPI Group (UK) Ltd, Croydon CR0 4YY

A CIP Record for this book is available from the British Library

ISBN 978 0 7486 4893 1 (hardback)
ISBN 978 0 7486 4892 4 (paperback)
ISBN 978 0 7486 4894 8 (webready PDF)
ISBN 978 0 7486 5062 0 (epub)

Contents

List of Figures, Tables and Maps   iv

1. Introduction   1
2. Diaspora: Defining a Concept   16

SECTION ONE   THEMES

3. Scotland: The Twa Lands   37
4. Scottish Migrants: Numbers and Demographics   56
5. The Emigration Experience   77
6. Encounters with Indigenous Peoples   95
7. Associational Culture   114
8. Return Migration   132

SECTION TWO   GEOGRAPHIES

9. Within the British and Irish Isles   153
10. The United States   171
11. Canada   188
12. Africa   204
13. Asia   222
14. The Antipodes   239

Epilogue   257
Bibliography   263
Index   294

Figures, Tables and Maps

FIGURES

2.1	Diaspora as category and concept	19
3.1	Index of average agricultural wages: Scotland and England & Wales, 1790–1900	46
3.2	Regional rates of employment growth: occupied males, 1851–1911	50
4.1	UK net migration: Scotland compared with England & Wales (excluding Ireland), 1841–1931	57
4.2	Decadal net migration (overseas and internal) expressed as percentage of natural increase: Scotland, England & Wales, 1841–1930	65
4.3	Net migration (overseas and internal) expressed as percentage of population: Scotland, England & Wales, 1841–1930	65
4.4	Percentage distribution of total emigration from Scotland by destination, 1853–1930	67
4.5	Scottish population growth by sex, 1801–1961	71
5.1	Emigrants bound for Canada boarding the *Metagama* at Glasgow docks, 1923	79
5.2	Nurse inspecting Hebridean children who are immigrating to Canada on board the *Marloch*	90
6.1	Large meeting of settlers and Maoris at a native village near Napier, Hawke's Bay, New Zealand	97
6.2	Buffalo Bill's Wild West Show Indians posing on rocks near Fraserburgh	103
7.1	Caledonian Society outside Commercial Hotel, Lockhart	121
7.2	Girl performing a Scottish dance at the American Highland Games in Greenwich, USA	126

8.1	Returning emigrants from New Zealand, Glasgow, 1940	138
9.1	Lord Mayor Sir James Millar of London with Caledonian Lodge members	165
10.1	Allan Pinkerton with Abraham Lincoln, c. 1861	181
11.1	Settlers in Western Canada	191
12.1	Mary Slessor and Mrs J. MacGregor at the Church of Scotland Foreign Mission, Calabar	211
12.2	Grantown-on-Spey soldiers enlisted to fight in the Anglo-Boer War	215
13.1	General Sir David Baird discovering the body of Sultan Tippoo Sahib after having captured Seringapatam on the 4 May 1799	225
13.2	Hong Kong, wood engraving by Frederick Grosse, 1866	232
14.1	Scottish immigrants bound for the Group Settlement Scheme, 1926	251

TABLES

3.1	Annual average percentage increase in population	41
3.2	Crude birth rate and crude death rate, expressed per thousand people: Scotland and England 1755–6 and 1861	41
3.3	Comparative population growth: Scotland, England & Wales and Ireland, 1755–1951	42
3.4	Scotland's sheep, 1870–1901	47
3.5	Main production categories: Scotland, 1841–1951	49
3.6	Urban percentage of total population in selected territories, 1700–1800	52
3.7	Percentage population in Scottish towns, showing increase over previous decade	52
4.1	Overseas emigration from Europe by country and by decade, 1851–1960	58
4.2	Overseas emigration, 1851–1913: average annual rate per 1,000 population	59
4.3	Proportion of migrants enumerated elsewhere in UK	60
4.4	Estimates of Scottish migration, 1600–1700	62
4.5	Birth and death rates, population change and emigration: England & Wales and Scotland, 1861–1920	64
4.6	Net out-migration from Scotland, 1861–1920	66
4.7	Emigration from Scotland to non-European destinations, in thousands, and as percentage, 1853–1930	68
4.8	Principal Canadian destinations of sample of highland and lowland emigrants in 1871	69

4.9   Population growth and sex distribution, 1755–1961   70
4.10   Internal migration: all females to all men in 1881   71
4.11   Sex ratios of Scots in New Zealand: NZSG and PNZ surveys   72
4.12   Percentage of females married at 20–24 years, Scottish and New
        Zealand regions, 1878, 1881   72
4.13   British and Irish as percentage of foreign-born in New Zealand
        and in asylums   73
4.14   Stature of Australian Imperial Forces and Canadian
        Expeditionary Forces enlistees by birth region   74
9.1   Scots migrants to other parts of the UK, per decade, 1841–1931   155
9.2   Scots-born in England and Wales, 1841–1951   156
9.3   Administrative counties and large towns in England with the
        highest proportion of natives of Scotland (1911)   157
14.1   Scots as a percentage of the total population and foreign-born
        population in New Zealand   247
14.2   National composition of UK immigrants to New Zealand   247
14.3   Estimated percentages of Scots in relation to the Australian
        population   248
14.4   Scots as a percentage of the total population and foreign-born
        population in Australia   248

MAP

8.1   Map of William McHutcheson's trip   143

CHAPTER I

Introduction

'Scotsmen', observed *Chambers's Edinburgh Journal*, 'are proverbially inclined to roam abroad in quest of fortune. This is true not less of the humble than of the higher ranks'.[1] The Scots' wanderlust has been a notable characteristic indeed, with an estimated 2.33 million Scots making their way across the Atlantic or to the Antipodes between 1825 and 1938 alone. In view of these numbers, the upsurge in scholarly interest in Scottish migration history does not surprise, and has seen demographers, sociologists and historians explore the causes and consequences of migration from Scotland to a multitude of destinations near and far. There is as yet, however, no comprehensive examination of Scottish diaspora history in which 'diaspora' moves beyond its traditional use as a category describing the movement of people through outward migration, commonly identifying victimhood and exile as its key characteristics. The idea of such an 'enforced diaspora'[2] of Scots is largely misleading. What we offer here is an alternative definition of diaspora: as a concept that captures diasporic actions and consciousness by tracing not only the tradition of Scottish emigration from the failure of the late-seventeenth-century Darien venture through to 1945, but also the Scots' as agents in diaspora, their diaspora experiences and interactions with different host societies, and the impact of the diaspora upon Scotland.

Split into sections that address key theories, themes and geographies, the book captures the diverse settlement experiences of the Scots overseas. Bringing themes and geographies together in this way, and underpinning them with central theoretical concepts and primary material, will provide readers with a unique opportunity to assess the movement of Scots abroad, as well as their impact in the new worlds in which they settled, including places often overlooked such as South-east Asia. The book's comparative focus and its broad time-frame give recognition to the distinctive developments in a diverse range of Scottish diaspora locations, spanning the 'near diaspora' of England and Ireland to as far afield as New Zealand.

A   WHAT MAKES A SCOT?

In late October 2012, shortly after the Scottish and UK governments had signed the Edinburgh Agreement which sets out how both governments will 'work together to ensure that a referendum on Scottish independence can take place',[3] Jon Kelly raised the question whether there is a 'formula for Scottishness' in the *BBC News Magazine*. 'It's not about being able to tolerate the sound of bagpipes, or preferring Irn Bru to Coca-Cola', noted Kelly, '[i]nstead, it all comes down to where you bide – that is, live.'[4] Whatever one's stance on the matter of Scottish independence, the referendum has brought to the fore the question of what makes a Scot – and what criteria can be used to establish it. First, and for the purpose of the referendum, 'Scottishness' is determined by **residency** in Scotland. This means that while people born in England now living in Scotland will be able to cast a vote in the independence referendum, Scots living in England – or elsewhere in the UK and abroad – will not. The choice to focus on residency has come at the expense of a second criterion: that of **citizenship**. This complicates matters for two reasons. First, there is no Scottish citizenship at present but there is British citizenship and nationality – hence a citizenship of the very constitutional arrangement that is being challenged by the referendum. Secondly, at the time of writing, those Scots who have relocated abroad do not lose their UK citizenship after applying successfully, for example, for Canadian or Australian citizenship. With that in mind: is their interest in the future of Scotland any less valid than that of English or Welsh-born residents of Scotland? For the purpose of the referendum, where residency in Scotland trumps citizenship, it would be. In an independent Scotland, however, the story might be a very different one if the Scottish National Party (SNP) remained in office as it seeks to entitle émigré Scots to citizenship in very much the same way as Ireland does. By bringing into the mix the criterion of **descent** beyond the first generation – the Irish model potentially entitles even the great-grandchildren of Irish citizens to acquire Irish citizenship – a large number of next-generation Scots from throughout the diaspora could become citizens in an independent Scotland. As the leader of the SNP Alex Salmond has noted, 'the maximum entitlement to citizenship' is their goal, using Scotland's 'global reach in the most effective way'.[5] Such ideas for the future of an independent Scotland are underpinned by homecoming policies designed to encourage next-generation Scots to return, there being the assumption that, as ethnic descendants of the homeland, these returnees are culturally similar to the Scottish population. At this juncture of UK identity politics and constitutional debate, the question of the role played by descent is, of course, strongly politicised. It is not, however, a novel one, nor one confined to taking place in Scotland. In late 1928 and early 1929, for example, a contribution about what made a 'bona-fide Scot' that first appeared on the pages of Edinburgh's *Weekly Scotsman* was picked up by both Australian and New Zealand newspapers. 'Must one be born in Scotland of Scots parentage?' asked the writer, concluding:

> I understand that in Canada there are hosts of children of Canadian birth who speak only Gaelic, the language of their parents or even grandparents. Are not these young Gaels as much Scots as if they had been born at Auchtermuchty, Auld Reekie, or Glasgow?[6]

Beyond residency and citizenship as potential criteria for defining what makes a Scot lie a plethora of other measures of Scottishness that can suitably be grouped under the heading of **ethno-cultural identity**. While many outward symbols of that identity, including those adopted from the Highlands such as bagpipes and the kilt, are often dismissed as either cultural remnants of a past long gone or modern fabrications,[7] for many a Scot and next-generation descendant, they nonetheless hold strong meaning. This is the case too because they are so easily identifiable. As Scottish writer and comedian Janey Godley notes, '[t]he main thing I love about Scottish identity is that it travels . . . It's not hard to figure out. The scenery, Billy Connolly, haggis . . . everyone recognises it straight away.'[8] Scots have utilised many such symbols for the purpose of connecting with other Scots abroad ever since they first departed from Scotland – a factor that has contributed to their perceived 'clannishness'. This, *The Scotsman* reported in 1860, certainly set the Scots apart from the English, stating that

> the old story of the two Oxford men, belonging to the same College, who meet at the crater of Vesuvius and didn't speak because they had not been introduced, is scarcely a caricature of the frosty reserve with which our southern neighbours treat one another in 'foreign parts'.[9]

For the purpose of this study the inclusion of ethno-cultural identity in the definition of what makes a Scot is certainly crucial: be it through their own actions or through the ascriptions of others, Scots maintained ethnic boundaries in diverse ways and it is, in part, through these boundaries that we can identify them as a distinct diaspora group today. Moreover, for many, ethnicity, and an active expression of it, was by no means an obstacle to life in new worlds.[10] Physically removed from the homeland yet with many migrants and next-generation Scots still strongly connected and oriented towards it, expressions of a Scottish identity overseas facilitated the maintenance of that connection, promoting a global Scottish World. Looking at it in this way, we can only speak of 'the Scots' when we categorise the *Scottish* diaspora since it would make no sense to divide Protestant from Catholic, lowland from highland, or second generations of English and Irish migrants into Scotland who then emigrated abroad.

B APPROACHING THE SCOTTISH DIASPORA

Having established what criteria might make a Scot, the test for a definition of diaspora is how well the concept supports scholarly investigation of the people who left the homeland in which they were raised to live their life in another country. The first issue we draw attention to is the length of time one lives outside the homeland. Does being part of Scotland's diaspora require permanent settlement? There are two distinct cases where permanency is not an intention: the seasonal migrant and the sojourner. A seasonal migrant is someone who leaves his or her homeland in search of work. They might never secure employment or that work might be academic instruction, but the principle is that people leave their homes on a seasonal basis to secure work in another part of the country, or outside their homeland, to then return at the end of the season. This pattern would be repeated each year. A sojourner is also someone who intends to return to the homeland. Again the search for employment is key, but rather than seasonal employment the sojourner intends to spend a specific period away from the homeland. The distinction is not always clear, and some Scottish sojourners worked seasonally in Canada before returning home each year, but the guiding principle is the temporary stay. Relocating for a set time outside of Scotland, the intention of the sojourner is always to return, ideally after raising sufficient funds to enable economic advance in Scotland.

Muddying the waters further is the indentured migrant. In this case the migrant is travelling overseas with insufficient funds for the cost of the journey or the wherewithal for establishing a life upon arrival, and opts to sign an indenture. Such an agreement may take many forms, but is generally along the lines of performing an agreed period of service in exchange for the cost of passage to a new country and some level of accommodation and sustenance. In some instances a return ticket was also part of the bargain, but the majority of Scottish indentured servants were looking for a permanent move.

A subcategory of all three is the Scottish migrant overseas who moves to another overseas territory of Empire or country where the Scottish diaspora is to be found. These movements could be seasonal, temporary or funded by indenture, and while identified mostly with British subjects not born within the British Isles, they did include the movement of Scots as economic opportunities arose. What the example of this migration highlights is the global scope of the movement of Scots; that movement was not always one-directional, and it certainly was not always finite.

Acknowledging the danger of simplification there is validity in employing the most straightforward definition of the people of the diaspora: establishing a permanent or semi-permanent change of national residence.[11] But the length of time, the intention to stay, and the financial commitment to that migration pinpoint a range of subcategories. Return migrants include those who always intended to return, but also those who were forced to return because of illness, financial straits, homesickness, or deportation for criminal activity.

An important element in the classical definition of a diaspora is that the movement of people from the homeland or territory was the result of directly enforced eviction or from some other economic or physical threat that compelled people to leave. Baumann notes that the creation of a diaspora resulting from 'emotion-laden connotations of uprootedness, precariousness and homesickness' of dislocation provides explanation for ethnic associational culture that clings to the Old World.[12] One can present evidence that no group was victimised out of Scotland. The last civil war on British soil was the battle of Culloden in 1746, and involved land and cultural confiscations, and some but no mass exiles; not banned from worship in the modern period, in 1829 Roman Catholics were freed of the restrictions on holding office and government position in Britain; in 1832 the electoral franchise was opened to those men who owned property to the value of £10 although not until 1929 were women and men granted equal access to the ballot box. Those Irish fleeing famine were not denied entry to Scotland or England, although a claim for relief was met with an invitation to return across the Irish Sea to the parish of birth. Indeed, London and later Glasgow can attribute the openness of British society for the growth of each city's Jewish community, a number of whom arrived fleeing Russian persecution in the 1870s.

Short-distance migration was carried out when work was needed. Workers would circle the countryside and the towns around their home as opportunities dictated, and in some sense this migration was multi-directional as the cyclical economy worked its way over time. Like temporary migration, this may not have involved a break in society, so that the migrant was still operating within the rhythms and mores of the familiar. Nor was it unusual for employment to be gained upon the good word of a relative. Before trades unions and employment exchanges, some industries only employed people on the basis of family reputation or other connection. The shipyards and the skilled trades offer examples of this kind of hiring process.

Migrating overseas in an attempt to secure better employment was a personal decision about self-improvement. But this, and the choice of destination, was also cognisant of family, friends and other known information. Chain migration is the term used for migrants who trod a pathway to a settlement trailed by those known to them: the wife following the husband, the grandmother joining her grandchildren, the brother joining his sister, the villager joining villager and the clan member joining those of the clan. Chain migration is important to gain understanding of why there is clustering both in the departure and the settlement of migrants. As we will see in the numerical analysis of Chapter 3, there was no random distribution of leavers and settlers with identifiable clusters at the end of each 'chain'. The destination offered advice and knowledge to the migrant, information that was otherwise difficult to acquire, especially in earlier periods. The chain tends to refer to longer migrations where the destination was less knowable and the cost of return, and therefore the imperative to make the migration work and to be successful over a longer period of time, was greatest. Longer distances were travelled more often as the technology of transportation made the journey easier and more frequent, and the opportunity cost of the passage less.[13]

As part of the chain, the town may have drawn in migrants from its hinterland and this fits with the concept of step migration. Migrants tend to have experience of short-term and temporary moves before making longer-distance migrations. We find distances of a few miles in the pre-industrial period, and longer distances in the industrial period, although not elongated by the arrival of the railway as it might be assumed. The decision to move to elsewhere in Britain, or overseas, was often presaged by a local move. We find steps in the migrant's history – short- and medium-distance movements before a longer journey with the intention of permanent settlement was undertaken.

Within this wider context of the diverse types of migration and movement overseas, we suggest that analysis of Scotland as a nation vis-à-vis the English nation is no longer tenable in light of the wealth of Scotland's history now found within diasporian scholarship and the number of Scots about whom this history is written. This idea follows in the footsteps of J. G. A. Pocock's call for a four-nation approach to British history,[14] giving recognition to the distinct experiences of Britain's constituent parts both at home and abroad. Within this wider framework, the concept of diaspora allows us to escape the tyranny of the nation-state.[15] This follows because diasporic actions are, by definition, transnational, crossing borders through migration. Moreover, diasporic actions are also often facilitated by communication networks that span not only the distance between old and new worlds, but reach across the globe.[16] For these networks to develop, however, Scots first needed to make their way to destinations beyond Scotland's borders.

Significant levels of Scottish emigration can be traced back as far as the late fourteenth century. Early destinations included France, the Low Countries, Scandinavia and England, where Scots pursed economic, educational and military opportunities.[17] An estimated 10,000 Scottish soldiers served in France during the fifteenth century, while the Scottish presence of pedlars was such in Denmark that the King acted in 1496 to restrict their activities.[18] Recent studies on Scottish-Polish relations also highlight the growing trade between the two nations with tax records for the period 1469–71 showing a considerable number of names of Scottish merchants.[19] Both soldiers and pedlars emigrated in increasing numbers to Prussia, Denmark, Sweden and Poland-Lithuania in the sixteenth century, there being small but distinctive communities of Scots scattered throughout these territories.[20]

Some change occurred in the pattern of migration following the Scottish Reformation, most notably among the allegiances of Scottish soldiers as a result of the subsequent changes in political alliances. Thousands of Scots, for example, joined their fellow Calvinists during the Dutch Revolt against Spain in 1568, beginning an association with the Dutch military which would last until 1780, the outbreak of the Fourth Anglo-Dutch War.[21] Scots also served in increasing numbers in the Protestant armies of Denmark-Norway and Sweden including 1,600 Scots who were levied for Sweden in the 1570s, and it was during the Thirty Years War (1618–48) that the Scottish military presence in Europe peaked.

While mercenary motivation cannot be dismissed as the primary reason why so many Scots became involved, recent research has given more credence to theological and dynastic loyalty as factors.[22] Certainly the marriage of James VI's daughter Elizabeth Stuart to Frederick V, the Elector of Palatinate in 1613, formed a strong connection between the Scots and Protestant Germany which had serious implications when events in Europe began to unfold. This occurred in 1619 when Archduke Ferdinand II of Austria was deposed by Bohemian Protestant nobility who crowned Frederick, making Elizabeth the new Queen of Bohemia. When Habsburg forces attacked Bohemia, many of the Scottish nobility and gentry came to the defence of Queen Elizabeth and her family. The war in Bohemia drew in many Scots and led to a significant Scottish presence in several European armies thereafter, including 1,500 Scots who were recruited to the Bohemian army and who fought alongside 1,000 men 'borrowed' from the Scottish forces in the Dutch Republic.[23]

Scots were also involved in Danish and Swedish campaigns, some 13,700 entering the Danish army between 1626 and 1629 alone, and 25,000 serving in the Swedish campaigns over the whole conflict.[24] Elsewhere, 11,000 joined the French army while many continued to enlist in the army of the Dutch Republic. This does not include the many Scots who were already living abroad, including 900 members of the Scottish diaspora who were recruited by the Poles.[25] In all, 48,080 official warrants were issued by the Scottish Privy Council for the anti-Habsburg armies throughout the course of the war. While questions exist over the validity of this figure, recent scholarship does estimate the Scottish military presence at around 50,000, not including the several thousand who served in the armies of the Habsburgs and their allies. If correct, 20 per cent of the adult Scottish male population was engaged in the war.[26]

Many of the Scots who fought in the Thirty Years War remained abroad after it was brought to an end in 1648. This was in part due to the Cromwellian conquest of Scotland in 1650 which spurred another exodus of soldiers among uprising Scots who were offered foreign service over imprisonment as an enticement to halt their activities. In 1689 a further exodus occurred, this time among Jacobite supporters following the accession of William of Orange to the Scottish throne, who dispersed themselves in armies as far apart as Russia, Sweden, France and Spain.[27] Although these were the last mass enlistments of Scots to non-British armies, as will be seen in this volume, it was by no means an end to Scotland's military presence abroad.

While not as numerically high, commercial migrations following the Reformation were also significant in this early period. Previously established Scottish communities continued to grow, with some estimates placing the number of Scots across Europe by the middle of the seventeenth century as high as 50,000.[28] Scottish pedlars were of sufficient magnitude to create tension with their host communities, being the subject of revoke in Norway and Poland-Lithuania. In 1624 Scots in Danzig complained to James VI about measures ordering 'the removal of all strangers' from the town, which they blamed on the arrival of poorer Scottish migrants fleeing meagre harvests at home. In response the King issued a proclamation prohibiting young people boarding ships without letters of invitation from relatives in Poland or proof of their ability to sustain themselves.[29] Gauging the number of Scots is fraught with problems but in Poland-Lithuania some 5,969 settled Scottish merchants have been identified, 500 of whom were in Danzig.[30]

Scottish communities abounded in Norway where they engaged in the timber trade, still known in Norway as the Skottehandelen ('the Scottish trade'), and in Sweden where Scots exerted significant influence over the Swedish iron industry. Scottish merchants enjoyed considerable political influence in Stockholm, and in Gothenburg where two seats on the council were reserved for members of the Scottish nation.[31] In the Netherlands, the city of Veere was another Scottish enclave, having been designated as the Scottish staple port of the Dutch Republic, through which all Scottish trade theoretically passed. A Scottish conservator remained in residence until 1799 during which time the city retained a small Scottish community.[32] The Scottish presence was larger in Rotterdam, the strength of which is evident from the establishment of a Scottish Kirk in 1642.

The earliest ventures 'abroad' also brought the Scots to the 'near diaspora' of England and Ireland. Be it London, Liverpool or Belfast, many early modern Scots were found working in trading houses or in private business. Scots have also been travelling to North America since the sixteenth century, but these very early movements were small in scale. Larger numbers of Scottish migrants only arrived in the United States from the late seventeenth and early eighteenth centuries. By 1729 the coastal areas around North Carolina were populated by Jacobites who were forced to emigrate after the failure of the 1715 uprising.[33] The largest migration, however, only occurred from the mid-nineteenth century, when significant portions not only of Scots but also migrants of many other European ethnic groups became part of what was the age of mass migration.

Whether we look at the earlier or later migratory streams, many are characterised by a combination of 'pull' and 'push' factors. While clearances and exile from the Highlands did not play as significant a role in Scottish migration as popular beliefs have it, they were a push factor for some. Crucial pull factors included the provision of free passages to particular destinations, but also economic facors, such as the discovery of gold. As a result, the gold rush in California in 1848–9 and the 1862 Homestead Act did much to attract impoverished Scots.[34] Other migrants from Scotland made it abroad in quest of an adventure. The example of the Orcadian doctor John Rae (1813–93) is an interesting one in this respect. He worked for the Hudson's Bay Company, a fur trading company in Canada, but was also an active surveyor and student of flora and fauna. He was interested in indigenous society – to the extent that there exists a portrait of him in full Cree dress.[35] So in this book we ask: did Scots leave because they expected to attain a higher standard of living than at home? We look at this from two directions, basing discussion on the information the Scots had and the impressions they gained from family, friends, agents and others they knew. Secondly, we look at the macro indicators that historians have used to evaluate the evidence. So while scholarship has moved to give greater attention to the colonies, 'to recover the decentralized narrative', equally we 'must be careful not to forget the centre and get lost in post modern antiquarianism.'[36]

C BUILDING A DIASPORA

We build our book from its foundations – the diaspora concept (Chapter 2). If a literary survey were conducted upon the state of historical scholarship on the Scots who lived in other nations of the world – say, as was current three or four decades ago – then the 'Scots abroad' or the 'Scots overseas' would be found, with no mention of the diaspora concept. A discrepancy from the language of today would also be found if the records of the Scottish Office in that period were compared to the current policy initiatives of the Scottish Government. And not just in Scotland, but internationally, too, there has been a flowering in the use of the term 'diaspora' in recent decades to describe and analyse nationals who live their lives in countries outside their natal or ancestral home. The interest comes in the potential of the diaspora concept to help scholarship and policy analysts make sense of various aspects of human agency that are attached to the action of migration. The creation and promotion of ethnic identity, of ethnic boundaries, of group and associational behaviour, enacted in relationship to a homeland – be it a longing to return or a sense of rejection or alienation – diasporic living is an inescapable social phenomenon. A phenomenon, indeed, that is profoundly widespread. Between 1815 and 1914, some 55 to 60 million migrants left Europe for the New World – a number almost equivalent to the whole population of the UK today. The history of that movement has shaped the sending and hosting nations, recalibrating geopolitical, economic and political power on a massive scale. It is not simply the movement that is of interest to scholars, while greatly significant in itself, it is the new societies, the new economies, the new politics and new worlds created in the 'New World', and the relationship of the 'New' with the 'Old'.

Scots, we know, were prodigious migrants, and have been throughout their history. In Chapter 3 we present the Scotland they left behind. From the conclusion of the 1745 Jacobite uprising until the end of the Second World War, Scotland's society and structure underwent fundamental change. For one, the nation's population increased fourfold. Most of that growth happened before 1901 and the rise in Scotland's population was always less than in England and Wales. A major reason was that per capita rates of out-migration were always greater north of the border. Scotland, we show here and in Chapter 4, was one of Europe's greatest exporters of people. But it was not simply a consequence of taking to heart the predictions of the Revd Thomas Malthus that persuaded Scots to migrate. Population pressure upon insufficiently productive land was a fundamental challenge to Scots' generational stability. This was not necessarily new, for the Scots were already habitual movers – to Europe, to England and to Ireland, and back again – following work seasonally to the towns and regions alike. Life was marked by fragility, of income and food, but also distinguished by transformation, in rates of urbanisation and the shift from an agricultural to an industrial workforce. The Scots' standard of living was slowly on the rise, and the people were hurrying to the towns and into industrial jobs, but so were those migrating abroad, and relocating to England and Ireland. And despite decadal fluctuation, they did so in ever increasing flows. Just how great were those flows, and where the Scots ended up, is the subject of Chapter 4. By examining this socio-economic transformation we explore whether Scots who migrated to the towns went directly from the countryside, or took a number of 'steps' in order to try their hand in a nearby settlement before making the decision to head for the jute mills of Dundee or the thread-making factories of Paisley. Alternatively, did these men, women, kin and clan decide to head straight for Greenock and a transatlantic voyage to North America? The Victorian statistician Ernest Georg Ravenstein's produced eleven 'laws of Migration' to explain this movement, and we put his laws and the evidence to the test (pp. 58–63).

The decision to migrate is just that: a decision. However much agency this involves is a matter for the case at hand. The transported criminal would certainly have less say in the decision than the gold-prospector encouraged by a new find in California leading him to down tools and get on the first boat out. The emigrant experience examined in Chapter 5 weighs up the information Scots were exposed to when considering the option of departure. Did the boat have proper passenger decks, was the captain honest, was the boat new, was it under sail or steam? The on-board experience, the welcome that awaited them, and the land and job opportunities they found, are part of the experience of diasporic Scots, and the formative knowledge of potential migrants that circulated at home.

The uncertainty Scots exhibited on their first encounters with indigenous peoples of the New World is exposed in Chapter 6. Orcadians picked up at Stromness for work with the Hudson's Bay Company were some of the first Scots to encounter Native people with any regularity, and some of the first to marry and raise mixed-race families despite initial opposition from their employer. A strong narrative of affinity between highland Scots and indigenous peoples has been suggested because of the commonality of their experiences in the face of the processes of 'civilisation' and imperial expansion. Certainly there is evidence of Scots' material culture permeating Native society, as well as trade in the opposite direction. Scots learnt of indigenous culture from guidebooks, art works, and from high-profile visits, including the Ojibbeway tribe who toured Scotland in the 1840s, or from American icon William Cody's 'Buffalo Bill Wild West Show', which he brought to Glasgow in 1891 and 1904, on the second occasion also touring the troupe around the north-east in three special trains. Yet the majority of Scots migrants accepted the forced removal of indigenous people from the land, and were keen to procure the best properties for themselves.

The Scots were well aware of the hardship of life in the New World and admired Native peoples for their abilities and knowledge of successful settlement. Helping fellow Scots to find their feet upon disembarking the boat has been a feature of Scots' settlement from the off. The oldest charitable society in America, the Scots Charitable Society of Boston (founded in 1657), was just such a provision. Philanthropic help from St Andrew's societies in North America, and cultural, political and social help through Caledonian and sporting societies in the Antipodes – examined in Chapter 7 – have helped Scots to mark their ethnic boundaries: these societies, and the annual commemoration of Robert Burns or St Andrew, can also be found in Argentina, China, India, Japan and more places besides. Associationalism also involved the Scots transplanting their culture to new settlements. Not just adapting the institutions they found upon arrival, giving them a tartan tinge, as it were, but bringing over their own institutions, unadulterated, and helping to build new societies from that basis.

Scots philanthropic and cultural societies were formed to help migrants to integrate, find jobs and social networks, and meet a need to be amongst one's own kind. Not all Scots did remain, or ever wanted to stay, and the emigrant experience includes those who returned to Scotland – the theme of Chapter 8. And while associational culture signals the Scots' presence in the diaspora, return migration indicates the fluidity of this experience. One third or more migrants were thought to have returned to Scotland throughout the 1870–1914 period. Some travelled back and forward seasonally, or yearly, while others only ever intended to emigrate for a short period of time, sojourning in the hope of making enough money to advance their lives upon return. The mercenary soldier or the Indian trader – the 'nabobs' – or the slave drivers were examples. With the return of Scots people, so came the arrival of new ideas and ideologies. Visiting Scots searching out their ancestors are another category again. The so-called roots tourists were a feature of mature migration, of descendants rather than first-generation migrants returning to their natal home.

With such numbers re-establishing their lives in Scotland, despite the momentousness of the decision to leave in the first place, Chapter 9 explores why more Scots did not choose to migrate within the British and Irish Isles. It was closer, it was (mostly) under the same state, and the climate, social conditions and people were familiar. London was the preferred location for those that did migrate south, and the towns and counties closest to the Scottish border were preferred over more distant non–Metropolitan destinations. Only in the inter-war decades of the twentieth century did more Scots emigrate to England and Wales than overseas and, by 1951, over 600,000 Scots-born people were enumerated there – enough to comprise Scotland's second largest city after Glasgow. In this case, Scots were moving to an economy and society even more mature than their own, and in England and Ireland they came upon two great rivals amongst Europe's leading migratory peoples. Still, the Scots who went were part of the diaspora, retaining an orientation to home and a sense of difference, creating associational and religious institutions to help with both.

On the whole, migrating Scots preferred to look outside the British and Irish Isles for their new life, and after a slow start before the 1760s, their main preference was 'Amerikay' (Chapter 10). 'A dance called America' summed up this passion, as the dancers twirled round and round, bringing everyone in to join them 'till the whole neighbourhood was afloat'. From soldier settlement in Georgia to family settlement in New York, North Carolina and Chicago, the Scots flocked across the Atlantic to America. Scots were instrumental in the ideas behind the Declaration of Independence, with Scots-trained John Witherspoon a signatory as well as the first president of the college we know as Princeton University. This was an intellectual exchange that has sustained scholarly connections as well as affinities in popular culture, from philosophical and medical training, to the cowboy and the cultural pull of the western amongst Scotland's cinema-going public of the 1930s.

Before America took the crown as the destination of choice, Canada – for its 'Britishness' – had a particular hold over Scots (Chapter 11). The Scots were involved in the fur and timber trade and in explorations across this great land mass. Canada provides some of the best examples of chain migration. The Earl of Selkirk's purchase of land in Prince Edward Island where he planned to settle 800 highlanders is an instructive example of planting a settlement, linking it with home, and of attempts to intervene against increasingly high odds. From settling first in the Maritimes, the Scots increasingly settled further west, encouraged by the agents employed by Minister for Immigration Clifford Sifton and the Canadian Pacific Railway to take them into the interior.

Africa, by contrast, experienced few Scottish settlers until the twentieth century, but had been a destination for many a missionary, soldier and sojourner prior to that – Mungo Park, David Livingstone and Mary Slessor were Victorian heroes for their missionary work in Africa (Chapter 12). Scots, inevitably with their trading influence, were involved in the slave trade through their work in London and on the plantations in the Caribbean, but there was much popular and intellectual opposition to the practice, and the Scottish ports did not figure as London and Liverpool did in the transportation of slaves. Indeed it was as soldiers and miners that Scots left a second lasting impression on Africa, with the result that numbers settling increased most in the first decades of the twentieth century.

Enterprise, and being enterprising, characterised the Scottish diaspora in Asia (Chapter 13). Working within the formal and informal trading opportunities of the British Empire, the nations of the Far East became 'business outposts' for Scottish sojourners. Before trade westward to North America picked up, Scots looked to Bombay, Madras and Calcutta, often reached first by a Scottish presence in the East Indian Company and the trading houses of London. Military patronage led to commercial patronage, and the Scots benefitted from post-Union access to those networks. Of all the Scots trading companies, Jardine, Matheson & Co. were the most successful. Formed in 1832, and benefiting from trading in tea and opium, the partnership rose to become the largest British trading company before 1914. And there were other successes, too: twelve of the first seventeen trading houses in Singapore were Scottish.

Between 1861 and 1945 the Scots made up around 15 per cent of all UK-born migrants to Australia, which was a bigger proportion of Scots than in the UK (Chapter 14). From sending a much lower number of convicts to Australia than came from the English courts, Scots then arrived to work the land as they did in New Zealand. Scots migrants began increasingly to choose the two Antipodean destinations from the 1830s and 1840s, with organised migration schemes helping to swell the numbers. Otago, for instance, became the Scottish preference above all, and both countries encountered inflow as news spread of the discovery of gold. In the Antipodes, as in all the locations we examine, the Scots left a cultural legacy that continues to resonate.

Of all these legacies, perhaps none matches the Burns Supper as an outward sign of the Scottish diaspora. We devote our epilogue, then, to what is not the essential, but is undoubtedly the essentialist diasporan experience: 'The Immortal Memory of Robert Burns'.

NOTES

1. *Chambers's Edinburgh Journal*, 13 October 1849, p. 225.
2. Harper, *Emigration from Scotland between the Wars*, p. 1.
3. 'Agreement between the United Kingdom Government and the Scottish Government on a referendum on independence for Scotland', Edinburgh, 15 October 2012, http://www.scotland.gov.uk/About/Government/concordats/Referendum-on-independence (accessed 19 January 2013).
4. BBC News Magazine, 26 October 2012, http://www.bbc.co.uk/news/magazine-20048521 (accessed 19 January 2013).
5. *The Herald*, 17 January 2013.
6. *The Argus* (Melbourne), 15 December 1928; see also *Evening Post* (Wellington), 21 March 1929.
7. Most famously this argument has been made in Hobsbawm and Ranger (eds), *The Invention of Tradition*.
8. BBC News Magazine, 26 October 2012.
9. *The Scotsman*, 4 July 1860.
10. E.g. for 'working-class collectivism', see Belchem, 'Hub and diaspora', p. 24.
11. Lucassen and Lucassen, 'Migration, migration history, history', p. 32.
12. Baumann, 'Diaspora', p. 314.
13. Tilly, 'Migration in modern European history', pp. 53–6.
14. Pocock, 'British history'.
15. Akenson, 'The historiography of English speaking Canada and the concept of diaspora', p. 386.
16. For the extent of such networks and how they underpinned ethnic networks and associational life, see also Bueltmann and MacRaild, 'Globalizing St George'.
17. Devine, *Scotland's Empire*, p. 6.
18. Smout, Landsman and Devine, 'Scottish emigration', p. 77.
19. Bajer, *Scots in the Polish-Lithuanian Commonwealth*, p. 5 (Introduction).
20. Smout, Landsman and Devine, 'Scottish emigration', p. 77.

21. Murdoch and Mijers, 'Migrant destination', p. 323.
22. Murdoch, *Scotland and the Thirty Years' War*, p. 16.
23. Murdoch, 'Scotland, Europe and the English "missing link"', p. 893.
24. Murdoch, *Scotland and Thirty Years' War*, pp. 10 and 11.
25. Ibid., p. 13.
26. Ibid., p. 14.
27. Murdoch, 'Scotland, Europe and the English "missing link"', p. 894.
28. Ibid., p. 895
29. Smout, Landsman and Devine, 'Scottish emigration', p. 82.
30. Murdoch, 'Scotland, Europe and the English "missing link"', p. 897.
31. Ibid., p. 898.
32. Grosjean and Murdoch, 'Scottish communities abroad in the early modern period', p. 17.
33. Bryan, *Twa Tribes*.
34. Ibid.
35. Ibid.
36. Bayly, 'The British and indigenous peoples', p. 21.

CHAPTER 2

Diaspora: Defining a Concept

In this opening thematic chapter, the meaning of 'diaspora' is introduced. Quite deliberately the term is split two ways: diaspora is defined as a noun, a description of people; then as a verb, a description of actions.

Scholars develop concepts as analytical tools to better order and define complex evidence. They do this to gain insight into social behaviours and structures. Concepts are not facts, but ways of understanding. Forged chiefly in the balance of generalisation and case study where the median example is prioritised over the outlier, concepts can also be configured as 'ideal types' against which social behaviours are compared. Deepening explanatory power further is the application of social theory. Concepts are the base upon which social theories are derived. Social theory can inform concepts directly 'from above' (grand theory) and 'from below' (grounded theory). In so doing the notion of a dialectical relationship is added to explain the circularity of concept and theory, each modifying the other. In all cases, the definition of a concept must be clearly stated else analytical precision is lost.

The development and deployment of concepts is an established technique in both the social sciences and the humanities. Social class, gender and race are concepts comprehensively debated and refined by sociologists seeking insight into the rise of Western civilisation. Class, gender and race are also descriptive categories that allow observations to be gathered in the form of tallies and proportions.

The category of diaspora, traditionally associated with the movement of people, is an old one, but the concept of diaspora is relatively recent. Scholars have struggled to master either form because of the need for both interdisciplinarity and empirical knowledge of more than one national history. The observation that all of the world's peoples today can be regarded as part of the earliest diaspora out of Ethiopia and Africa more generally is suggestive of the challenge.[1] Moreover, migration in not unique to any one period: throughout human history people have walked and sailed to other places, often in tribes, groups or communities, and only archaeological evidence survives to illuminate journeys where no written records lie extant. For illegal immigrants it can be that records are created only after arrivals have been recognised by authorities, sometimes after generational distance. Yet as more and more variation of human experience is brought forward, allied to the inherently international and comparative nature of what is being described, a greater analytical range of instances compels us to adapt or replace previously established paradigms of diaspora. Consequently scholars such as Rogers Brubaker and Cairns Craig have questioned the validity of the very concept itself.[2] They, and those who follow their reasoning, argue that the term diaspora has lost functional value by its uncritical application to all kinds of migratory experiences. This bloating is all the more noticeable because the concept began from very narrow origins.

A AN EPISTEMOLOGY OF DIASPORAN STUDIES

From his standpoint as editor of the academic journal *Diaspora*, Khachig Tölölyan responded to the many examples of diaspora he encountered by inviting the journal's readership to submit illustrations of the most egregious deployment of the term in popular culture. Examples unearthed ranged from a 'corporate diaspora' where company restructuring resulted in middle managers dispersed from their jobs, to grisly murders and body parts dispersed as an 'anatomical diaspora'. Tölölyan's wider point is the casual acceptance within certain areas of academia that the British diaspora was, and should be, readily knowable to scholars without any great need for specialist precision.[3] Such uncritical use has been labelled by Rogers Brubaker as a '"diaspora" diaspora', in other words 'a dispersion of the meanings of the term in semantic, conceptual and disciplinary space'.[4]

The analytic worth of a concept is determined by its explanatory value. Ideally the concept is near universal in application and sufficiently robust over more than a short period of time. If semantically imprecise – being susceptible to misinterpretation – then the concept will be modified or abandoned all together. As a descriptive category of migration, the term diaspora is first used to identify those peoples who have left their nation's land and settled elsewhere. From its origins in Greek, the noun διασπορά derives from the composite verb 'dia-' and 'speirein'. In English the noun refers to a scattering: to peoples leaving one homeland and living amongst other peoples in their homeland.[5] In Greek diaspora means to scatter and disperse; in the original Hebrew the word means movement to any place, with no (minimum) limit on the number of places or the permanency of their relocation.

Diaspora has its lineage in Judaic and Christian traditions, with the description in Deuteronomy being one of forced dispersal:[6] 'The LORD shall cause thee to be smitten before thine enemies: thou shalt go out one way against them, and flee seven ways before them: and shalt be removed into all the kingdoms of the earth.'[7] From these etymological roots the category of diaspora stands in its elementary form as the peoples of a nation who have settled in at least two but up to and including multiple locations (where numbers are not so insignificant that no meaningful community of descent could be said to form).

B MIGRATION AND DIASPORA

Migrants, *tout court*, are not a diaspora as either category or concept. Migration is characterised by the seasonal and temporary removal from one's homeland. A migration might happen more than once in a year and is generalised as movement to a single destination. Migrants also leave permanently for a location or range of locations outside of the nation. But the straightforward fact of emigration does not in itself make a diaspora. If Scots only left their nation to live in England or only to live in Australia, the analysis would be in terms of migration. The same would be the case if Scots migrated to these two nations in very small numbers, for only short periods, perhaps seasonally, or with the firm intention of returning. Migrants can tick all the measurement criteria we would expect to find in diaspora, and indeed can be totalled together and presented as the category of diaspora, but in itself that is insufficient to define the concept.[8] To restate the distinction: the concept of diaspora is defined here as capturing diasporic actions. Importantly, this also acknowledges agency in diaspora, 'recognising that a diaspora is actively maintained, promoted and utilised by its members.'[9] This applies to the movement of peoples as it does to the movement of ideas. So while the spread of religion can be studied within a diaspora framework, the spread of adherents can be conceptualised as part of a diasporic consciousness.

Living and acting in diasporic ways defines the concept from which investigative purchase then flows. What, then, are the social phenomena – the diasporic actions – that are captured by this concept? The first core element is orientation to homeland as diasporic permanence co-exists with a desire to return. The active component here is sustaining a relationship with the homeland. An orientation to homeland is expressed by migrants and their descendants as a longing to return, and includes the homesick and those experiencing anomic disorientation by their life outside the nation of their birth. Moreover, the aspiration to return is often sustained throughout generations of descent. At this point the concept of ethnicity is brought into the analysis. Scottish migrants become Scottish diasporans because they prioritise their ethnicity through an orientation to home. Even if done by non–ethnic means,

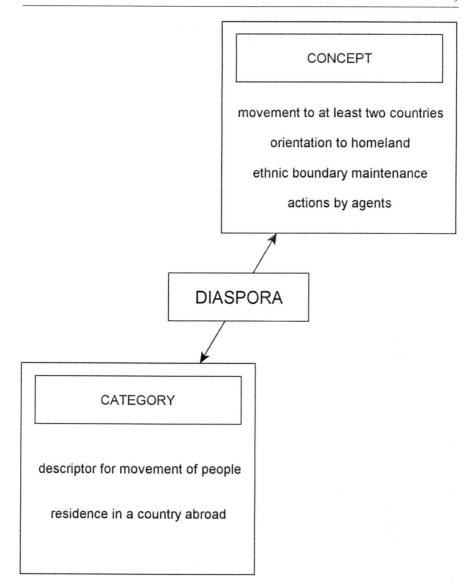

Figure 2.1 Diaspora as category and concept [source: the authors]

their boundary making demarcates an ethnic diaspora. Figure 2.1 summarises the central differences between diaspora as category and concept.

But the orientation to the old homeland also includes those who consciously reject it. There are migrants who maintain no wish to return, and there are those who are economically, physically, politically or legally unable to return; this includes those who are expulsed and exiled. Baumann identifies negativity in the earliest use of diaspora, with loss of homeland and forcible isolation being characteristic.[10] Here the parsing of diaspora presupposes departure was not always voluntary. The African diaspora, for example, was a creation of the sixteenth-century slave trade involving the forcible transportation of slaves to the Caribbean and to South and North America – perhaps as many as 12 million people over the period, with slavery not abolished within Britain until 1807, until 1833 within the British Empire, and until 1865 in the United States.[11] The greatest movement of Europeans happened when between 55 and 60 million people left their continent for distant parts of the globe in the period between the ending of the Napoleonic War and the start of the First World War.[12] In both these examples the reason for dispersal is narrowly stated: an element of direct force precipitated flight from a homeland, even if only for a minority. For some scholars that is a necessary pre-condition of a diaspora definition. The history of the Jewish people from the eighth century until the creation of Israel in 1948 is a widely cited example of diaspora for this very characteristic. Scholars including critics point out that until recently the Jewish example did not simply categorise a diaspora but conceptualised the phenomenon.[13]

The adjective 'force' marks out the conceptual definition of diaspora from other movements because social action is so strongly shaped by the nature of departure. In some contemporary accounts, and most commonly in popular memory, the Scottish diaspora has been framed by the forcible clearance of highland and crofting families, even when the history of diaspora – such as the Scots in Europe – pre-dates these historical events. Reference to victimhood and exile has given credence to the Scottish example being redolent of the Jewish case.[14] Burning cottages and physical threat backed up by the rule of law, police and military force compelled short- and long-distance migration. There is also the economic rationale to migrate, with the choice being starvation or a life of subsistence poverty. Compulsion, then, was another imperative to stand alongside forcible eviction, but even here one must assign agency to migrants however unfavourable the circumstances or ideology faced. Women were generally much more reluctant to emigrate than men – with potential domestic servants noted for pulling out 'at the eleventh hour' of the journey to New Zealand.[15] Yet overwhelmingly the migrations from Scotland and Britain were voluntary without any direction or organisation from local or central government. As Shepperson has noted:

> it was not within the British tradition to actively foster emigration or colonization . . . what national state could or would tell its people that they could no longer exist at home, but were only wanted or needed by distant colonies or a foreign power?[16]

This is not to suggest that infrastructural and institutional encouragement was absent from the emigration policies of successive governments – Empire

Settlement schemes after the First World War provide one example – but expulsion and banishment were one part, insufficient on their own to create the Scottish diaspora.

Both category and concept of diaspora assume permanence in another land after migration, but here the category encounters porosity. Permanent residency after migration is not a choice made without acceptance from the host nation. When dealing with major movements of people, legal and bureaucratic definitions may be all we have to hand. The consequence of deploying administrative definitions is that groupings and coherence are assigned to migrants in ways that generally stand distinct from theoretically or empirically defined understandings. Over time the host country will classify migrants under different headings depending on political expediency, labour market needs, and perceived or real national threats. Migrants may be admitted when there are labour shortages for unskilled labourers, skilled workers or trained professionals; others may be admitted on humanitarian grounds as refugees fleeing religious or military threat, or granted right of settlement on the grounds of long-standing colonial relations. Significant movements of Indians within the territories of the British Empire for example were part of wider trends in inter-diasporan movement. There are also limits on those qualifying categories, with particular groups, or races, excluded from some countries. Australia operated a 'whites only' immigration policy in the years from the Immigration Restriction Act 1901 until a softening of the restrictions in the 1960s and 1970s. In response to near neighbour Japan entering the Second World War in 1941, Australian Prime Minister John Curtin declared '[t]his country shall remain forever the home of the descendants of those people who came here in peace in order to establish in the South Seas an outpost of the British race'.[17]

Some migrants had no wish for permanent residency. Gypsies, tinkers and tramps are continually on the move, within the same country, and across countries.[18] With neither the right to permanent residence in the receiving country, nor emotive connection to a homeland, nor even an acknowledged homeland to return to, such transients are outliers to the definition of diaspora and are in most cases treated separately. With transient peoples there was not, nor could there be, a myth of return.[19]

C DISPERSING THE CONCEPT

Despite emphasis on actions orientated to homeland as an idealised place of eventual return or as a place of rejection, difficulties in definition and the transnational nature of the evidence have meant practitioners of diaspora studies remain as fleeting as their subject matter. Labour, trading and religious dispersions have also been labelled diasporas for maintaining some element of connection with home, yet really their primary characteristic is their dispersion above all else.[20] Armstrong's shaping of the debate pins the diasporic label 'to any ethnic collectivity which lacks a territorial base within a given polity'.[21] The many who have followed his migratory focus help explain the proliferation of studies in the academy, coincident with the mass movements of peoples that evolved from labour and immigration policies of the 1960s.[22] The technologically improved ease with which people relocate to other countries and the proliferate international division of labour and outsourcing of employment consequent of globalisation have meant heavy flows of people, with governments then adapting their immigration policies to fit domestic needs.

The enhanced immediacy of connecting people that followed developments such as international agreement on standard time, the transatlantic telegraphic cable, and the steamship, let alone the immense communication advances that then followed, have encouraged scholars to conceive of diasporic actions in ways that do not require either specific territories or an empirical migratory connection. Long-distance nationalists can shape the politics of a homeland to which they have no direct association, yet their actions be claimed as analogous to a diaspora. The Republican movement in Ireland has received significant financial help from Americans at various times since the mid-nineteenth century, not all of whom have Irish ancestry. In Quebec the Francophone and Anglophone communities have each been assigned internal coherence as well as the connections of an international diaspora that is deterritorialised other than through a loosely conceived loyalty to France and Great Britain respectively. Such examples question how much a diaspora is, by necessity, defined in relation to the territory of a homeland over an imagined community. The dislocation of two world wars, and the proliferation of refugees fleeing ethnic and religious conflicts have also added new case studies that have pushed for inclusion, to the extent a 'Diasporama' has now formed.[23] Inevitably this dispersion of the term compromises its analytical value by hollowing out rather than deepening understanding with nuance – a situation exacerbated in most university departments where the required personal and institutional commitment for Area Studies is downplayed in favour of national histories. Focus is primarily directed upon (only) one sending nation and two or more host nations where the historian's case study erects geopolitical limits to the research. Historians also prefer to periodise their research as either pre-modern or industrial, tending not to study cycles of movement throughout history. And attention predominantly, and almost exclusively for the modern period, has examined transatlantic migration from Europe to the New World, ignoring intra-territorial movements such as within the British Empire.[24]

D   MAXIMUM AND MINIMUM PRE-CONDITIONS

The history of international migration is one of people moving from their country of birth to reside for a period of time in another country. The story of diaspora is of the people from one country moving to two or more different countries, conceiving attachment and longing to their homeland, and engaging in activities that can form ethnic boundaries in distinction to other ethnicities and nationalities. Fitting the discussion so far presented, William Safran's schemata – based on the Jewish diaspora – defines the concept of diaspora as an ideal type:

1. They, or their ancestors, have been dispersed from a specific original 'center' to two or more peripheral, or foreign, regions.
2. They retain a collective memory, vision, or myth about their original homeland – its physical location, history, achievements, and, often enough, sufferings.
3. Their relationship with the dominant element of society in the hostland is complicated and often uneasy. They believe that they are not, and perhaps cannot be, fully accepted by their host society and therefore feel partly alienated and insulated from it.
4. They regard their ancestral homeland as their true, ideal home and as the place to which they or their descendants would (or should) eventually return – if and when conditions are appropriate.
5. They continue to relate, personally or vicariously, to that homeland in one way or another, and their ethno-communal consciousness and solidarity, which reach across political boundaries, are importantly defined in terms of the existence of such a relationship. That relationship may include a collective commitment to the maintenance or restoration of their original homeland and to its independence, safety, and prosperity. The absence of such a relationship makes it difficult to speak of transnationalism.
6. They wish to survive as a distinct community – in most instances as a minority – by maintaining and transmitting a cultural and/or religious heritage derived from their ancestral home and the symbols based on it. In so doing, they adapt to hostland conditions and experiences to become themselves centers of cultural creation and elaboration.
7. Their cultural, religious, economic, and/or political relationships with the homeland are reflected in a significant way in their communal institutions.[25]

Being required to produce empirically observable evidence for each of the seven criteria reduces the number of examples that might mirror or even come close to the Jewish case. Indeed, only the Indian, Armenian and African diasporas can be said with any confidence to meet this standard. To follow Safran's criteria, then, is to limit drastically the opportunity for comparison.

Additionally, scholars remain wary of too prescriptive a concept. They fear that too many examples will be rejected which are best examined under the rubric of diaspora than by any other concept. It is for this reason that Safran's definition is envisaged as an ideal type and in order to navigate a path between a prescriptive and an uncritical model, scholarship converges upon a less inflexible track.[26] Limiting the concept further is recognition that the evidence uncovered cannot be cleaved from its historical context of labour flows, global capitalism, and political and social dislocations. The concept is required to reflect the empirical evidence of why migrants pack up their belongings for the opportunities of a life elsewhere, and the social consequences that result. Cohen holds that there are four key aspects to this: the first is 'victim migration', those who are fleeing one nation to seek safety in another; including those forced from their land. This, of course, can be variously defined since in all cases of migration there is hope of a better life after social, economic or physical distress. Labour migration, Cohen's second category, identifies those who move in the expectation of improved earning opportunities. These movements are determined by internal economies and trading relations, and are impacted by the forces of globalisation (his third grouping). Finally, Cohen suggests, the international nature of migration is a feature of imperial relations, and a particular feature of the British Empire was the movement of people within its economic, political and constitutional boundaries. The flows of these people carry a concomitant spread of culture – constructing and spreading diasporic consciousness.[27]

E   PRESCRIPTION AND AGENCY

While the relative merits of expanding or restricting the conceptual definition of a diaspora should be weighed when theorising patterns of migration and permanent settlement, the range of empirical evidence to be included presents a further set of challenges. Migrants are not the first group of people in history to think and act in more ways than the historian can imagine, even when broad classifications such as Cohen's are discerned. It would be wrong to deploy the concept of diaspora in a way that lacks flexibility and downplays human agency. Many migrants were proactive in their decision to move and in choosing a distant settlement. Even those 'forced' out of their native homeland, or those who travelled as indentured servants or supported by savings or the offer of employment, reflect levels of agency in their actions. As individuals, and not in groups, Scottish clerks and apprentices travelled to the colonies to take up positions with companies linked to Scottish-based businesses,[28] and Scottish ethnic networks ensured the presence of many a Scot in businesses overseas, such as Jardine, Matheson and Co., the largest foreign trading company in the

Far East by the late nineteenth century. Yet the Scottish diaspora is neither holistic nor homogenous across all host countries. Migrants are found to be proactive in maintaining ethnic homogeneity and 'difference', as Safran predicts, but many, perhaps the majority, were proactive towards assimilation. For some migrants the old homeland might be a nation (Scotland), but it might not be a nation-state (as Britain is not). Complicating the pathways further is the definition of home that is conceived of and enforced by a foreign power. African migrants might have no conception of nation to call their homeland, certainly not until Europeans carved national boundaries in straight lines upon their maps, nor even so after that.[29] By contrast Orcadians and Shetland Islanders have a strong sense of their island identity and its Norse heritage that has been found to supersede their Scottish and British identities.[30]

More besides, the concept of diaspora also includes those migrants who come to dominate, rather than assimilate into, the land in which they settled – the Boers and the British whites of southern Africa are two such instances. Taken together as ethnically homogeneous, Europeans in Australia and New Zealand, and in North and South America, overwhelmed the respective indigenous populations of these countries in historically rapid times. That we do not signal these takeovers for what they were leads Akenson to label the great European movement of people as 'casual genocide'.[31]

The agency deployed in establishing a diaspora within a larger already habitual community can also be analysed as nation-building. Although a minority would cling to the old ways irrespective of the new life around them, a further connection between migrants and their homeland was the replication of institutions, bureaucracies and style of doing things from the Old World to the New. The structure of Ontario's education system and its reliance on Irish National Readers, and the Scottish influence on the New Zealand education system, on Princeton in the USA and the wider higher education sector in Canada, including medical education, are examples of how Scots shaped the New World with what was familiar to them.[32]

There remains a counter-interpretation of evidence such as this, that when working within a conceptualisation of diaspora the recreation of a culture outweighs the myth of origin and the desire to return.[33] Taking this approach, Cohen suggest that a group's consciousness of home, whether or not there was a choice to return home, and whether the option was available to make the move permanent, should not be regarded as essential.[34] Both maximalist and minimalist definitions can be criticised for a focus on return and a constant connection with the home rather than assimilationist lives in the host nation. Also, and contradictory as it might at first seem, the ability to return made easier by rising relative living standards and technological changes, de-objectified 'home'. Regular steam crossings and jet airplanes had a significant effect, as Chapter 8 explores in more detail, making home a simple journey rather than an ideological construct. And this makes the historian pause when attempting to make empirical comparisons on the balance of want, means, cost and time required for temporary or permanent return, differentiating practical issues from the imagined community. Added to the latter are those who identify with Scotland without ever wishing to return, or of subsequent generations who have never known Scotland, and may or may not wish to visit, and those who identify with Scotland as 'home' for reasons of cultural or fortuitous choice rather than lineage. Their orientations to 'homeland' are distinct from first-generation migrants. 'Affinity Scots' have no blood link or return impulse, but identify with cultural constructions of the diaspora. Scots benefiting from higher socio-economic conditions in North America, Australia and New Zealand find no contradiction in working to preserve their connection with Scotland, and celebrating vociferously that heritage, without any intention to 'return', knowing that would be to their economic disadvantage.

F ETHNICITY, NATION AND TRANSNATIONALISM

Elemental to the transition from diaspora in itself to diaspora for itself is the concept of identity, primarily ethnic identity. Anderson's 'imagined community' – which explains how identity is maintained by groups of people who will never meet and have no immediate interaction – allows us to better understand this process.[35] Moreover, it is not unusual for research to uncover later generations of Scots identifying more strongly with the romantic or intellectual pull of homeland despite having no first-hand experience of Scotland. The territory, the nation, and the homeland to which orientation is claimed may not even exist. The idea of cultural and literary diaspora is defined as a place without roots where creativity forms in the imagination rather than in reality of a territory.[36] But unlike Cohen's de-emphasis of the homeland connection and its decoupling after cultural and institutional transplantation, empirical research still shows signs of the homeland being difficult to shake off. For this reason Belchem laments the decline of evidence-based multi-generational studies of migrant communities in time and space.[37] While a diaspora of the imagination is important for creating the cultural conditions within which the attachments between ethnic affiliates are formed, it is far removed from the actual cheek by jowl living together that characterises an ethnic enclave in a host country. The concept of 'diaspora space' is introduced to refer to an area or town or city where a range of different nationalities intermix in settlement.[38] The idea of the Polonia, the 'fourth province of Poland',[39] the Jewish quarter, or 'Little Italy' speak to this, and the census of 2011 records the number of French residents in London being of a magnitude that, were they in France, would qualify as the fifth largest French city. 'Little Aberdeen' in early twentieth-century

Sunderland and the 'Scotch Block' in mid-nineteenth-century Milton near Toronto flag areas where Scots have been found to congregate.

Talk of ethnic enclaves leads to another set of identity questions that arise with those who settle in another country: does the hyphenated diasporic identity of, say, Scottish-Americans or Scottish-Australians override their American, Australian, Scottish, British and/or British Imperial identities; and, if so, when and under what circumstances might the tipping point have been? They are not questions easily met. Diasporic subjects are, by definition, imbued with dual and multiple identifications that mark hybridity as the norm. One element in the proliferation of theoretical interest in diaspora comes from concomitant interest in the modern nation. From current thinking it would seem that the nationalist perspective of the nation has been replaced by the internationalism of diaspora. Tölölyan and Clifford examine how the nation-state is the 'primary conceptual "other" against which the diaspora is defined – and often celebrated'.[40] Yet while diaspora is transnationalist in scope, this does not make it synonymous with transnationalism. People are moving from one nation or nation-state to another nation or nation-state, leaving neither undermined.[41] Indeed few have believed that migrants broke decisively from their nations to become increasingly and overwhelmingly assimilated.[42] No 'melting pot', but a 'salad bowl' where national loyalties persist within transnational space. Too often such debate ascribes an idealistic teleological coherence to the concept of the nation, and from the age of mercantilism to the rise of globalisation, the 'island nation' has long been akin to an ideologically presented golden age rather than an international reality.

To conceive the boundaries of diaspora within the pulls of transnationalism, social theorist Homi Bhabha explains that 'it is by living on the borderlines of history and language, on the limits of race and gender, that we are in a position to translate the difference between them into a kind of solidarity'.[43] In this sense a border is not an outer limit, or mark where something has ended, but a place from which 'something begins its presenting'.[44] Boundaries are created by endogamy and by some form of social inclusion and signposts where we learn about ourselves. Boundaries are used both for presenting categories, and for presenting identity. Scotland's diasporic identity was formed 'out of place', in the boundaries of its national symbolic representations and out of its everyday institutional and cultural characteristics.[45]

For most Scots migrants, names, clans, and ethnic associations such as St Andrew's societies offer an outward sign of collective boundaries, the latter being a defining characteristic of the Scottish diaspora (see Chapter 7). Language has also played a role. Both Scots and Gaelic, the latter especially, have brought and kept Scots together as groups and communities in many different settlements, including regional, island and religious communities. Dunedin (in New Zealand) takes its name from the anglicised Gaelic version of Edinburgh (in Gaelic, Dun Eadinn) and around 14 per cent of place names in Otago and Southland have Gaelic origins.[46] In North Carolina's Cape Fear Valley the largest highland settlement in the United States was established, leaving strong cultural imprints, and Gaelic communities also flourished in British North America, for instance in Quebec.[47] Most comprehensively of all, the administrative pull of the English language brought disparate strands together as the lingua franca of Empire. Religion has also been a major pathway to Scottish diasporan identity, with Presbyterianism maintaining a link to the Church ordinances in Edinburgh and Roman Catholics to the re-established Scottish Hierarchy in 1878. By working within the Scots' boundaries of presentation, the researcher is better able to understand the depth of social relationships amongst and between Scots migrants. Some of these connections were direct – the reaction to the Disruption in the Church of Scotland was a live debate within the colonies and directly facilitated diaspora links. The importance attached to the worldwide Presbyterian community meant Free Church leader Revd Dr Candlish sailed immediately to New York to explain the issues, taking with him the hope of raising funds. Clusters of Orcadians were seen to leave their homes for a life in New Zealand when the religious split separated them from their usual Sunday succour.[48] Yet for others the connection was opaque. The diasporan experience is defined not by being pure, but by recognising and managing imprecise connections with the host society – by dealing with 'hybridity and heterogeneity' in Stuart Hall's emphasis, the hyphenated, partial and contradictory reality of identities that are never zero-sum.[49]

Involvement of the diasporan group in the host nation's politics and socie-ties is not only part of the host nation's history, but also part of the sending nation's version of diaspora. Emphasising how diaspora is a concept not a category, research acknowledges aspects of Scots' lives in a host country that may be studied in ways that are not diasporan. Welfare, social class and labour market analysis may in some cases be more relevant to the discussion. 'Being diasporic' does not override race, gender and social class, or stand separate from those and other powerful social divisions.[50] Diaspora, simply, is another layer of hybridity. New arrivals will always tend to maintain some sort of boundary of difference upon arrival, at least at first. How those boundaries are maintained over subsequent generations is both central to the definition of diaspora and academically significant to framing analysis. The concep-tual openness required suggests the answer to be a framework, rather than a theory, of diaspora.[51] Diaspora is not a thing to be hunted, but a way of understanding the lives of ordinary people. High or low numbers of migrants are simply that: flows of people. Numbers of generational and affiliated Scots are, again, simply head counts. Without the conceptual framework for dias-pora outlined in this chapter, or one similar to it, identifying diasporic Scots on the grounds of their ancestry does not explain boundary maintenance and affiliation across nations.

G AN INTRODUCTION TO DIASPORIC ACTIONS

We have argued that there is a distinct difference between diaspora as entity with quantifiable memberships and diaspora as a set of inter-related actions. To gain analytical purchase, scholars look to people as they present themselves as a diaspora, the boundaries of their diasporic formation, the fluidity of these boundaries, and the uncertainty and chimeric nature of their diasporic memberships. In this deconstruction, diaspora is a set of actions, not an entity: accepting diaspora as a mercurial category, one 'of practice, project, claim and stance, rather than as a bounded group'.[52]

Throughout these chapters the reader will encounter Scotland's diaspora broken down by its constituent features. Mapping any diaspora is a jagged picture beyond simple movement and settlement. Reflecting this open-endedness, two forms of return migration are analysed: those who return to their homeland from the diaspora during their lifetime – their natal homeland; and those who return to the country of their parents, grandparents or ancestors – their ancestral homeland. The choice to return 'home' rather than migrate to an alternative destination shows some element of ancestral preference, one that historians can chart and evaluate over time, plus some preference by the homeland to welcome those considered to be its descendants. At the time of writing Scottish migrants do not lose their British citizenship after gaining citizenship elsewhere. Different rights exist for Commonwealth and natural-ised citizens and for those of British overseas territories. Although not equal, ancestral links maintained through the remnants of the British Empire proffer a favoured route to residency in the UK. Homecoming policies encourage migrant ancestors to join the deterritorialised diaspora by visiting the ter-ritorial nation – an approach followed by the Scottish Government in the Homecomings of 2009 and 2014. There is the assumption that these ethnic descendants are culturally similar to the homeland population. Evidence from a range of investigations into other nationalities has shown that economic reasons are prioritised in the decision to return.[53] While Scotland was not an impoverished country, ethnicity claims a significant role in the return decision because both in reality and in perception the economic pull is weak, and there is a significant opportunity cost to return. The pull of ethnicity and ethnic familiarity therefore has to be strong enough to overcome short- and medium-term economic disadvantage.[54]

Coming under the term **sojourner** are migrants who plan to work in another land for a set period of time, or until a financial goal has been achieved.

Two years working for the Hudson's Bay Company, a few years trading in the Far East through the East India Company, three years of work experience on the North American railroad, or in the New Zealand gold fields until a find is made – but always with the intention to return to Scotland – typify this migrant. Migrants without such a specific goal to their migration, but absent from their homeland for only a limited period of time, are **temporary migrants**, some of whom may then be characterised as **odyssey migrants**, 'exploring a new world' without a definite plan of residence. There is an opportunity cost involved in migration, from preparation and travel costs to the loss of earnings while travelling to the expenses of establishing a home in the New World. Research shows that generally it was not the poorest who emigrated from Scotland, simply because they could not afford it. To migrate as an **indentured servant** meant to guarantee one's labour for a set period of time to whoever paid the cost of the passage. Children might have their passage paid for or subsidised by a charity such as Quarrier's or Barnardo's. Adults, too, might find **philanthropic migration** their only hope to afford the cost of passage. Twenty-seven groups of emigrants from the Sutherland estate were granted aid to facilitate their travel to Australia, New Zealand, Canada and India, with no discernible pattern of age, marital status or occupation amongst these groups.[55] Those who are forced from their homes or fled threats or persecution are classed as comprising a '**victim diaspora**'. Soldiers were offered land to settle as a reward for service, but also to protect the colony as a reserve army of farmers who could fight; for instance lawyer John Campbell was hired by the Colonial Office to help relocate Scottish ex-soldiers from the Napoleonic campaign to the Ottawa valley.[56] This policy also benefitted the homeland by keeping the costs of their subsistence off the poor roll while employment was sought after demobilisation. **Settler settlements** exist in various parts of the diaspora, including Canada and South Africa. The **homeland** is the land from which the migrant originated or to which the ancestor or affinity migrants orientate themselves, but memories of homeland will be negative for those forced to leave, and at best ambivalent amongst those compelled to migrate to achieve a standard of living they imagined should have been available at home. However it is framed, migration involves some level of rejection of home – either by the subjects or those who sent them. Migrants would often follow the lead of their family, their neighbours or other community members they might know. **Chain migration** is a term used to explain the blood, kin and knowledge links across great distances that connected one community in Scotland with one overseas, comprising a metaphorical chain that facilitated movement between two distant locations. In the years immediately following the Earl of Selkirk's purchase of land on Prince Edward Island around 3,000 settlers from Skye and the West Highlands joined him. And with help from the British government, 2,700 unemployed weavers from

Glasgow and the western Lowlands immigrated to the Ottawa area between 1820 and 1821.[57] The Revd Norman McLeod brought a significant number of settlers to Waipu in New Zealand – a final destination reached by the group only after sojourns in Nova Scotia and Australia.[58] The chain can lead to a preponderance of overseas visitors to the newly settled migrant and a source of information for potential emigrants from ones who then returned,[59] in each case stimulating the diasporic-homeland connection. Organisations and institutions like the Orange Order, mechanics' institutes and sporting clubs can follow that chain to become established in the new country just as they were in the old; they can be organic to the new setting, reflecting the host country as much as Scotland itself. Where Scottish institutions are found in the host country which to all intents and purposes are direct reflections of what would be found in the homeland, then the term **transplanted** is used. Transplanted communities range from the Aberdonians who moved as a group to Elora in Upper Canada to the Orcadians who migrated as kin and neighbour groups to New Zealand's South Island. Once settled, native-born Scots and their descendants may continue to work to maintain an ethnic difference in their chosen land, or they may downplay or eschew their Scottishness and either by unintentional osmosis or by deliberate linguistic or social activity achieve **cultural assimilation,** where they prioritise their assimilated lives. Those that persisted in prioritising their Scottish lineage, and worked to pass on that identity to their children, grandchildren and others are said to have left **inter-generational legacies** – where Scottishness in the diaspora is carried forward by these legacies.

Finally in this exploration of social action and behaviour of Scots furth of the nation, we examine their diasporic **stances, projects, claims and idioms**; in other words, how Scots people behave as diasporic Scots. This shift from category to concept in the analysis takes hold by ascribing social processes to the numbers enumerated, investigating whether diaspora locates behaviours that scholars can then generalise in meaningful ways.

NOTES

1. Palmer, 'Defining and studying the modern African diaspora', p. 1.
2. Craig, *Intending Scotland*, pp. 203–44.
3. Tölölyan, 'Diasporama' (1994) and 'Diasporama' (2000).
4. Brubaker, 'The "diaspora" diaspora', p. 1.
5. Baumann, 'Diaspora', p. 315.
6. Ibid., p. 320.
7. Deuteronomy 28: 25, King James Bible.
8. Butler, 'Defining diaspora, refining a discourse', p. 202.

9. Bueltmann, *Scottish Ethnicity*, pp. 181–2; see also Bueltmann, Gleeson and MacRaild, 'Locating the English diaspora', p. 8.
10. Baumann, 'Diaspora', p. 316.
11. Braziel and Mannur, 'Nation, migration, globalization', p. 2.
12. Akenson, 'The Great European migration and indigenous populations', p. 22.
13. Brubaker, 'The "diaspora" diaspora', p. 2.
14. That definitions were accepted on their basis to the paradigmatic victim diaspora of the Jews, Armenians and Greeks is noted in Brubaker, 'The "diaspora" diaspora', p. 2.
15. McLean, 'Reluctant leavers?', p. 109.
16. Shepperson, *British Emigration to North America*, p. 249.
17. Fact Sheet 8: Abolition of the 'White Australia' policy, http://www.immi.gov.au/media/fact-sheets/08abolition.htm (accessed 12 November 2012).
18. Lucassen and Lucassen, 'Migration, migration history', pp. 14–19.
19. Safran, 'Diasporas in modern societies', p. 87.
20. Brubaker, 'The "diaspora" diaspora', pp. 2–3.
21. Armstrong, 'Mobilized and proletarian diasporas', p. 393.
22. Baumann, 'Diaspora', p. 313.
23. Butler, 'Defining diaspora, refining a discourse', p. 190.
24. Lucassen and Lucassen, 'Migration, migration history, history', p. 26.
25. Safran, 'The Jewish diaspora in a comparative and theoretical perspective', p. 37.
26. Butler, 'Defining diaspora, refining a discourse', p. 192.
27. Cohen, *Global Diasporas*, pp. x–xi.
28. McCalla, 'Sojourners in the snow?', p. 85.
29. Akenson, 'The historiography of English-speaking Canada and the concept of diaspora', pp. 383–5.
30. Harland, 'The Orcadian odyssey'.
31. Akenson, 'The Great European migration and indigenous peoples', p. 25.
32. Ibid., pp. 403 and 407; Kehoe, 'Catholic identity in the diaspora', p. 93; Brooking, 'Sharing out the haggis', p. 59; Murray and Murray, 'The seed, the soil and the climate', pp. 190–8.
33. Clifford, 'Diasporas', p. 307.
34. Cited in Butler, 'Defining diaspora, refining a discourse', p. 192.
35. Anderson, *Imagined Communities*, pp. 6, 25–6.
36. McCleod, *Beginning Postcolonialism*, pp. 33, 210.
37. Belchem, 'Hub and diaspora', pp. 21–2.
38. Boyle, 'Towards a (re)theorization of the historical geography of nationalism in diasporas', pp. 430–1.
39. Belchem, 'Hub and diaspora', p. 23.

40. Brubaker, 'The "diaspora" diaspora', p. 10.
41. Braziel and Mannur, 'Nation, migration, globalization', p. 8
42. Brubaker, 'The "diaspora" diaspora, p 7.
43. Smith, '"Bordering on identity"', p. 20.
44. Ibid.
45. Morton, 'Identity out of place', pp. 256–80.
46. Brooking, 'Sharing out the haggis', pp. 55–6.
47. Bennett, *Oatmeal and the Catechism*.
48. Harland, 'The Orcadian odyssey'.
49. Cited in Brubaker, 'The "diaspora" diaspora', p. 6; Hall, 'The question of cultural identity', pp. 273–5.
50. Braziel and Mannur, 'Nation, migration, globalization', p. 5.
51. Butler, 'Defining diaspora, refining a discourse', p. 194.
52. Brubaker, 'The "diaspora" diaspora', p. 13.
53. Tsuda, 'Why does the diaspora return home?', pp. 22–3.
54. Ibid., pp. 21 and 25.
55. Richards, 'The last of the clan and other Highland emigrants', pp. 46–7.
56. Vance, *Imperial Immigrants*, p. 53.
57. Harper, 'Exiles or entrepreneurs?', pp. 23–4.
58. Molloy, *Those Who Speak to the Heart*.
59. McCarthy, '"For spirit and adventure"', p. 125.

Themes

CHAPTER 3

Scotland: The Twa Lands

Canadian novelist Alice Munro's finely crafted short stories, inspired by her family roots in the Scottish Borders, begin with two brothers – one a minister of the sternest Presbyterian variety, the other a teller of tales and a firm believer in fairies.[1] Munro is a Laidlaw, part of a family history traced down the line to another harvester of stories, James Hogg, fellow Borderer and long-time friend of the historical novelist Sir Walter Scott. Munro's ancestors were like many lowlanders in the 1830s that had suffered too long the economic difficulties of a downturn in the hosiery trade. In hope, they had bundled up their belongings and searched for prosperity and a new life in Canada. *The View from Castle Rock* is the most personal of Munro's publications, structured from her own genealogical research reflecting on a life long-lived. It concludes with an incidental consequence: the narrator's encounter with an immigrant who had known her father and brother when once he worked on a nearby farm in Ontario upon arrival from Eastern Europe. The meeting is a powerful one, connecting memories from Munro's youth to stories passed through the generations, to archival work done to document this history and to legwork undertaken to find the markers, the gravestones and homesteads, with which they are associated across the ocean to her homeland. Equally incidental is the mention of Jane Porter's *The Scottish Chiefs*; popular fiction first published in 1810, chosen to illustrate the type of reading that nourished a transplanted culture.[2] Munro's stories deal with how the memories from the past can be transmitted through the generations, by interactions and events throughout individual lives. We cannot remember what we were not alive to experience, yet these 'memories' can somehow be acquired and then articulated as diasporic legacies.[3] Indeed it would appear that these remembered connections could be transmitted through our own lives and more widely through the lives of others across land and ocean, between 'twa lands'.

The genealogist knows a connection between leavers and stayers is maintained psychologically – evidenced in mementoes and personal testimonies preserved, and most usefully for their research in the form of grave markings. A wander through the nation's kirkyards will find plots inscribed with the names and dates of family members who died abroad, recorded alongside the names of those who lie beneath the ground. Hence John Jack, who emigrated to New Zealand in the early 1880s, consciously chose to be cremated in New Zealand so that his ashes could be sent back to Scotland to be placed in the family grave in Dundee.[4] The impetus for connecting with migrant relatives long gone can be seen in other settings where families are fractured by distance. After the great battles of the First World War were over, the British government made funds available for families to bring home the bodies of the fallen. Some took up the offer; others preferred to think of the foreign field as a little part of Scotland.[5] The campaign's most popular English language poem, 'In Flanders Fields', published in *Punch* in 1915, was written by Scottish Canadian military doctor Colonel John McCrae. As relatives remembered their dead, 'homeland' had become and was to remain the poppy fields and graves of Flanders fields:

> In Flanders fields the poppies blow
> Between the crosses, row on row,
> That mark our place; and in the sky
> The larks, still bravely singing, fly
> Scarce heard amid the guns below.

For those living in the diaspora, Scots gatherings might start with a toast: 'Yer guid health my friends, and guid health to the twa lands!' Popularised at nineteenth-century Burns suppers, glasses were raised to the diasporic connection between that land now lived in and the land left behind. With the physical connection to their nation at an end, as well as loyal and sometimes dewy-eyed toasts, Scots migrants relied on letters from the old country, news from relatives, neighbours, and communal groups, and an expectation of reunion in the afterlife to maintain a bond with home.

In the previous chapter a migrant's relationship with his or her homeland was underlined in the conceptualisation of diaspora, maintained through both personal knowledge and social memories passed down through families, and through constructions within the imagined community of the diaspora. As well, the maintenance of an active homeland relationship was seen to involve diasporic actions in the creation and negotiation of ethnic boundaries. The evidence taken from outside of Scotland to test this abstraction is presented in the case study chapters, but a pre-emptory task is to examine the Scotland left behind – that is, the structural factors that led to the nation's heavy per capita rates of emigration. To do this, attention falls on the socio-economic pressures that provide the backdrop for the decision to emigrate.

A STRUCTURE AND ACTION

Dudley Baines argues that while it is common for historians to regard migrants as deviants because they are dissatisfied with the place the majority have chosen to remain, if there is a long tradition of migration in that community then their actions must be regarded as closer to the norm. If that is the case, as it was for Scotland, then at some point in the lifecycle there comes the decision to remain or to seek pastures new.[6] To help explain the context for this choice, we turn to a central analytical relationship in the social sciences: the relationship between structure and action. Looking to rationalise the decisions ordinary people take, scholars weigh up 'free will' and 'structural' factors. Did the emigration decision make little or no regard for the socio-economic conditions within which Scots found themselves, or can it be shown that structural factors gave pattern to this movement? Of equal importance, analysis of the nation left behind examines the historical framework of the spiritual connection to homeland that has also been conceptualised as essential to diasporic formation. The homeland connection existed in terms of an imagined community, and one that was generated also through the socio-economic fragilities of everyday life. By flirting with the dangers of national generalisation over regional and local variation, four broad factors can be identified to frame the decision to migrate:

1. demographic pressures
2. standard of living
3. occupational change
4. urbanisation.

B DEMOGRAPHIC PRESSURES

The warnings of the Revd Thomas Robert Malthus (1766–1834) shaped debate on rural over-population from 1798, speaking to the need for dramatic change to highland society.[7] Malthus predicted that population growth would simply bloat the numbers living at or below subsistence, deepening the poverty of those already in want. Writers such as Archibald Alison, William Thornton and John Stuart Mill carried this debate into the middle of the next century. The headline concern was over-population – and the moral, economic and social dislocations contemporaries associated with it. Hidden within the highland crisis was the regional distribution of the population. Seeking out temporary employment in the farms of East Lothian or Tayside was one solution for the poor, as was fishing and gathering kelp around the coasts. Out of necessity the Scots had long undertaken temporary migrations as a solution to the Malthusian darkness. In the 1840s Scots from Caithness and Sutherland in the country's north-east made the seasonal trek south-west to the Clyde fishing fleets near Glasgow. This established an historical memory of temporary absences as part of the regular pattern of life, for stayers and leavers alike.[8]

Increasing demographic pressures deepen scarcity of resources, raise levels of un- and underemployment and, as a consequence, encourage population movement in the hope that these stresses might be alleviated. The evidence is not straightforward, however. For the eighteenth century there were cases where rural population growth may have helped boost agricultural productivity. It was not without reason that landlords were found resistant to their tenants leaving the land, attempting to create employment through improving infrastructure with work on roads, bridges and canals – the Caledonian Canal especially – and by developing new economic opportunities.[9] Rather than growth leading inevitably to idle hands, a large number of labourers ready to work could maximise output, producing enough to improve the calorific quality of the diet.[10] Still, not all regions could or did absorb such pressures equally and consistently, with land holdings becoming subdivided to the extent that the ability to support livelihoods became life-threateningly precarious, encouraging the decision to leave for employment and subsistence elsewhere.[11]

It is difficult to discern the regional impact of demographic change with any certainty in the eighteenth century, nor its relationship to migration. We have no national census until 1801, nor are estimates of the death rate known with any great confidence until civil registration in 1855. Prior to that there are only limited and uneven burial registers, their coverage challenged by migrations to the towns and overseas.[12] Scotland's average population gain from Webster's estimate of 1,265,000 in 1755 until the first census was 400,000 people or an annual growth rate of 0.5 per cent. Between then and 1851, the population increased by 1,281,000, more than trebling the previous span at an annual average growth of 1.6 per cent (Table 3.1 and Table 3.3). Demographers assign the greatest portion of this rise to heightened levels of marital fertility sustaining a high birth rate alongside what was still a high death rate (Table 3.2).

Although death rates did not fall with any great rapidity until the twentieth century, expectation of life increased from thirty-three years and six months in the 1790s to thirty-nine years and three months by the 1850s.[13] In 1910–12 the expectation for newly born boys was 50.1 years and for girls it was 53.2 years.[14] These rates have risen to 75.8 years for men and 80.4 years for women in the returns for 2008–10, although confirming the connection to rising standards

Table 3.1 Annual average percentage increase in population [source: Tranter, *Population since the Industrial Revolution*, p. 43]

	1750–1800	1800–50	1850–1910
Scotland	0.5	1.6	0.9
England & Wales	0.7	1.8	1.6
Ireland	1.1	0.6	0.7

Table 3.2 Crude birth rate (CBR) and crude death rate (CDR), expressed per thousand people: Scotland and England 1755–6 and 1861 [source: Anderson, 'The demographic regime', p. 13]

	Scotland		England	
Year	1755–6	1861	1755–6	1861
CBR/1000	41	35	33	36
CDR/1000	38	22	26	21

of living, these modern-day results show variations of 13.2 years for men and 8.9 years for women between the most and least deprived areas of Scotland.[15]

When aggregated, the Scottish population grew by around 27 per cent in the period 1755 to 1801. In comparison, the highland population grew at a rate of around 20 per cent over the same decades. Taking these bald figures suggests that population pressure was not as extreme in eighteenth-century highland Scotland as elsewhere in the nation, yet it was to have greater consequences for access to land, employment opportunities and the ability to stave off starvation.[16] Under the old Poor Law, administered by the Church of Scotland, the cost of funding poor relief came from fines levied by the church through the disciplinary regulations of the Kirk Session (mainly for sexual offences) and by church collections (a role confirmed by the state in 1592). Otherwise the cost fell on the small numbers of heritors of the parish; but with little help forthcoming many of the smaller landowners had to pay subsistence rates simply to keep the population in place. As it was, the faster rate of growth after 1801 proved to be uncontainable, and instead of absorption of this growth through greater labour numbers on the land, the impetus for removal gained traction.

In 1951 four times as many people lived in Scotland as at Webster's estimate of 1755. The bulk of that growth – some 3.2 million people – had happened by 1901, and was fastest through the first half of that century. It is noticeable that the population of England and Wales grew at an even faster rate, and Scotland's size relative to these nations declined from a high of 18 per cent in 1801 to 11.6 per cent in 1951. To put the flatness of Scotland's twentieth-century growth in comparison, the nation's highest ever population

Table 3.3 Comparative population growth: Scotland, England & Wales and Ireland (millions, and by percentage), 1755–1951 [source: Mitchell and Dean, *Abstract of British Historical Statistics*, pp. 6–7]

Year	Population in Scotland	Population in England & Wales	Population in Ireland (Republic of Ireland & Northern Ireland after 1926)	Population in Scotland as percentage of population in England & Wales	Population in Scotland as percentage of population in Ireland (Republic of Ireland & Northern Ireland after 1926)
1755	1.265				
1801	1.608	8.893		18.1	
1811	1.806	10.164		17.8	
1821	2.092	12.000	6.802	17.4	30.8
1831	2.364	13.897	7.767	17.0	30.4
1841	2.620	15.914	8.175	16.5	32.0
1851	2.889	17.928	6.552	16.1	44.1
1861	3.062	20.066	5.799	15.3	52.8
1871	3.360	22.712	5.412	14.8	62.1
1881	3.736	25.974	5.175	14.4	72.2
1891	4.026	29.003	4.705	13.9	85.6
1901	4.472	32.528	4.459	13.7	100.3
1911	4.761	36.070	4.390	13.2	108.5
1921	4.882	37.887	4.229 (1926)	12.9	115.4
1931	4.843	39.952	4.248 (1936/7)	12.1	114.0
1951	5.096	43.758	4.332	11.6	117.6

return on 27 March 2011, recorded at 5,295,000, was a relatively modest 624,000 people more than in 1901.[17] Yet even with only incremental gains, Scotland's population turnaround in comparison with Ireland is startling – from standing at under one third of Ireland's population in 1801 to declaring at nearly 20 per cent in excess by 1951. This transformation tells of the dramatic exodus of the Irish around the globe rather than of Scots turning from the emigration path. The proportional decline of the Scottish population in comparison with England and Wales highlights the greater level of out-migration from the northern country, despite a common demographic regime. Improving rates of child mortality and widespread use of contraceptive methods in the 1950s contributed to fertility decline in both Scotland and England. And it became easier to sustain a stable population as technological developments in agricultural production and wider and cheaper imports of food eased some of the previous nutritional pressures, except, most clearly, during wartime and into the 1950s as rationing, which ended in 1954, and supply shortages persisted.

Hesitant growth reflected eager out-migration, and whatever structural discouragements took root, it did not hinder emigration rates from exceeding immigration rates in almost every year of twentieth-century Scotland.[18]

The first release of pressure from population rise at the start of our period came from internal movement. Contracts of six and twelve months created structural breaks in employment that led to resettlement as new employment was sought. Apprenticeships and seasonal work added to the experiences of a people who understood internal migration as part of the seasonal rhythms of life. The predominance of rented farms contributed to a rural population in flux. Highlighting the distinctiveness of this lifestyle, Anderson notes that

> [t]he substantial proportions of the population of rural France and
> Germany who were born, lived and died in the same parish were never
> matched in Scotland: two thirds of the families listed in the village of
> Kippen in Stirlingshire in 1789 were not resident there in 1793.[19]

The migration of female harvest workers was sufficiently widespread to acquire a moral dimension – both in terms of the morality of unsupervised young women with money in their pockets and the 'lowering' effect of such a transient lifestyle – only to be 'saved' upon their return.[20] The intra- and inter-regional movement of women seeking out paid work in the second half of the eighteenth century was to have another effect: raising the age of first marriage and reducing the number of children born within marriage. This same process took men away from familiar courting customs, and early marriage, to an environment of single-sex living and working, with a further need to move in order to seek out partners. Examples here are the highland men employed in railway construction in the 1840s and again during the fast-paced construction phase of the 1860s, joining with the Irish navy as the backbone of the industry.[21]

One study suggests that in the 1840s most highland families had at least one member engaged in seasonal work in lowland Scotland.[22] In another investigation, of 334 highlanders who were identified as having followed stepped migration prior to settling in Glasgow during the period 1852 to 1898, 50 per cent took one intermediate step before settling in the city while 15 per cent had five or more steps.[23] We can also identify this movement by looking at the occupational structure of the urban settlements. Highlanders and the Irish in 1851 were only slightly under-represented in the metal, machinery and ship-building industries of Scotland's towns, with two-thirds of highlanders classed as skilled.[24] The mid-century town of Perth, for instance, received migrants from highland Perthshire as did Dundee although it was the main destination for migrants tramping from Argyll, Invernessshire, Ross and Cromarty, and northern Skye.[25] Out-of-region income, and temporary removal from the local economy of a stomach to be filled, sustained the population in rural Scotland, in the highland counties especially. Such migrations, importantly, were also part of a series of movements eventually leading to permanent settlement in one of the nation's towns and cities or to a place outside the nation.

C STANDARD OF LIVING

Thus it was not just population growth but population redistribution that strained infrastructure and turned the Scots into a people for whom internal migration was a regular occurrence. Few, however, argue that the pressures predicted by Malthus were on their own sufficient to cause European migration. Additional factors such as developments in transportation and the internationalisation of markets not only impacted on local economies but also, more decisively, undermined rural industry.[26] Over the two centuries from 1750 Scotland can be characterised as having experienced an uneven but general rise in standards of living despite lower average wages and higher rental costs than in England. From the evidence recorded in household budgets, and by matching wages to average food prices, it is estimated that around two-thirds of the Scot's budget was spent on food each year.[27] Even at that high proportion, little of those scarce resources went towards eating meat, which was an expensive purchase for most and had been for many decades. Indeed, one attraction of signing up for military action in the seventeenth century was access to a regular meat diet. From the standpoint of the 1790s, contemporary estimates of the amount of meat consumed by the people of Ayr forty years earlier, then a town of around 4–5,000 in size, was only fifty cattle. And it appears that meat was still absent from the Scottish diet in the 1790s, with one calculation for Edinburgh finding less than 6 per cent of nutrition gained from its consumption, whereas 70 per cent came from meal, although there is evidence of greater meat consumption elsewhere.[28] The last famine or famine-like conditions in Scotland were in 1782, whereas the everyday shortage of food and their narrow diet worsened Scots' resistance to the effects of the infectious epidemics of 1808, 1831, 1836–7 and 1846–9.

The general picture of the eighteenth and nineteenth centuries is that oatmeal became the dominant food of lowland Scotland, a trend that was being followed more slowly in the highland parts of the nation as animal consumption declined. The predominance of oatmeal and potatoes was out of necessity, with the middle ranks and elites more likely to add meat to their diet because they could afford to. The consumption of milk was found to be widespread by the Poor Law investigations of 1843, generally acquired from bartering. In evidence running from 1847 until the early part of the twentieth century, women born in Scotland's cities were a third more likely to deliver babies of low birth weight than mothers born in the Lowlands more generally, the north of Scotland and the Borders. Labouring women in Scotland and those in white-collar but low-paid clerical occupations were 50 per cent and 46 per cent respectively more likely to deliver low-weight babies than women within domestic service and food handling occupations.[29] Overall Ward's analysis points to low and declining nutritional standards amongst the ordinary urban dweller, yet still Scots were leaving their counties for an urban life in consistently heavy flows.

Scarcity of food and oversupply of rural labour comprised the environment that was near enough constant through to the end of our period. Marriage was delayed until sufficient funds could be accumulated to rent and furnish a house, including those of the middle classes, and in some areas of the north-east one-fifth to one-quarter of children were born illegitimate, in part because marriage was deferred. Crofters had to wait for the death of the father to inherit land and were found to marry late, reducing the numbers of children being born despite recording high levels of fertility; in industrial areas by contrast, the timing of marriage was influenced by the trade cycle.[30] With good reason the rhetoric of emigration agents focused on the availability of cheap land overseas and the cheaper costs of grain, meat and tools to tend the land, as well as the availability of regular work. Letters sent home to family made mention of diet, food costs and the relative expenses of daily life, a feature also of the emigrant guides which could not resist comparison with Scotland (Chapter 6).

Changes in rural society contributed to wresting people from older patterns of life. The Improvers of the mid-eighteenth to mid-nineteenth centuries began from the principle that changes had to be made to economy and society. Farming by means of runrig – small strips of land individually owned or rented – was replaced by the use of fields with fencing to enclose them. These processes took land away from the cottars, reducing the numbers who were directly employed by growing crops and tilling the land. Many of these people then became rural labourers – not upon the land by their own ownership or rental, but by cash contract. Once the cottars became labourers they became as moveable as any other property. The strains of capitalism had been felt in nearly all aspects of the rural economy. Stated at its broadest, the farms outside of the more fertile areas of East Lothian and Ayrshire lacked self-sufficiency, being unable to feed those that worked them, and requiring interventions into the market to raise funds to buy (or to barter for) grain.[31] Most rural Scots prior to the final quarter of the nineteenth century were living near, or below, levels of subsistence. Evidence from the 1850s and 1860s concludes that around £40 to £50 of value had to be generated from land in highland Scotland for a family to feed itself without income from an alternative source, yet the annual value produced by the crofts averaged out at £33.[32]

The Scots had long come to regard rental or ownership of land as a means to obtain subsistence if all other employment was absent. Removal of that option hastened departure for other counties and burghs, easing the number of

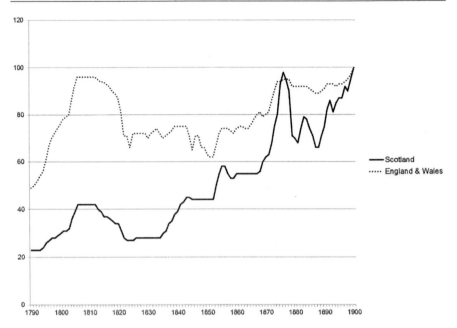

Figure 3.1 Index of average agricultural wages: Scotland and England & Wales, 1790–1900 (1900=100) [source: Mitchell, *European Historical Statistics*, pp. 78–9; based on average labouring wage]

mouths to be fed, yet not necessarily improving the nutritional intake of those that remained. The reward for agricultural labour was persistently lower than might be gained for similar work in the counties of England (Figure 3.1).

What Figure 3.1 also indicates is that the income earned from agricultural work was most disadvantaged when the number employed in this sector was greatest; equality was only reached after the sector had contracted. The agricultural depression of 1873 which kept prices low through to 1896 was a period of pronounced haemorrhaging of the rural workforce, with Scots leaving for the towns to take up industrial occupations while also contributing to the numbers who left Scotland behind. And while Scotland's lowland wages had generally caught up with comparable wages in England, a Board of Trade report in 1912 estimated that still incomes in urban Scotland were 10 per cent lower than in England once the higher-cost foods such as beef, eggs, cheese, butter and tea were accounted for.

D   OCCUPATIONAL CHANGE

The fundamental economic change experienced by Scots in the age of migration was the contraction of the agricultural and textile sectors and the rise of

Table 3.4 Scotland's sheep, 1870–1901 [source: Ministry of Agriculture, *Agricultural Statistics*][37]

Year	Number of sheep
1870	6,750,854
1871	6,882,747
1877	6,968,774
1884	6,983,293
1885	6,957,198
1901	7,401,409

industrial work. The number of people employed in agriculture and on the land declined from 316,000 in 1851 to 218,000 in 1911 – in percentage terms a falling-off from 20 per cent of Scots' employment to just over 13 per cent.[33] The clearing of the runrig towns for sheep had begun in the 1750s, and was inevitably accompanied by a decline of tenants. This started out with small areas and small numbers of sheep but both increased into the 1790s.[34] There is strong testimony from those forced to move under legal and physical threat, epitomised by the ruthlessness of the Countess of Sutherland and her factor Patrick Sellar. In May 1814, for example, 430 tenant families were evicted from their homes on the Sutherland estate and forced to move to coastal villages. In Sutherland the number of sheep increased from 15,000 in 1811 to 1,300,000 in 1820; the numbers in Argyll increased at a similar rate, reaching 1 million by 1880.[35] The importance of sheep production to the Scottish and indeed British economy was felt beyond the period of land clearance. In the 1870s there were 28 million sheep in Britain, of which Scotland was home to around 7 million. In 1952 there were just over 20 million sheep that represented forty-two sheep for every 100 persons, making Britain the third densest sheep nation and the tenth largest sheep producer in the world.[36]

The trauma of removal, which continued from various locations into the post-famine years, has long sustained diasporic connections with the homeland – narratives of exile and enforced removal – for clearance was directly responsible for Scots leaving to re-establish their communities in the diaspora, in Cape Breton and Glengarry, most notably.

Yet if there was to be one solution to the Malthusian darkness of a rural society increasingly unable to feed itself, then the introduction of the potato rather than sheep seemed to be the answer. The creator of the Statistical Account of Scotland, Sir John Sinclair, estimated that four times as many people could be supported by an acre of potatoes than by an acre of oats, and it was a crop more resilient to the mild and damp Scottish climate. The use of the potato also meant non-arable areas were now being inhabited where once they were empty, creating population spread but also dependence on the crop that meant its catastrophic failure in 1847–8 had profound repercussions.

The formation of the Central Board of Management for Highland Relief in 1847, coming together from the Edinburgh and Glasgow relief committees, showed a quick realisation of the unfolding dangers. An unprecedented £210,000 was raised by the Board, and relief came in the form of seed and meal doled out from two vessels stationed as meal depots at Tobermory in Mull and Portree in Skye, with work given in exchange.[38] In some parishes as much as three-quarters of the population was dependent on hand-outs to avoid starvation. Yet this was imposed unevenly and there was fear that the help was either too generous or it was turning the highlander into an indolent pauper, dependent (forever) on charity. Estimates of the number left hungry or starving by the potato blight suggest around 200,000 were affected, and the economic, health and nutritional challenges of the crisis were significant to earnings and nutritional intake for at least another decade. The costs of the relief on the landowner were also noticeable, with land being sold off and others using what funds they had left to assist in the emigration of their tenants. In one study it was found that 9,000 more emigrants left Scottish ports in 1847–9 compared with the departures recorded in the three years before famine struck. For many contemporaries, emigration was the only response to the crisis, but as the report on Lunacy in Scotland makes clear, it tended always to be the young and able that left: 'Often the intention is there to send for the weak, the imbecilic, the deaf and dumb, but as a rule this rarely happens.'[39] And there was no immediate abandonment of the Highlands, with preference first for internal movement. In most cases of western and island depopulation – ranging from 12 per cent in South Uist to 21 per cent in Barra and 23 per cent in Coll – much was already in progress before the blight took hold. The parishes of Invernessshire and Sutherland in the east and the towns of Dingwall, Tain, and Stornaway increased in population between 1841 and 1851. It is suggestive that emigrant flight during blight was not coterminous when accounting for the 60,000 highland Scots who were displaced in the period 1841 to 1861. Only after the Emigration Act of 1851 was there government finance to help with the cost of passage for those otherwise held in place by the debt of rent arrears.

A 'thickening and widening of economic activities' is Whatley's description of the nation's economic transformation in the second half of the eighteenth century. Linen sales and the import and re-export of tobacco proved lucrative to the Glasgow merchants.[40] The shipping needs of the 'tobacco lords' and the impetus that came from canal development created demand for the output of the Carron iron works (founded in 1759). This inter-dependency, part of an economy maturing and expanding, showed signs of connection with Empire and global markets that would become so remarkable over the next century. Trade in goods but also in financial services, and investment in overseas trade were key, indicated by bank assets increasing from £329,000 to £3.1 million and a fifteen-fold increase in the circulation of banknotes between 1744 and 1772 alongside the development of a regional banking system.[41]

However we interpret the occupational restructuring that might lead us to discern patterns in Scotland's emigration, more jobs than ever before were created as the nineteenth century progressed and the standard of living (albeit not dramatically) did rise. The industrialising phase from the mid-eighteenth century was predicated on textile work. By working looms in their homes, rural Scots, in the Borders, Highlands and Islands especially, were able to obtain some much-needed cash to sustain a family's working life in the fields. By the 1830s, seven out of ten adult jobs were involved in work associated with the textile industry, and the handloom industry still employed 100,000 workers in 1880s although by then the work was no longer the engine of Scotland's economic output. As the nineteenth century unfolded from the 1830s, textile work had become heavily feminised and the average wage had dropped. Thread spinning instead of cotton spinning was the new cotton-kingmaker, although hosiery work in the Borders and knitting in the Western Isles retained regional significance. Textile and clothing employed 20.3 per cent of the occupied male labour force in 1851 but only 7.2 per cent in 1911, a decline second only to that of agriculture. By contrast, shipbuilding, engineering and metal work increased over the same period from nearly 7 per cent to 16 per cent. New skills were created, older skills lost out, and work patterns shifted: the estimate that 25 per cent of Glasgow's labour force was casually employed in 1830 was seen to drop to a fraction by the end of the twentieth century as regular full-time work triumphed.[42] The sectoral nature of this industrial transformation is shown in Table 3.5.

The growth in demand for coal came from the heavy industries of iron, steel and shipbuilding. Between them, 300,000 jobs were added from 1851 to 1911. The percentage of the occupied male population involved in hewing coal from the ground increased from 6.2 per cent (1851) to 11.2 per cent (1911). So different was this new economy that not only were many more jobs found in emerging sectors, but also new kinds of jobs came into being: employment in transportation increased by 17 per cent, the result of railway

Table 3.5 Main production categories: Scotland, 1841–1951 [source: Census of Population (Scotland), 1841–1951][43]

Year	Agriculture services	Mining	Manufacturing	Construction	Utilities	Services
1841	231,629	25,202	352,016	52,437	71,726	252,897
1931	199,185	125,253	567,504	89,797	254,308	757,716
1951	170,437	85,045	559,251	131,662	438,464	864,168

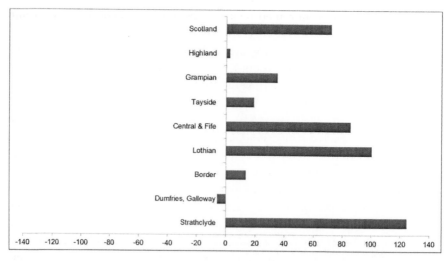

Figure 3.2 Regional rates (per cent) of employment growth: occupied males, 1851–1911 [source: adapted from Treble, 'The occupied male labour force', p. 176 (Table 1)]

growth and transportation demands from new endeavours. Scotland's shipbuilders employed 4,000 people in 1841, 51,000 in 1911 and 122,000 in 1921. The Clyde produced less than 5 per cent of Britain's shipping output in 1835, a figure that rose to one-third in 1870–1911 and, by 1913, 18 per cent of world shipping launched from its docks. The North British Railway Works (1903) – with the largest output in Europe – exported its steam engines and rolling stock to the diaspora, the Empire and the world. With the exception of the Dumfries and Galloway, every region of Scotland gained from male employment growth in the second half of the nineteenth century (Figure 3.2).

The economic changes of the first half of the nineteenth century meant much internal movement and generally, for most, better wages. And while it was not until the last quarter of that century that the professions rose in prominence, the earlier period found an expansion in the middle classes, with bookwork, supervisory and knowledge-based positions looking to be filled.

While it is difficult to get precise evidence beyond the life course data of the genealogist, the nature of Scotland's economy suggests that amongst an abundance of personal reasons, male Scots especially were choosing to migrate overseas for improved remuneration for their industrial skills rather than a straightforward end to under- or unemployment. Wages at home were rising, but still more could be got elsewhere. The effect of Scots workers emigrating was not necessarily negative, however. A hypothesis can be proposed that the search for better paying employment had mitigating effects on the domestic economy because of a continued diasporic connection between the host and sending nation. Novelist and secretary of the Canada Company John Galt reasoned that the glut of goods the new emigrant would need, and likely to be acquired in quick order and without time for haggling away the seller's profit, would be of benefit to Scotland's manufacturers. As well, industrious migrants, and those of the middle classes with some capital and savings of their own, provided a market for Scots goods and a means for manufacturers in Scotland to acquire raw material. Such connections also developed opportunities for investment of Scots' capital. In this vein it has been argued that the influence on overseas trade by Scottish merchants was of greater significance than the impact of that trade upon domestic businesses.[44] Between 1865 and 1914 the UK invested $5 billion in the United States alone.[45] Scotland's wealth relied significantly on overseas investment, with estimates suggesting this increased from around £60 million in 1870 to £500 million in 1914. Approximately 8 per cent of Scotland's income came from investment and business ventures overseas in 1910. This was a higher proportion than found down south: equating to £110 for every person in Scotland compared to £90 per person in England.[46] Other evidence suggests that Scottish investment overseas ranged between £390 million and £520 million in 1914.[47] Aberdeen speculators invested in the USA, beginning with the Illinois Investment Company in 1837, and the Scottish Australian Company in New South Wales. Robert Fleming's Scottish American Trust formed in the 1870s when risk capital became available. Not much of this investment came from Glasgow, but when the City of Glasgow Bank collapsed it had many overseas commitments.[48]

E URBANISATION

The milieu of demographic and nutritional pressures outlined so far, along with the counter-attractions of industrial employment linked into British and imperial markets, accelerated the ongoing transformation in where Scots lived. With Lanarkshire home to more Scots than any other county in 1801, by the time two more decades had passed nearly half of all Scots lived in the industrialising central belt between Glasgow and Edinburgh; in 1801–41 83 per cent of Scots lived there.

By the middle of the nineteenth century Scotland was one of Europe's most urbanised nations when measurement is taken at towns over 10,000 (Table 3.6). These trends continued – from 31 per cent of the population in 1831 to 59 per cent in 1911 were to be found living in towns of 5,000 people and above (Table 3.7). And when measured at the more substantial level of 20,000 people, then Scotland lagged only England as Europe's most urbanised nation mid-century, with England standing at 61 per cent and Scotland at

Table 3.6 Urban percentage of total population in selected territories, 1700–1800 (in towns ≥10,000) [source: DeVries, *European Urbanization*, p. 39 (Table 3.7 adapted)]

Territory	1700	1750	1800
Scandinavia	4.0	4.6	4.6
England & Wales	13.3	16.7	20.3
Scotland	5.3	9.2	17.3
Ireland	3.4	5.0	7.0
Netherlands	33.6	30.5	28.8
Belgium	23.9	19.6	18.9
Germany	4.8	5.6	5.5
France	9.2	9.1	8.8

Table 3.7 Percentage population in Scottish towns (≥5000), showing increase over previous decade [source: Flinn, *Scottish Population History*, pp. 313 and 315]

Year	Population in Scottish towns >5000 (per cent)	Increase over previous decade (per cent)
1831	31.2	28.2
1841	32.7	16.2
1851	35.9	17.3
1861	39.4	16.2
1871	44.4	23.6
1881	48.9	12.8
1891	53.5	17.6
1901	57.6	19.7
1911	58.6	8.1
1921	61.3	7.3

50 per cent, followed by the Netherlands at 40 per cent. Geographically this urbanisation was concentrated, although each county had its towns. As early as 1821 Glasgow had overtaken its east-coast rival to be Scotland's largest city and Britain's second largest.[49] Dundee's population increased five-fold in the period 1820 to 1890; Aberdeen grew at rates of just under 30 per cent per decade until 1831 and by 1851 the population had more than doubled.

After 1800 and especially from the middle of the nineteenth century forward, Scotland was, per capita, one of Europe's greatest exporters of urban industrial people to the New World (Chapter 4, Table 4.2). More were employed in agriculture in Scotland than in England, but compared with Britain's major competitors in 1911 the proportion making their living from the land was remarkably low: Scotland 13 per cent; England 9 per cent; France 43 per cent; Germany 37 per cent; the USA 31 per cent.[50] Starting from the mid-eighteenth century, 200 years of land improvement and occupational change had turned Scots males into wage earners, employers and labourers

– no longer renters or owners of land, and as a consequence less wedded to the land. Between 1841 and 1911 the newly created jobs were overwhelmingly male, at a rate of around 3:1, and increasingly so after 1918 with male paid employment peaking at 1.57 million.[51] Yet this is a story of social dislocation. The successes of the great capitalists, inventors and industrialists, with immense resources under their command, and that of the many small capitalists who proliferated the economy, masked the sheer instability of the working lives created by their endeavours. More so than in England, Scottish capital looked overseas for investment returns and to fill order books. Yet overseas orders came with economic dependency upon the international trade cycle, as well as Britain's own periods of cyclical prosperity and shortage, including reliance upon industries equally tied to export markets. Wages improved relative to costs while remaining on average lower than for comparable work in England. The 'economic miracle' of Scotland's Victorian age was remarkably fragile, a point made by matching periods of economic depression with the great peaks in emigration in the 1840s and 1850s, the mid-1880s, 1906–13 and the 1920s.[52] Life expectancy was longer in the countryside than in the towns, yet migration to the industrial areas was the norm.

F   CONCLUSION

In the period covered by this volume, Scotland was a European urban nation *par excellence*. The demographic pressures that challenged the Scots' standard of living and the occupational opportunities of industrialisation each fed movement to the towns. Along with rural–urban migration must be added inter-city migration and the natural increase in population. The results were dramatic: half of Glasgow's population was born outside the city in the middle of the nineteenth century, a higher rate than the London metropolis. These kinds of evidence suggest that overseas migration can only be analysed within the context of internal migrations. The trauma of eviction and clearance in the Highlands region widened as the forces of the free market pressed the Scots to leave their homes for a livelihood elsewhere. The first half of the twentieth century experienced yet further economic realignment as well as the suffering of two world wars. It was no paradox that Scots left an industrialising economy that was one of Europe's most urbanised nations. The destinations might have been different as were the strains and contexts, but internal and overseas migrations had long been the pattern to Scotland's economic and social history. The twa lands – in spiritual and structural union – were not for separating.

NOTES

1. Munro, *The View from Castle Rock*.
2. Harper and Vance (ed.), *Myth, Migration and the Making of Memory*, pp. 29–37.
3. Morton, 'The social memory of Jane Porter', pp. 312–15.
4. Bueltmann, *Scottish Ethnicity*, pp. 41 and 202.
5. Winter, *Sites of Memory, Sites of Mourning*, pp. 24–7.
6. Baines, *Migration in a Mature Economy*, p. 35.
7. Malthus, *An Essay on the Principle of Population*.
8. Morton, *Ourselves and Others*, p. 24.
9. Richards, *A History of the Highland Clearances*, ii, pp. 158–60.
10. Gibson and Smout, 'Scottish food and Scottish history', p. 11.
11. Ibid., p. 84.
12. Blaikie, 'Rituals, transitions and life courses in an era of social transformation', pp. 90–1.
13. Whatley, *Scottish Society*, p. 2.
14. Anderson and Morse, 'The people', p 30.
15. www.gro-scotland.gov.uk (accessed 1 February 2012).
16. Anderson and Morse, 'The people', pp. 8 and 31.
17. See http://www.scotlandscensus.gov.uk (accessed 2 February 2012).
18. Anderson, 'Population and family life', p. 17.
19. Withers, *Urban Highlanders*, p. 62; Anderson, 'The demographic regime', p. 20.
20. Withers, *Urban Highlanders*, pp. 64–5.
21. Ibid, pp. 66–7.
22. Anderson, 'The demographic regime', p. 21.
23. Withers, *Urban Highlanders*, p. 76.
24. Corrins, 'The Scottish business elite in the nineteenth century – the case of William Baird and Company', pp. 58–83.
25. Withers, *Urban Highlanders*, p. 101.
26. Baines, *Migration in a Mature Economy*, p. 12.
27. Devine, *The Scottish Nation*, p. 125.
28. Gibson and Smout, 'Scottish food and Scottish history', pp. 62 and 68.
29. Ward, *Birth Weight and Economic Growth*, p. 44.
30. Blaikie, 'Rituals, transitions and life courses', p. 94.
31. Dodgshon, 'Everyday structures, rhythms and spaces of the Scottish countryside', p. 37.
32. Morton, *Ourselves and Others*, pp. 23–4.
33. Treble, 'The occupied male labour force', p. 167.
34. Dodgshon, 'Everyday structures, rhythms and spaces', p. 35.

35. Devine, 'The Highland Clearances', p. 136; Stewart and Watson, 'Land, the landscape and people', p. 28.

36. Hart, 'The changing distribution of sheep in Britain', p. 260.

37. This work is based on data provided through www.VisionofBritain.org. uk and uses historical material which is copyright of the Great Britain Historical GIS Project and the University of Portsmouth (accessed 1 February 2013).

38. Devine, *The Scottish Nation*, p. 413.

39. Levi, 'On the economic condition of the Highlands and Islands of Scotland', pp. 386–7.

40. Whatley, Scottish Society, p. 65.

41. Ibid, p. 67.

42. Treble, 'The occupied male labour force', pp. 171–2, 186.

43. This work is based on data provided through www.VisionofBritain.org. uk and uses historical material which is copyright of the Great Britain Historical GIS Project and the University of Portsmouth (accessed 1 February 2013).

44. Campbell, 'Scotland', p. 21.

45. Devine, *To The Ends of the Earth*, p. 97.

46. Lee, 'Scotland, 1860–1939', p. 444. Although some of this capital may have originated from England, Devine, 'Industrialization', p. 57.

47. Devine, *To The Ends of the Earth*, p. 231.

48. Campbell, 'Scotland', pp. 19–20.

49. Whatley, *Scottish Society*, p. 2.

50. Knox, 'A history of the Scottish People'; www.scran.ac.uk (accessed 20 February 2013).

51. Lee, *Scotland and the United Kingdom*, p. 25.

52. Devine, *To the Ends of the Earth*, p. 105.

CHAPTER 4

Scottish Migrants: Numbers and Demographics

A Teddy Bear said to his parents one day,
'Dear Father and Mother I'm going away;
I love these big mountains and valleys and trees.
But I long to see beauties far greater than these.
There's a place in Pennsylvania a grand State
Where I am told everything is kept right up to date;
The people are honest and happy and wise –
To please all his neighbors each citizen tries,
That's where I am going, for if I am there
I know I'll grow up a good, useful old bear.'
He kissed them all good-bye and with his heart light and gay,
In his fur overcoat Teddy trudged on his way,
He soon met his cousin who smiled and then said:
'I'm going there also–how's that, Cousin Ted?'
They trotted along through the valley so fair,
At last they were joined by another young bear,
More Teddies were met as the bears marched along,
And they soon formed an army about ninety strong.
There were Teddies from England and Scotland and Wales.
And others from Russia and Cork and Versailles;
The Dutchman, the Darkey, the Chinese, the Jap,
And teddies from every old town on the map.
They kept right ahead with a hop and a skip
Til they land at Beaver, the end of their trip.
The people ran out and screamed with delight,
For these Teddy Bears made a very odd sight . . .[1]

Between 1815 and 1914 an estimated 55 to 60 million migrants left Europe for the New World nations of South America, North America, the Caribbean, Africa and Australasia.[2] Over 2 million of these Europeans were Scots, disproportionately contributing to an unprecedented population redistribution that altered irretrievably the globe's geopolitical balance. Just why emigration came to be such a common experience requires focus upon the numbers of migrating Scots who journeyed south to England and Wales and in even greater numbers overseas. By sketching out the flow of people prepared to overlook the economic, physical and mental dangers that accompanied settlement in another country, we present outcomes from the structure/action equilibrium.

Scots knew the issues that precipitated their removal from the countryside and from the towns. Having surveyed the pauper parishes of Edinburgh in 1849, the social reformer and Secretary of the Edinburgh Ragged School Dr George Bell described the 'excuses', rejecting them as reasons, for the eviction of highland Scots and the encouragement to emigration that followed. He railed against the suggestion that the Scots lacked self-motivation, or that the weather was detrimental to agricultural life, or the ground and coasts would not support them. In his mind it was the lack of support from the landlord class who should instead give the peasantry the chance to labour: '[t]his is as true of Scotland as it is of Norway, Belgium, Switzerland and France'.[3]

Around 11.6 million people left England, Wales and Scotland between 1825 and 1930. Scotland's share was 2.3 million of that total, and always fewer people left Scotland per decade than from England (Figure 4.1).[4] Italy (8 million), Germany (5 million) and a significant amount from Spain and

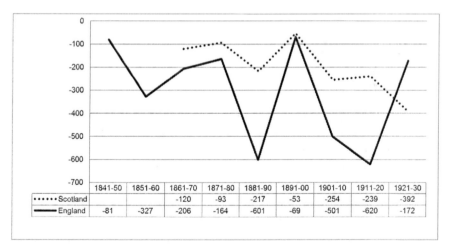

	1841-50	1851-60	1861-70	1871-80	1881-90	1891-00	1901-10	1911-20	1921-30
⋯⋯ Scotland			-120	-93	-217	-53	-254	-239	-392
▬▬ England	-81	-327	-206	-164	-601	-69	-501	-620	-172

Figure 4.1 UK net migration: Scotland compared with England & Wales (excluding Ireland), 1841–1931 (000s) [source: derived from Baines, *Migration in a Mature Economy*, p. 61 (Tables 3.1 and 3.2)]

Table 4.1 Overseas emigration from Europe by country and by decade, 1851–1960 (in 000s) [source: Mitchell, *European Historical Statistics*, p. 47]

	1851–60	1861–70	1871–80	1881–90	1891–1900	1901–10	1911–20	1921–30	1931–40	1941–50	1951–60
Austria-Hungary	31	40	46	248	440	1,111	418	61	11		53
Belgium	1	2	2	21	16	30	21	33	20	29	109
Denmark		8	39	82	51	73	52	64	100	38	68
Finland				26	59	159	67	73	3	7	32
France	27	36	66	119	51	53	32	4	5		155
Germany	671	779	626	1,342	527	274	91	564	121	618	872
Italy	5	27	168	992	1,580	3,615	2,194	1,370	235	467	858
Netherlands	16	20	17	52	24	28	22	32	4	75	341
Norway	36	98	85	187	95	191	62	87	6	10	25
Poland								634	164		
Portugal	45	79	131	185	266	324	402	995	108	69	346
Russia			58	288	481	911	420				
Spain	3	7	13	572	791	1,091	1,306	560	132	166	543
Sweden	17	122	103	327	205	324	86	107	8	23	43
Switzerland	6	15	36	85	35	37	31	50	47	18	23
United Kingdom & Ireland	1,313	1,572	1,849	3,259	2,149	3,150	2,587	2,151	262	755	1,454

Portugal (4.5 million) were the principal counterparts, although throughout every decade after 1851 for a century, the United Kingdom and Ireland sent out more emigrants than any other European state.[5]

A   RAVENSTEIN AND THE 'LAWS' OF MIGRATION

Scotland's migration history gains its place within the analysis of the Great European migration of the modern period when measured in per capita terms: then Scotland was, along with Ireland and Norway, one of the leading emigrant nations (Table 4.2).[6]

Presently we will examine the reasons for this national exodus, but first attention turns to an influential set of 'laws' of migration first proposed over one century ago. The 'laws' are derived from evidence collated from the 1871 and 1881 censuses of Scotland and England and Wales and were formulated by Ernst Georg Ravenstein, Frankfurt-born and an immigrant to England in 1852. A renowned cartographer and demographer, backed by statistical training in Germany, Ravenstein received the first Victoria gold medal of the Royal Geographical Society in 1902.[8] He was spurred into exploring patterns

Table 4.2 Overseas emigration, 1851–1913: average annual rate per 1,000 population [source: Baines, *Migration in a Mature Economy*, p. 10 (Table 2.1, adapted)][7]

Rank	European country	1851–60	1861–70	1871–80	1881–90	1891–1900	1901–10	1913
1	Ireland	14.0	14.6	6.6	14.2	8.9	7.0	6.8
2	Norway	2.4	5.8	4.7	9.5	4.5	8.3	4.2
3	Scotland	5.0	4.6	4.7	7.1	4.4	9.9	14.4
4	Italy			1.1	3.4	5.0	10.8	16.3
5	England & Wales	2.6	2.8	4.0	5.6	3.6	5.5	7.6
6	Sweden	0.5	3.1	2.4	7.0	4.1	4.2	3.1
7	Portugal		1.9	2.9	3.8	5.1	5.7	13.0
8	Spain				3.6	4.4	5.7	10.5
9	Denmark			2.1	3.9	2.2	2.8	3.2
10	Finland				1.3	2.3	5.5	6.4
11	Austria-Hungary			0.3	1.1	1.6	4.8	6.1
12	Switzerland			1.3	3.2	1.4	1.4	1.7
13	Germany			1.5	2.9	1.0	0.5	0.4
14	Netherlands	0.5	0.6	0.5	1.2	0.5	0.5	0.4
15	Belgium				0.9	0.4	0.6	1.0
16	France	0.1	0.2	0.2	0.3	0.1	0.1	0.2

of migration by the suggestion from William Farr that no laws existed that could explain the many varied movements of people around Britain. Farr was superintendent of the statistical department of the General Register Office and determined to establish his own laws, of the spread of disease, that might benefit sanitary reform.[9] Responding to Farr's summons led Ravenstein to publish his laws of migration in the *Geographical Magazine* (1876) and the *Journal of the Statistical Society of London* in 1885 and 1889.[10] By studying birthplace data he advanced the following generalisations upon the migration experience:

1. The majority of migrants go only a short distance.
2. Migration proceeds step by step.
3. Migrants going long distances generally go by preference to one of the great centres of commerce or industry.
4. Each current of migration produces a compensating counter-current.
5. The natives of towns are less migratory than those of rural areas.
6. Females are more migratory than males within the Kingdom, but males frequently venture beyond.
7. Most migrants are adults; families rarely migrate out of their country of birth.
8. Large towns grow more by migration than by natural increase.

9. Migration increases in volume as industries and commerce develop and transport improves.

10. The major direction of migration is from the agricultural areas to the centres of industry and commerce.

11. The major causes of migration are economic.[11]

Grigg has made the strongest case for the enduring relevance of Ravenstein's proposals, although others suggest the assumptions are misplaced, the analysis mechanical, and the results impossible to prove from the evidence.[12] A survey of the scholarship concludes that these 'laws' are simply hypotheses, and as such shape rather than define the parameters of analysis.

Applying the Scottish evidence to test Ravenstein's observations, however, finds a mixture of insight and exception. Scotland offers structural explanations for the first proposition that the majority of migrants tend to travel short distances (law one). In most of the nation's rural regions agricultural labourers were hired on six-month contracts where livelihood and home were lost whenever a contract was not renewed. In the towns where rental was the norm, Scots were used to moving fairly often. Even with leases being for twelve months, and because of the landlords' requirement that agreements be signed in advance, locking in tenants for around sixteen months, considerably longer than the shorter leases found in England, moving day was a flurry of motion.[13] The Scottish example provides a range of evidence of internal movement, often inter-regional, circular, contra- and frequently inter- and intra-urban. Despite uncertainty as to what distance counted as short or long,[14] Ravenstein's law identifies short-distance migrants as those who move to an adjacent county or to a bordering country. Table 4.3 shows the preponderance of small moves by English and Welsh migrants to elsewhere in the same kingdom and to the border countries is marked compared to the small moves of the Scots and Irish to their sister kingdoms. Yet the generalisation that local migration tended towards neighbouring counties remains valid, militating against movement to progressively larger destinations.[15]

Universality should be avoided, however, with the notion of step migration (law two). The hypothesis is validated to some extent in the highland example

Table 4.3 Proportion of migrants enumerated elsewhere in UK [source: Ravenstein, 'The laws of migration' (1885), p. 182]

Proportion of migrants enumerated in:	Border countries	Elsewhere in the same kingdom	Sister kingdom
Migrants of Anglo-Welsh birth	52.4	45.1	2.5
Migrants of Scottish birth	46.0	29.8	24.2
Migrants of Irish birth	16.2	24.1	59.7
Migrants of British birth	46.2	39.9	13.9

presented by Withers (Chapter 3), but there is evidence both for migration in stages as well as migration by long distance without any intervening passages of residence elsewhere. Indeed, Ravenstein's suggestion that perhaps one quarter of migrants move straight to their final destination without any intervening steps, meaning three-quarters took any number of steps, is impossible to prove from the snapshot census. We also suggest it is too simplistic to claim that migrants' longer movements are only to 'large industrial and commercial towns' (law three). Scotland's urban network was remarkable for the appearance of towns in all its regions. From the eighteenth century onwards Scotland housed its people in towns to an extent that neared European highs. Their inter-urban movement has to be accounted for, not least because it was both short and long in distance.[16] The life course analysis of Pooley and Turnbull finds just as many large to small movements, as small to large – and no discernible pattern of ever more distant movements, although this was not consistent over time.[17]

Two other aspects of Ravenstein's laws are similarly less than convincing when applied to the Scottish evidence: the notion of counter-currents (law four) and the supposition that more people migrate from the countryside than the towns (law five). Scotland sustained higher levels of net loss than England (Table 4.5) notwithstanding the influx of Irish migrants in the second half of the nineteenth century. Neither does the Scottish pattern easily fit the law that rural people migrate more than urban people. Indeed Grigg points out that Ravenstein's own evidence can be interpreted to show urban migrants sustained proportionately greater flows.[18] Underpinning this migration was a rising population that could no longer be sustained in the countryside (law ten), yet most Scots had long mixed industrial work in rural settings. By contrast under-population in the 'white colonies' was a problem that created a demand for migrants, especially for workers who had some experience of industrial work. A number of spinners who found their wages and then their jobs diminish in the 1830s were attracted to the opportunities overseas. And highlanders, most of whom had some familiarity with seasonal work in the manufacturers of lowland Scotland, made up the bulk of Scottish migrants before the 1840s, to then be replaced by lowlanders who had endured the cyclical employment of urban industry. The rural/urban, agricultural/industrial distinction is far from clear, and made more complex still by inter-censal movements and the limitations within the historical records for distinguishing between recent, temporary, return, short- and long-term migration.

The gender ratios found in Scotland and in the host nations around the world confirm the tendency for young single men to predominate in migration flows, a feature long in existence (law six). The lack of Poor Law support for unemployed men who were otherwise fit and healthy encouraged them to seek employment wherever it was available. Single men were especially mobile,

Table 4.4 Estimates of Scottish migration, 1600–1700 [source: Smout, Landsman and Devine, 'Scottish emigration in the seventeenth and eighteenth centuries', pp. 85–90 (Tables 5.1 and 5.2)]

Destination	Minimum	Maximum
1600–1650		
Ireland	20,000	30,000
Poland	30,000	40,000
Scandinavia	25,000	30,000
Elsewhere	10,000	15,000
Totals	85,000	115,000
1650–1700		
America	7,000	7,000
Ireland	60,000	100,000
Elsewhere	10,000	20,000
Totals	78,000	127,000

with marriage delayed until some level of financial stability could be secured. That women did not match them in overseas migration can be attributed to a reluctance to participate in pioneer life and single women being dissuaded from emigrating by kin and community. The persistence of this pattern can be seen in the rate of young men leaving Scotland being not so different in the mid-seventeenth century as it was in the mid-nineteenth century. The evidence from the earlier period shows Scots travelling east in substantial numbers to Scandinavia and the Baltic to pick up work as traders, pedlars and as soldiers: perhaps around 2,000 per year and likely more in the famine decades of the 1680s and 1690s when Ireland was the preferred destination. Because young men predominated in these numbers, likely around 20 per cent of Scotland's fifteen- to thirty-year-olds were involved, a figure not too dissimilar to the number of young men who left between 1851 and 1861.[19]

Much of the evidence from Scotland confirms that adults did predominate in overseas migration (law seven), and to a lesser extent in shorter-distance migration, although other examples question whether families 'rarely' migrated. Census evidence suggests that while in a minority, families did migrate in good numbers, and also that family groups followed to join their pioneering kin settlers. The Scots who headed to New Zealand tended for Otago and Gaelic-speaking highlanders to Glengarry in Upper Canada show the reliance of the chain, with letters home almost perpetually exhorting wider family kin to join in the emigration adventure, sharing stories of abundance and social freedoms. So while families did not dominate the flows, Ravenstein's conclusions appear to assign too much weight to the over-representation of single men.[20] Showing how the 'laws' can be undermined by exogenous events, gender ratios were highest in the 1840s in New Zealand before a policy focus on family and female migrants during the Vogel period closed the gap (see Chapter 14).[21] Also, while it has been the case that more men moved overseas than women, this is not the same as saying men moved longer distances than women. Examining longitudinal data, Pooley and Turnbull find women moving long distances in the period 1850 to 1930 when using sample evidence to highlight those who migrated for family reasons. Older women were prepared to move longer than average to join their family, countering the suggestion that such migration was simply about work and dominated by men (law eleven).[22]

Similarly the law that 'towns grow more by migration than natural increase' (law eight) can be accepted to some extent, but is difficult to sustain over time and between examples. In the UK London is out on its own for its ability to overcome distance decay, and Glasgow was one of the leading migrant destinations in the middle of the nineteenth century, yet the demographic transition as well as more general local fluctuations impacted on the natural increase of these cities. Exceptions are also found in Ravenstein's assumption that transformation in transportation (law nine) shaped patterns of migration. While intuitive, this is difficult to prove and counter-factors are legion: for instance, governments, not shipowners, established the criteria for right of entry and settlement. There is little to suggest that the arrival of steam locomotion and an expansion of the railway network in the 1830s and again in the 1860s changed the preference for short-distance migration.[23] The train was relatively expensive and it was not until the second phase of its expansion that railway stations were generally sited in the heart of the city rather than its edge. Although Ravenstein was writing during the 'age of the railway', and the steamship was the preferred mode of oceanic travel from the 1870s, sea travel under sail and rigging remained an important carrier of people and goods. Steamships, though, quickened first by refinements of the screw propeller and then the turbine engine at the start of the twentieth century, allowed for faster and more regular crossings, bringing down fares and facilitating both return migration and visits to friends and family.

B   NUMBERS OF MIGRATORY PEOPLE

The introduction of the Scottish evidence confirms the wider view that Ravenstein's laws are in fact hypotheses formed from empirical observation. What also transpires is that these observations are not theoretically informed – a tendency identifiable in a range of migration studies.[24] As was argued in Chapter 2, high or low numbers of migrants are simply that: flows of people. Without the conceptual framework of diaspora, counting or categorising migrant Scots and their descendants does not explain boundary maintenance and ethnic affiliation across nations. In other words, we are unable to say anything meaningful about the Scottish diaspora at all. To emphasise again our key point: the value of the diaspora concept is that it adds analytical depth to the empirical observation of migrant flows.

With the conceptual parameters in place and added to Ravenstein's hypotheses, the remainder of this chapter will focus on what we know about Scotland's migrant population. A continuous run of emigration statistics is only available from 1825, based on ship muster rolls. Prior to 1863 the figures obtained through the Passenger Acts include only steerage not cabin passengers, and the Scots who left from English and Irish posts before 1853 are not traced (and most likely it is emigrants to Australia and New Zealand who were under-reported here).[25] There are disembarkation statistics for America (1820) and Canada (1829), but the evidence is not comprehensive.[26]

Scotland's population grew from just over 3 million in 1861 to 4.8 million in 1921 (Chapter 3, Table 3.3) an increase of 55 per cent. While significant, this compared with England's growth over the same period of 79 per cent and that of Wales of 87 per cent. Noticeably, we are unable to explain away this difference by comparing each nation's crude death and crude birth rate (Table 4.5): these rates were remarkably similar despite other data showing marital fertility in Scotland was between 8 per cent and 21 per cent higher. Scottish women concentrated on having children in the early years of marriage and stopped earlier, but were hindered in getting married by the relative lack of available young men.[27] Whereas one woman in five aged forty-five to fifty-four was single in 1871, one woman in eight in England and Wales was unmarried – meaning that Scotland's nuptiality returns were dampened although those that did marry had higher rates of child-bearing than women in England.[28] That this pattern continued is seen from evidence collected in the 1911 census which shows Scottish fertility levels above those for England and Wales for all ages of marriage, although fertility rates were by then declining.[29]

Table 4.5 Birth and death rates, population change and emigration: England & Wales and Scotland, 1861–1920 [source: Anderson and Morse, 'High fertility, high emigration, low nuptiality', p. 8 (Table 3)]

	Per cent population change		Crude birth rate		Crude death rate		Net out-migration/ 1000		Gross emigration/ 1000	
	E&W	Scot	E&W	Scot	E&W	Scot	E&W	Scot	E&W	Scot
1861–70	13.2	9.7	35.2	35.0	22.5	22.1	1.0	3.9	2.8	4.6
1871–80	14.4	11.2	35.4	34.8	21.4	21.6	0.7	2.8	4.0	4.7
1881–90	11.7	7.8	32.5	32.3	19.2	19.2	2.3	5.8	5.6	7.1
1891–00	12.2	11.1	29.9	30.2	18.2	18.5	0.2	1.3	3.6	4.4
1901–10	10.9	6.5	27.3	28.4	15.4	16.6	1.5	5.7	5.5	9.9
1911–20	4.9	2.6	22.7	24.0	14.6	15.3	1.7	3.5	4.0	7.3

Instead the major contribution to slowing Scotland's population growth came from the very high out-migration rates. Both the rate of gross emigration and the rate of net out-migration show a higher percentage of people leaving Scotland than England and Wales during each decade (Table 4.5). The relative drag of these outflows on Scotland's population growth is confirmed as a percentage of natural increase (Figure 4.2) and population (Figure 4.3). Over

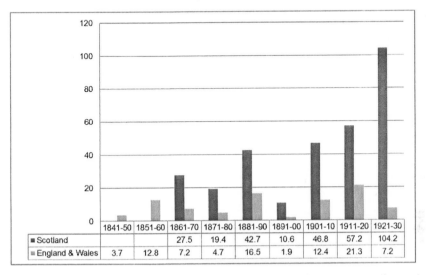

	1841-50	1851-60	1861-70	1871-80	1881-90	1891-00	1901-10	1911-20	1921-30
■ Scotland			27.5	19.4	42.7	10.6	46.8	57.2	104.2
■ England & Wales	3.7	12.8	7.2	4.7	16.5	1.9	12.4	21.3	7.2

Figure 4.2 Decadal net migration (overseas and internal) expressed as percentage of natural increase: Scotland, England & Wales, 1841–1930 [source: Baines, *Migration in a Mature Economy*, p. 61, derived from Tables 3.1 and 3.2]

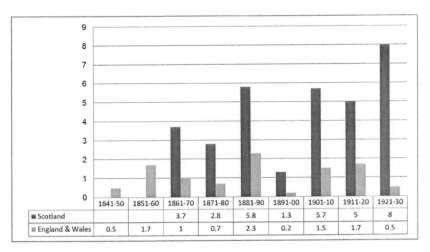

	1841-50	1851-60	1861-70	1871-80	1881-90	1891-00	1901-10	1911-20	1921-30
■ Scotland			3.7	2.8	5.8	1.3	5.7	5	8
■ England & Wales	0.5	1.7	1	0.7	2.3	0.2	1.5	1.7	0.5

Figure 4.3 Net migration (overseas and internal) expressed as percentage of population: Scotland, England & Wales, 1841–1930 [source: Baines, *Migration in a Mature Economy*, p. 61, derived from Tables 3.1 and 3.2]

the period 1853–1930, some 61 per cent of Scotland's natural increase was lost to out-migration whereas England and Wales lost around 36 per cent.[30] When we are able to factor in return migration to the analysis for the period 1861 to 1911, Scotland lost 30.2 per cent of its natural increase to out-migration, compared with less than 9 per cent in England.[31]

Proportions and timings of migrations were different either side of the Scottish-English border, too, despite the growing influence of the central state after 1840. In the period 1853–1930 Scotland contributed 19 per cent of Britain's emigrants while comprising 14 per cent of its population at the start and 11 per cent at the end of that time-frame. Scottish migration also happened later than in England: half of the English total had left by 1899 whereas half had not left Scotland until 1906. And it was at the start of the twentieth century that the rate of emigration from Scotland far exceeded that for England, leaving at nearly twice the rate between 1901 and 1914 (11.2 per cent per thousand compared to 6 per cent per thousand).

C FOLLOWING THE FLOW

From what demographers have been able to gather from the official record, an estimated 1.9 million people left Scotland between 1861 and the start of the Second World War (Table 4.6), a figure that rises to 2.3 million when the start point is 1825.[32] Every region of Scotland experienced net outward emigration in every decade between 1861 and 1914, with net migration near universal for all the counties.[33]

The numbers of Scots migrating can be split pre- and post-Famine, giving 1860 as the tipping point. The numbers who left Scotland in the seventeenth century were anything between 163,000 and 242,000 (Table 4.4), averaging

Table 4.6 Net out-migration from Scotland, 1861–1920
[source: Flinn, *Scottish Population* History, p. 441 (Table 6.1.1)][34]

Decade	Net out-migration
1861–70	116,872
1871–80	92,808
1881–90	218,274
1891–1900	51,728
1901–10	253,894
1911–20	226,768
1921–30	415,768
1931–39	47,973
1861–1939	**1,875,324**

around 2,000 people per year; an estimate of the Scots who left for overseas between 1763 and 1776 is put at 25,000 or again around 2,000 per year.[35] The flow of migrants in 1825–50 has been estimated at around 10,000 per year; whereas in 1850–75 this flow had risen to just under 20,000 per year. The regional impact of this phase of migration is illustrated by the Western Highlands losing a third of its population between 1841 and 1861.[36] By the early 1900s the numbers leaving Scotland had reached 20–30,000 per year and by 1914 this had gone up to 60,000 per year.[37]

How much were the flows determined by the pull of the host nations versus the push from Scotland, and did tales of disproportionate success help the former? In the American census of 1850 Scots were the fifth largest group of foreigners (born outside the US), standing at 70,550.[38] So while the number of Scots leaving was a very significant proportion of Scotland's population, it was less relevant to the host countries where Scots were routinely outnumbered by English and Irish arrivals. Still, Ferenc Morton Szaz follows the disproportionate argument, that 'Scottish ideals of individual achievement, economic advance and opposition to privilege and caste' proved attractive, a suggestion we examine further in Chapter 10.[39]

Of all overseas migrants leaving Scottish ports, around one quarter of Scots left for the United States in the period 1830–1844, rising to 55 per cent during 1845–53, peaking at 76 per cent in 1890–4. In the 1830s and until 1844, Canada

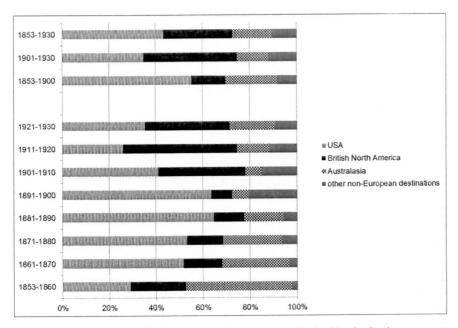

Figure 4.4 Percentage distribution of total emigration from Scotland by destination, 1853–1930 [source: Baines, *Migration in a Mature Economy*, p. 64 (Table 3.4)]

Table 4.7 Emigration from Scotland to non-European destinations, in thousands, and as percentage, 1853–1930 [source: Baines, *Migration in a Mature Economy*, p. 64 (Table 3.4)]

	USA		British North America		Australasia		Other non-European destinations		To all non-European destinations	
	000s	per cent	000s	per cent	000s	per cent	000s	per cent	000s	per cent
1853–60	35.1	29	28.4	23.5	54.6	45.2	2.8	2.3	120.9	100
1861–70	76.7	51.8	24.3	16.4	42.3	28.5	4.9	3.3	148.2	100
1871–80	88.1	53.2	25.8	15.5	41.1	24.8	10.7	6.5	165.7	100
1881–90	178.2	64.8	35.2	12.8	45	16.4	16.8	6.1	275.2	100
1891–1900	118.4	63.7	16.6	8.9	13	7	38	20.4	186	100
1901–10	187.6	41	169.6	37.1	31.1	6.8	69.2	15.1	457.5	100
1911–20	91.1	26	169.9	48.6	48.1	13.7	40.8	11.7	349.9	100
1921–30	157.4	35.3	161.6	36.2	85.8	19.2	41.5	9.3	446.3	100
1853–1900	496.5	55.4	130.3	14.5	196	21.9	73.2	8.2	896	100
1901–30	436.1	34.8	501.1	40	165	13.2	151.5	12.1	1253.7	100
1853–1930	932.6	43.4	631.4	29.4	361	16.8	224.7	10.4	2149.7	100

was the preferred destination for these migrants, although we cannot discount those who then moved on to the US. Canada then took anything between 10 and 25 per cent of the total, spiking in 1910–14 at nearly 60 per cent. Australia temporarily took a majority of Scotland's migrants after 1853 – the discovery of gold proving a major pull factor (Chapter 14). The Scots accounted for on average 22 per cent of UK immigrants to New Zealand in the period 1800 to 1945.[40] Taking the year 1878 as a snapshot, Lenihan enumerates the English at 54 per cent of New Zealand's population born in the British and Irish Isles, with the Scots at 24 per cent and the Irish at 22 per cent, concluding that New Zealand was two and half times 'more Scottish' than the British Isles (where Scots totalled just over 10 per cent of the population).[41] South Africa only attracted reasonable numbers at the end of the century, taking 20 per cent of Scots migrants as the century turned, but return migrants from the Cape were almost equal in number as those arriving, indicating that conditions were not as favourable as was hoped.[42] In 1913–14, 47 per cent of Scottish migrants (compared to 36 per cent from England Wales) described themselves as skilled and over 50 per cent did so in the 1920s. Of those for whom we have occupational information in this year, the skilled tended to head for the US and South Africa and the unskilled for Canada.[43]

A number of scholars have attempted to break down these national flows by examining their regional destination. The Scots who migrated to New Zealand, for example, headed primarily for Otago and Southland in the South Island, but settlement patterns varied over time. Hornsby's sample of 7,478

Table 4.8 Principal Canadian destinations of sample of highland and lowland emigrants (per cent) in 1871 [source: Hornsby, 'Patterns of Scottish emigration to Canada', pp. 401–2]

	Ontario	Nova Scotia	Quebec	New Brunswick	PEI	Manitoba
Highland	42	31	11	6	6	3
Lowland	60	10	17	7	3	2

emigrants who chose Canada looked to analyse the flows of Scots coming from (broadly defined) the highland and lowland regions (Table 4.8).[44]

Highland migrants tended to prefer the Maritime Provinces where their forebears first settled a century previously, while lowland Scots headed for the commercial and industrial parts of Ontario and Quebec. The study also indicates that few highlanders were migrating to the urban centres of Toronto, Hamilton, Ottawa and Kingston, whereas the lowland migrants who favoured Ontario were tracked to Toronto and Hamilton, with half of Quebec's lowlanders turning up in Montreal.[45] The evidence also suggests that two-thirds of the highland migrants followed 'channels of migration', what we have called chain migration in Chapter 2, whereas less than one third of lowland migrants followed a particular channel, and that was likely related to government or commercially sponsored schemes: the move of Orcadians to Manitoba, for example, was the result of a sponsored scheme by the Hudson's Bay Company, although Baines estimates only 9 per cent of British migrants received a travel subsidy throughout the 1815–1914 period.[46] Finally, here, Hornsby's study confirms the bigger picture presented so far: that all regions of Scotland experienced outward migration, and no one region dominated the flow.

D GENDER OF MIGRATION

Micro studies can also help the researcher to better analyse the preference of men and women to migrate. A point raised by Ravenstein that is confirmed in long-run census returns is that young males preponderate in the flow of over-seas migrants. In the period 1861 to 1911, male migrants outnumbered female migrants both in proportion and in volume for every decade, and this tended to be the pattern for earlier decades, too.[47] Might this suggest that men also took a lead in the family's decision to emigrate? Married in 1802 to Mary Black, the West Lothian-born Secessionist minister the Revd William Bell provides one example of a male migrant who took little notice of the wishes of his family. With his ordination secured in 1815 Bell found the oversupply of ministers too great to compete against. His first hope was New Zealand, but Mary refused to go, and the cost was too great. Bell turned his attention to British

North America, writing to Earl Bathurst, Secretary of State for the Colonies, to request free passage for ministers and teachers. Aged thirty-seven he had clearly made up his mind to leave Scotland, so when an opportunity arose with a petition to the Church of Scotland from the Presbyterians of Perth in Upper Canada, Bell was convinced this was his calling. Such was his haste, he only told his wife once plans were well under way, and did so by letter while absent preaching in Dunbar. After Mary laid bare her opposition in her written reply, William's response, while making peace, insisted he would go regardless of her decision to accompany him: 'My Dear Mary, I love you so much, but I love God more,' he wrote, before reminding her that 'in Heaven you will see all your friends that are worth seeing, and I trust that you will find that to be your native country.' Mary relented and on 5 April 1817, she, William and their six children set sail for Canada.[48] But this was clearly his decision.

While one example is scarcely sufficient to assess comprehensively the degree to which wives were involved in the decision-making process or not, a characteristic of Scotland's remaining population was that it was predominantly female. Ranging from around seventy-seven to eighty men per 100 females mid-century, only by the end of the century did equivalence near, with around ninety-four men to 100 women in 1901 and 1911 before widening in distribution through to 1961 (Table 4.9 and Figure 4.6).[49]

While more men than women went overseas, if we deploy gender ratios as a rough indicator of movement, then women were more likely to migrate

Table 4.9 Population growth and sex distribution (millions), 1755–1961 [source: Mitchell, *Abstract of European Historical Statistics*, p. 8]

	Scotland's population	Males in Scotland	Females in Scotland
1755	1.265		
1801	1.608	0.739	0.869
1811	1.806	0.826	0.980
1821	2.092	0.983	1.109
1831	2.364	1.114	1.250
1841	2.620	1.242	1.378
1851	2.889	1.375	1.513
1861	3.062	1.450	1.612
1871	3.360	1.603	1.757
1881	3.736	1.799	1.936
1891	4.026	1.943	2.083
1901	4.472	2.174	2.298
1911	4.761	2.309	2.452
1921	4.882	2.348	2.535
1931	4.843	2.326	2.517
1951	5.096	2.434	2.662
1961	5.179	2.483	2.697

	1801	1811	1821	1831	1841	1851	1861	1871	1881	1891	1901	1911	1921	1931	1951	1961
Male	0.74	0.83	0.98	1.11	1.24	1.38	1.45	1.60	1.80	1.94	2.17	2.31	2.35	2.33	2.43	2.48
Female	0.87	0.98	1.11	1.25	1.38	1.51	1.61	1.76	1.94	2.08	2.30	2.45	2.54	2.52	2.66	2.70

Figure 4.5 Scottish population growth by sex (millions), 1801–1961 [source: Mitchell, *Abstract of European Historical Statistics*, p. 8]

within their country of birth, and Scots and Irish women were more or less evenly split in their choice of another part of the UK, and did so more than Englishwomen (Table 4.10).[50]

Agreeing with the assessment that women were less likely to leave the British mainland, one contemporary analysis of internal movements produced evidence that women are greater migrants than men when measured over shorter distances. It is one of the reasons why there are close ratios amongst Scots migrants in the towns and cities of England (Chapter 9, Table 9.3), although in part this is also because the death rate for men was higher than for women at most ages.[51] The figures in Table 4.10 also show the greatest difference from men is that women were much more likely to move to another county within the same country.

Table 4.10 Internal migration: all females to all men (=100) in 1881 [source: Weber, *The Growth of Cities in the Nineteenth Century*, p. 277]

	England & Wales	Scotland	Ireland
Residing in county of birth	104:100	108:100	104:100
Residing in another county of same country	112:100	114:100	116:100
Residing in another part of the UK	81:100	91:100	92:100

E SCOTS AFTER MIGRATION

We should not be surprised, then, to find more Scotsmen than Scotswomen in
the diasporic locations. Two local studies examined by Lenihan confirm this
pattern for New Zealand, although the proportions vary (Table 4.11). Samples
are used because there are no ethnic specific fertility data available. Deploying
another set of data, where Otago the town most preferred by Scottish migrants
is used to represent all Scots migrants, Pool finds the availability of a large
male marriage market played some (but not a full) part in Scotswomen being
quick to marry upon arrival (Table 4.12).[53] Over the period 1840 to 1920, the
mean age of arrival in New Zealand ranged between 23.5 and 26.4 years.[54] In
Scotland the mean age of first marriage was 26.8 in 1871 and 26.6 years in

Table 4.11 Sex ratios of Scots in New Zealand: NZSG and PNZ surveys (women = 100)
[source: Lenihan, '"Counting" migrants', p. 81 (Table 1, adapted)][52]

Period	Sample	Ratio	N
Pre-1852	NZSG	121:100	659
	PNZ	143:100	219
1853–1870	NZSG	127:100	2,816
	PNZ	137:100	745
1871–1886	NZSG	114:100	1,708
	PNZ	116:100	684
1887–1900	NZSG	149:100	162
	PNZ	168:100	142
1901–1920	NZSG	119:100	558
	PNZ	119:100	496

Table 4.12 Percentage of females married at 20–24 years,
Scottish and New Zealand regions, 1878, 1881 [source: Pool, 'A
"Caledonian" conundrum', p. 109 (Table 2)]

Scotland (1881)	27
Far North	17
Highland	15
North-west	24
Western Lowlands	32
Eastern Lowlands	25
Borders	20
Towns	29
Cities	28
Rural areas	24
New Zealand (1878)	53
Canterbury 'English'	47
Otago 'Scottish'	51

1911[55]; for white New Zealanders it was below twenty-three before slowly rising to twenty-four years by 1896.[56]

This evidence indicates different characteristics and values amongst the Scots migrants that were not simply a structural response to the availability of marriage patterns.[57] The nuptiality of Scotswomen aged within the twenty to twenty-four range was much higher after migration than if she had stayed at home (Table 4.12). That Scots changed their behaviours in their new settlements, perhaps beyond what we might think of as 'diasporic actions', will be assessed further in the case study chapters to follow, but health indicators can also be used to estimate how successful Scots were as settlers.

Of course, some Scots returned home scarred by the experience:

> There is a strange old man often to be noticed wandering about
> Gairloch. He is a native of the parish, but is now homeless and in his
> dotage. He goes about seeking, as he says, the road to America. It seems
> that many a year ago he emigrated with his wife and family to the
> United States. They all became more or less insane, and all died except
> the father, this old man.[58]

Whereas in terms of migrants' mental health, research remains tentative, but in comparison to the Irish-born, the Scots-born residents in New Zealand were not to be found over-represented in the nation's mental asylums (Table 4.13).

To make sense of these comparisons, examination must be made of poverty and also institutional decision-making which might serve, as has been seen in case study evidence in Belfast, to assign the Catholic Irish to the asylum but their Protestant brethren to the community.[59] Indeed, height data points to the Irish doing well from migration. The native-born in Canada and Australia were taller than the British-born emigrants who enlisted into military service at the time of the First World War, but Irish- and Scots-born migrants outgrew

Table 4.13 British and Irish as percentage of foreign-born in New Zealand and in asylums [source: McCarthy, 'Exploring ethnicity and ethnic identity in New Zealand asylums', p. 192 (Table 4)]

Census year	Scotland-born		Ireland-born		England-born	
	Census	Asylum	Census	Asylum	Census	Asylum
1878	20.0	21.9	18.2	29.0	44.3	38.5
1881	19.8	18.3	18.5	31.7	44.7	36.8
1886	19.7	17.9	18.5	32.1	45.2	37.9
1891	20.0	18.1	18.3	33.0	45.0	37.8
1896	19.3	18.1	17.6	31.0	44.5	38.0
1901	18.6	19.0	17.0	29.7	43.6	38.1
1906	16.9	17.7	15.0	28.4	41.3	38.6

Table 4.14 Stature of Australian Imperial Forces (AIF) and Canadian Expeditionary Forces (CEF) enlistees by birth region [source: Cranfield and Inwood, 'Stayers and leavers, diggers and Canucks', p. 7 (Table 4)][60]

Birthplace	AIF	CEF
Native born	168.21	167.21
Scotland	167.09	167.15
England	167.05	166.85
Ireland	168.39	168.35
Wales	166.59	166.59

the English-born. Possibly there were smaller migrants who left, but this is likely not enough to explain the differences. Scholars assign access to recourses and improved nutritional intake as the reason for generational gains in stature.

What this kind of health evidence is allowing us to explore is that diasporic actions were not confined to boundary maintenance or the feeding of collective memories flagged through ethnicity. Instead environmental aspects can be added to socio-economic dynamics as determinants of Scots' behaviour after migration. Mental health and diet are both determinants and outcomes of diasporic actions.

F   CONCLUSION

To explain the reasons why Scots chose to leave their country, the previous chapter foregrounded the relationship of structure to action, with four structures identified: (1) demographic pressures; (2) standard of living; (3) occupational change; and (4) urbanisation. The delineation of the Scots' patterns of migration and emigration is the outcome of that balance, yet in Chapter 2 we concluded our analysis of the concept of diaspora by arguing that mapping the Scottish diaspora requires us to go beyond the observation of movement and settlement. A number of categories of migrant were introduced: the sojourner, the returnee, the temporary and the odyssey migrant, those who moved because of government, charitable or philanthropic help, and those who moved as indentured servants or harboured a grievance of exile stemming from forced removal. Other than when the historical record is able to provide evidence of return migration, the decennial census is little help with any of these categories, nor with how individuals, families and groups might comprise the conceptualised Scottish diaspora through their agency. What the data presented in this chapter do show are patterns of emigration – the extent and timing of the flows, the preferred destinations whether they be short or long, or to which overseas location, and the preference to migrate by men or women, and from where in Scotland they originated. The data also show, quite clearly, that outward migration was a pronounced drag on Scotland's population growth and shaped the ratio of men to women in the nation and the diasporic locations alike.

NOTES

1. *The Daily Times* (Beaver, Pennsylvania), 20 March 1908.
2. Akenson, 'The Great European migration and indigenous populations', p. 23.
3. Bell, *Day and Night in the Wynds of Edinburgh*, p. 22.
4. Baines, *Migration in a Mature Economy*, pp. 59–61.
5. The only exception being the decade 1901–10, when Italy exceeded the UK and Ireland total by 465,000.
6. Devine, *To the Ends of the Earth*, p. 87.
7. Where the rank order is calculated as the mean emigration rate from the four heaviest decades.
8. Baigent, 'Ravenstein, Ernst Georg (1834–1913)', http://www.oxforddnb.com/view/article/41114 (accessed 23 July 2012).
9. Eyler, 'Farr, William (1807–1883)', http://www.oxforddnb.com.subzero.lib.uoguelph.ca/view/article/9185 (accessed 20 February 2013).
10. Ravenstein, 'Census of the British Isles, 1871', pp. 173–7, 201–6, 229–33; Ravenstein, 'The laws of migration' (1885); and Ravenstein 'The laws of migration' (1889).
11. Grigg, 'E. G. Ravenstein and the "laws of migration"', pp. 42–3.
12. Ibid.; Pooley and Turnbull, *Migration and Mobility in Britain*, pp. 300–1.
13. Rodger, *The Transformation of Edinburgh*, p. 278.
14. Pooley and Turnbull, *Migration and Mobility*, p. 300.
15. Grigg, 'E. G. Ravenstein', p. 47.
16. Pooley and Turnbull, *Migration and Mobility*, pp. 300–1.
17. Ibid.
18. Grigg, 'E. G. Ravenstein', pp. 48–9.
19. Smout, Landsman and Devine, 'Scottish emigration in the seventeenth and eighteenth centuries', p. 85.
20. Pooley and Turnbull, *Migration and Mobility*, p. 302.
21. Pool, 'A "Caledonian" conundrum', p. 103.
22. Pooley and Turnbull, *Migration and Mobility*, p p. 189. The data come from life histories produced by genealogists.
23. Grigg, 'E. G. Ravenstein', pp. 43–6.
24. A point made in Pooley and Turnbull, *Migration and Mobility*, p. 302.
25. Morton, *Ourselves and Others*, pp. 248–9.
26. Flinn (ed.), *Scottish Population History*, p. 94.

27. Ibid., pp. 8–9.
28. Ibid.
29. Anderson, 'Fertility decline in Scotland, England and Wales, and Ireland', p. 4.
30. Baines, *Migration in a Mature Economy*, p. 60.
31. Anderson and Morse, 'High fertility, high emigration, low nuptiality', p. 9.
32. Flinn, *Scottish Population* History, p. 447.
33. Lee, 'Scotland, 1860–1939', p. 430.
34. The figures for 1911–20 include those Scots who died abroad during the 1914–18 conflict.
35. Baines, *Emigration in a Mature Economy*, p. 58.
36. Devine, *The Scottish Nation*, pp. 468–9.
37. Brock, *The Mobile Scot*, pp. 23, 25.
38. *Merchants' Magazine and Commercial Review*, vol. 34 (January-June 1856), p. 109.
39. Szasz, *Scots in the North American West*, p. 79.
40. Phillips and Hearn, *Settlers*, p. 52 (table 2).
41. Lenihan, '"Counting" migrants', p. 74.
42. Flinn, *Scottish Population History*, pp. 450–1.
43. Ibid. and also pp. 452–3.
44. Hornsby, 'Patterns of Scottish emigration to Canada, 1750–1870'; sample derived from Whyte, *A Dictionary of Scottish Emigrants to Canada Before Confederation*.
45. Hornsby, 'Patterns of Scottish emigration to Canada', pp. 402–4.
46. Ibid, p. 407; Baines, *Migration in a Mature Economy*, p. 53.
47. Brock, *The Mobile Scot*, p. 135.
48. Hinson and Morton, 'Observations of a Scottish moralist', pp. 222–3.
49. Morris, 'In search of twentieth-century Edinburgh', p. 13.
50. Brock, *The Mobile Scot*, pp. 146–7.
51. Anderson and Morse, 'The people', p. 31.
52. PNZ: Peopling New Zealand Project; NZSG: New Zealand Society of Genealogists.
53. Pool, '"A "Caledonian" conundrum', p. 99.
54. Lenihan, '"Counting" migrants', p. 82.
55. Anderson and Morse, 'High fertility, high emigration, low nuptiality', p. 7, n. 8.
56. Pool, 'A "Caledonian" conundrum', pp. 102, 107.
57. Ibid.
58. Dixon, *Gairloch in North-West Ross-shire*, p. 115.
59. Morris, 'Urban Ulster since 1600', pp. 130–3.
60. Our thanks go to the authors for making this research available to us.

CHAPTER 5

The Emigration Experience

When James Good emigrated from Scotland with his wife and children in 1841 he did so to escape Paisley's temperamental weaving industry to become a farmer in Ontario, Canada. That the decision to emigrate to distant shores across the Atlantic had been the right one seems to be confirmed in a letter James wrote to his brother during the family's first year away:

> I received your letter of the 3rd January after many a call at the Post Office and I was both vexed and glad, glad at getting word from you but vexed at hearing of the state of you and the rest of my Paisley friends. I cannot but think I have escaped very narrowly. We came through some hardships but it is past like a dream in the night and God has been very kind to us in all things . . . You say my Mother would like to come here. We would be very happy if she would. I think I have the happiest family in America but if she would come here it would add to their happiness.[1]

The positivity, which is repeated in subsequent letters from James, is a characteristic of many emigrant accounts, commonly serving the purpose not only of reassuring worried families at home of the émigrés' wellbeing, but also to justify to themselves that they were indeed better off in the New World than had they remained in the Old. It was not until the Goods' third winter in Canada that cracks began to appear: the family was struggling to make ends meet, leading James to appeal to his brother for the loan of five pounds to tide him over the winter; assurances were given that the sum would be repaid immediately upon their reaping of the next year's harvest. This, however, was not to be, as thirty years later, upon hearing of James's death, his brother requested repayment of said five pounds. This episode of one family's emigration experience, characterised by genuine hope for a better life after arrival as well as later problems, gives perspective not only on the hardships which prevented James from repaying his brother, but also on the fact that his brother decided to request the repayment of the money thirty years later – conditions in Dundee too had remained difficult. Yet while James may never have reached a level of comfort to pay off his debt, upon his death his land was paid for and he left his wife in good circumstances. These contradictory impressions reflect the mixture of highs and lows experienced by many Scottish emigrants.

A   CROSSING THE OCEAN

While Scots intent on emigrating may have consulted advice handbooks, newspaper articles or spoken to family members and friends who had either emigrated themselves or knew of the experiences of people who had done so, for most emigrants the quest for a new life only truly began as they boarded the ship which would take them to a far-off land that was to become home. Not all emigrants required sea passage to reach their destination, but of those who did many already had to travel considerable distances before even reaching their port of embarkation; for those destined beyond Europe, this was the point from which, realistically, there was no turning back. When the Jack family left Edinburgh for London to then journey on to New Zealand in October 1883, an assemblage of family and friends had made their way to the port of Leith to bid the Jacks farewell. Those gathered were well aware, as one friend observed in a letter, that they would probably not be seeing each other again 'in the flesh'.[2] As the hour for departure approached emigrants were faced with conflicting emotions: sadness at knowing they were seeing loved ones for the last time mixed with excitement at the prospect of a new life ahead, and anxiety at the challenges that could entail.

The experience that followed was largely dependent upon where the emigrants were destined and the period in which they were travelling. Parallel to the Industrial Revolution was a revolution in transportation, with the development of steam and the introduction of iron and later steel dramatically altering oceanic voyages from the late nineteenth century. North America, which had previously taken several weeks to reach by sailing ship, was now reachable in a little over a week, while journey times to the Antipodes were cut from over 100 days to less than half that. Together with their better safety and comfort, steamships quickly became the preferred method of transportation, the proportion of transatlantic emigrants travelling by sailing ship declining from more than 50 per cent in the early 1860s to all but a small minority by 1870.[3] When the Clyde-built *Servia* was launched in 1881, newspaper reports about the 1,000-passenger 'floating palace'[4] (the largest carrying vessel afloat at

Figure 5.1 Emigrants bound for Canada boarding the *Metagama* at Glasgow docks, 1923
[source: SCRAN; Resource Rights Holder: Hulton Getty; SCRAN ID: 000-000-201-282-C]

the time) reflected that the days when ocean travelling was attended with any degree of misgiving had long since passed.

Although oceanic voyages by steamships were not free from risk,[5] conditions stood in stark contrast to those faced by Scottish emigrants of an earlier time.[6] Evidence presented by the Highland Society of Scotland to a House of Commons Select Committee in 1802 reveals the extremes that could be faced. Of an emigrant ship bound for North Carolina in 1773 it was stated:

> The Number of Persons on board were about 450, of whom 25 had, at coming on board, no Birth nor Bed of any sort, nor could any be afforded them during the Passage, except as furnished by Vacancies owing to death. The Water became scarce during the Voyage, which lasted Twelve Weeks and Three Days. The Thirst of the poor People was of course stimulated by feeding entirely on Salt Meat. For the last Fortnight the Allowance to each Passenger was only an English Pint of Water for 24 Hours; and many of the Casks having been made of Staves used in the Tobacco and Indigo Trade, the Water was often so impregnated with these nauseous Ingredients, that the People sickened and threw it up. The Consequence was, that they were seized with a

Dysentery, and 23 of them died before reaching Carolina, and the rest were landed in the most exhausted and dilapidated State.[7]

Another vessel, which left from Skye with 400 passengers, had berths a mere 18 inches broad and 2 feet high, and evidence was given of 700 emigrants being crammed into two vessels in Fort William, one of which lost fifty-three passengers before reaching America.[8] Appalled at what they heard, the Select Committee resolved that action had to be taken and within a short space of time legislation was winding its way through Parliament which was to radically alter how emigrant shipping was regulated.

As well as limiting the number of passengers to a ratio tied to a ship's tonnage, the Passenger Act of 1803 stipulated daily quantities of rations and required a qualified surgeon on board all vessels that carried fifty or more passengers. Whether or not it was the intent of legislators to bring about passenger fare increases beyond the reach of the majority of potential emigrants is debatable, but for those concerned at the growing rapidity of Scottish emigration, the resultant decline on overseas movement was welcome. For a quarter of a century the legislation remained in place with only relatively minor alterations. Only as Malthusian concerns about overcrowding gained popularity did attitudes towards emigration and passenger regulation change. In 1826, for example, the *Edinburgh Review* asked for an almost complete repeal of the Act arguing that

> though it is true that cases did occur in which emigrants were exposed to great hardships . . . we are not sure that they were of sufficient magnitude to call for any interference on the part of the Government, and certainly afforded no apology whatever for the existing regulation.[9]

If the reported abuses that led to the legislation's introduction were the exception, those that followed its complete repeal were not.[10] With protests coming from even some of the more reputable shipowners, a new bill was introduced to Parliament in 1828 once again establishing minimal standards for passengers. Although various attempts were made to further regulate emigrant shipping, these could not guarantee that minimal standards would be met.[11]

While it was not until the old sailing vessels gave way to steamships that conditions improved significantly, it would be wrong to suggest that by boarding an emigrant ship passengers were knowingly subjecting themselves to grave misery. One problem was that the ships used in emigration usually served a primary function as cargo ships and were thus only temporarily fitted to accommodate emigrants. Steerage accommodation was undoubtedly basic, consisting of wooden planking over crossbeams, with berths along the sides.

With no portholes, ventilation was poor and in the case of storms, when the hatch had to be kept down to prevent water from getting in, the stench would have been quite unbearable. In his account of the voyage previously encountered, James Good complained about the quality of water and scarcity of provisions, but with the exception of widespread seasickness, most passengers appear to have remained healthy.[12] Writing of his voyage to Melbourne in 1853, former Glasgow councillor James Black noted that '[t]he "Abdalla" is a comfortable ship. Provisions, as yet, both abundant and excellent. All classes of passengers give the same testimony.'[13] Similar sentiments were expressed in an address to the captain signed on behalf of 140 passengers from the emigrant ship *Nelson*:

> On leaving Glasgow we had doubts as to the favourable issue of the voyage. But we are happy to say that these apprehensions were entirely removed, not only by the attention paid to our comfort, but also by the liberal supply of provisions and pure water for all out wants.[14]

Insurance records document that most ships used for Scottish emigration were of a relatively high quality. As a major insurer of shipping, Lloyd's inspected and rated vessels, of which a high proportion were 'A1' or 'AE' – either in first-class condition or without defect and fit for safe conveyance.[15] Rather than fear or destitution, the overall impression gained from emigrant accounts of voyages is one of civility, with the majority of passengers uncomplaining of their situation.[16] Describing a steerage passenger's day, Mrs Hinshelwood, who travelled on the *Nebo* from Glasgow to Rockhampton, wrote:

> We rise before six, get the children bathed and ready for school, and our bed folded up on hinges by half-past seven; breakfast at eight. We wash our dishes, while the husbands sweep our floors, and we are all expected on deck by nine o'clock for the day. We have a free library, and read and chat till one – dinner time. Tea about five, then comes time for getting ready for bed our little ones, who are all very merry. The first mate scrambles sweets among them, had put up a swing, and seems to enjoy their company. We generally bed about nine, as it gets chilly in deck.[17]

Life on board clearly revolved around routine, with free time being spent reading, playing cards, listening to music and dancing in the evenings. For most the biggest challenge was addressing the monotony of travel. Even among the higher-class cabin passengers, who had access to greater comforts and activities, the tedium of weeks at sea could not be escaped. It is, therefore, of little surprise that, regardless of conditions on board, it was of immense relief to all passengers when they arrived at their destination.

B EXPECTATIONS AND REALITY

In spite of what they were told by emigrant agents or family members who had left prior to them, few emigrants could really anticipate what their new life would entail. Although usually driven by the desire for a better quality of life, it is difficult to generalise about emigrants' actual expectations and whether or not these were subsequently met. Some were certainly highly optimistic about their prospects, like Neil McCullum who emigrated to Geelong, Australia and, presumably in anticipation of finding gold, wrote in 1854: 'I will be wealthier at the end of one year here than I was at the end of seventeen years of slavery' back in Scotland.[18] Few, however, were so lucky, and while there were exceptions, such as James Paterson, David Syme and Sir John McIntyre, each of whom struck it rich by discovering gold, most Scottish emigrants probably had more realistic ambitions.[19]

Important too was the reputation Scots began to earn for their accomplishments overseas. Writing about Australia and New Zealand, Anthony Trollope claimed, in 1873, that '[t]he Scotch have always been among the best, – or perhaps the very best, – colonisers that the world has produced'.[20] In the United States, Neal Dow, the entrepreneur and prohibitionist, wrote in 1880 that 'of all immigrants to our country the Scotch are always the most welcome. They bring us muscle and brain and tried skill and trustworthiness of our greatest industries of which they are mangers of the most successful ones.'[21] Even in the remoter reaches of Africa, Tom von Prince of the German East Africa Company observed that the Scots were 'a breed of men which is very clever in monetary affairs. They combine the pleasant with the useful, are the best soldiers of England, and are very precise as businessmen.'[22]

Elsewhere Scottish contributions were no less impressive, with stories abounding of Scots excelling in business, politics and other professional pursuits. Most alluring are the accounts concerning the self-made man, perhaps best epitomised by Andrew Carnegie's rags-to-riches tale, but of which there are many others. One is that of George Russell, a pastoralist who had emigrated to Australia in 1831 at the age of nineteen in response to the difficult economic conditions in his Aberdeenshire home. By 1839 he was managing 8,000 sheep and, in 1858, he was able to purchase 8,500 acres of his own which he eventually increased to 28,000. When he died in 1887 he left £318,000.[23] Or John McKenzie, one of ten children to a tenant farmer, who emigrated to New Zealand in 1860, and, after five years working for others, could buy 80 acres to farm himself. In the same year he went into public office, eventually going on to become Minister of Lands and Agriculture, as which he oversaw many important land reforms, rarely failing to draw on his antecedent experiences in Scotland.[24] Arguably it was in Canada where the Scottish contribution was most felt, with popular histories often suggesting that they in fact 'invented' the country, although equally indicative of the examples of Scottish accomplishments overseas were two joiners named Young and Sterling, who having raised capital carrying out their original trade in Buenos Aires, bought lands in Uruguay in 1823, and by the mid-century were exceedingly prosperous.[25]

Despite the many success stories, however, it is important to note that the experiences of men like Carnegie, Russell and McKenzie were not shared by the majority of migrant Scots, thus making up only a fraction of the multi-layered Scottish emigrant experience. The personal testimony of migrants provides the most immediate and most valuable insights into that wider experience. Though not without its problems in terms of representativeness and subjectivity,[26] migrant letters in particular document the reality of life in new worlds of settlement of many a Scot. Upon disembarkation from their ship, most migrants had to journey overland, after which they had to quickly find employment and habitation. The early stages, particularly for those taking up land, were the most challenging. In the case of Andrew Kennedy, who immigrated to the United States in 1809, the prospect of what lay ahead was too much to bear. Upon meeting old acquaintances who had settled thirty years earlier, he was so discouraged at the poverty of their settlement that he returned to Scotland the following summer.[27] For those who had exhausted their limited resources in making the overseas crossing, however, returning was not an option, leaving them little choice but to meet the challenges thrown their way. One emigrant from the Isle of Raasay put his feelings into a song entitled *Gearain air America* (Complaint about America) part of which has been translated as follows:

> I am lonely here
> in Murray Harbour not knowing English;
> it is not what I have been accustomed to, for I always spoke Gaelic.
> My neighbours and I
> used to chat at length together;
> here I see only scoundrels,
> and I do not understand their language.
>
> I am offended at my relatives
> who came before me;
> they did not tell me about this place
> and how it has tried them.
> Going through the wilderness

> there is nothing but a blazed trail;
> this is a truly lonesome place
> For one who lives by himself.[28]

But even those migrants who struggled less with adjustment and settlement often noted the challenges of migrant life. These were more numerous for pioneer migrants – that is those arriving at the commencement of settlement in a particular country or area. As Bazil Thomson, who had emigrated to New Zealand, observed, life was often 'rough and ready'.[29] Thomson found consolation in the fact that he had emigrated together with his two brothers – a fact indicative of the importance of kinship and wider ethnic networks in the Scottish emigration experience.

That emigration was the prelude to further trauma and deprivation, particularly among those caught up in the economic transformation sweeping the Highlands and Islands in the eighteenth and nineteenth centuries, is often the popularly perceived experience of Scottish emigrants. Yet while those who did leave Scotland during the Clearances had to contend with a new physical environment under different climatic conditions, with the added difficulties of language, shortage of funds and sickness, perhaps not faced in the same extreme by other Scottish emigrants, in the long run most found themselves in a better situation than had they remained at home. So rather than the highly evocative descriptions given in poems and songs, or images like Thomas Faed's *The Last of the Clan*, a more objective way of measuring the fate of these emigrants, are the remittances sent back home – payments which enabled the highland economy to sustain its remaining people better than would otherwise have been the case.[30] Evidence would suggest that any initial hardships experienced, in most cases, eased with time.

A questionnaire sent by the Saskatchewan Archives in the 1950s to settlers and their descendants who had come to the Canadian prairies between 1878 and 1914, as well as giving a voice to those who mostly otherwise did not record their experiences, enables some direct comparisons to be made. Of the respondents, sixty-two were Scots, who answered questions on a range of issues related to their settlement experiences. In her analysis of the responses of British settlers, Marjory Harper found that they were characterised by their uniformity rather than diversity of experience, with little disparity between those from different parts of the British Isles.[31] While there were exceptions like John Laidlaw from Rossshire, who recalled that his parents felt they had been misled by advertising, having been enticed to Canada believing they would be able to retire to Scotland on their profits after a few years but were not in fact able to do so, dissatisfaction was rare. Harper concludes that 'most respondents had emigrated with optimistic expectations, and, despite hardships, had not been disappointed by more than half a century of life in Saskatchewan.'[32]

Those who responded had, of course, remained on the land, with replies thus perhaps offering a biased view of land settlement. Not everyone persevered and as is seen in the contrasting fortunes of two Scottish settlements in the Canadian north-west – at Killarney and Saltcoats – the line between success and failure was fine. Part of the same government-assisted colonisation scheme involving crofter and cottar families from the Western Highlands and Islands, the settlements were established a year apart, with the first settlers arriving in 1888. Despite initial difficulties in both locations, after a decade the Killarney settlers were described as being 'in the way of becoming substantial and successful farmers', whereas all but one of the Saltcoats settlers had abandoned their lands.[33] According to the government's final report on the scheme,

> had the [Saltcoats] settlers remained on their homesteads they might ultimately have achieved the same measure of success as those at Killarney. They were however, led away by bad advice, and many of them did not realize the fortunate position they were placed, or the opportunities open to them.[34]

This unsympathetic view does not take into account that many of the crofters were fishermen unaccustomed to farming, nor the difficult market conditions and unfavourable weather they were faced with.[35] Such lack of recognition of the migrants' background and abilities proved the nail in the coffin of several settlements, including, for instance, some of New Zealand's so-called 'special settlements' (see also Chapter 14). It is not known what happened to the Killarney and Saltcoats migrants in the long term, but even as the settlement around them was failing, they were by no means condemned to destitution. Rather than working their own land, most took up work as labourers, where they could make respectable wages bringing in the harvest, cutting wood or working on the railway.[36]

While owning land was one of the major pull factors behind emigration, this was not so for everyone, and as with immigrant farmers it is equally possible to find contrasting experiences among those who did not take up land. John Ronaldson, for example, was a flax hackler from Kirkcaldy, who immigrated to the United States in 1852. His wife was supposed to follow, but Ronaldson appears to have determined that life in America was no better than in Scotland. Frustrated at having to move around so much to find work, he also reflected that factory wages were not in proportion to the work performed and that the working hours were particularly long.[37] In a letter home he stated:

> The people has good meat here, but they are generally as hard up as in Scotland . . . There are thousands in this country would be better at home, but then them at home wont believe it, so before they would

submit to jeering at home they stop still. For my part my chance has
been average, when you take sickness and other expenses into account
. . .[38]

After two years, and in spite of being able to save at least twenty-two pounds,
Ronaldson returned home to his wife in Scotland. Another migrant who
recommended against family coming out, and experienced mixed fortunes
himself, was David Laing who immigrated to the Unites States in the 1840s.
Having worked most of his life as a day labourer, in 1871 he split up with his
wife and moved to take up work in a railway maintenance shop. In letters to
Scotland he discussed the high unemployment and ensuing economic difficulties engulfing the country. Although Laing had to accept a cut in wages, he
did retain his own job, and, by the time the correspondence ended in 1876,
had experienced a considerable reversal in his economic fortunes, having been
promoted to foreman.[39] The impression that life started out tough but became
easier is also supported by the experiences of Joseph Delaney recorded as
part of the Ellis Island oral histories project. After his arrival in 1922 he got
work unloading boiler ashes in a cable factory. Because of the low pay he left
after six months, returning to the mining trade for which he had been trained
in Scotland. Here, however, due to the work being much tougher than in
Scotland, he lasted only three months, deciding instead to become a driller's
helper. In this trade Delaney stayed and became a driller in his own right,
working for various different companies throughout his career. Although he
acknowledged that his first year in America had been difficult and that he often
felt homesick, when asked if he would make the same move again he replied
emphatically that he would, stating that had he stayed in Scotland he would
have had a much tougher and poorer way of life.[40] Endurance, a willingness
to adapt and also perseverance were crucial ingredients for Scots all over the
world to successfully make home in a new country. As was observed by a Scot
who had emigrated to New Zealand: 'McGregor didn't stay long enough to
know if he liked it . . . I didn't like it at all the first year either. I could have
come home at any time then with pleasure, but I've got over that now'.[41]

While accounts such as these cannot be seen as representative of all
migrants, among non-farmers, early hardships also appear to have eased, being
replaced over time with economic security. That this was indeed the case for
most Scottish migrants is supported by two different studies of Scots in New
Zealand. The first, a study of 784 letters from fifty-seven individuals and
families sent to or from Scottish settlers in New Zealand shows that while life
was not always easy, particularly amongst the earliest settlers, if immigrants
were willing to be flexible and show perseverance, they were able to succeed.[42]
Also striking among the New Zealand study was the sense noted by Scottish
immigrants that they had joined a more egalitarian society in which their hard

work would be rewarded by better opportunities. That Scots did achieve upward occupational mobility is supported by the second of the studies, using a database containing the names of 6,612 Scottish immigrants based on information provided by the New Zealand Society of Genealogists, Scottish Interest Group (NZSG). Enabling the occupations of immigrants to be traced over the duration of their working lives, this quantitative analysis reveals that Scottish immigrants were able to attain, if not prosperity, certainly economic stability in their new homes.[43] In particular, if land ownership can be taken as a guide to success, there were many who achieved this. As well as those who were able to acquire land upon immediately moving to New Zealand, there were those who worked for others in agriculture before becoming farmers in their own right. Similarly, while the majority of gold miners may not have struck it rich, many who did work in the gold fields and later in other forms of mineral extraction, do appear to have used their accumulated earnings to purchase land which they then farmed. Upward mobility was not limited to agriculture, also occurring in several other sectors, including manufacturing. Individual examples include Robert McKinlay who initially worked in New Zealand as a leather cutter but went on to found a boot and shoe factory, and William Dawson Douglas, classified in the public sector and professional category, who trained and worked as an accountant, rising through his career to become manager of the company he initially worked for. Both could easily be included in those high-achieving Scots highlighted earlier in the chapter. And while similarly atypical in the significant level of their success, their generally positive overseas experience appears to be one shared by a majority of Scottish emigrants.

An important key to many such success stories was the Scots' ability to utilise kinship and ethnic networks to their benefit. These 'were comprised of dense and penetrating personal, commercial, and public layers. They were about friendship, just as much as business opportunities, and could span large distances. Relationships intersected and connected different groups of people.'[44] In so doing, patronage flows were channelled, and migrants could generate social capital in their new home. While migrants with diverse ethnic backgrounds also made use of such networks, the Scots were particularly adapt at drawing on their ethnicity in a way that facilitated their integrations into diverse colonial worlds – this was also the case because of their extensive use of ethnic associational culture (see Chapter 7).

C WOMEN AND CHILDREN

The proportion of women among Scottish emigrants was less than men, but their emigration experiences are equally instructive. Although there were high achievers like Catherine Helen Spence, Australia's first professional woman journalist and first female political candidate, Jennie Gowanlock, Canada's first licensed female physician, and Mary Slessor, whose missionary work in West Africa is remembered to this day, women feature much less prominently than men in success stories of overseas Scots. Similarly, while there are notable exceptions, such as Catharine and Susanna Strickland whose narratives of their experiences overseas have been widely read, surviving published accounts and personal testimonies of female Scottish emigrants are considerably fewer than those of men, making their lives generally less well documented.

Unfortunately it is among the largest component of female emigrants that exists greatest anonymity: those who emigrated as part of family groups and were in charge of household and child-rearing responsibilities. While this labour may have been unwaged, it was essential to successfully functioning families, and by no means shielded women from any of the hardships experienced through emigration. Indeed, with many women having uprooted at the primary instigation of their husbands, to then be left isolated at home, this could make adjusting to their new life even more difficult than for men. Although wives of farmers, shopkeepers or even missionaries regularly carried out work beyond the household, it was unusual for married women to enter the workforce, and only occurred if necessity dictated. Such circumstances included the death of a husband, where the spouse still had children to support.

Most emigrant women who entered the paid workforce were not, however, married when they emigrated. The subject of considerably more attention from contemporaries and historians alike, the proportion of single women emigrating peaked in the late nineteenth and early twentieth centuries when those relocating overseas rarely fell below 50 per cent.[45] This was in large part down to attempts to address the gender imbalance of the British Empire by recruiting women to help 'civilise' the colonies, while at the same time helping to remove 'surplus' women from Britain. Represented by all levels of class and education, included amongst their ranks were governesses, teachers, nurses, factory workers, and, following the First World War, clerical workers and secretaries. By far the most common occupation among single Scottish female migrants was, however, that of domestic servant – and one that was not overtaken by women in other occupational categories until the Great Depression of the 1930s.

Enticed by the prospect of greater opportunities than in Scotland, for many of these women emigration was made feasible by the availability of heavily subsidised or loaned fares that were being offered by recruiting agencies, emigration societies and employers themselves. One of the most active female emigration agencies in Scotland was the Aberdeen Ladies' Union, which oversaw the emigration of 330 women between 1883 and 1914.[46] In return for the passage out the women had to work for a designated period of time (an arrangement not dissimilar to that of indentured servitude), or until they had paid off the value of their fare. By travelling under the auspices of such organisations they were being safeguarded both during and after passage against vulnerabilities to which single women in particular were considered open. According to the Union's annual reports the women fared well, and in 1895 several girls returned to Aberdeen to persuade friends to accompany them back to Canada.[47] Not all were, however, so happy with their experiences: many organisations were criticised for their oppressive management of the women in their care.[48] During the voyage references can be found to overzealous matrons who, responsible for upholding proper behaviour on board, instigated military-like procedures for cooking and cleaning, ensured that spare time was spent productively, and crucially, prevented the women from coming into contact with the ship's male passengers.[49] Upon arrival many women felt that what they had been promised did not meet expectations, but because of the debts they had incurred, they were forced to endure poor pay and conditions until their debts were cleared. Jean Burns, who had been selected for a position looking after a baby on an Ontario farm, found that the only other hired help in the home was a young immigrant girl recruited through Quarrier's Orphan Homes of Scotland, and so, beyond caring for a baby, Jean had to cook, clean, do the laundry and ironing – a workload considerably heavier than she had anticipated. After three months, having paid off her debt, Jean left the position, taking up factory work instead. Paid $4 per week, which only covered her board, Jean thus found herself in a worse financial situation than as a domestic. Not until she received a pay increase, and moved into cheaper accommodation, did Jean's situation finally improve.[50] Such experiences were not limited to those who had emigrated as part of a wider group. Mary Dunn paid her own way to get to Pennsylvania in 1923 where she took up work in a fabric store. Frustrated at what she had to pay for room and board she decided instead to seek employment as a domestic where she was paid on top of receiving lodgings. She started out at $7.50 a week and, by the time she married in 1928, was on a weekly rate of $15. Clearly, as with Jean Burns, Mary Dunn's expectations were not initially met, but, in time, both women were able to improve their situations. While these women did have genuine cause for complaint, what is significant is that in spite of the restrictions they faced on the voyage and after their arrival, they still possessed a considerable degree of agency, first in the decision to migrate, but also in the longer term, once they had become settled in their new homes.

Children on the other hand had little or no say in the decision to emigrate or in what happened to them afterwards. Most accompanied their parents and probably adapted quickly to their new surroundings, enjoying the sense of adventure but always with the comfort of their families being close at hand. More controversial though were the thousands of children who were dispatched to overseas destinations without the company of a parent or guardian.

Figure 5.2 Nurse inspecting Hebridean children who are immigrating to Canada on board the *Marloch* [source: SCRAN; Resource Rights Holder: Hulton Getty; SCRAN ID: 000-000-201-060-C]

Initially the practice was seen as a means to cure juvenile criminals, although, by the mid- to late-nineteenth century, it had become a preventative measure by those who feared neglected, abused, homeless and poor children would drift toward criminal habits. It also served to reduce Britain's surplus population, while providing cheap labour to the receiving countries. Most prolific in the practice was Dr Barnardo, who, by his death in 1905, had sent 60,000 children overseas, although only a relatively small proportion of these came from Scotland.[51] Scotland's most important player in child migration was William Quarrier whose organisation sent as many as 7,360 children until the practice was ceased in 1938; almost all of them went to Canada.[52] Comprised primarily of children from his orphan home at Bridge of Weir, they included those whose parents were deceased, ill or could not or, in the case of illegitimate children, did not want to care for them, as well as those removed from neglectful or abusive home situations. In promoting emigration, Quarrier believed 'that we can do nothing here for the class of children we help that will at all compare with what can be done in Canada.'[53] And he was not alone in such beliefs. Although on a smaller scale, other Scottish children's homes and organisations, like the Salvation Army and Boys' Brigade, engaged in child emigration, as did individual philanthropists like Dr George C. Cossar, who ran a scheme which helped boys emigrate to Canada in the 1920s. While those involved in such schemes may have had little doubts about their merits, there were criticisms about their general accountability, and some individuals had second thoughts about letting their children depart. It was not, however, until after the First World War that concerns about the general principle of child emigration began to emerge.[54]

Few today would condone such a policy, and the knowledge that children were removed whose parents remained alive, separated from siblings and in some cases, victims of abuse, make retrospective criticism easy. But the proponents of child emigration were led by a well-intentioned belief that they were rescuing children from a bad situation, giving them an opportunity that would otherwise be unavailable to them. In many cases the organisers' driving beliefs were vindicated by the success stories and thanks received by the very emigrants who were sent. While the letters published in the reports of the sending organisations give the impression of unqualified success, the careful selection which these would have undergone mean that they cannot be taken at face value. More balanced are accounts given years after their emigration, such as that by William Donaldson who emigrated to Canada as part of Dr Cossar's scheme. Acknowledging that a good many boys remained in Canada and fared quite well, he stated: 'I think the Cossar boys were looked upon as a source of cheap labour.'[55] This is not an inaccurate view and is supported by the reality that in spite of what was hoped, few children were adopted by the families with whom they were initially placed. Foster families were paid to look after children until they had reached the age of eleven or twelve, after which they were sent to households where they were expected to perform light duties in return for their keeping. Having reached school leaving age, they often faced a further move to a guardian who could afford to employ them as full-time apprentices. That they were allowed to move on clearly shows that they were never considered an integral part of the family with which they were placed – a reality which was no doubt only too obvious to the children themselves. While they may not have been physically mistreated, and in the long run prospered in their lives, the removal of children from their home environments in most cases probably did not meet the aims of those behind it.

D   CONCLUSION

Crossing the ocean – or any number of the seven seas – was the first and one of the more daunting aspects of migrating to a life outside of the British and Irish Isles. Although there was no shortage of stories circulating of 'coffin ships', unscrupulous captains and mendacious agents to keep migrants on their guard, for most the reality proved less dire than feared. Steamships reduced journey times, increased the regularity of crossings, and competition between shipping lines necessitated improvement in on-board conditions in order to attract passengers – the passage of the twentieth century was far improved from that of the eighteenth century.

In reflections upon Scots journeys to the diaspora and the extent to which expectations matched reality upon first impression, or after a period of time, successful migration required an element of good fortune, a certain attitude and personal energy, plus the support of kin, the host community, and sufficient financial reserves to adapt as opportunities arose. More than most, young single women and children transported by Quarrier's or Barnardo's were in need of a lucky break and benevolence to gain a foothold in a society bereft of family networks. Expectations were linked to the information migrants had prior to departure. This came to them in the form of letters from family and friends, agents' summaries, newspaper and government reports, and the often-detailed portrayals of diasporic life found in emigrant guides. It is to these latter sources that we now turn to examine Scots' encounters with the indigenous peoples of the New World.

NOTES

1. Good Family Letters, University of Guelph Archive, XS1 MS A200.
2. Bueltmann, "'Where the measureless Ocean between us will Roar'", p. 243.
3. Devine, *Scottish Nation*, p. 475.
4. *Glasgow Herald*, 2 March 1881.
5. In January 1883 for example the *Wild Deer* ran aground off the coast of Ireland en route from Glasgow to Otago. See *Dundee Courier and Argus*, 15 January 1883.
6. Harper and Constantine, *Migration and Empire*, p. 302.
7. Extracts from reports of the Highland Society of Scotland, 12 January 1802, appendix to First Report from the Committee on the Survey of the Coasts, &c. of Scotland (Emigration), p. 8.
8. Ibid., p. 9.
9. *Edinburgh Review*, 45 (1826), p. 61.
10. MacDonagh, *A Pattern of Government Growth*, p. 67.
11. In 1855, for example, the *Hugh Walker* had to throw thirteen casks of beef and five casks of pork overboard for being so offensive in spite of it having passed government inspection before leaving from Glasgow. See *Glasgow Herald*, 14 May 1855.

12. Good Family correspondence.
13. *Glasgow Herald*, 17 June 1853.
14. *Glasgow Herald*, 13 January 1864.
15. Campey, *An Unstoppable Force*, pp. 164–90. See also Lucille Campey, '"Fast sailing and copper-bottomed"'.
16. Hassam, *Sailing to Australia*, p. 21.
17. Ibid., p. 141.
18. Richards, *Scots in Australia*, p. 33.
19. Prentis, *Scots in Australia*, p. 116.
20. Trollope, *Australia and New Zealand*, p. 184.
21. Aspinwall, 'The Scots in the United States', p. 80.
22. MacKenzie and Dalziel, *The Scots in South Africa*, p. 5.
23. Richards, *Scots in Australia*, p. 34 and entry for George Russell in the Australian Dictionary of Biography, http://adb.anu.edu.au/biography/drysdale-sir-george-russell-12439 (accessed 10 February 2013).
24. McKenzie had witnessed Highland clearances when he was a child, noting in a debate on his Land Bill in 1892 that he 'got his ideas as a boy when he saw the poor people evicted from their houses in the most cruel manner, and unable to get a place for their feet to stand upon except they went to the cemeteries.' Quoted in Brooking, *Lands for the People?*, p. 21.
25. Fernandez, 'The Scots in Latin America', p. 235.
26. For a discussion of the utility and problems inherent to migrant personal testimonies, see Bueltmann, '"Where the measureless Ocean between us will Roar"', pp. 246–7.
27. Richards, *A History of the Highland Clearances*, vol. 2, p. 228.
28. MacDonnell, *The Emigrant Experience*, p. 119.
29. Bazil Thomson to his sister Jane, 8 January 1880, Alexander Turnbull Library, Wellington, New Zealand, MS-Papers-5174.
30. Richards, *A History of the Highland Clearances*, vol. 2, p. 263.
31. Harper, 'Probing the pioneer questionnaires', pp. 28–46.
32. Ibid., pp. 32 and 44.
33. *Eleventh Report of Her Majesty's Commissioners Appointed to Carry Out a Scheme of Colonization in the Dominion of Canada of Crofters and Cottars From the Western Highlands and Islands of Scotland*, (HMSO, 1901), p. 4.
34. Quoted in Stuart, 'The Scottish crofter colony, Saltcoats', p. 50.
35. See Rebecca Lenihan, 'From Alba to Aotearoa', especially pp. 199ff.
36. Stuart, 'The Scottish crofter colony', p. 46.
37. Ronaldson Series, in Erickson, *Invisible Immigrants*, p. 376.
38. Ibid., p. 375.
39. Laing Series, in Erickson, *Invisible Immigrants*, p. 361.
40. Interview with Joseph Delaney, part of the Ellis Island Oral History Project, accessed through the North American Immigrant Letters,

Diaries, and Oral Histories, http://solomon.imld.alexanderstreet.com (accessed 10 February 2013).

41. James M. Baxter to a James, 28 February 1882, Hocken Library: Dunedin, Misc-MS-0878.
42. Bueltmann, '"Where the measureless Ocean between us will Roar"', p. 250.
43. Lenihan, 'From Alba to Aotearoa'.
44. Bueltmann, *Scottish Ethnicity*, p. 120.
45. Carrier and Jeffrey, *External Migration*, p. 104.
46. Harper, *Adventurers and Exiles*, p. 275.
47. Ibid., p. 276.
48. Chilton, *Agents of Empire*, p. 99.
49. Hassam, *Sailing to Australia*, p. 70.
50. Barber, 'In search of a better life', pp. 13–16.
51. Haper, *Adventurers and Exiles*, p. 165.
52. Harper and Constantine, *Migration and Empire*, p. 254.
53. Quoted in Harper, *Adventurers and Exiles*, p. 168.
54. Ibid., pp. 181 and 194.
55. Taken from an account by William Donaldson in Harrison, *The Home Children*, p. 243.

CHAPTER 6

Encounters with Indigenous Peoples

They might be imagined only from sketches reproduced in periodicals or novels, but indigenous encounters were a thread that bound the experiences of those who migrated to non-European destinations. Anxiety about a life away from the safety and comfort of the familiar had to be faced by the intending migrant. For those wondering which new peoples would be met upon landfall, a potential encounter with Natives meant trepidation. Some migrant nationalities were known: the Irish and the English were familiar at home and were customary companions on emigrant boats, although there would always be some for whom this was their first meeting with the southerner or a Roman Catholic. Continental Europeans and Americans were described colourfully in domestic newspapers, but it was less likely that Scots had ever met those nationals face-to-face. The printed press had long chronicled the racial difference between lowland and highland Scots, but indigenes were less recorded; they were a different race, and ignorance brought fear.

An upshot to travelling to non-European destinations and to trading and socialising amongst Native peoples was how these encounters slowly permeated Scottish life and thought back home. Scottish encounters with indigenous peoples around the world were not straightforward nor were they unidirectional. Responding to the urging of Daunton and Halpern to incorporate the interaction with colonised peoples into domestic history, this chapter explores how indigenous encounters shaped the conceptions of race and class domestically and how these encounters fed the homeland–diaspora connection.[1]

A FIRST CONTACT

It is difficult to do more than speculate what sway Christopher Columbus's reports on the New World, first stepping foot upon American soil in 1492, had upon contemporary Scots. Europe had long been travelled by Scottish emigrants, but it was not until the sixteenth century that Scots contributed to settlement in the North American continent and not until 1670, with formation of the Hudson's Bay Company (HBC), that their most sustained encounters with indigenous peoples occurred. The pursuit of profit took Scots into uncharted territories. Traders-cum-explorers like cousins Alexander Mackenzie and Roderic McKenzie from the Isle of Lewis established forts in the Canadian wilderness,[2] while the tobacco trade channelled through Glasgow brought Scots into trading partnerships with North American indigenes on a par with the trapping and movement of pelts. Further afield in New Zealand early interactions between Maori and European settlers centred on the trade in sealskin and agricultural produce.

Yet while these initial encounters were an intrinsic part of British imperial expansion and settlement around the world, we must be careful not to see these historical events as the inevitable corollary of the rise of Western civilisation. The 'Great European Migration', and the Scots' role within it, was not simply the normal and regular outcome of economic development, of equalising colonising economies. Akenson warns that to think in such a way would be to ignore the imperialism that carried these developments beyond simple logic stemming from self-interest and trade. The Scots encounters with indigenous peoples were the product of imperialist ideology, and its direct outcome, 'the theft of territory', took place on a massive scale.[3]

B   SETTLING THE LAND

When the Reverend William Bell warned his fellow Scots in *Hints to Emigrants* (1824) of a 'moral as well as a natural wilderness', he was referring as much, if not more, to the highland Scot and Irish labourers he was familiar with, as the Algonquin and the Mississauga Indians he had come across in the New World.[4] Bell's discoveries were reflections and negotiations around race embedded in familiar cultural constructions. Strengthening the relevance of such encounters to both Scottish ethnic and diasporic consciousness was the claimed affinity between highland Scots and various indigenes, both being 'from the land'. These Old and New World people, so the argument has been made, had experienced similar cultural, economic and political oppression, and had similar orientations to land ownership, to stratifications of rank and to deferential social order. Highland-born Donald MacDonald was a noted campaigner for Maori rights in the 1860s and 1870s who embodied this affinity, arguing that 'Highlanders who have learnt to speak the Maori tongue can enter into the feeling of a Maori . . . better than most Europeans'.[5] In that country's twentieth-century reflections on its history, connections were made between Scots and Maori around the legacies of social organisation and land ownership.[6] Elsewhere, Szasz observes that '[a]lthough these indigenous peoples lived on opposite shores of the North Atlantic, they share a commonality evinced through their oral cultures, based on myth; their societies, based on kinship; and their mutual dependence on the natural resources available for their survival.'[7] Calloway has taken a similar view, noting that 'having been colonized and "civilized" themselves, highland Scots sometimes identified and sympathised with Indian people they saw going through the kind of experiences they or their parents had suffered'.[8] The loss of common land to enclosure and the consolidations that came with the eighteenth-century Improvement ideology shaped parallels between Scots and colonial indigenes.

At various points in the period under examination, debate flourished within Britain and colonial administrative and ruling circles about the right to own land. Awareness of the hardship caused by the Scottish court system being less protective of customary rights than the English legal system furnished some amount of sympathy in colonial dealings. Tiree-born Donald McLean was charged by the British government with negotiating for the 225,000-acre Rangitekei-Turakina block with the Ngati Apa, settling on recompense of £2,500. Being trusted on both sides, McLean was to become the most influential civil servant in nineteenth-century New Zealand.[9] Another highland Scot who gained the goodwill of the Maori was the legal campaigner Alexander

Figure 6.1 Large meeting of settlers and Maoris at a native village near Napier, Hawke's Bay, New Zealand [source: *Illustrated London News*, 31 October 1863]

MacDonald. MacDonald was less revered by the Crown and was imprisoned for his efforts, yet was gifted 800 acres and a sum of money by those Maori for whom he fought so hard.[10] Behind this empathy was a philosophical connection: both highland Scots and indigenes, separately but with enough common ground for contemporaries and historians to focus upon, questioned the moral basis upon which anyone has the right to own land. This, more often than not, is a question for those who have lost land, and those who have been cleared from the land at the behest of its legal owner.

With all that being said, land acquisition was the essence of imperial expansion. Investment in overseas land purchase was a significant source of income that subsidised investments at home; Scots investors were hawkish towards any challenge to that capital flow.[11] So while sympathy might be exercised in colonial land dealings by those on the ground, there was a hard-nosed capitalist relationship between the Scots at home, their factors and agents in the diaspora, and the indigene who surrendered legal entitlement to that land.

C   GLIMMERS OF INDIGENOUS LIFE

It is a hapless task to attempt to measure just how aware Scots were of indigenes, but there is a smattering of evidence that indicates the breadth of knowledge that was circulating. While living in San Gabriel in southern Mexico Hugo Reid made a number of perceptive observations on indigenes in letters to his friend Abel Stearns. Educated in Scotland, Reid spent two years at Cambridge University before returning north to work in his father's shop and then for Henry Dalton's trading, then gold mining company in Peru.[12] Reid's letters to the *Los Angeles Star* in 1852 highlighted the plight of the local Indians. He found their language 'simple, rich, and abounding in compound expressive terms', yet its use had waned 'since conquest'. He highlighted indigenes' diet where food was generally eaten cold ('which helped maintain the good health of the teeth'), and salt was hardly used for fear one's hair would turn grey. Later letters address issues of birth and burial, medicine and diseases, and customs such as wild tobacco being used to induce vomiting.[13] The ordinariness of indigene life was intriguing here, but it was the clues to survival in unfamiliar climates and hostile environments that were scanned most carefully by recent and potential migrants.

More than the mark of a name, tattooing was one signifier of indigene culture that was copied by the Scottish sailors who travelled abroad or found indigenes as fellow crew members. Such Scots who 'went native' took to marking their bodies with artwork.[14] Ship surgeon David Ramsay, Perth-born but later resident in Australia, showed his fascination with these designs by donating two tattooed Maori skulls along with Maori ceremonial knives and capes to his hometown Perth Library and Antiquarian Society in 1842.[15] Inevitably the settlements established by early pioneers would take them close to various indigenes, paving the way for close observation. In settling over eighty families within the environs of New York, Islay's Captain Lachlan Campbell left his fellow Scots to seek accommodation with the Huron, Mohawk, Iroquois and Delaware tribes.[16] Traders, both ordinary Scots and those whose origins or career were exceptional, recorded encounters. The early traders went into an environment where following Native patterns of life was the best means to survive.[17] Scholars have speculated that the success of Scots in the North West Company was because of their familiarity with the social structure they encountered, and their adaptation of English, French and local dialects, just as they filtered Gaelic and English. Examples can be found of Scottish-born translators throughout nineteenth-century North America, such as Robert Dickson, Robert Stuart, John Stuart and Donald Mackenzie.[18] Yet while the principle can be proposed, the personal aptitude required suggests this was not the norm.

Despite everyday observations shaping familiarity, the extremes of scalping, torture and cannibalism were all fears that permeated early and subsequent Scottish impressions of North-American Indians. Cannibalism was also a concern with respect to Maori – and one already voiced by Captain Cook.[19] Imperfect knowledge heightened fears in wildernesses and pioneer settlements far from the rule of law and the safety of community controls. That such 'abominations' were exacerbated by European contact, and that the Europeans were equally as violent, did little to assuage concerns. With harsh discipline commonplace within regiments, soldiers of the British army were involved in scalping and in turn offered rewards for scalps received.[20]

Many Scots, though, remained fascinated by the people they were encountering for the first time. William Hunter, founder of the Hunterian Museum in Glasgow, acquired a number of differently styled Maori cloaks and whalebone hand clubs from Captain Cook's voyages in the 1770s. Another well-known explorer, the Orcadian Dr John Rae (1818–93), developed a strong affinity for the Inuit during his explorations of the Arctic, bringing home a deerskin bag he designed in the Inuit style.[21] Rae had gained an unwelcome reputation for his role in searching for Sir John Franklin's ill-fated 1845–7 expedition to find the Northwest Passage across the Arctic north of Canada, discovering from Inuit hunters in 1854 the dark descent into cannibalism of the stranded sailors. But Rae gained sufficient trust of the Cree community around James Bay and at Moose Factory to copy their designs in the manufacture of canoe paddles and snowshoes, in return being gifted a caribou-hide octopus bag embroidered with stylised thistles. The thistle is indigenous to the James Bay area, and was later imported too, but the plant did not appear in iconography until after Rae's arrival.[22] Later on in the nineteenth century Scottish physician and anthropologist Neil Gordon Munro was the first Westerner to study the Ainu people of Hokkaido in Japan, and many more explorers and missionaries were paramount in providing early accounts of indigenous life and peoples from Africa to Australia.

D INDIGENOUS CULTURES TRAVEL TO SCOTLAND

There is also scattered evidence that indigenes were open to learning more about Scotland and to making their culture and society more empathetic. The interchange of knowledge was not simply about the indigene artefacts being transported to Scotland's museums. In the Strath Taieri region of New Zealand combinations of Scottish and Maori place names are common and similar examples can be found throughout the country.[23] McCormack has unearthed evidence of increasing consumption of tartan fabric by Aboriginal communities in Canada in the nineteenth century, just as those products are being mass-produced in the same period in Scotland.[24] The ubiquitous Portneuf spongeware pottery found in the second half of the nineteenth century mostly came from Scotland. Glasgow potters Robert Cocharan and Co. built their own factory in America to supply the local market and John Marshall and Co. from Bo'ness produced designs specifically for Canada.[25] Observing artefacts indicative of various indigenous cultures was a means for Scots to gain knowledge of what they might encounter upon emigration. Travelling shows and fairgrounds also offered insight into these dark worlds, along with descriptions in periodicals such as *Blackwood's Magazine* and *Tait's Magazine*. In Gaelic culture, literary representations as well as first-hand observations ranged in tone from empathy to hostility. Words were coined for the colour of indigene skin and hair, and commentators mixed a general fear of reprisal alongside an equally vague spiritual respect for the Native American as 'green men' (woods people), something akin to those who appear in local tales from the highland woods.[26]

Other insights came from returnees where the accent was on the fantastical. Upon Sir William Drummond Stewart's return to Scotland after seven years in the American West he brought home a range of artefacts, mementos, plants and live animals.[27] He had first journeyed to America in 1832 to hunt buffalo, initially joining a group of Scots and Indians at their trappers' rendezvous. Between 1837 and 1842 Stewart commissioned the American Alfred Jacob Miller for twenty-eight oil paintings and eighty-seven sketches to record his adventures. A number of these images were displayed in New York before being transported to Murthly Castle. The images featured Native daily life: eating, talking and sharing a pipe when visiting at camps to which he was taken by his Métis guide Antoine (who appears in one third of the sketches). In these images, the appearance of Indian observers adds authenticity to 'the Buckskin Baronet's' encounters with Native Americans. Perhaps the most conspicuous of Stewart's imports were the buffaloes introduced to Perthshire in the hope they would breed. Stewart brought back plants and fauna and trees to replenish his estates. Two beautifully carved 'buffalo chairs' commemorate the link with a far-off place, and, perhaps more exotic still to the local society, Antoine was at the castle along with at least two Indians who immediately became curiosities in local society.[28]

Another example is that of George Caitlin who brought Indians across the Atlantic Ocean to Scotland, in their case accompanying a gallery of over 600 paintings of Indian life and culture in 1843.[29] In November that year a group of Canadian 'real, red denizens of the wilds', but of course 'born subjects of her Majesty Queen Victoria' travelled to join him.[30] Caitlin's show was of sufficient prominence to make him a guest of the Royal Highland Society and be introduced as honoured invitee at the Caledonian Ball. Upon arrival in Edinburgh in 1845, 'their novel appearance created a great excitement' and 'filled our hall with the most respectable and fashionable people'.[31] Addressing the crowds, war chief Walking Rai acknowledged the applause which he found respectful for 'strangers amongst you, and with red skins'. He continued:

> My friends, we have just arrived in your beautiful city, and we see that you are a different people from the English in London, where we have been. In going into a strange place, amongst strange people, we always fear that our dances and our noise may not please – we are showing you how we dance in our own country, and we believe that is what you wish to see. (Applause and '*How, how, how!*')[32]

Interestingly, they assumed England had conquered Scotland, believing it a shame the northern kingdom did not have a king of its own. A crown, it was suggested, should be worn, not 'shut up in a dark room'. And if the crown was not to be used, then the red and green stones could be used for watch-seals, and the gold melted down to make sovereigns to give to the poor. After four days in Edinburgh the group took the steamer to Dundee and then on to Perth. Caitlin tells of a story on board the steamer to Dundee where between them the Indians raised the fare for a young girl travelling without a ticket, telling the girl to remember that 'the heart of a red man is as good and as kind as that of a white man'. Going to Glasgow they enjoyed daily rides in an omnibus and visited the Hunterian Museum, throwing money to the poor children they saw, with the city's beggars soon gathering outside their quarters for 'when the savages came out'. The visitors, however, became tired of attempts to Christianise them, having each been handed a Bible with their name inscribed upon it. The indigene's stock retort was that they had expected to find sober and kind Scots people with so many preachers available to interpret the Bible, but this was not the case. Encountering so much poverty, especially amongst the children, that 'we think it would be good for all your teachers to stay at home . . .' was a quite devastating retort to 'egalitarian Scotland'.[33]

There is also evidence indicating that during indigenous encounters with Scots the failure of the clan system was recognised alongside reluctance to romanticise the past. So while the Ojjibye who visited Scotland in the 1840s bemoaned the lack of roots and herbs their doctor was used to using, several Native American tribes gathered together in 1850 to send word of their thanks to Dr Charles Jenner for his inoculations against smallpox.[34] During a farewell soirée to Ka-ge-ga-gah-Bowh (also known as George Copway) held at Edinburgh's Queen Street Hall in December 1850, the old ways were no cause for celebration. Copway was commended for his plans to return to America and 'unite his scattered race around common laws' and 'induce them to exchange the sectarian feeling of clanship for that of a high and devoted nationality; and further to lead them to the pursuits of agriculture, literature, and religion'. Copway did not eschew romanticism, appearing dressed as a highland chief, yet chose the modern political path of lobbying the American Congress to secure land that could be used for the Native American tribes to unite upon. Copway also made the case for removing the rank of Chief by presenting it as a hindrance to the modern development of the tribes.[35]

Not all Native American visitors to Scotland had the courage or capacity to disparage Scotland's home civilisation with such effect as the Ojibbeway and Ioway, but many had comparisons to make. Of greatest profile and lasting cultural influence was Buffalo Bill's Wild West extravaganza, which came twice to Scotland, in 1891 and 1904. American-born William Cody (1846–1917) gained his military prowess as an army scout before becoming a showman in 1872. The troupe was formed in 1883, and having previously toured England as part of Victoria's Golden Jubilee celebrations, Cody brought 'Buffalo Bill's Wild West' and its cast of 250 people and 175 animals for a six-month stay in Glasgow in 1891. Housed in a former Boys' House of Refuge to perform twice a day, the Glasgow venue held 7,000 spectators. For a backdrop Cody displayed seven pictures measuring 200 feet by 35 feet mounted on a cyclorama of large drums.[36] A cultural connection was achieved by the use of 'authentic' performers. Included amongst them were Kicking Bull who survived the Battle of Little Bighorn (1876) and other Lakota survivors of the Ghost Dance War (1890–1). As a further mark of authenticity, a representation of the performers sold a ghost shirt to Kelvingrove Museum in 1891 where it remained for over a century before repatriation.[37] Locals would tell stories of Cody's generosity to the poor of the city along with evidence of the touring Indians sending money home and maintaining some element of fame upon

Figure 6.2 Buffalo Bill's Wild West Show Indians posing on rocks near Fraserburgh [Source: SCRAN; Resource Rights Holder: North East Folklore Archive; SCRAN 000-000-480-112-C]

their return. Yet again the hardship of poverty marked the Scots out to these indigenes.

The Scots response reflected both what they read about in their local newspapers and the knowledge already gained and circulated within reports and stories returned to them by migrants and soldiers. These stories ranged, perhaps inevitably, from the mundane to the heavily objectified. The renowned writer John Buchan who later became Canada's Governor General (1935–40), made the harsh realities of Native welfare a particular concern of his time in office and the subject for his final, posthumously published novel *Sick Heart River* (1941).[38] But it was the Native American conceptualised by Cody's shows that came to dominate twentieth-century Scottish culture. The earliest cinema-goers showed strong demand for the western movie over domestic product in the 1930s.[39] The 'Indian' as a stylised character was epitomised by 'Tonto', first as a radio character from 1933 and then on comic strip and television from the 1950s. The landmark American Western *Apache* in 1954 inspired the hit song by the same name by The Shadows in 1960. Specifically making the Native American indigenous to Glasgow was the comic strip 'Galsgae Cowboy' Sheriff Lobey Dosser, illustrated by Bud Neill from the 1940s until the 1960s, and with much retrospective appeal thereafter.

E   EMIGRANT GUIDES TO LIVING AMONGST INDIGENOUS PEOPLES

From inspecting indigene artefacts and observing indigenous visitors, Scottish society had some idea of what indigenous peoples might look like as a race and some idea of what they would wear. They might also have picked up some concerns that Scottish civilisation was not as unquestionably superior as they might have believed. Trappers, explorers and adventurers gave clues to life in the wild, but missing from the narrative was settler life. Ordinary tradesmen and domestics and families dominated the flow of emigrants in the nineteenth century, so alternative information was sought upon the likely indigenous encounters they would face. Here emigrant guides were used.[40] These guides would stress the Europeanness, or not, of these people. Indigenes were not discussed in their own terms, but as sub-Europeans.[41] The hot climate was used to explain African appearance, and Australia was described by rival nations' agents as too hot for the European body, certainly compared to the more temperate New Zealand.[42] From their Enlightenment thinkers the Scots had learned of the supposition that variations in climate explained the path of civilisation around the world: David Hume and Adam Ferguson argued that Europe's temperate climate was one reason behind that region's lead in the path of social development.

To illustrate how pioneer impressions were presented to potential and intending migrants, we have chosen to conduct a close reading of two of these guidebooks, with Canada providing the case study. Around two dozen accounts were published on Upper Canada in the 1820s and a steady trickle thereafter, with similar numbers produced for the main locations of the diaspora.[43]

The first to consider comes from John Howison (1797–1859), an Edinburgh-born doctor who journeyed to Lower Canada in 1818. Arriving first in Montreal he made his way to York (Toronto) before settling to practise in St Catharines. He stayed in Canada for only two years before joining the East India Company as assistant surgeon, heading for Bombay where he remained for twenty years; he died in London (England) in 1859. Howison's *Sketches of Upper Canada* was published with the Edinburgh publisher Oliver and Boyd in 1821 (with further editions in 1822, 1825; and a German edition in 1822) and was followed by a series of essays in *Blackwood's Magazine*.[44] John Galt, the Scottish novelist, one-time secretary of the Canada Company, and author of his own travel books, reviewed the guide with pleasure,[45] and the classified advertisements in a number of Scottish newspapers described *Sketches of Upper Canada* as offering 'Practical Details for the Information of Emigrants of every Class'. The book is packed with stories that served to show the humanity of Native Americans. In November 1821 Edinburgh's *Caledonian Mercury* chose one of these accounts as an 'affecting story' for its readers. The narrative concerns a young boy separated from his mother while she searched for berries in the woods and he sought shells on the beach. Upon the wind blowing and the lake rising, the boy was left clinging to a tree while the distraught mother could only watch and wait as darkness came. Just when she thought he had died, and she had flung herself to the ground in anguish, the boy scrambled up the bank towards her, only to slip as he tried to catch her hand, falling under the billowing lake to his death. This sad but overtly melodramatic story of the boy's death was typical of the favourable light Howison shone upon Native Americans.

In another vignette of Native life and conduct, Howison tells of visiting an Indian wigwam one cold day which he found to be 'extremely comfortable' with an open fire at the front. It was an encounter made favourable because it was conducted in English and the Native had just helped him to ford an iced stream.[46] Howison was impressed with the hospitality he received and told of a young artist – whose depiction of the battle of Waterloo displayed much bloodshed and slaughter ('in the Indian taste') – who he thought sufficiently talented that he purchased some of his artwork. Howison, here, was pleased with the spread of European culture, speaking positively of those native peoples taught to read and write using a version of the gospel of St John and hymns translated into Mohawk by missionaries. Howison had also encountered interactions between Natives and Europeans that were less successful, concluding that little of the civilising and more of the 'vicious propensities' had rubbed off. Rather than improvement, Indian intercourse with Europeans has 'been the means of divesting them of those rude virtues and barbarous qualities which alone give a sort of respectability to the savage'. Howison lauded the Indian's faculties for observation, to an extent the Europeans could never hope to match. He described their finding their way through even the thickest wood without recourse to a compass, observing the moss which always grows on the north side of the tree trunk, and he extolled their hearing, vision and marksmanship as near perfect, whereas civilisation 'destroys the acuteness of the senses'.

These comments refer to what Howison called the 'boast and glory' of the Indian who in turn often expressed pity for white people who spent so much time 'learning how to live' in their pioneer settlements. Howison regarded the Indians as being heavily protected by the British government, with medical and material help provided from government representatives each year. The potential migrant was told that they had something to emulate, not fear, in the deportment of the Indian. Nor, however, should they regard themselves as a superior race. Nowhere was this better explained than when Howison was journeying near Talbot Settlement and came across a mix of Scottish highlanders, Indians and Americans that gave him the opportunity for direct comparison:

The Scots were smoking tobacco and speaking in Gaelic; the Indians
– in full hunting costume – were watching a child blow on a miniature
windmill, the New England Americans were talking politics, their own
successes and mixed vulgarity and piety in their speech. The Scots were
weighed down by poverty, servitude and ignorance, the Americans had
a great evaluation of themselves, and the Indians possessed a sort of
negative superiority over both parties. Though untutored, they were
not in a state of debasement, and they seemed more entitled to respect
than either the Scotch or the Americans.[47]

Comment that sought parallels between Scots and Native Americans came
from the pen of Robert MacDougall (Robert MacDhùghaill, 1813–87). He
journeyed across the Atlantic from his Perthshire home with his father and
sister in 1836, joining his two brothers who had arrived earlier. MacDougall
was another who did not live out his life in Canada, returning to Scotland
in 1839 before leaving for Australia in the year he published, in Gaelic,
The Emigrant's Guide to North America (Glasgow, 1841). MacDougall's
approach was not to judge Native American behaviour against a European or
Presbyterian measure, but to engage known analogies to describe this race of
people. As a measure of how otherworldly he found the Native American, he
resorted to likening their skin tone to an industrial procedure back home: like
'lichen-dyed cloth, immersed in the tub three times'. His range of analogies
varied from animals, to trees, to the Scots people themselves: Native American
hair was 'rough as a piece of shaggy hair of the grey horse'; their eyes like the
'earth berry'; and, 'although the Indians are a different colour than the Gael,
they are neither black nor yellow, as some maintain. Neither are they the
colour of copper, nor can I name anything that I have ever seen that is exactly
the colour'.[48]

Writing directly to a highland audience, MacDougall sought parallels in
familiar activities common to the lives of both races: while 'the men among
them walk elegantly and cheerfully, with backs as straight as a rod of ewe
wood' he finds the women 'have [a] heavy, undulating gait, like the Highland
women who are used to carrying the creel'. He identifies a gender divide in
their society, where men will carry gun, shot, powder, bow and quiver of
arrows, but the women are left to lug the remainder of their belongings.[49] And
while Howison regarded Native Americans as 'feeble and useless allies, but
dangerous enemies', MacDougall labelled them better on the hunt than standing on the battlefield, compliant most when in the presence of their chief ('like
the clan chiefs who were once among the Gaels').[50]

MacDougall drew several parallels between the two peoples, likening
the role of tribal chief to that of the old highland clan chief, comparing the
hardworking character of Native women to that of highland women, and even

perceiving similarities between their respective languages. The Natives had 'a slow, soft, pleasant speech, merely a branch of the Gaelic language . . .'[51] This Gaelic-speaking chronicler concluded that the European could only marvel incomprehensibly at Native American hunting skills – knowing where the salt spring runs and where the deer are found – and their infinite patience when fishing. MacDougall was particularly impressed with the dignity they showed in raising children, clothing them, transporting them, and keeping them free from bad habits. He found Native Americans to be respectful to one another and noted that many were now abandoning their hunting and gathering life-styles to build permanent settlements and cultivate crops. To contemporaries, this was a sure sign of progress.

As they stared out at the Atlantic Ocean en route to their new life, these were some of the stories Scots had in mind. They had read that Native Americans were a different race, physically and culturally distinct. They had learned that Christianity had spread amongst some of them, sometimes for the good, sometimes not, and that the Europeanisation of Native Americans was not unreservedly favourable to a proud and honest race. Where their worries might have darkened was for their own people, and for themselves.

F FROM THE 'AGE OF HUMANITARIANISM' TO THE 'AGE OF IMPERIALISM'

The mixed and often negative indigene response to Europeanisation and Christianity reported in North American emigrant guidebooks was part of wider reflection on slavery, ethno–centric improvement and the path of civilisation. The work by Scottish missionaries to spread Christianity shaped a range of metropolitan attitudes to other races. Thus when the Society for the Propagation of the Bible in Foreign Parts plied its work around the territories of the British Empire in the eighteenth century, its operatives perceived little difference between colonial heathens and those they encountered at home. But as the metropolitan engagement with the colonies evolved, the concept of race was redefined away from the non-industrious white population, with the term 'indigenous' used to mark distinction from the European heaven.[52] This difference was firmly in place by the 1840s when increasing awareness of racial characteristics, irrespective of class, dominated analyses. *The Dundee Courier* in 1846 explored 'The capacities of the Negro race' showing their military, political, commercial and artistic successes.[53] Writing in *Fraser's Magazine* in 1849 on the 'Occasional discourse on the Negro question', Thomas Carlyle contrasted different races with the 'racial whiteness' of the working classes.[54] An article from the *North British Review* on the 'Permanence of the Negro', reproduced in the *Caledonian Mercury* in 1862, claimed a 'law' that all savage races are doomed in the face of civilisation. Here it was argued the Central African Negro was an exception: 'their barbarism, or semi barbarism, seem fully capable to live side by side with our civilisation'.[55] The Mohicans and the Maori was intellectually and morally more advanced than the Negro, it was continued, but still the latter is the strongest.

Despite what they might have learned from observers of their own society, from the middle of the nineteenth century the Scots' world-view of indigenes was fixed upon a contrast between the 'beastly living' of the indigene and civic world of the homeland. The indigene's nakedness ('the people goeth all naked') was both observational and metaphorical.[56] It was also a cultural marker full of sexual as well as theological underpinnings, of indigenous men poorly treating their women, redeemable only by British 'rescue'.[57] By late in the nineteenth century Africans in the Cape or in the Caribbean were no longer 'excused' by their circumstances, and contemporaries were quick to make accusations of immorality and drunkenness.

Like most European settlers, the Scots generally accepted the forced removal of indigenous people from their land as a necessary step in the progress of humanity. Scots, highland Scots included, exhibited all the prejudices and exploitative practices engaged in by other immigrants. There were some important exceptions, but diasporic Scots were actively engaged in colonising rather than sharing empathetically their colonised experience, and by any choice of figures the outcome always favoured the Europeans. In ninety short years, the European-derived population of America increased from 7.9 million (1820) to 81.8 million (1910), while the Native American population dropped from 0.7 million (c. 1815) to 0.237 million (1900).[58] In *The Imaginary Indian*, Daniel Francis identified several nineteenth-century writers who travelled in Canada and came down on the inevitability of progress. However much they regretted the plight of the Native population, they were convinced that their own civilisation must prevail, that the Indian must assimilate or die.[59] The image of the Indians as 'naked' and 'savage' was used to rationalise this process.

Attitudes were not static, however. The HBC was initially hostile to interracial sexual relations before later accepting the value of such relationships for trade and for social and commercial stability. Other land, investment and trading companies simply accepted the attraction of the 'country wife' in an environment where so few European women were to be found. Yet it is not straightforward to assume that the different Native cultures involved understood marriage to mean the same thing.[60] Some European men were no more than transients, seeking sexual gratification or the equivalent of a wife's help around the house or upon the land before moving off, while other men remained and added their surnames to the local community. The mix shows that intimacy went alongside trade and exploitation within personal relationship between Scots, Métis and First Nations.[61] Rather than the union itself, it was the mixed-race children who faced the more significant prejudice. While there is some evidence of mixed-blood leaders who came to the fore in Indian culture, with names such as Ross, McGillivray and McIntosh playing an important role in early US history,[62] such influence was unusual. The apparent advantage for mixed-race children on both sides of the blood divide was conditional. The 1869 Indian Act removed 'status' from any Indian women who married a non-Indian, and the legislation stayed in place until 1925.[63] Alternative examples find discrimination in each society, and varying levels of integration throughout the diaspora. Amongst twenty-first-century indigenes, the issue of pure- and mixed- blood became one not just of social status, but of welfare and educational rights. Mixed-race children in Africa did better, for example, than such children in Rupert's Land in what is now Canada.[64]

More so than the emigrant guides which tended to be prosaic in their descriptions, travel literature highlighted the sexual allure of Indian women, an attraction that appealed most strongly amongst working-class migrants. The myth of the 'Black Peril' and the 'Black Rapist' in Australia, India and South Africa added to the exotic charm *and fear* of indigenous populations.[65] Life outside the Indian compound was as intriguing as it was repellent. In part through the sexualising of the indigene, the humanitarianism of the early phases of Scottish colonialism gave way to debates on racial inferiority and fear that racial impurities were weakening European society at different rates. The Scots – like the British and Europeans more widely – applied notions of race to frame their imperialism. Individually and cumulatively the Kat River rebellion (1846–7) in the Cape, the Indian Mutiny (1857), the Morant Bay Rebellion (1865) in the West Indies, and the Waikato War (1863) in New Zealand were taken as heinous breeches of trust quickly ascribed to racial failings of the 'scheming and immoral oriental' in popular and colonial discourses. This transition has been characterised by scholars as a shift from the 'age of humanitarianism' to the 'age of imperialism'.[66] The massacre of Cawnpore (Kanpur) and the murder or women and children at the Bibighar well (1857) shocked British society and hardened their racialisation of Indians. The British state took over administration of India from the East India Company, and the military's response was to favour men from the Punjab, Nepal and Afghanistan, which indicated both where they believed greatest loyalty lay, but also suggested the relative fighting prowess they assigned to different ethnic groupings. Indigenous peoples had been used by each of the European powers in the respective battle for imperial supremacy, until the recruitment of indigenes fell away as these conflicts were played out. By the late Victorian period there was little desire to include indigenes within the regiments of the imperial forces, the British War Office believing sepoys unsuited for fighting in colder climes. Likely out of necessity rather than cultural revaluation, this changed by around 1915 when casualty rates reached such levels during the

First World War that recruitment was spread as widely as possible. Perhaps sensing the continuation of attitudes from the 'age of imperialism', Canadian Aboriginals were reluctant to be enumerated in the 1916 census for fear it would lead to their conscription.[67]

This administrative and military racialism of indigenes was sustained by theories of scientific racism built upon the ideas of Social Darwinism. Robert Knox, the Edinburgh anatomist who had received cadavers from the notorious grave robbers William Burke and William Hare in the 1820s, carved his influential theories and images of race in *The Races of Man* (1850) from a mix of these ideas and from his work as a military surgeon with the Xhosa in West Africa.[68] Making the point for the Cape, but one that can be applied more generally to the Scottish diaspora, Smandych and McGillivray argue that even within the basic humanitarianism of the abolitionist cause, the stadial arguments of the Scottish Enlightenment meant there was an implicit racial underpinning to the stages of progression.[69] Contemporary experiences also saw progression. Early pioneers found relative peace and equanimity in their indigenous encounters, with affinities and mutual respect won over long years of settlement, cultural exchange, and personal and economic interaction. As the 'age of imperialism' took root in the nineteenth century, however, despite high-profile visits from Native Americans to Scotland, contemporaries framed their encounters in terms of indigenous racial inferiority and religious and personal 'nakedness'. In each phase, the dialectic of race and indigene held the Scots' non-European diasporic experiences in a firm grip.

G   CONCLUSION

Creating New Scotland (*Nova Scotia*) and naming settlements after towns and representations of home – Hamilton, Edina, Aberfoyle, Bona Accord, amongst many more – was predicated on a reimagined civil society uncorrupted by the traumas and dislocations of a previous life of struggle. What 'civilisation' meant in pioneer life was never going to be straightforward, and however it was imagined, the place of indigenes within the New World had somehow to be figured in. Scots, like most European migrants, expected the New World to be 'empty', populated only by migrants such as themselves. They did, though, have some knowledge of indigenes from the guidebooks read before departure, and in the letters and stories they read and heard from family and friends. Importantly, also, they had some experience (at least) of Native Americans visiting Scotland – only for short periods, but suitably different to make impressions that lasted. These impressions, of course, were highly objectified, feeding notions of affinity between two peoples dispossessed of their land. Yet notwithstanding that and other empathies, the Scots were willing imperialists

– accepting the forced removal of indigenous people from their land, so they might build the nation that was their new home.

NOTES

1. Daunton and Halpern, 'Introduction', p. 45.
2. McCormack, 'Transatlantic rhythms', pp. 253–4.
3. Akenson, 'The Great European migration and indigenous populations', p. 28.
4. Bell, *Hints to Emigrants in a series of Letters from Upper Canada*, Letter XIV.
5. Patterson, '"It is curious how keenly allied in character are the Scotch Highlander and the Maori"', p. 153.
6. MacKenzie, 'A Scottish empire?', p. 29.
7. Szasz, *Scottish Highlanders and Native Americans*, p. 6.
8. Calloway, *White People, Indians and Highlanders*, p. 17.
9. Patterson, '"It is curious how keenly allied in character are the Scotch Highlander and the Maori"', p. 147.
10. Ibid, p. 154.
11. Bayly, 'The British and indigenous peoples', p. 22.
12. Dakin, *A Scotch Paisano in Old Los Angeles*, pp. vi, 12.
13. Ibid., pp. 230–1.
14. Morgan, 'Encounters between British and "indigenous" peoples', pp. 60–1.
15. Hooper-Greenhill, *Museums and the Interpretation of Visual Culture*, p. 114.
16. Bryan, *Twa Tribes*, p. 9.
17. Ibid., pp. 18–19.
18. Ibid., pp. 10–11.
19. Hulme, 'Introduction', p. 21.
20. Way, 'The Cutting Edge of culture', pp. 131–5. See also British Museum: Ethno Q78.Am.39. for an exhibit of a scalp.
21. National Museums Scotland: A.LOAN 304.128.
22. Oberholtzer, 'Thistles in the North, pp. 100–2.
23. Brooking, 'Sharing out the haggis, p. 56.
24. McCormack, 'Transatlantic rhythms', p. 255.
25. Dalgleish, 'Aspects of Scottish-Canadian material culture', p. 130.
26. Newton, '"Going to the land of the Yellow Man", p. 237.
27. Strong, 'American Indians and Scottish identity in Sir William Drummond Stewart's Collection', p. 127.
28. Ibid, pp. 130–3, 141, 148.

29. *The Scotsman*, 1 April 1843, p. 3.
30. *The Scotsman*, 11 November 1843, p. 11.
31. Caitlin, *Adventures of the Ojibbeway and Ioway Indians in England, France and Belgium*, Vol. II, p. 162.
32. Ibid, pp. 162–3.
33. Ibid, pp. 168, 170, 173–6.
34. *The Scotsman*, 19 January 1850.
35. *The Scotsman*, 7 December 1850.
36. Bryan, *Twa Tribes*, pp. 87–8.
37. Ibid, p. 9; Hooper-Greenhill, *Museums and the Interpretation of Visual Culture*, pp. 157–61.
38. Hutchings, '"Teller of tales"', p. 342.
39. Griffiths, *The Cinema and Cinema Going in Scotland*, pp. 198–208.
40. A version of this section was previously published in *History Scotland* (Autumn, 2011). We are grateful to its publishers for permission to use this material.
41. Morgan, 'Encounters between British and "indigenous" peoples, c. 1500–c. 1800', p. 89.
42. Ibid, p. 90.
43. Waterston and Talman, 'John Howison'.
44. John Howison, *Sketches of Upper Canada*.
45. Waterston and Talman, 'John Howison'.
46. Howison, *Sketches of Upper Canada*, p. 205.
47. Ibid., p. 196.
48. MacDougall, *The Emigrant's Guide*, p. 30.
49. Ibid., p. 31.
50. Howison, *Sketches of Upper Canada*, p. 165.
51. MacDougall, *The Emigrant's Guide*, p. 39.
52. Bayly, 'The British and indigenous peoples', p. 21.
53. *Dundee Courier*, 10 November 1846.
54. Daunton and Halpern, 'Introduction', pp. 4, 12.
55. *The Caledonian Mercury*, 27 June 1862.
56. Morgan, 'Encounters between British and "indigenous" peoples', pp. 82, 88.
57. Ibid., p. 67.
58. Akenson, 'The Great European migration and indigenous populations', p. 33.
59. Francis, *The Imaginary Indian*, pp. 58–60.
60. Brown, 'Partial truths', pp. 60–1.
61. Innes, 'Multicultural bands on the Northern Plains and the notion of "tribal" histories', pp. 137–8.
62. Cunningham, *The Diamond's Ace*, p. 49.

63. Winegard, *Indigenous Peoples of the British Dominions and the First World War*, p. 41.
64. Morgan, 'Encounters between British and "indigenous" peoples', p. 66.
65. Winegard, *Indigenous Peoples of the British Dominions*, p. 36.
66. Smandych and McGillivray, 'Images of Aboriginal children', pp. 364–5.
67. Winegard, *Indigenous Peoples of the British Dominions*, pp. 73, 150.
68. Smandych and McGillivray, 'Images of Aboriginal children', p. 380.
69. Ibid, pp. 367–8.

CHAPTER 7

Associational Culture

When, in late 1901, 300 Scots gathered in Calcutta for their annual St Andrew's Day dinner, they wired 'hearty greetings' to fellow Scots in Singapore who had also come together to celebrate Scotland's patron saint.[1] Next to Burns Night, St Andrew's Day was the key event in the social calendar of the Scots overseas, offering an opportunity for them to gather annually, celebrating their Scottish heritage not only with fellow Scots in their respective place of settlement, but with many others throughout the Scottish diaspora – a global 'imagined community'[2]. Hence, in New York in 1890, 'the music of the bagpipes and the pungent aroma of the haggis' filled the banquet room of Delmonico's restaurant, which frequently served as the venue for the city's Scottish community. Traditional Scottish songs were sung, and Scottish stories were told, and, as the *New York Times* did not fail to note, 'the names of Wallace, Bruce, Burns, and Scott had only to be mentioned to start a fresh round of cheers or another song.'[3] In many cities throughout North America similar sentiments were expressed, with balls and dinners evidently the most common celebrations. Well over 100 guests came together in St Paul, Minnesota, for the local St Andrew's Society ball in 1886, exchanging greetings with the Winnipeg St Andrew's Society in Canada. In Hong Kong, also in 1886, the annual ball was, as the *China Mail* observed, one of great sociability, with an illustrious round of 700 guests gathered at the City Hall, which had been superbly decorated for the occasion. Even further afield, in Australia, about 500 guests gathered for the 1881 St Andrew's Day celebration of the Caledonian Society of South Australia in Adelaide and a 'procession representative of the Society, headed by the chief piper and his assistants, and Mr John McDonald – all in highland costume – and swelled by a goodly number of Caledonia's lassies as well as of her lads, drew up near the Chiefs residence [Chief of the Caledonian Society]'.[4] Once assembled there, a number of speeches were given. One speaker 'proceeded with the assurance that those of them who were fortunate enough to be "brither Scots" had reason to be proud of their native home.' And the 'history of Scotchmen was the history of a gallant race; the Scotchmen of to-day were the inheritors of many noble memories of deeds of gallantry and self-sacrifice (Hear, hear)'.

At the helm of organising balls and other St Andrew's Day events, now as much as in the eighteenth and nineteenth centuries, were a plethora of Scottish ethnic associations around the globe – many with a long history that dates back to the Scottish migrants' first foot-fall overseas. As new research suggests, Scottish associationalism was not only strong, but Scots effectively spearheaded the development of ethnic associations worldwide. In North America, St Andrew's societies were established as philanthropic organisations in the eighteenth century, giving support to new immigrants in distress, while, in the Antipodes, the Scots exercised remarkable influence through their Caledonian societies and the promotion of sports. With these varied roles of Scottish ethnic associations in mind, this chapter will trace their development and function for diasporan Scots.

A SCOTTISH ASSOCIATIONALISM: A GLOBAL PHENOMENON

It was an often told joke at St Andrew's Day dinners that if two Irishmen were wrecked on a desert island they would inevitably start a fight. If it were two Englishmen they would never speak because there was no one to introduce them, whereas if it were two Scotsmen, they would form two Kirks and a Caledonian society.[5] While such ethnic characterisations would undoubtedly have been challenged at any St Patrick's or St George's Day dinner, the propensity of Scots to establish clubs and societies is one of the Scottish diaspora's defining characteristics. A directory published in 1935 lists more than 1,000 Scottish associations operating outside of Scotland at the time, ranging from Caledonian societies, St Andrew's societies and Burns clubs, to regional societies, pipe bands, dancing groups and sporting clubs.[6] They could be found across the globe, being present in countries as diverse as Argentina, Brazil, China, Egypt, India, Japan, Kenya, Nigeria and Peru. It was, however, in the traditional emigrant destinations, chiefly including the United States, Canada and the Antipodes, where Scottish associational culture was most vibrant. By the early twentieth century, Australia and New Zealand were each home to around 100 Caledonian societies alone,[7] while in South Africa the same organisation could be found in all major population centres and continued to spread to many smaller ones. In North America it was St Andrew's societies that dominated the early Scottish associational landscape, although by the end of the nineteenth century, they had become outnumbered in Canada by the Sons of Scotland Benevolent Association, and in the United States by the Order of the Scottish Clans. At their peak, these mutual benefit societies had 200 and 250 branches respectively and a combined membership of more than 20,000.[8]

Often these clubs and societies could be found operating alongside each other, particularly so in areas of heaviest Scottish settlement. Early-twentieth-century Toronto, for example, was home to ten separate Scottish associations, Chicago had a total of seventeen, while Melbourne had no fewer than three different Caledonian societies, two Highland/Gaelic societies, five Thistle clubs, five Scottish societies, and one Burns club, each of which operated separately from the others.[9] It was, however, London that was the indisputable heartland of Scottish associationalism, boasting more than eighty clubs and societies by 1935 that represented all aspects of Scottish sport and entertainment and catered to most regional areas of Scotland.[10]

Although the total membership of London's Scottish clubs at the beginning of the twentieth century has been estimated at between 4,000 and 5,000, not all would have enjoyed particularly large followings.[11] Memberships of Scottish clubs and societies, generally, could vary from a loyal few to several hundred. The St Andrew's Society of Thorah and Adjacent Townships in rural Canada never exceeded thirty members, while, by contrast, the Caledonian Society of Melbourne had a total membership of well over 500 in 1886.[12] Membership numbers varied as a result of several factors. While, at the outset, all associations operated under an ethnic banner, serving as sites of memory and allowing their members to maintain a link with the old homeland, 'the Scots' associative behaviour, and the associational structures put in place, were by no means uniform throughout . . . [the Scottish] Diaspora.'[13] As well as the size of Scottish immigrant population from which members could be drawn, another key to understanding membership numbers were the eligibility criteria set by the different Scottish associations. In most cases membership was conditional upon the payment of a membership fee, and women were generally excluded from most associations – a trend concurrent with patterns of associational culture more broadly. New research on English ethnic associations documents, for instance, that they too largely 'drew upon masculine traditions' until the First World War.[14]

Apart from gender there was often an ethnicity requirement stipulating that none but 'Scotchmen', and the children, grandchildren, and great-grandchildren of natives of Scotland, were able to join. Such rules based on ethnic criteria were less strictly implemented in New Zealand, however, where 'there is no evidence to suggest that ethnic origin exclusively determined or prevented membership in . . . Caledonian societies' in particular. Hence Cumberland-born Robert Lawrence Rule acted as the Oamaru Caledonian Society secretary for thirty years (1879–1909), and Sew Hoy, a prominent Chinese merchant and investor based in Dunedin, can be found on the Otago

Caledonian Society membership roll for 1882.[15] The degree of variation between membership rules is further underscored by the case of London's Caledonian Society, which capped membership at 100 as a means of maintaining the organisation's social exclusivity. According to a contemporary account of the Society, 'there are few Scots in the last generation or two who having attained distinction in their career in London have not sought to crown it or seal it by entering its limited circle.'[16] To ensure that members were of the right calibre, some Scottish ethnic associations required that candidates for membership be proposed in writing by another member and consented by a majority of meeting attendees. This was a process common to St Andrew's societies whose memberships comprised mostly of high-level professionals such as lawyers, merchants and business proprietors.[17]

St Andrew's societies in North America sat at the top of an unofficial hierarchy of Scottish-American organisations.[18] Although memberships overlapped, less prestigious were Caledonian societies, Scottish societies and Burns clubs, and at the bottom of the pyramid were the widely accessible mutual benefit societies, whose members tended to be made up of skilled manual and non-manual workers. This classification, however, cannot be uniformly applied throughout the Scottish diaspora. In New Zealand, for example, St Andrew's societies were virtually absent from the Scottish associational scene, which was spearheaded by the country's Caledonian societies: it was these societies that exerted the greatest influence, particularly through the promotion of Caledonian Games.[19] It is also worth noting that further variations in outlook and objectives can be found among the more specialised Scottish associations, including, for instance, regional societies such as Dunedin's Caithness and Sutherland Association, all of which catered more exclusively for their respective regional immigrant group.

Yet, in spite of the differing membership bases and varying objectives of many Scottish clubs and societies, when the occasion required, they were able to come together for the good of the Scottish immigrant community. In Toronto, all the city's Scottish clubs and societies were represented, along with 2,000 onlookers, for the unveiling ceremony of a memorial cairn on the St Andrew's Society's burial plot for destitute Scots in 1891.[20] The fundraising effort for the cairn was the first joint collaboration of its kind in the city and was soon followed by another, this time to establish a highland regiment in the city, which also ended successfully with the formation of the 48th Highland Regiment. Similarly, in Chicago, more than sixty men from thirteen of the city's Scottish organisations attended a meeting in 1888 to draw up plans to erect a statue of Robert Burns.[21] Several years later they took things a step further by forming the United Scottish Societies. While such umbrella organisations were not particularly common, they did exist from place to place. In Australia, a number of Victoria's Scottish clubs and societies formed the

Victorian Scottish Union in 1905 with the auspices of fostering harmony and a sense of common purpose.[22] The Union's greatest challenge came in 1911 when the Australian government announced the disbandment of the country's Scottish kilted volunteer regiment as part of a comprehensive overhaul of its military. The Victoria Scottish Union engaged in a campaign that elevated the issue to a nationwide protest. Although they were able to prolong the move for two years, with war looming in Europe the Ministry of Defence went ahead and disbanded the Scottish volunteers. The Union did, however, later recommence its campaign and in the mid-1930s the Ministry of Defence saw fit to restore the Victorian Scottish Regiment in both name and uniform. Such united efforts represent a high point in Scottish associationalism, and although there was no dramatic disintegration, the number of clubs and societies, the extent of their memberships, and the efforts to unite for the greater good of the Scottish community would never again reach the same levels as they did in the late nineteenth and early twentieth centuries.

B   PHILANTHROPIC BEGINNINGS

That the Scottish diaspora developed such a vibrant associational culture should perhaps not be considered surprising in light of the levels of associationalism in Scotland itself. Georgian Edinburgh became a brilliant centre of associational life, and many considerably smaller communities could boast a plethora of clubs and societies.[23] Yet in comparison to the literary and learned societies which adorned Scotland's associational culture, the earliest clubs and societies of Scotland's diaspora were much more pragmatic in purpose. The first known Scottish society in North America was the Scots Charitable Society of Boston. Founded in 1657, it was modelled on the Royal Scottish Corporation, which from as early as 1611 had helped impoverished Scottish merchants and crafts-men not entitled to parish poor relief in London.[24] The philanthropic aims of the Boston charity would characterise Scottish associationalism in North America for at least two centuries to follow. Other Scots societies, Thistle clubs and Scots Benevolent societies were established for that purpose, as were regional organisations such as the Dumfries and Galloway Society, which was founded in 1803 'for the relief of indigent natives of Dumfries-shire and Galloway and their children.'[25] It was, however, St Andrew's societies that came to dominate in providing relief to indigent and poor Scots.[26] Comments prefacing the New York State St Andrew's Society Constitution of 1794 succinctly summarise the sentiments behind the organisation:

> When people fall into misfortune and distress in any part of the world, remote from the place of their nativity, they are ever ready to apply for

relief to those originally from the same country, on the supposition that they may possibly have connections by blood with some of them, or at least know something of their relations. For these reasons, the natives of Scotland, and those descended of Scotch Parentage, in the State of New York, have formed themselves into a Charitable Society, the principal design of which is to raise and keep a sum of money in readiness for the above laudable purpose.[27]

The first St Andrew's Society was established in Charleston, South Carolina, in 1729, and there is evidence of at least thirty others springing up across the United States with the same purpose.[28] In Canada the earliest Scottish society was the North British Society, founded in 1768, 'for the benefit of ourselves and assistance of each other, who may be afflicted with disease or any other casualty or misfortune,'[29] although as in the United States, it was St Andrew's societies that soon took the lead in providing such services.

Relief usually took the form of small sums of money given to those determined by a society's board of mangers to be most in need. How much any family or individual received was usually limited to a specific amount, and the total given out by a society in any year could not exceed the revenue brought in over that same period. For smaller societies in the nineteenth century relief was usually between $2 and $5 per family, whereas, for larger organisations such as the New York St Andrew's Society, it could be up to $15.[30] The Charleston St Andrew's Society was more generous, awarding nineteen individuals sums ranging from $30 to $80 in the year 1841,[31] although this was most likely due to the Society's stipulation that assistance was limited to members and their families. This was unusual among St Andrew's societies, where usually two conditions prevailed: first, that recipients of aid were a native or descendant of Scotland, and secondly, that they were deserving of aid. Who fit the latter category can be gleaned from an appendix attached to the 1880 managers' report of the St Andrew's Society of Toronto:

Mrs J – has one child four years old, and is within a few days of her confinement, a perfect stranger in the city and destitute, her husband at present in Scotland and lying sick in hospital there.
A McN – widower with one child suffering from Rheumatism in his joints, [. . .] a very painful case.
Mrs S – from Edinburgh, her husband gone to the States and left his family to starve.
Peter T – eighty years of age, from Argyleshire, has no friends here.
A C – from Ayrshire had wife and four children here in the country five months and most of that time in the hospital, he is still very weak and totally out of means.

The distinction between the 'deserving' and 'undeserving' poor was usually down to whether they were seen as being victims of misfortune and bad luck. Whereas widows, the elderly and those physically unable to work were given direct aid, those who were seen as being responsible for their own fate were usually given assistance in other ways, for instance through the installation of proper values of industry and thrift. Although assistance was granted in most cases, much scrutiny went into the decision-making process, and there were certainly instances where relief applications were turned down. The careful examination of cases was time-consuming. Indeed, it was because of the time involved that, in 1905, the New York St Andrew's Society appointed a Scottish woman to visit the aged and infirm; her designated task was to ascertain their immediate needs and report their condition to the Society's Board of Managers.[32]

Beyond giving one off payments to individuals, St Andrew's societies met their philanthropic goals by several other means. In 1853 the Charleston Society violated its own rules by donating $250 following an appeal from the St Andrew's Society of New Orleans calling attention to the 'prevailing epidemic [of Yellow Fever]' in their city and asking for assistance.[33] The St Andrew's Society of Illinois also made an appeal to its sister societies following the Great Chicago Fire of 1871 in which 90 per cent of the Society's membership suffered a complete loss of their homes and property.[34] Other provisions made by St Andrew's societies included travel expenses, pensions, burial costs, and use of the Society's burial plot if available. More unusual was the school run by the Charleston Society from 1804 until the passage of the Free Schools Act in 1811, the former of which endeavoured to provide an elementary education to poor children, or the Scottish Home run by the Illinois St Andrew's Society. The latter undertaking commenced when, in 1901, the Society rented a two-storey building to accommodate elderly men and women of Scottish ancestry. Within a decade the venture had grown, having its own purpose-built home on a five-acre site outside Chicago. Although the house was completely destroyed by a fire in 1917, subscriptions were received from across the country; with all the money raised within two weeks, the Home could be completely rebuilt within six months,[35] and continues to operate to this day as 'a small, private community that provides both assisted living and nursing care services'.[36] Another example is the home run by the St Andrew's Society of Montreal, which, from 1856, provided temporary accommodation for Scottish immigrants and other homeless Scots. When it closed its doors in 1925, more than 6,500 immigrants had passed through the home,[37] although, as the Society's Charitable report from 1867 shows, this was but one way in which it provided relief:

> 180 individuals had enjoyed shelter of the home; that 105 persons had
> been helped on their way, at a cost of $224.65; that 192 cords of wood

Figure 7.1 Caledonian Society outside Commercial Hotel, Lockhart [source: National Library of Australia, nla.pic-an23154584–v]

had been distributed to the city poor, with 1,120 loaves of bread, 2,400 lbs. Meal, and $69.47 in small sums of money – the whole work of the committee costing $1,341.05.[38]

According to the President of the St Andrew's Society of St John, New Brunswick, between 1798 and 1885 more than $30,000 had been expended on its behalf in charity.[39] In doing so the society provided a safety net for those Scots who had no one but their fellow countrymen to turn to in their time of need post-emigration.

C FROM CHARITY TO SCOTTISH CULTURE

The development of a philanthropic associational culture in North America was not, however, a pattern that was replicated in all major overseas Scottish emigrant destinations. In Australia, New Zealand and South Africa, where Caledonian societies dominated the associational landscape, there were never more than a handful of St Andrew's societies or any other organisation committed to providing benevolence to fellow Scots. Although some Caledonian societies did state benevolence as one of their aims, this objective was infrequently acted upon. In New Zealand, for example, Caledonian societies often 'outsourced their benevolent work by donating funds to local charitable institutions for distribution'.[40] And while some, such as the Otago Caledonian Society based in Dunedin in the South Island of New Zealand, provided scholarships and small sums of relief, by and large the attention of these societies was focused on the promotion of Scottish traditions, chiefly that of Caledonian Games.[41] The contrast with North America can most likely be attributed to its earlier emergence as an emigrant destination, and the fact that it attracted a different type of migrant. Immigration to Australia, New Zealand and South Africa did not gain momentum until considerably later, and it was not until 1839 that the first Scottish association appeared in Australia, with New Zealand following in 1862 and South Africa in 1870. This later time-frame, combined with the usually more expensive shipping fares, acted as a filter to those most likely to need assistance, and resulted in there being a lesser demand for a philanthropic support network.

The United States and Canada, however, also saw a change in the priorities of Scottish clubs and societies throughout the nineteenth century through the evolving function of their Caledonian societies. The first was established in Cincinnati in 1827, with the objective 'to relieve such of our countrymen as may arrive among us in distressed circumstances, and to give them information and advice for locating themselves in the western country.'[42] As can be seen from the Chicago Caledonian Club's Constitution and By-Laws half a century later, the objects of the club were stated as: (1) 'the preservation of the Ancient Literature and Costumes, and the encouragement and practise of the ancient Games of Scotland'; (2) 'the establishment of a Library and Gymnasium, and employment of Lecturers before the Association'; and (3) 'charity, which, in its amount, character, and mode of distribution, shall be dependent on the will of the majority of its members.'[43] Little more than a decade after this, when the Caledonian Society of Chicago was formed, charity was not even listed as an objective; sociability among Scots, the encouragement of national costume, and the perpetuation of Scottish music, history, and poetry being its priorities.[44]

The general aim of promoting Scottish culture became the focus of most Scottish associations in the late nineteenth and early twentieth centuries, and was even evident among North American St Andrew's societies. Although the organisations had always taken a lead in organising St Andrew's Day celebrations, that they were diversifying their role is demonstrated by the efforts of the St Andrew's Society of Philadelphia, which, in 1910, resolved to build a 'Scotch library' with works on Scottish history, biographies of eminent Scots, maps, volumes of prose, poetry and fiction, and Scottish music and songs.[45] St Andrew's societies did maintain benevolence as their primary objective, but by 1935 they were only twenty-three of the 269 Scottish clubs and societies across the United States, the vast majority of which made no pretence of sharing this goal. Even among the Order of the Scottish Clans, which provided

a specific service to its members, the promotion of Scottish culture was used
to entice members, over the many other competing mutual benefit societies.

What a typical meeting entailed can be gleaned from an account from the
Sons of Scotland Burns Camp which took place in June 1891:

> Pipe Major Munro opened proceedings with Scots wha hae, the
> world renowned war song of Scotia on the national instrument. This
> roused the enthusiasm of his brethren, so that they were well prepared
> to enjoy the next event, viz, an essay by Neil Mackinnon, entitled,
> 'Bannockburn and its results.' Bro. Logan of Waverly Camp sang 'the
> land where I was born' and in response to a vigerous encore gave 'Robin
> Tamson's Smiddy.' Chief McCorkindale of Bruce Camp, with his usual
> eloquence, recited a very humerous piece, viz., 'The Western Lawyer'
> which was highly appreciated . . .[46]

Music, singing, lectures and storytelling dominated club and society programmes, with gatherings taking place on a monthly or, in some cases,
fortnightly basis. Many societies also organised concerts or entertainment
evenings such as the 'at home' that opened the 1926 session of the Tasmanian
Caledonian Society and was attended by over 100 members; it was, however,
the celebrations marking key dates in the Scottish calendar that attracted most
attention and were most eagerly anticipated.[47] Similarly, so-called inglesides
were held throughout New Zealand from the late nineteenth century, with 'the
promoters of the ingleside . . . actuated by the desire to lighten the hearts and
strengthen the friendships of themselves and their numerous guests.'[48]

As early as 1664 the London Scottish Corporation held an annual St
Andrew's Day dinner to celebrate the occasion while raising money for needy
Scots living in London.[49] By 1880 it had over 400 attendees and was the largest
and most prestigious St Andrew's Day celebration in Britain. Although such
traditions were slow to establish themselves in Scotland itself, among the
diaspora they were enthusiastically embraced, with annual dinners and balls
being organised by Scottish societies throughout the world. As in London
such events tended to be high-society affairs, and could include distinguished
guests such as governor generals, British and foreign ambassadors, mayors,
or in the case of the St Andrew's Society of Montreal's 1878 ball, Princess
Louise, the fourth daughter of Queen Victoria, who was the wife of the
Marquis of Lorne, Canada's Governor General. In acknowledgement of the
occasion's importance and exclusivity, the names of those in attendance were
often published in newspaper reports. Newspaper coverage per se was extensive, with particular attention being paid to who attended, what the ladies were
wearing, the decoration of the venue, the dinner, and what was said during the
toasts. Typical were the Toronto *Globe's* comments in 1900 when it claimed

'the scene in the Pavilion after the ball began was one of great splendour. Never were there more beautiful gowns, more brilliant uniforms or a more distinguished assemblage at a St Andrew's ball.' In a report from another year it was noted that 'the menu [was] far above what one gets at the usual ball supper – There was everything to eat and ditto to drink, and the tables, set for eight were most cosily and elegantly arranged.' High praise indeed from Toronto's high-society magazine, *Saturday Night*. Among the largest St Andrew's Day celebrations were those held in the Asian city entrepot of Hong Kong. Estimates suggest that the city's St Andrew's Society, which had been established in the early 1880s, regularly attracted well over 1,000 guests to its annual St Andrew's Day Ball. It was, as the *China Mail* observed in 1901, 'the leading event of the social calendar'.[50]

Whether it was the opportunity to network with likeminded individuals or whether those attending were genuinely inspired by a desire to help raise funds for their less fortunate fellow Scots is open to question, but what these occasions certainly demonstrate is a desire of those involved in their organisation and those attending as guests to celebrate Scottish culture. This, in turn, helped to create solidarity among many diasporan Scots by invoking a common Scottish identity.[51] That this extended beyond those in attendance at such events is documented by the sending and receiving of goodwill messages from neighbouring sister societies and those further afield. The connection between South Africa's Scottish diaspora can be seen from the greetings read out at the Durban St Andrew's dinner, which came from Martizburg, Kokstad, Bloemfontein, Kimberly, East London, Kingwilliamstown, the Cape Caledonian Society from Cape Town, and Port Elizabeth's Scottish Association.[52]

While, in terms of the public attention they received, St Andrew's Day festivities were certainly the most visible Scottish gatherings, other key dates in the Scottish calendar were also widely celebrated. Burns Night, Halloween and Hogmanay were widely marked with concerts, dances and dinners. While usually not as salubrious as some St Andrew's Day celebrations, many parallels existed, with Burns Nights in particular proliferating worldwide, often serving as a national day proxy.[53] Venues were decorated to remind those assembled of their origins, with flags, tartan bunting and other Scottish symbols in abundance. Haggis and other traditional Scottish fare would be served at dinners, and the company would be entertained throughout the evening with tales, songs and poetry of Scotland, while toasts would be heartily drunk with large amounts of whisky. According to the *Western Argus*, on New Year's Eve of 1927 the Salmon Gums Caledonian Society held its usual Hogmanay social which began at 4 pm with a banquet: 'After the usual toast given by the chief, the company was regaled with song and story. Then the hall was cleared for the dancers, who tripped to the music of the pipes.'[54] On Halloween activities often centred around children. Rooms were decorated with lanterns and black cats, while committee members disguised themselves as witches and told ghost stories. The customary games and entertainment on such occasions were dookin' for apples, treacle bun eating contests, prophesying fortunes, and the handing out of mystery bags.[55] While such activities may have closely reflected parallel celebrations in Scotland, certain additions distinguished them as having been adapted by the diaspora. Along with the customary games organised by the Perth Caledonian Society in 1910, the children were handed cards explaining the meaning of Halloween as well as a sprig of Scottish heather. The supper consisted of haggis and 'cham pit tatties' and the evening concluded with the singing of 'Auld Lang Syne'.[56] Similarly the Nelson Scottish Society intertwined traditional celebrations with music from the Society's pipe band.[57] This combination of explicitly Scottish symbolism with tradition demonstrates the desire to be in keeping with how such events were marked in the homeland, but also documents the need to reinforce the Scottishness of such occasions with more explicit markers of Scottish ethnicity. The desire for such reinforcements increased, as evidence from New Zealand suggests, from the early 1900s.[58]

D   ASSOCIATIONALISM THROUGH SPORT

Another example of the changing role of St Andrew's societies in North America was the inclusion in some of their constitutions of a commitment to the encouragement of the national athletic games.[59] Although more commonly organised by Caledonian societies, Caledonian Games were one of the most visible outpourings of Scottishness across the world. The Games overseas emerged soon after their inaugural appearance in Scotland, with the first reportedly taking place in 1819 under the auspices of a Highland Society in Glengarry, Ontario.[60] In the United States the first Games were held in Boston in 1853, although it was only after the Civil War that they began to flourish.[61] By 1875 there were at least eighty Scottish clubs and societies holding annual Games across the United States.[62] So prolific was the pattern elsewhere that, by the end of nineteenth century, Caledonian Games were a common feature around the globe, reaching from their home in Scotland to North America, the Antipodes and South Africa: '"Caledonia" was commodified, and developed as a successful brand'.[63]

Crowds grew quickly. Ranging initially from a few hundred to a few thousand, by 1870 the Brooklyn Caledonian Club Games drew 5,000 spectators, Detroit 6,000, Boston 8,000, Toronto 15,000 and New York 20,000.[64] Two years later, the New York Games attracted 25,000 visitors, which was probably the largest attendance of any Games throughout the nineteenth century. While

Figure 7.2 Girl performing a Scottish dance at the American Highland Games in Greenwich, USA [source: *SCRAN;* Resource Rights Holder: Hulton Getty; SCRAN ID: 000-000-200-924-C]

no other single Games could match this, arguably their popularity was greatest in New Zealand, where 'on New Year's Day 1888 around 45,000 people participated in, or more generally were spectators at, Caledonian Games'; this was about 'seven per cent of the total colonial population at the time.'[65] Based on the attendance numbers, or estimates provided in newspaper accounts and associational records, at their peak between 1880 and 1895, individual Games at Invercargill, Oamaru and Wellington attracted in the region of 6,000, while attendance in Dunedin occasionally reached over 10,000. Particularly remarkable, however, was the number of 7,000 spectators who attended the Oamaru Caledonian Games at its peak in 1888: a small settlement 70 miles north of Dunedin in the South Island of New Zealand, Oamaru had a population of about 5,500 at the time.[66] Even prior to this, 'dense crowds . . . thronged the platform'[67] of Oamaru's railway station, with spectators gradually making their way to grounds where the Games were held.

Games attracted people from far afield, becoming both magnets for tourists and important annual meeting places for family and friends who were scattered across the region. In North America, Games customarily took place between July and September, often coinciding with local public holidays. By contrast, in Australia and New Zealand – and as a result of reversed seasons – the period between Christmas and New Year was most popular, with New Year's Day itself being the preferred date. As well as the Games being a draw for spectators, competitors were willing to come from far afield. Organisers tried to ensure that Games did not clash and societies in close proximity coordinated so that competitors could travel from one Games to the next.[68] Admission fees funded prize money, which attracted the best athletes; these, in turn, provided an even more significant pull factor for spectators. Particular crowd pleasers were Scottish athletes who, because of their popularity, were sometimes offered appearance fees on top of any winnings they received from the events in which they participated. The most famous of these athletes was Donald Dinnie who came to North America for the first time in 1870. At the age of thirty-nine Dinnie was acknowledged as Scotland's greatest athlete, having competed for sixteen Highland Games seasons in his native land. Because of his reputation North American Caledonian clubs were willing to pay heavy appearance fees for him to compete, including $100 from the Chicago Caledonian Club and $50 from Montreal. On his 1870 tour he attempted seventy-five events of which he won sixty-eight, collecting several thousand dollars in prize money. Two years later he returned to North America with friend and fellow athlete James Fleming, where he toured once more before going to Australia and New Zealand in the 1880s where he spent several years competing.[69]

Caledonian Games often started with a procession to the venue, headed by pipers, a band and association officials. Thereafter, programmes incorporated traditional competitions including caber tossing, hammer throwing, quoiting, highland dancing and piping, along with less traditional events such as wheelbarrow and three-legged races. Less popular events were organised for the morning with those favoured by the public taking place in the afternoon. Over time Games became increasingly competitive and sophisticated professional sports meets, and they are correctly acknowledged as making an important contribution to early track and field sports. Ironically the growing popularity of amateur athletic clubs came at the expense of Caledonian Games, which by the end of the nineteenth century were suffering from declining attendances and were looking back at former glories.

As well as organising Caledonian Games, Caledonian societies were also responsible for establishing shinty clubs and supporting other sports in which members of the Scottish diaspora engaged. According to newspaper reports from South Australia in the late nineteenth century, shinty was slowly but surely taking its place among popular outdoor games, and a match between Port Gawler Athletic Club and Adelaide Caledonian Society in 1882 was watched by as many as 500 onlookers. Curling, football, rugby and bowling were likely even more popular and although not limited to Scotsmen, their connection with Scottish associationalism can be seen through the Caledonian Society of Toronto's decision, in 1890, to allocate funds for the purpose of obtaining trophies for competition amongst the curling, football and bowling on the green clubs of bona fide standing in the city.[70] Such sports were participated in and watched by members of the Scottish diaspora across the globe and perhaps as much as any St Andrew's Day dinner or Burns supper enabled them to come together and engage in an activity which consciously or subconsciously helped to reinforce their Scottish identity. Perhaps even more importantly, though, these activities also reflect the wider civic value of Scottish ethnic associationalism. While catering primarily for fellow Scots, through charity and the maintenance of Scottish traditions, the majority of Scottish associations examined here were not cut off from wider civic life, but connected to it in fundamental ways.[71]

E   CONCLUSION

All three core criteria of the diaspora concept are indicated through Scottish associational culture: orientation to homeland, boundary maintenance, and residency in more than one location outside of Scotland. Ethnic membership of philanthropic organisations, while never immutable, is the strongest possible indicator that participation, and qualification for pecuniary relief, were tied to ethnicity. The chosen names – St Andrew's, Caledonia, Sons of Scotland, Robert Burns – are again the clearest evidence of orientation to home. Support was mobilised *because* of the homeland connection. Sporting and cultural societies similarly orientated themselves to home, recreating culture from Scotia and introducing new hybrid cultures in conjunction with the host society, using simple ethnic language – 'brither Scots' – as a distinguishing mark. There were myriad opportunities for Scots to come together as Scots or even, if aloof from such activity, to be aware of others operating within this diasporic framework. These societies worked together on occasion, and sometime umbrella organisations came along to co-ordinate their activities in more systematic ways, together offering social, political and patronage linkages for the community.

Of course, many more Scots did not join such associations, nor required philanthropic help, nor would welcome an invitation to participate in Highland Games; but then diasporic Scottish associations could also be ethnically neutral.

Mechanics institutes and subscription libraries are not overly Scottish, but were part of transplanted institutions of a kind familiar to all Scots migrants. Again membership of these societies and associations was not a requirement to indicate diasporic action, but their existence was part of a developing civil society within which Scottish diasporic actions operated.

NOTES

1. *Singapore Free Press and Mercantile Advertiser*, 3 December 1901.
2. Anderson, *Imagined Communities*; see also Chapter 3 – Ethnicity, Nation and Transnationalism.
3. *New York Times*, 6 December 1890.
4. *South Australian Register* (Adelaide), 1 December 1881.
5. Robertson, 'Hints on forming a Scottish Society', p. 70.
6. *Scots Year Book*, 1934–5.
7. Ibid.; see also Bueltmann, *Scottish Ethnicity*, p. 66.
8. The *Scottish Canadian*, October 1897 and December 1900. According to Celeste Ray, the Sons of Scotland had 5,000 members compared to the Order of the Scottish Clan's 16,000, 'Scottish immigration and ethnic organization in the United States', p. 67.
9. Sullivan, 'Scottish associational culture in early modern Victoria, Australia', p. 154.
10. *Scots Year Book*, 1934–5.
11. Harper, 'Transplanted identities', p. 24.
12. Records of the Thorah St Andrew's Society, Archives of Ontario; Prentis, *Scots in Australia* (2008), p. 200.
13. Bueltmann, *Scottish Ethnicity*, p. 206.
14. Bueltmann and MacRaild, 'Globalizing St George', p. 81.
15. Bueltmann, *Scottish Ethnicity*, p. 96.
16. *Scots Year Book*, 1934–5, p. 95.
17. O'Connor, '"Nowhere in Canada is St Andrew's Day celebrated with greater loyalty and enthusiasm"', p. 109.
18. Ray, 'Scottish immigration and ethnic organization', p. 68.
19. Bueltmann, 'Manly games, athletic sports and the commodification of Scottish identity'.
20. *The Scottish Canadian*, 25 June 1891.
21. Noble, 'The Chicago Scots', p. 146.
22. Sullivan, 'Scottish associational culture in early Victoria', p. 156.
23. Morris, 'The Enlightenment and the thistle', p. 57.
24. Taylor, *A Cup of Kindness*.
25. Harper, 'Transplanted identities', p. 23; reference made to a Scots

Benevolent Society in Cist's *Cincinnati in 1841*; reference to the Dumfries and Galloway Society made in Whatley, *Two Hundred Fifty Years*, p. 26.

26. Ibid., p. 3.
27. Ibid., p. 14.
28. Easterby, *History of the St Andrew's Society of Charleston South Carolina*, p. 8. The development pattern of Scottish associations along the eastern seaboard of the United States mirrors that of other ethnic groups, for example that of the English; see Bueltmann and MacRaild, 'Globalizing St George'.
29. MacDonald (ed.), *Annals of the North British Society of Halifax, Nova Scotia*.
30. Whatley, *Two Hundred Fifty Years*, p. 23.
31. Easterby, *History of the St Andrew's Society of Charleston*, p. 81.
32. Whatley, *Two Hundred Fifty Years*, p. 32.
33. Easterby, *History of the St Andrew's Society of Charleston*, p. 81.
34. Noble, 'The Chicago Scots', p. 145.
35. Ibid., p. 148.
36. See http://www.chicagoscots.org/thescottishhome/ (accessed 22 February 2013).
37. Calculated from St Andrew's Society of Montreal Register of Emigrants, available at http://www.standrews.qc.ca/sas/archives.htm (accessed 10 February 2012).
38. Annual Report of the St Andrew's Society of Montreal for 1867.
39. Jack, *History of the St Andrew's Society of St. John N. B. Canada*, p. 139.
40. Bueltmann, *Scottish Ethnicity*, p. 185.
41. Bueltmann, 'Ethnic identity, sporting Caledonia and respectability', p. 171.
42. 1827 Constitution of Caledonian Society of Cincinnati, quoted in Clipson, 'The Caledonian Society of Cincinnati', available at http://www.caledoniansociety.org/societyhistory.html (accessed 10 February 2013).
43. Constitution and By-Laws of the Chicago Caledonian Club, 1872, quoted in Rethford and Skinner Sawyers, *The Scots of Chicago*, p. 111.
44. Ibid., p. 113.
45. Beath, *Historical Catalogue of the St Andrew's Society of Philadelphia*, p. 28.
46. *The Scottish Canadian*, 18 June 1891. Note that the cairn dedication took place on 20 June, while the parade took place the following day. The error appears to be on the part of the newspaper.
47. *The Mercury* (Hobart, Tasmania), 29 April 1926.
48. *North Otago Times* (Oamaru, New Zealand), 2 December 1891; see also Bueltmann, *Scottish Ethnicity*, pp. 72–3.
49. Buettner, 'Haggis in the Raj', p. 221.
50. *China Mail* (Hong Kong), 30 November 1901.

51. Buettner, 'Haggis in the Raj', p. 227.
52. Morton, 'Ethnic identity in the civic world of Scottish associational culture', p. 43.
53. See also Bueltmann, '"The image of Scotland which we cherish in our hearts"', pp. 78–97.
54. *Western Argus* (Kalgoorlie, Western Australia), 17 January 1928.
55. *New York Times*, 31 October 1866; also *Nelson Evening Mail* (Nelson, New Zealand), 3 November 1909.
56. *The West Australian* (Perth, Western Australia), 5 November 1910.
57. *Nelson Evening Mail*, 3 November 1909.
58. Bueltmann, *Scottish Ethnicity*, pp. 85ff.
59. Donaldson, *Scottish Highland Games in America*, p. 25.
60. This is disputed by Gillespie in 'Roderick McLennan, professionalism, and the emergence of the athlete in Caledonian Games'. Gillespie argues that society records suggest that the event in question was solely a piping contest, with no athletics taking place.
61. Donaldson, *Scottish Highland Games in America*, p. 32.
62. Zarnowski, *Heroes of a Forgotten Sport*, p. 14.
63. Bueltmann, 'Manly games', p. 224.
64. Zarnowski, *Heroes of a Forgotten Sport*, p. 14.
65. Bueltmann, 'Manly games', p. 225.
66. Bueltmann, *Scottish Ethnicity*, p. 130.
67. *North Otago Times*, 3 January 1878.
68. See for instance the Waitaki District (New Zealand) Caledonian Games circuit in Bueltmann, *Scottish Ethnicity*, pp. 135–6.
69. Zarnowski, 'The amazing Donald Dinnie', p. 3.
70. *The Scottish Canadian*, 18 December 1890.
71. See also Bueltmann, *Scottish Ethnicity*, pp. 122–3 and conclusion.

CHAPTER 8

Return Migration

In July 1909 the love story of Gabriel R. Gibson of Kilsyth – a small town halfway between Stirling and Glasgow – and Myrtle MacIntyre made headlines in the *San Francisco Call*. Gibson had fallen in love with MacIntyre and 'wooed his sweetheart' during his school days in Kilsyth.[1] But, in 1903, Gibson left for the United States, seeking to make a better life for himself in Berkeley, California. His departure from Scotland did not put an end, however, to his love for Myrtle: the two kept in touch, corresponding regularly by sending many a letter across the Atlantic Ocean. But '[s]ix years of correspondence' eventually 'proved unsatisfactory to Gabriel . . . and he left for his native land . . . to wed Miss Myrtle MacInyre, the woman of his choice.'[2] Together the newly-wed couple then made home in Piedmont, California.

One story of transatlantic ties maintained between Scotland and the United States says little, of course, of the wider Scottish emigrant experience of the return home – be it temporary or permanent. What the story points to, however, is the fact that emigration was not as finite and 'conclusive in the later nineteenth and early twentieth centuries as perhaps it had been half a century before.'[3] People, their culture and their ideas flowed between places of Scottish settlement overseas and the old homeland, and the return home, made for a multiplicity of reasons that included factors such as Gabriel's desire to wed his school sweetheart, but also illness or family obligations, was more common than one might assume. The return movement of Scots remains an under-explored aspect of Scottish diaspora history although Scots have been returning to Scotland as sojourners or for business reasons since their first foot-fall abroad, contributing to the significant number of emigrant Scots who did not permanently relocate overseas. This much holds true from the late nineteenth century in particular, when improved and increasingly cheaper means of transport made the return more viable even from places in faraway Australasia. The mother of nationalist Douglas Young, for example, braved

yearly sailings between India and Scotland in the early decades of the twentieth century, numbering twenty-six in total.

Estimates suggest that the proportion of Scots returning home was higher
than a third between 1870 and 1914. Given the wider diaspora framework of
this book, these numbers provide important evidence of the fluidity of the
Scottish diaspora, as well as transnational connections that existed across
borders. To grasp the complexities of this fluidity, this chapter is not restricted
to the permanent return of Scots to Scotland. Instead, the chapter provides
insights into the diverse reasons for which Scots ventured home, including
returning in mind but not body, the temporary return, and early roots-
tourism. Conceptualised in broader categories, this chapter compares two
fundamentals of the first and subsequent generational return: the economic
and ethnic rationale. The latter gained momentum from the late nineteenth
century, with qualitative data offering important insights into the deep,
mutual and sustained connections that it helped to maintain between Scotland
and its diaspora.

A SOJOURNING SCOTS

An estimated 150,000 Scots had left Scotland by the close of the seventeenth
century, with the majority making their way to Ireland, but then also other
parts of Europe (see Chapter 4, Table 4.4); these Scots were primarily engaged
as merchants and soldiers.[4] A significant number of these early Scottish
migrants, however, were not seeking to permanently relocate overseas. They
were sojourners and, as such, their intent from the outset was to live overseas
for a set period of time only and for the purpose of achieving a particular goal
– one often connected to a job or a business venture. As noted in our discussion
of the concept of diaspora, the eventual return to Scotland was an intrinsic part
of their migration.

Among the earliest examples of these returnees were many of the soldiers
who went to fight in European wars of the seventeenth century, including, for
instance, the Thirty Years War. With its conclusion, soldiers were decommis-
sioned from the army, with many returning home to Scotland happily, but also
a large number 'forced to return from the wars abroad as invalids'.[5] At about
the same time there we can also find many next-generation Scots in Europe
who, born to Scots abroad, made their way to Scotland for reasons as diverse
as the desire to claim an inheritance, or 'to do some service for their parents'
country.'[6] While these foreign-born Scots may not have felt the same attachment to Scotland as their parents and were unfamiliar with many aspects of
Scottish life, they nonetheless were an important group making its way 'back'
to Scotland in the seventeenth century.

Moving beyond this early period, which already highlights the extent of connections and travel, migration and sojourn to and from Scotland, even more substantial movements occurred from the eighteenth century onwards. A fascinating example on a small scale, but one clearly reflective of the wider movement patterns of diasporan Scots and the impact made by returnees, can be found in the small parish of Belhelvie near Aberdeen which, over three centuries, has been shaped to a significant degree by returning Scottish migrants. The earliest returnees included those making their way home from the Baltic mercantile migrations of the seventeenth century, but we also find a large group of parishioners returning after the Union of 1707. Having been among the earliest Scots who sought to make their fortunes in the British Empire, especially in India,[7] these returnees quite literally left visible landmarks in the estates they built in the parish. One of the estates thus established was that of the Orrok family. With various family members having been engaged in trade with India, or serving in the East India Company in India itself, enough capital was generated abroad to facilitate and finance the development of the estate. But wider contributions to parish life were also supported with the money made overseas, including for instance the donation of two seats in Belhelvie kirk. Moreover, William Orrok was also among the first to subscribe to a fund for the building of a turnpike road in 1799, thus contributing significantly to the improvement of local infrastructure.[8] Another family from the parish whose wealth came from India was the Lumsden family. Colonel Thomas Lumsden had served in the military in India and, after his retirement, gave money to help finance the salary of the Belhelvie schoolmaster.[9]

Elsewhere the support of returning Scots was even more substantial. In 1815, for example, General Andrew Anderson bequeathed £70,000 to the Church in Elgin, thereby facilitating the establishment of an institution that provided a home for fifty children. Elgin, it seems, was fortunate in this respect, as another significant donation was made by Alex Gray. He had served in the Bengal medical service and gave £30,000 to the Elgin hospital.[10] The most impressive example of how Scots who had made a fortune overseas funded developments and philanthropic pursuits back in Scotland, however, is that of James Matheson, co-founder of the famous trading company of Jardine, Matheson & Co. (for details on the Company itself, see Chapter 13). Born in Lairg, Sutherland, James Matheson was educated in Edinburgh, first at the city's Royal High School and then at the University of Edinburgh, before relocating to London, where he commenced working for an agency house. It was from there that he made his way to the Far East, departing for Calcutta in India to work in a firm managed by his uncle. Matheson later moved to Canton, where he met William Jardine, his future business partner, in 1818. Jardine, Matheson & Co. flourished quickly after its establishment, dominating the Asian opium trade with its fast opium clippers and a strong network of merchants, many of whom were also Scottish. Both Jardine and Matheson acquired significant wealth in the Far East and looked to Scotland to spend some of it in their retirement there. Jardine thus purchased Lanrick estate in Perthshire, hoping 'to lead the life of the country gentleman',[11] while Matheson bought the Isle of Lewis for half a million pounds in 1844; together with his other estates in Scotland, Matheson owned substantial acreage, including 220,433 acres in Ross alone.[12] On the Isle of Lewis he built Lews Castle near Stornoway, and, more significantly, provided funds during the highland famine to give support to the local community.[13] As a result, Matheson 'was made a baronet . . . for his generosity to the people of Lewis during the famine'.[14] He also provides us with a significant example of Scottish diasporan action, with his money made abroad facilitating the emigration of a large number of Scots to Canada. From 1851 to 1855, Matheson provided funds for well over 2,000 people to emigrate to Canada, at a cost of £10,000.[15]

Those Scots returning to Scotland from India were commonly referred to as 'nabobs'.[16] Having made their fortune in India, or the Far East more generally, nabobs were typical Scottish sojourners, following in the tradition of planning the eventual return to Scotland from the outset of their departure overseas. It was the very way in which they acquired their wealth abroad, however, that could complicate their return to Scotland. A common view was that nabobs had made their wealth in 'untraditional' ways:

> [c]ommercial nabobs made money from what seemed to be murky sources, such as speculation in shares and contracts that were highly unstable, transient and prone to corrupt abuse. Where they did deal in commodities these tended to be frivolous luxuries like tea, silks and brightly painted cotton calicos.[17]

Customarily, means of acquiring wealth in Scotland had focused chiefly on the acquisition of land. Combined with the fact that many of the sojourning Scots who had made substantial financial gains abroad were from a different class background to the Scottish aristocratic elite, thus reflecting the often more flexible class system and the opportunity of upward social mobility open to diasporan Scots overseas (see also Chapter 5), the 'nouveau riche' were often met with hostility. In light of these views, held in Scotland and elsewhere in the British Isles, returning nabobs had to re-assimilate after their return from the East. In the case of Sir Hector Munro of Novar, for instance, the knowledge of him having accepted gifts from the nawab (rulers of princely states) and his role in the defeat at Pollilur were obstacles to his return.[18] What this highlights is that it was crucial to plan the return home to Scotland carefully prior to actually commencing it. Strategies employed by intending returnees were primarily based on re-invigorating and nurturing their networks and patronage systems in Scotland. Hence many a Scot in India was keen to help Scots already resident there, or to expedite the journey of those seeking to make it there, believing that the patronage thus dispensed by them might facilitate a cordial welcome back in Scotland.[19] Such patronage flows and ethnic networks were crucial and document, as Andrew Mackillop has convincingly argued, 'how sojourner homecomings became self-perpetuating, mutually reinforcing and ultimately the basis of a multiplier effect. The very desire to return home prompted the initial individual to encourage and assist others from his region to follow him.'[20]

While, as we have seen in other chapters, ethnic networks were generally an important aspect of the Scottish migration process and the migration experience throughout the diaspora and over time, the ways in which they could connect Old and New World was especially important for sojourning Scots for whom residency overseas was always intended to be temporary rather than a permanent settlement. The connections maintained with Scotland often helped facilitate careers in politics for those returning, but direct investment of money was also important. Munro invested significant sums, for example by giving loans to landlords.[21] This example underlines again how riches acquired overseas could shape the Old World in very direct ways – in this case by facilitating land purchases and land development, making a contribution to decreasing local poverty.

The elite character of Scottish migration to the East – it was primarily that of the professional middle class and landed gentry – also helps explain why many sought to return home. Their ventures overseas were not in quest of seeking a better life or escaping the constraints of an established class system – although the often more flexible class system overseas could be beneficial to some. Instead, the crucial point is that the majority of sojourning Scots in the East sought to utilise their time abroad as a means to improve their status at home. Service in the East India Company or engagement as manager of a trading house were seen as a stepping stone, not as the end goal. This migration of Scots to the East was, therefore, always a more transient one, comparable to the earlier trading ventures in the West Indies and the Chesapeake in the West, but not the large-scale mass migration that occurred in the mid-nineteenth century. As Karras explains, 'transients, because of their goals, would have found some places much more attractive than others.'[22] Chief among these transients in the West were those seeking to make their fortune in the tobacco industry. While English merchants had dominated the trade until the 1740s, it was from then onwards that Scottish merchants made their mark, with Glasgow's tobacco lords shaping the city's fortunes, and, more visibly, its architecture,[23] supplying further evidence of the flow of Scottish diasporan capital and people back to Scotland.

Not all Scottish sojourners located to faraway lands, however: London's

Scottish community was sufficiently large[24] and so was that of many English port cities, including Bristol and Liverpool (see also Chapter 9). Given the proximity to Scotland, the Scots residents of this 'near Scottish diaspora' of England and Ireland maintained strong ties with the homeland, returning at regular intervals. Among the Scots in London were many of the political elite, but also a large number of merchants – a group that included those who McGilvary aptly describes as the 'nabob mainstream of southern England'.[25] Among them were, for instance, Alexander and Abraham Hume, two brothers who, for a good four decades, had supported the patronage system of Scots in London, and within the realms of the East India Company, extending the system's reach back to Scotland.[26]

B DIASPORAN IDEAS AND TEMPORARY RETURNEES

It was not only capital and patronage, however, that flowed back to Scotland with Scottish returnees: many also brought with them new ideas that then informed their actions in Scotland; this was often a reciprocal process, with a migrant's behaviour in the New World customarily being shaped by antecedent experiences made in the Old World. One example of this, explored in more detail in Chapter 12, relates to trade union leader James Thompson Bain. While, after his arrival in South Africa, his actions there were informed by his Scottish heritage and the training he had received in Scotland, the experiences he made on the Rand, in turn, shaped his ideas when he returned to Britain. While this was a forced rather than voluntary return, and only a temporary one,[27] Bain's case emphasises the degree to which the Scottish return movement is not only about people but also ideas. Another example of this is provided in what might suitably be called the 'return flow' of nationalist sympathies. In some cases, such as that of Richard McCallum, such sympathies only made it back on paper. While McCallum was born in Blenheim in the South Island of New Zealand, his father's Scottish heritage had influenced him significantly – so significantly, in fact, that he developed sympathies for the Scottish Home Rule movement in the 1890s. Convinced that the Scots' 'national life and patriotic feelings' were very much 'alive', McCallum argued that the Union of 1707 had been flawed, and that Scotland should become independent.[28] Influenced too by an Australian Scottish nationalist, McCallum wrote up his ideas in a pamphlet entitled *Home Rule for Scotland*.

Such sentiments would surely have been shared by James Grant and Theodore Napier, two outspoken nationalists who both returned to Scotland from abroad, engaging in the fight for Scottish national expression in several ways. Grant, who had been born in Edinburgh in 1822 but was raised in North America, returned to Scotland from England after having followed his

Figure 8.1 Returning emigrants from New Zealand, Glasgow, 1940 [source: SCRAN; Resource Rights Holder: Scottish Life Archive, National Museums of Scotland; SCRAN ID: 000-000-003-830-C]

father into a military career there. Grant made his name as co-founder of the National Association for the Vindication of Scottish Rights – the only Scottish effort in the mid-nineteenth century to mount a sustained campaign for Scottish rights. Napier made his way to Scotland from Melbourne in a quest for education, 'becoming more showman than politico in his promotion of

Bannockburn Day and a very singular version of home rule'.[29] Neither Grant nor Napier were particularly successful in their nationalist enterprises – a fact reflective, in broader terms, of the comparatively weak national movement in Scotland at the time. Yet the fact that two of Scotland's leading figures in this movement had grown up outside of Scotland – and left again – tells us a lot about the strength and endurance of diasporan Scottishness.

Moreover, the case of Napier also reveals a final type of temporary returnee: those who made it back in search of education. Children of Scots resident abroad were regularly sent home to study, particularly when it came to the study of medicine and theology. The reputation of the Scottish education system provided a strong pull factor, but it was also family ties that could provide an incentive in this respect. Further to the body of younger students, there was also a group of older Scots who returned for such educational pursuits – or rather re-educational pursuits.[30]

C WAR AND THE RETURN

One group of returnees among which the Scots are disproportionately highly represented is that of military pensioners, especially in the early nineteenth century. Existing scholarship has largely focused on soldiers settling in the colonies at the end of their service, for instance in North America or South Africa – a pattern related to the provision of land grants in these locations. Soldiers were perceived as valuable settlers, securing frontiers and supplementing colonial populations in areas where settlement was only sporadic. While the Empire Settlement Act of 1922 was the first act to specifically facilitate the settlement of ex-servicemen, with the UK government co-operating with governments in the Dominions to provide assisted passages and land settlement schemes, there had been earlier initiatives that soldiers could utilise after being discharged if they were keen on remaining abroad.[31] Overall, however, Scottish soldiers settling overseas were outnumbered by those who chose to return home.

In the early nineteenth century, approximately 16 per cent of soldiers from the British Isles were Scottish – a percentage disproportionate in terms of the Scots' population share within the British Isles at the time, which was around 10 per cent. As is also observed in other chapters of this book, the over-representation of Scots is a common characteristic of the Scottish diaspora more broadly. What is notable, however, is that although the number of soldiers serving in the British army was disproportionate, the number of Scottish soldiers settling abroad after being discharged was not. As Cookson estimates on the basis of soldier pensioner data, 8 per cent of pensioners living in India in the early nineteenth century were Scots – a figure similar to that of

Scottish veterans in Upper Canada, which stood at 7 per cent.[32] While the low percentage of Scottish ex-servicemen remaining in India may be explained, at least in part, by the fact that departure to the East was, as we have seen, very much perceived as a sojourn only, this does not explain the even lower proportion settling in Canada. The point is that Scottish pensioners in the early nineteenth century generally 'were indisposed to settling overseas . . . [and] continued to be under-represented among "colonial" pensioners even with the next generation of soldiers.'[33] This reluctance of Scottish soldiers to settle in the Empire is the result of a number of factors.

First, it is important to consider the general social circumstances of soldiers at the point of discharge. Scottish soldiers tended to be single men when they joined the army. By the time they were discharged from service, many had reached their forties and were keen to marry and find employment. In the colonies, however, there generally was a deficit of females, contributing to unfavourable sex ratios. While Irish pensioners, who settled abroad in larger numbers than their Scottish counterparts, were part of a migratory stream among which single adult females were more prominent, the same cannot be said for the Scots.[34] In combination, the soldiers' age and the lack of single females in their age range thus 'impeded the marriage prospects of pensioners'.[35] Moreover, age patterns also restricted the pensioners' opportunities for finding employment because many of the colonies that would have been options for settlement were, at the time, small economies with limited job markets. Secondly, it is also worth noting that many of the Scottish soldiers returning home did not only return to Scotland, but to their county of birth or a county close by. As an analysis of soldiers' settlement patterns in Scotland after discharge of a number of regiments shows, well over 70 per cent of the returnees resided in their respective region of birth in both the periods 1814 to 1816 and 1840 to 1845.[36] Regional, even local, connections and kinship networks in Scotland appear to have played a vital role in the wish of soldiers to return home. As we have seen, kinship and local networks were also important in chain migration and migratory patterns to particular destinations overseas – a trend that we can now identify as equally relevant in the reverse.[37] Finally, Scottish soldiers who went back to Scotland were generally warmly received: hailed as builders of Empire, Scottish veterans were deemed respectable and law-abiding and were, therefore, able to live in relative prosperity.[38] Hence, and in terms of weighing up advantages and disadvantages of remaining in the colonies or returning home, many Scottish soldier pensioners decided that the return was the preferable option, with the economic rationale speaking largely in favour of Scotland.

The ways in which military service could connect soldiers with the homeland, however, was not restricted to ex-servicemen: war effectively promoted contact between the old world and the new. Throughout the diaspora, Scottish clubs and societies sought to promote the establishment of Scottish regiments, and patriotic funds in support of the war effort were set up. In even more direct terms, and identifiable as a specific type of the temporary return, military service in Europe provided an opportunity for many Scottish-born, or next-generation descendants, to visit their ancestral home. After the First World War, for example, a letter from New Zealand, sent jointly by a number of presidents of Scottish associations to the editors of *The Scotsman*, the *Glasgow Herald*, and the Moderator of the United Free Church of Scotland, reveals the value of the soldiers' visit to Scotland. 'Our gratitude', the letter's authors pointed out, 'is due to you [the people of Scotland] for making dear 'Auld Scotland' a second home to so many of our men while absent from their native land.'[39] While these trips had been facilitated by the tragic circumstances of war, they nevertheless document the increased popularity, in the early twentieth century, of roots-tourism.

D   ROOTS–TOURISTS

In 1900 New Zealand Scot W. J. Crawford embarked on a 'bicycle journey through the fair land of Scotia'.[40] While the majority of late nineteenth and early twentieth-century travellers in Scotland will not have used Crawford's chosen means of transport, his journey is still representative of the growing number of tourist trips to Scotland by émigré Scots and their descendants. Hailing from North America, South Africa or Australasia, these Scots embarked on such trips to explore, in person, the Scotland they remembered themselves from their childhood days or – if born overseas – the one they had been told about in stories by their parents and grandparents. These travelling Scots were early roots-tourists, visiting Scotland in search of their ancestral history and culture.[41]

Roots-tourism is a distinct type of the Scots' return movement. Until recently it has primarily been viewed as a modern phenomenon, reflecting the desire of an increasing number of next-generation Scots – many with an interest in genealogy – to trace their family's ancestry and to explore their heritage in Scotland itself.[42] As recent scholarship shows, however, the roots of roots-tourism can be found much earlier, namely in the late nineteenth and early twentieth centuries.[43] Importantly, the identification of this earlier roots-tourism offers a novel perspective on the transnational connections maintained within the Scottish diaspora, providing sustained evidence not only of the deep ties that existed between Scotland and Scots resident abroad, but also of how the temporary return served to cement them. Sparked by the specific desire to return to the ancestral home, roots-tourism thus sheds light on the meaning of the return itself, flagging the ethnic rationale we identified at the outset.

Two types of roots-tourism can be traced, first that of the individual return of émigré Scots like Crawford and secondly, the return of Scots in groups.

By the time Scots resident overseas began to travel to Scotland in more significant numbers the country was already a popular destination for tourists. Travellers from within the British Isles had toured the Western Isles in the late eighteenth century, while tourists from continental Europe were attracted by the famous, albeit fabricated, tales of Ossian – an increased interest reflected too in the growing number of guidebooks on travelling and tours in Scotland published in the late eighteenth and early nineteenth centuries.[44] Scotland's popularity as a tourist destination increased further in the course of the nineteenth century, and particularly when Queen Victoria began to travel annually to Balmoral, with reports of her visits also finding their way into newspapers overseas. Together with new promotional literature and a still growing plethora of guidebooks,[45] travel to Scotland was encouraged in several ways. Visitors' books at popular Scottish tourist attractions document the growing number of visitors from abroad. As the Visitors' Book kept at Sir Walter Scott's home, Abbotsford, reveals, for example, the number of visitors from the United States increased from twenty-eight in 1833 to 2,362 in 1913. Given that 375 Canadians also made their way to Abbotsford in the same year, at least 2,737 North American visitors passed through its doors in 1913.[46]

Scotland's appeal as a tourist destination would not have been sufficient in itself, however, to attract tourists from overseas had there not also been significant improvements in transport. Decreased travel time – a result of the introduction of steamships – and cheaper fares were crucial in bringing home to Scotland a steadily growing number of Scottish roots-tourists. As we have seen in Chapter 5 (in reverse direction), compared to the strenuous journeys of the early and mid-nineteenth century, conditions for travellers had been much improved. While it could take well over three months at sea to reach the British Isles from New Zealand in the 1860s, steamship travel in the late nineteenth century reduced this to about six weeks. Crossing the Atlantic had always been shorter, but the travel time was reduced for this passage too, and well coordinated shipping timetables provided further enhancements. The accommodation on ships was also much improved, with more spacious berths being available even for steerage passengers. Not only did this make travel more comfortable, it reduced health risks. Further improvements were introduced by shipping companies in the early twentieth century – some in recognition of the burgeoning market for tourists travelling 'home'.[47] Advancements in travel provisions within the British Isles further benefitted tourism, with the iconic *Flying Scotsman*, which offered speedy travel from London to Edinburgh, becoming a sight in itself.

Among the individual Scots returning home to Scotland was the Revd James Chisholm. Born in Scotlandwell, Kinrossshire, in 1842, Chisholm immigrated to New Zealand with his parents in 1858, arriving in Port Chalmers, Otago, on the *Three Bells* directly from Glasgow. As the *Cyclopedia of New Zealand* documents, Chisholm soon joined the rush to the interior of Otago when gold was first discovered at Gabriel's Gully.[48] He successfully mined enough gold to allow him to return to Scotland to study as a minister at Edinburgh University, then returned to New Zealand after his ordination in 1872. There he was put in charge of Milton, a small settlement a good 30 miles south of Dunedin in the South Island. It was two decades later, in 1892, that the Revd Chisholm embarked on his second home trip. Though initially instigated on medical grounds, the trip nonetheless offered him an opportunity for roots-tourism. After leaving New Zealand, the Reverend first explored Rio de Janeiro en route to Scotland. Such interim stops were common, particularly for travellers from far afield. Fellow New Zealander William McHutcheson, for instance, went on an expansive journey through North America on his trip, visiting Hawaii, San Francisco and many more cities and sights before eventually making it to the east coast of the United States, from where he then went on to Scotland.[49]

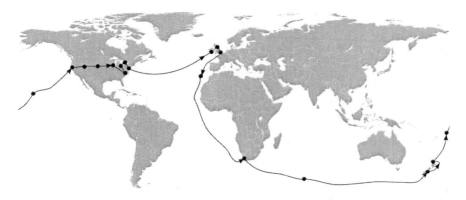

Map 8.1 Map of William McHutcheson's trip [source: the authors]

Whether they came via the United States, the lower route around Cape Horn or Asia, many Scottish roots-tourists initially arrived in London and then proceeded to Scotland. Chief objective among the travellers was the visit of family members, but also families and friends of New World acquaintances. This extended the number of contact points in Scotland, but also provided a very immediate communication network for diasporan Scots. The Revd Chisholm, for instance, took with him many letters from members of his congregation in New Zealand, promising to deliver these in person to the respective relatives in Scotland. Itineraries were also arranged around the sites roots-tourists wished to visit, and these commonly included Burns's cottage, Bannockburn and Loch Katrine.

What makes accounts of return travellers of particular interest is that descriptions of Scotland's natural beauties and these historic sites were often contrasted with compelling observations about Scottish life and social conditions – there could easily be a clash between the romanticised Scotland travellers had created in their minds and the real Scotland visited.[50] Moreover, the meaning of 'home' had also changed for many roots-tourists: within the new worlds in which returnees lived, Scotland was still considered 'home',[51] but it was the New World that was the measure of Scotland. Hence it was to his great delight that Revd Chisholm discovered several plants native to New Zealand in the Edinburgh Botanic Gardens.[52] And as another traveller, George Grant, noted, 'I never before understood what is meant by the expression "a flood of memories". Homecoming was very delightful.'[53] Memories were to be welcomed but, for both, their everyday lives had moved on.

Apart from such individual return trips to Scotland, the early twentieth century also witnessed a growing number of organised group returns, with trip planning often facilitated by Scottish associations such as St Andrew's and Caledonian societies (Chapter 7). One such group return, that of over 600 Australians of Scottish descent, took place in the summer of 1928. Described by Australian newspapers as a 'national pilgrimage to Scotland', the visit was jointly organised by the Victorian Scottish Union and similar bodies in other Australian states.[54] The idea for the trip was first discussed in 1927, when the hope was expressed that 200 to 500 people of Scottish descent would make the journey with the purpose of making Australia better known in Scotland. The trip thus served a dual purpose: it was designed as a homecoming to Scotland but also as an advertising ploy for Australia, with each Scot travelling to Scotland meant to directly encourage Scots to migrate to Australia.[55]

The trip's chief organiser was Archibald Gilchrist, the general secretary of the Victorian section of the New Settlers League. Scotsmen interested in going could submit their names for consideration to be included in the travelling party to Mr Gilchrist, with selections then being made on the basis of state quotas.[56] A reduced fare for the passage was offered, with the trip's itinerary developed around the following milestones:

> The delegation is to leave Brisbane on March 27, 1928; Sydney, April 3; Hobart, April 7; Melbourne, April 11; Adelaide, April 14; and Fremantle, April 19. The journey will be via Colombo, Suez, and Port Said, arriving in London on May 18. The party will leave for Scotland on the morning of May 23. From May 24 to May 30 will be "Australia Week" in Edinburgh, and a similar week will be held in Glasgow from May 30 to June 5. After leaving Glasgow the cities to be visited will include Perth, Dundee, Aberdeen, and Inverness, where the main tour will end on June 15.[57]

A piper was present on the group's arrival in England, 'playing "The Road to the Isles"', and famous Scottish singer Sir Harry Lauder sent a welcome message.[58] The group boarded the *Flying Scotsman* for Edinburgh at 8 am on 23 May at King's Cross, stopping at York and Newcastle en route. As one Australian correspondent noted, 'It was 9.30 p.m. as we entered Edinburgh and 10 p.m. by the time we were standing on the platform . . . Luckily my hotel was just over the Railway Station, the North British Station Hotel'.[59] The correspondent then went on to describe that banners stretched across the streets of Edinburgh saying 'Welcome Australia', and that shop windows displayed Australian products prominently. The group next laid a wreath at the National War Memorial at Edinburgh Castle, and visited the Leith shipyards, and a civic reception was held under the auspices of the Lord Provost and Town Council.

Later in the twentieth century, such organised return visits focused more specifically on particular areas in Scotland. The Wellington Shetland Society, for example, organised its first Hamefarin in 1960 – a return home that proved successful enough for the Society to organise further trips in 1985 and 2010, as well as a special 'Millennium Hamefarin' in 2000.[60] The idea to organise a trip specifically to Shetland was first muted by a Mr Arcus from Wellington in 1958 when he contacted a number of local councils on the Shetland Islands, suggesting that a group return be organised. A special welcoming committee was set up in 1959, and a number of events were run. The so-called 'hamefarers', numbering nearly eighty people, arrived in Lerwick on 20 May 1960, having made their way north from Southampton where they had originally reached the British Isles. The travellers had been welcomed in Southampton by a delegation from the Shetland Islands, and were entertained with church services, concerts, tea parties and talks throughout their stay, visiting, among other places, Lerwick, Dunrossness and Tingwall.[61]

Organised returns were, for many, the culmination of their lifelong passion for their roots, and one perhaps expressed in the New World through membership of a Scottish association, a Scottish sports club, the Presbyterian church or an interest in genealogy. This passion for heritage is even more evident at present, traceable, in fact, in the growing number of descendants of Scots who actively seek to explore their ancestry in Scotland. With clan societies, as well as the Scottish Government, keen on further promoting that interest, a new phase of roots-tourism has emerged in the twenty-first century that may be virtual as well as real.[62] For some heritage tourists the return to Scotland takes place on Facebook or Ancestry.com, while for others Homecoming Scotland in 2009 and 2014 provided an incentive to visit the ancestral home. In either case, the connection with Scotland helps nourish a strong sense of Scottish diasporic identity. The physical visit of sites connected, for instance, to the history of their respective clan allows the descendants of Scots to better understand where they come from, framing their own 'belonging'.[63]

The question of belonging was also a theme of importance in the literary tradition of Scotland's diaspora, reflecting, in a wider sense, the return of the mind. As much is certainly evident in John Liddell Kelly's *Heather and Fern*:[64]

> From this isle in the wide Southern Ocean,
> How oft does my swift fancy flee,
> On pinions of love and devotion,
> Dear home of my fathers, to thee!
> In a land lapped in bright summer weather,
> I sigh for one rugged and stern;
> I long for the bloom of the Heather
> In the Land of the Kauri and Fern.
> [. . .]
> Though dear to my heart is Zealandia,
> For the home of my boyhood I yearn;
> I dream, amid sunshine and grandeur,
> Of a land that is misty and stern;
> From the Land of the Moa and Maori
> My thoughts to old Scotia will turn;
> Thus the Heather is blent with the Kauri
> And the Thistle entwined with the Fern.

For writers like Kelly, Scotland had remained a spiritual home – a sentiment mirrored by fellow New Zealand Scot, James Baxter.[65] Spiritual or real, Scotland was, and continues to be, visited for multiple reasons, ranging from the desire to tour historical sites to the promotion of emigration to the New World. Entwined with these was the desire to revisit the old homeland, exploring ancestral roots. Hence, while the idea of pilgrimage became more prominent in the later twentieth century, the roots of the 'route home' can be found much earlier than that, providing important new evidence of the deep connections the diverse types of the return to Scotland sustained throughout the Scottish diaspora.

E CONCLUSION

This chapter has highlighted a key characteristic of the Scottish diaspora that our conceptualisation of it as a set of actions seeks to capture: the orientation of a diaspora towards the homeland. This orientation can take a variety of forms and does not have to culminate in the physical return home. This did, however, happen more frequently than one might assume, especially as one group of migrants – those who were sojourners – were intent on returning from the outset of their departure from Scotland. But those who had set out to permanently relocate overseas were also, at times, making their way back. As we have seen in Chapter 5, for example, the experiences of emigrants were not always positive, and a significant number struggled with their relocation overseas – a fact that undoubtedly contributed to a longing for the old home in many cases. Among those who stayed in the diaspora such longing could still be significant, and find expression in a strong, possibly a heightened, sense of ethnic identity. This could be maintained, for instance, through associational culture (Chapter 7), which served as an effective site of memory for many migrants. These examples underpin what we have examined here as the economic and ethnic rationale for the return, which could work together or separately to action a return to Scotland. Migrants were weighing up their options and, as the case of returning soldiers has demonstrated, the economic rationale could be a very compelling one. For roots-tourists it was not part of their decision to return to Scotland temporarily – though economic factors played their part in the sense that, at least in the late nineteenth and early twentieth centuries, and until further advances in long-distance travel, a return remained costly and was, therefore, not an option for everyone, especially for Scots who had settled in far-flung corners of the globe. With that in mind, the remaining chapters of this book will explore a diverse range of places where Scots settled, shedding light on overall settlement patterns of Scots over time, the experiences of the Scots in different locations, and the wider legacies the Scottish diaspora has left there.

NOTES

1. *San Francisco Call*, 23 July 1909.
2. Ibid.
3. Bueltmann, *Scottish Ethnicity*, p. 202.
4. Murdoch, 'Children of the diaspora', pp. 55–6.
5. Ibid., p. 60.
6. Ibid., p. 66.
7. Grosjean, 'Returning to Belhelvie', p. 217.
8. Ibid., pp. 221–2.
9. Ibid., pp. 223–5.
10. McGilvary, 'Return of the Scottish nabob', p. 99.
11. Pichon, *China Trade and Empire*, p. 26.
12. Ibid., footnote 73.
13. Devine, *To the Ends of the Earth*, p. 82; for further details, see also Devine, *The Great Highland Famine*, pp. 212–25.
14. Pichon, *China Trade and Empire*, p. 26.

15. Richards, *Highland Clearances*, p. 246.
16. Nabob is a term used to describe an East India Company servant who managed to acquire wealth through corrupt trade, or more broadly to refer to someone who made his wealth in the East. Nachtmann, *Nabobs*; see also McGilvary, 'Return of the Scottish nabob', p. 95.
17. Mackillop, 'The Highlands and the returning nabob', p. 237.
18. Ibid., p. 240.
19. Ibid., pp. 241 and 244.
20. Ibid., p. 242.
21. Ibid., p. 244; for details on Sir Hector Munro's expenditure, see Table 12.1 on p. 245.
22. Karras, *Sojourners in the Sun*, p. 4.
23. Cf. Devine, 'The golden age of tobacco'; and Devine, *The Tobacco Lords*; see also Karras, *Sojourners in the Sun*, chapter 3.
24. For example Nenadic (ed.), *Scots in London in the Eighteenth Century*.
25. McGilvary, 'Return of the Scottish nabob', p. 90.
26. McGilvary, *East India Patronage*, p. 98; similar systems, as well as support in government circles, was also dispensed in respect of the West Indies, cf. Hamilton, *Scotland, the Caribbean and the Atlantic World*, p. 169.
27. MacKenzie with Dalziel, *Scots in South Africa*, p. 231.
28. McCallum, *Home Rule for Scotland*; see also Bueltmann, *Scottish Ethnicity*, pp. 197ff.
29. Morton, 'Returning nationalists, returning Scotland', p. 109.
30. See Bueltmann, '"Gentlemen, I'm going to the Old Country"', pp. 152–3.
31. For instance Fedorowich, 'The assisted emigration of British ex-service-men'; Powell, 'The debt of honour'; and Raudzens, 'A successful military settlement'.
32. Cookson, 'Early nineteenth-century Scottish military pensioners as home-coming soldiers', p. 323 and Table 1 and Table 2 on p. 324.
33. Ibid., p. 323.
34. For details on why Scottish women were reluctant to emigrate, see for instance McLean, 'Reluctant leavers?'.
35. Ibid., p. 340.
36. Ibid., Table 3, p. 325.
37. For evidence of the role of kinship ties as a pull factor in the migration of Scots, see for example Lenihan, 'From Alba to Aotearoa'.
38. Ibid., pp. 334–5.
39. *The Scotsman*, 22 July 1919, p. 7.
40. *Otago Witness*, 3 October 1900.
41. Some parts of this section were published in *History Scotland* (Autumn 2011). We are grateful to the publishers for permission to use this material.

42. See for example the work of Paul Basu, including *Highland Homecoming*, and 'Macpherson country'.

43. Bueltmann, '"Gentlemen, I'm going to the Old Country"', p. 150.

44. See figures compiled by Nenadic cited in Table 1.1 in Durrie, *Scotland for the Holidays*, p. 21.

45. For instance *Handbook for Travellers in Scotland, With Travelling Maps and Plans*; Lawson, *The Famous Places of Scotland*.

46. Durie, *Scotland for the Holidays*, p. 140.

47. Harper and Constantine, *Migration and Empire*, pp. 333ff.

48. *The Cyclopedia of New Zealand*, Vol. 4, Otago and Southland Provincial Districts, p. 180.

49. McHutcheson, *The New Zealander Abroad*.

50. Bueltmann, '"Gentlemen, I'm going to the Old Country"', pp. 160–1.

51. This is evident, for instance, in personal testimonies. Cf. Bueltmann, '"Where the measureless Ocean between us will Roar"'.

52. Chisholm Diary, 10 July 1892, Hocken Library: Dunedin, 96–188.

53. George Grant Letters, 1885–1918, no date, Alexander Turnbull Library: Wellington, MS-Papers-0339.

54. *Cairns Post*, 3 November 1927.

55. See for instance *West Australian* (Perth), 25 July 1927.

56. *Brisbane Courier*, 23 June 1927.

57. *Mercury* (Hobart), 23 June 1927.

58. *Advertiser* (Adelaide), 21 May 1928.

59. *Cairns Post*, 10 September 1928.

60. Harland, 'Island heritage and identity in the Antipodes', p. 195; see also http://www.shetlandhamefarin.com (accessed 10 April 2012).

61. For details on the 1960 Hamefarin and subsequent trips, visit http://www.shetlandhamefarin.com/1960–shetland-hamefarin.php (accessed 10 April 2012).

62. For a detailed profile of these heritage tourists, see Basu, *Highland Homecomings*, chapter 3.

63. See for example Ray, 'Ancestral clanscapes and transatlantic tartaneers'. It is worth noting that this type of heritage tourism has recently also been embraced by so-called 'affinity Scots', see Hesse, 'Finding Neverland'.

64. Kelly, *Heather and Fern*.

65. For Baxter, Scotland was 'my spiritual home'. Quoted in Wright, 'The diaspora and its writers', p. 314.

Geographies

CHAPTER 9

Within the British and Irish Isles

In any analysis of Scotland's diaspora there lurks the question why more Scots did not leave for near neighbours England, Wales and Ireland. A shared land border offered access to potentially lower housing costs and to wages that were consistently 10 to 20 per cent higher. Why greater flows of labour did not match the technological interchange that ranged across industries, or the personal, intellectual and commercial exchange that linked these societies, has no single explanation. Ireland, indeed, was for most Scots even closer in an age when sea lanes were the superior option to roadways for traders and travellers alike. For good practical reasons, as well as political ones, Scotland's pre-1707 imperialism began in Ireland before it ever crossed the Atlantic.[1]

Very few Scots chose Wales as their diasporic location other than to the coal fields of Glamorgan and the South Wales steel plants in the first decades of the twentieth century. Analysis of the associational presence of Scots in London and the north of England, and in Ireland, tracks the ordinary lives of these migrants as well as their propensity toward further movements, including back to Caledonia. Research on Scots in this near diaspora has produced a number of distinct narratives. The Ulster-Scots are regarded as an outcome of Scotland's pre-1700 migration story, whereas for Scotland's elites and nascent middle classes the English capital held the opportunity for the kind of prestige not available anywhere else. The literary Anglo-Scots had a profound impact on Scotland's national self, and the 'Celtic agenda' with Wales and Ireland veered in and out of focus during the period. England offered a wider pool of marriage partners, and substantial trade and credit networks. Returning from the near diaspora, Scots brought culture, experiences and capital to their homeland, as likely as not to help maintain their cross-border inter-connections of family and business. What, then, was the Scots' pattern of migration to the other nations of the British and Irish Isles, and what evidence is there of diasporic actions once they got there? These inquiries structure this chapter.

A THE NEAR DIASPORA

Of anywhere, London held the greatest appeal. For all that James Boswell, the celebrated eighteenth-century author of *The Journal of a Tour to the Hebrides with Samuel Johnson* (1785), was bound up in his Scottish roots, 'his doomed, star-crossed love for London was one of the constant themes in his life'. The magnetism of the Imperial core was an attraction for tens of thousands of Scots who trod the same path and who, like Boswell, mixed settlement with regular returns north.[2] Among English cities, London was by a long way the prime destination for migrant Scots as it was for migrants from Ireland and for others foreign-born. In the 1911 census, 46 per cent of the non-London-born came from the south-east of England, with 29 per cent from Scotland, Ireland and overseas. The historic pull of that metropolis long overcame the normal levels of distance decay experienced by other British cities to surge in population from the early modern period.[3] In 1801 London was home to 10 per cent of the population of England and Wales; by comparison Glasgow housed 5 per cent of Scotland's population.[4] London and Glasgow were home to equal proportions of their respective national populations in 1851, but over the next ten years Glasgow took the lead, a sign of Scots' extreme levels of rural- and inter-urban migrations. In 1901 London attracted the largest raw number of migrants from all over Britain, when the census enumerators recorded 38.3 per cent of the capital's population having been born outside of the city. Marking the attraction of the new sectors of employment, however, proportionately more migrants (compared with those born within its boundaries) were at that time to be found in the great industrial cities of Glasgow (55.9 per cent), Liverpool (57.5 per cent), Manchester (54.6 per cent) and Birmingham (40.9 per cent).[5]

No matter how we choose to interpret the figures presented in this volume, they confirm as a general overview that migration was a common experience for Scots – as it was for most British and Irish people. Economically and politically successful Scots within England, and within the British capital, have claimed a disproportionate influence, often masking the place of ordinary migrants of no importance other than to their families and friends. Nenadic and colleagues have examined the Scottish cultural and political elites within eighteenth-century London, while Colley has emphasised Scottish political and military influence in the capital after 1746.[6] The literary successes of Sir Walter Scott and the churchman Thomas Chalmers brought Scottish values into English intellectual debates, each embraced and commodified further by Queen Victoria alongside an interlocking set of visual and aural tropes that centred around cultural constructions of highland life and society.[7]

The extent, timing and significance of the movement of ordinary Scots to and from England is difficult to gauge because we have no embarkation statistics or border controls whereby travel might be logged. The journeys across Hadrian's Wall were impressively fluid without undermining demographic differences that followed respective national patterns.[8] Assuredly also there were significant inter-national flows masked by the decennial snapshots. Searching other indicators of the Scottish presence in England for the period 1774–81 finds some 8 per cent of single men and 6 per cent of married patients treated at the Westminster General Dispensary being Scots-born.[9] Overall scholars estimate that about 10 per cent of all London's migrants came from Scotland in each decade of the nineteenth century.[10]

These estimates are not far removed from more recent evidence. Of those born in Scotland who lived in England in 2001, 13.7 per cent lived in Greater London, while the equivalent figure for migrants from Wales was 11.8 per cent. These numbers have seen a decline over the next two decades, yet are still enough to have comprised Scotland's fifth largest city. The 108,602 Londoners in 2011 who had been born in Scotland represented a fall of 4 per cent from the 113,117 enumerated in 1991.[11] In 2011 London had both the largest proportion of residents born outside the UK (37 per cent) and non-UK nationals (24 per cent), with Scots-born numbering 90,000 people or 1.1 per cent of the capital's population (being the ninth largest national group). In 2011 Scots-born made up 0.79 per cent of Wales's population.[12]

Some 748,577 Scots are estimated to have left Scotland for other parts of Great Britain and Ireland between 1841 and 1931. The peak for these flows occurred between 1861 and 1901 and in the inter-war decades, when – significantly – more headed for England than overseas (Table 9.1).[13]

While the inter-censal estimates give an indication of the number of Scots leaving for the near diaspora, to estimate how many Scots were living in England leads us to look at the census years. Table 9.2 shows the numbers

Table 9.1 Scots migrants to other parts of the UK, per decade, 1841–1931 [source: Flinn, *Scottish Population History*, pp. 442–3][14]

Decade	Estimated number
1841–51	74,314
1851–61	81,738
1861–71	96,274
1871–81	98,315
1881–91	90,711
1891–1901	98,210
1901–11	68,177
1911–21	63,069
1921–31	77,769
1841–31	748,577

Table 9.2 Scots-born in England and Wales, 1841–1951
[source: *General report, England and Wales*, Vol. IV, 1891,
p. 114; *General tables, England and Wales*, 1921, p. 189]

Year	Scots-born in England and Wales
1841	103,768
1851	130,087
1861	169,202
1871	213,254
1881	253,528
1891	282,271
1901	316,838
1911	321,825
1921	333,517
1931	366,486
1951	653,626

of Scots-born enumerated in England and Wales on census night. We do not
know if these people were temporary migrants or transients, recent or long-
standing residents, but they indicate the numbers who classified themselves as
Scots living in England in Wales.

In 1841, the proportion of Scots in the population of England and Wales
was 6.5 to every 1,000, rising to 7.3 in 1851, 8.4 in 1861, 9.4 in 1871 and 9.8
in 1881, before stalling at 9.7 in 1891. And while the Irish outnumbered the
Scots in England and Wales, they tended to locate in different areas – for
example the 65,056 Scots in Northumberland, Cumberland and Westmorland
outnumbered the 48,400 Irish. Only in Newcastle and South Shields did the
Scots number more than 5 per cent of the population; significant proportions
of the local population were found in Barrow-in-Furness (73 per 1,000),
Newcastle (60 per 1,000) and South Shields (44 per 1,000).[15] To accommodate these migrants, and a sign of their ethnic clustering, 'Scotch Flats' were
built in the 1870s for those migrant workers accompanied by their families to
undertake textile work in Barrow-in Furness.[16] And the general pattern was a
concentrated one: 37 per cent of all the Scots in England and Wales were found
in the mining areas of Durham, Northumberland, Cumberland, York, Derby,
Leicester, Stafford, Warwick, Gloucester, Monmouth and Glamorgan and 28
per cent in Greater London;[17] this is a pattern still found in 1911 (Table 9.3).

B DIASPORIC ACTIONS IN A MATURE SOCIETY

Analysis of the number of migrants does not per se comprise a diaspora, a
point we stressed in our discussion of the diaspora concept. There we stated

Table 9.3 Administrative counties and large towns in England with the highest proportion of natives of Scotland (1911) [source: Source: Table IX Birthplaces, Census for England and Wales, vol. IX, 1911, p. xii[18]]

Administrative counties	Proportion per 100,000 of each sex		Large towns	Proportion per 100,000 of each sex	
	Male	Female		Male	Female
Northumberland	4,149	4,037	Barrow-in-Furness	5,136	4,376
Cumberland	3,515	3,949	Newcastle-upon-Tyne	4,864	4,142
Westmorland	1,392	1,745	Tynemouth	3,123	2,751
Durham	1,486	1,319	Bootle	2,985	2,881
Middlesex	1,229	1,127	South Shields	2,971	2,646
London	1,156	1,101	Gateshead	2,880	2,550
Hampshire	1,306	873	Birkenhead	2,939	2,439
Surrey	968	1,147	Hornsey	3,081	2,245
Essex	1,085	858	Wallasey	2,368	2,349
Cheshire	908	1,009	Gillingham	2,455	1,603
Kent	896	788	Sunderland	2,217	1,804
Hertfordshire	783	900	Liverpool	1,993	1,838

the position that a diaspora was formed in and from the product of diasporic actions. In comparison to many of the Imperial case studies, the major difference between studying the Scots' transfer into the near diaspora is that they were moving to an already densely populated society. Indeed the Scots were migrating to a more mature economy than their own: to a nation which, as far as the raw numbers confirm, was losing five times as many people to emigration. Around 11.6 million people left England, Wales and Scotland between 1825 and 1930,[19] with Scotland's share of that total being 2.3 million. As a result we must frame any analysis of the Scots migration into England and Wales as movement to societies likewise shaped more by emigration than by immigration. Of significance too is that other nations of Great Britain were societies that had long experience and knowledge of the Scots. The English, Welsh and Scots have shared a monarchy since 1603 and a state since 1707, and did so with Ireland for the period 1801–1922. The Union of Crowns granted Scots 'the rights of Englishmen in England' meaning there was no need to confirm or extend residency rights in the 1707 bargain.[20] This participation in a united kingdom and the British state meant it was unlikely migrating Scots to England saw themselves as a minority, or unable to work alongside their fellow Britons. These migrants might be called 'minus one ethnics' – to borrow Michael Banton's phrase[21] – because they were not a visible minority nor, in most cases, did their religious preference for Protestantism, and their linguistic preference for English, undermine their simpler integration over Irish migrants despite their respective accents and cultural mores that spoke to ethnic granularity.

The English and those living in England worked within a range of personal and constructed impressions of their Scottish neighbours who had come to live amongst them, just as the Scots had impressions of the society they called their new home, each layering bricks of imperfect information to construct ethnic boundaries. The foundry men and the railway engineers would soon enough learn of each other's habits, their views on religion, politics, drink and the social issues of the day. Visiting Scotland in 1830 William Cobbett recoiled when faced with the Scots 'feeosophers', whereas the Cromarty stonemason Hugh Miller was somewhat taken aback by the lack of general religious knowledge found amongst patrons on the pubs and clubs of northern England in the 1850s, although generally he found the English franker as well as being more civil than the Scots, and less prying, too.[22] Some home-grown cultural divisions were not diluted by migration. In Yarmouth the Scottish fishing boats stayed in harbour while the English boats went to work during a dispute over Sunday fishing in the 1950s.[23] And the Scots imported Presbyterian services. Corby's Presbyterian church held a congregation of 400 in the 1930s, with its faith in the community strong enough to warrant a visit from the Moderator of the Church of Scotland in 1935 to open a new church hall.[24]

Alongside these face-to-face relationships which shaped the relative porosity of the Scottish diaspora in the rest of Britain, English readers, tourists and commercial travellers could summarise the history and society of Scotland by perusing Bradshaws', Baedeckers', Black's, and Murray's guidebooks, or those produced by the railway companies, or perhaps the travel writings of H. V. Morton, notably *In Search of Scotland* (1929) and *In Search of Scotland's Soul* (1930). These impressions would be modified and re-adapted as Scots integrated into their host society. Scots also read these accounts for themselves, absorbing their tropes, shaping how they presented themselves to English society as they sought to balance integration with boundary maintenance.[25] They had to, if T. W. H. Crossland's analysis of 1902 is to be taken at face value, when he warned the Scots against complacency and a too readily expressed claim of grievance: 'I have found it difficult to meet an Englishman who, if you questioned him straightly, would not admit that he has a rooted dislike for Scotchmen'.[26]

Contrasting examples serve to show the host English society contributing to Scots' own ethnic boundary-making in the southern nation. David Malloch (1705–65) left his native Perthshire to make his way as a playwright in the newly created Great Britain. Using an Anglicisation of his name to better appeal to English benefactors, Mallet (as he became known) is an example of a Scot's adaption to post-Union life. Mallet joined with James Thompson to write the British patriotic ode 'Rule Britannia' (1740), and attained sufficient literary celebrity – or notoriety as a Scot on the make – to be on the receiving end of jealous barbs from the likes of Samuel Johnson.[27] Other examples brought forth tensions both explicit and subtle, creating objectified impressions of Scots that were readily consumed and internalised. In the 1760s John Wilkes had fanned opposition to the incorporation of Scots into prominent positions within the Empire. The prime ministership of Lord Bute and the nabobs in India felt his caustic ire; the latter justified by the disproportionate presence of Scots within the East India Company (EIC) from the 1760s and into the 1780s (Chapter 13).[28] The Bank of Scotland held shares in the EIC as well as the Bank of England, showing the inter-linkages at the heart of imperial finances.[29] Wilkite opposition to the melting 'down' of the name 'England' into 'Great Britain' was one objection, and by highlighting the difference of Scots as a race it was a means of promoting English dominance within the Union.[30] Hogarth's 'The Caledonian voyage to Money-land' (1762) satirised the Scot on the make, ready to set sail for North America. Contributing further to this construction of post-Culloden Scotland as a poverty-stricken nation, prints of 'The Scots arrival in Money-land (1762) and 'Famine' (1763) depicted migration to England as an escape from nutritional, political and intellectual paucity, developments that the propagandists claimed were threatening to replace English liberties with Scottish ideas of arbitrary rule.[31]

By contrast, and more powerfully still, the diary of Queen Victoria idealised Scottish life and customs for an international audience. An entry for September 1852 records how she and Albert enjoyed a torchlight procession with 'magnificent pipers' adding to the atmosphere. She heard the cry of 'Neesh! neesh! neesh!' which she proceeded to anglicise as 'the Highland Hip! hip! hip!'.[32] The ancient Highlands had increasingly come to represent modern Scotland despite the evidence that 80 per cent of Scots lived in the counties of the Central Belt. Such evidence did not stop the editors of *Punch* collating a selection of its Scottish imagery in *Mr Punch in the Highlands* to poke fun at Scottish thrift, parochialism and the exorbitant costs and stingy service proffered by its nascent tourism industry.[33] But popular writing did showcase the benefits of political union. The Anglo-Scottish authors Lord Byron (1788–1824), Jane Porter (bap. 1776–1850), Thomas Carlyle (1795–1881) and Margaret Oliphant (1828–97) catered for both societies with stories and poetry rooted in Scottish themes that appealed to an English readership. Their constructions of the Scot shaped how the host and sending societies 'made sense' of the ethnic differences under a shared crown and parliament. Indeed, there was a narrative strain of the Scots as the great contributors to England's imperial agenda. Contemporary tropes stressed the Scottish influence within English culture from within England, the parameters of which are outlined by Morse with a deliberate whiff of contemporary hubris:

It was Hume and Mackintosh who laid the foundations for a modern history of England. It was Adam Smith who elaborated an economic theory that could serve as a framework for England's destiny as a trading nation. It was James Mill who in his classic *History of British India* (1818) mapped out Britain's future as an imperial power and legislator for mankind. It was Sir Walter Scott who in Ivanhoe produced the definitive myth of a proud Saxon race indomitably struggling against the Norman yoke. It was Thomas Carlyle who extended and developed this into a philosophy of the English character and a critique of industrialisation, and while Macaulay, who was perhaps the one single writer to produce a view of England that was more influential than Carlyle's, was not himself Scottish, he was deeply influenced by the ideals of the Scottish Enlightenment, the foremost protégé of Francis Jeffrey at the *Edinburgh Review* from 1839 to 1847, and from 1852 to 1856 MP for Edinburgh itself.[34]

William Thomson's experiments at the University of Glasgow that led to the transatlantic telegraph cable, for which he was knighted before his elevation to the title Lord Kelvin, is another name we could add to Morse's list; as is Lord Reith (John Reith), the stentorian first Director General of the BBC.[35] Both influenced communication of the Scots diasporic actions within England and out to the far diaspora, yet were central to a British identity that hardened the ground within which Scottish ethnic identity might hope to take root. Intellectual common interests sustained by the attraction of imperial expansion sustained the cultural assimilation of Scots into their southern host country. Before being returned to the Westminster parliament by the electors of Edinburgh, Macaulay wrote in 1835 about the centrality of the English language to Empire:

> The claims of our own language it is hardly necessary to recapitulate, it stands pre-eminent even among the languages of the West. It abounds with works of imagination not inferior to the noblest which Greece had bequeathed to us, – with models of every species of eloquence . . . Whoever knows that language has ready access to all the vast intellectual wealth which all the wisest nations of the earth have created and hoarded in ninety generations.[36]

This confidence came after parliamentary reform gave England and Scotland a democratic lead internationally (albeit temporarily) with the reform legislation of 1832. And the Scots' contribution to Empire was boosted through use of the English language, a predominant allegiance to Protestantism and a shared monarchy and state. Another influential voice, the educator Mathew Arnold, saw the progress of Anglicisation as inexorable to Britain's civilizing mission in the world:

The fusion of all the inhabitants of these islands into one homogeneous, English-speaking whole, the breaking down of barriers between us, the swallowing up of several provincial nationalities, is a consummation to which the natural course of things irresistibly tends; it is a necessity of what is called civilisation.[37]

Politically, too, by mid-century Scotland's governance were increasingly dominated by British and Imperial concerns, with little but the Kirk's Disruption of 1843 and crofters' discontent with their landowners in the 1880s taking up significant parliamentary time at Westminster.[38]

These kinds of evidence have fed into the analytic framework for Scottish national identity, but we should recognise that their audience was primarily an English one. Reflecting on his experiences of living in Chelsea where so many came to pay their respects to him and wife Jane Welsh, Dumfriesshire-born Thomas Carlyle surmised that 'the condition of England was for him the condition of Britain.'[39] These were debates of human ecology and socio-linguistics, but had practical application on the work floor. Hunger brought on by bad harvests encouraged Scots to seek opportunities in England, with industrial opportunities proving an attractive pull. Britain was at war from 1756 to 1763, from 1775 to 1783, from 1793 to 1802 and 1803 to 1815, drawing disproportionate numbers of Scots into the British army, with Scots-born military personnel stationed in the southern bases. Showing the links between Scottish military men and Scottish businessmen in London, Nenadic explains how London was often an irresistible attraction, where trade with Empire through the capital's port and the global reach of its clearing houses meant a London presence was a path to Scots' economic success. Military expansion led to business expansion, and the Scots' middling classes were keen to play a part, only returning north when the patronage that underpinned their success unwound.[40] A military career in Empire was a ready route to internal migration within Britain. Lieutenant John Grant, the father of Scottish nationalist James Grant (whom we introduced in the previous chapter), was on half-pay living in Edinburgh in 1832 when called back into service to command a barrack of veterans in Newfoundland. Edinburgh-born James followed his father to North America but returned to England in 1839 to the position of ensign in the 62nd foot regiment (the Duke of Edinburgh) at Chatham in Kent. James took charge of the depot in 1840 before eventually abandoning a military life for a career as an historical novelist. The fluidity of this peripatetic life found James fleeing Scotland's capital to settle permanently in England's capital after being cited in divorce proceedings in 1870. It was there that this Scottish family became integrated into English society: his youngest son became Father Roderick, priest at Brook Green in London, before Canon Grant rose to become most closely associated with Ingatestone in Essex where he served from 1904 until his death in 1934. Never ministering north of the border, it is at Ingatestone that Patrick is honoured with memorial windows depicting the saints of Scotland.[41]

C INDUSTRIAL ATTRACTION

While the intellectual and landowning elites of the eighteenth century focused on London and its opportunities for administrative influence within court and government as well as commercial trading opportunities not available elsewhere, the evolving pattern of Britain's industrialisation shifted the location of Scots' migrations. Around 10,000 craftsmen each year are estimated to have left for London in the closing years of the eighteenth century, with workers from Roxburghshire moving to Northumberlandshire and from Dumfriesshire to Cumberland. Nor was it solely industrial skills that were employed, with Scots going as far as Norwich to participate in the harvest to the extent that the Norwich Scots Society was formed in 1775 (although it changed its name to the Society of Universal Goodwill in 1787), and Ayrshire farmers were still to be found seeking work around East Anglia in the years before the First World War.[42] Yet it was industrialisation that was the main attraction, and the combined weight of Manchester, Leeds, Bradford, Sheffield and Hull tipped the balance of the economic core north of London and thus closer to Scotland's labour supply. Equally, the Celtic capitals of Cardiff, Belfast and Glasgow were economic leaders in the latter phase of the Industrial Revolution that drew on their own hinterlands and also from further afield. In one of the pioneering statements on the Scots migrations into England, R. A. Cage's rationale was to show the Scots in England helped to industrialise their southern neighbour, and to illustrate the importance of connections between Scotland and England to Britain's industrial revolution. The major industrial cities of England required multiple links to the Edinburgh–Glasgow corridor to sustain their growth, relying on manpower, finance, raw materials and markets, coupling production and consumption alike.[43]

Some of this interchange came from migrant entrepreneurs building up the boundaries of the Scottish near diaspora by looking back home for their labour. In the 1770s and 1780s mill master Adam Douglas hired his fellow Scots, finding them to be better-trained workers who were, for good measure, educated at Scotland's expense.[44] Others included John Gladstone who led one of the major Liverpool trading houses and prominent Manchester spinner George Murray, with some evidence of subsidies offered for Scots workers to bring their families south to join them,[45] and Scottish merchants making worldwide trading connections from their base in London.[46] Celebrated inventors James Watt (1736–1819), James Nasmyth (1808–90), and Sir

William Fairbairn (1789–1874), were all Scots who went to England to obtain working capital to continue their endeavours. James Taylor, a long-term trades unionist in London, worked to bring unskilled workers under the union support after arriving in the capital in 1881.[47]

Access to English markets and capital both delayed overseas migration and widened the opportunities outside the nation. Trade with England had long been in evidence, but after 1707 the southern markets were added to by export opportunities carved out by the British state. Under the protection of the Navigation Acts Scots were able to export about 25 to 30 per cent of the nation's production to the colonies. This post-Union arrangement meant avoiding the overpaid demographic growth that is so characteristic of a specialised economy locked into the needs and prosperity of a core economy.[48]

New forms of communication played a part in both these economic developments and the migration decision. Traders found it just as cheap to use the railway to bring fish purchased from the Scottish markets to consumers in England as it was to use markets from the Midlands and North of England.[49] The speed of the railway made it possible for the Edinburgh tradesman to be in daily communication with a counterpart in Newcastle, York or London, and female fish gutters and packers journeyed from Shetland, Wick and the northern fishing counties to Great Yarmouth and Lowestoft each year, a practice that continued until around the 1930s.[50] This sojourning was carried out first by boat then by chartered train, with Britain's total rail passenger numbers increasing from 111 million to 506 million in the third quarter of the nineteenth century.[51] The rail journey from Edinburgh to London was nine hours when the *Flying Scotsman* reduced this to less than seven and a half hours in 1888. Quicker still, the electrical telegraph allowed London news to be instantly transmitted to the provincial papers. These improvements in travel and communication were as crucial to maintaining the Scottish near diaspora as a community of Scots as they were for the diaspora further afield.

D ASSOCIATIONAL FOOTPRINTS

Not all the migration was the result of demand for skilled work, or a choice made freely. For instance some of Scotland's unemployed youth were sent by the Minister of Labour to take up work in the Midland factories of inter-war England as attempts were made by the government to regionally manage surpluses of labour.[52] Compared with the Irish, though, less noticeably were Scots resorting to poor relief, an argument made by Redford for Manchester, Liverpool and London.[53] Earlier evidence from 1819 suggests Scots migrants were not always so appreciated, with indications that the poor rate on the English side of the border was five times greater than on the Scottish side, with complaints that only six weeks of residence were required for assessment compared with three years in Scotland.[54] Just as they objectified the Irish in Liverpool, contemporaries feared that the Scots were the dregs of that society who had travelled the shorter distance south, while the more industrious were sufficiently energised to journey overseas.[55]

With the state reluctant to intervene in the poverty of migrants, the response was left to actions from within civil society. The Caledonian Society of London had as its object 'to promote good fellowship and brotherhood, and to combine efforts for benevolent and national objects connected with Scotland'.[56] One study suggests there were more Scottish associations in London than in any other city, sustaining twenty-eight ethnically Scottish clubs at the start of the twentieth century.[57] London also had the Royal Scottish Corporation to look after its Scots poor from 1603 and the Highland Society in 1788,[58] but most locations were not blessed by Scottish philanthropic and cultural societies until the nineteenth century.[59] St Andrew's societies were formed in Manchester (1876), Barrow (1878), Bradford (1886), Liverpool (1890) and York (1894) with London gaining a Caledonian Club in 1891.[60] Harper has found the minute books of the Cumbria Congregational and Evangelical Union teeming with records of Scots migrants coming and going in the nineteenth century.[61] Music and literary clubs formed ethnically neutral networks, sustaining mundane yet often intimate knowledge of Scots that contributed towards integration and the breaking down of the ethnic boundaries that form a diaspora. Burnett shows for the north-east of England the strength of the local community fundraising carried out through galas, dinners and balls to raise funds to help with the relief of highland Scots and rural Irish devastated by the potato famine of the 1840s.[62] It was a community response made possible by the involvement of Scots in St Andrew's and Caledonian clubs, in Burns clubs, and in piping and singing societies. In the second half of the nineteenth century, the Scots outnumbered the Irish numerically and proportionately in this region, a pattern contributed to by the industrial similarities with Scotland's west coast. Highland Scots and east coast Scots were, however, also to be found within the north-east shipyards, and in one case the residential area of these Scots in Hebburn, Tyneside became known as 'Little Aberdeen'.[63] Groups like the Darlington Burns Association (formed in 1906) started out helping the local Scottish enclave but became more open to all nationalities as the decades progressed.[64] At the inaugural dinner of the Sunderland Burns Club in 1897 there was much debate over members being 'only Scottish' or 'of Scotch descent'. 'Hail Brither Scots O' Coaly Tyne, We meet again for Auld Lang Syne' was the telegram which the Sunderland Burns Club sent to their Newcastle counterparts at their inaugural annual dinner of 25 January 1897.[65] A number of Burns clubs were in the region and affiliated to the Federation of Burns Clubs based in Kilmarnock. Significantly, the

Figure 9.1 Lord Mayor Sir James Millar of London with Caledonian Lodge members [source: SCRAN; Resource Rights Holder: The Scotsman Publications Ltd; SCRAN ID: 000-000-072-042]

Sunderland Burns Club hosted the first meeting of the Federation outside of Scotland in 1907.[66]

The philanthropic imperative was the primary objective of the Scots Society of St Andrew, formed in Hull in 1910 to 'Strengthen the ties which bind Scotsmen resident in or near Hull with their native land and to promote social intercourse amongst them particularly on St Andrew's Day'. It was a small community with Scots-born making up 1 per cent of Hull's population in 1891, with 2,700 Scots enumerated in 1921. Their help extended to those Scots passing through Hull who might get into trouble. A sense of self-preservation away from home motivated their ethnic boundary-making. As the Society's first President explained: 'They were in another country and they wanted to see each other as much as possible, and to help their poorer brethren'.[67]

By mid-century only around 10 per cent of migrant Scots made the journey over the Irish Sea, much less a proportion than, say, in the seventeenth century, and these were likely the children or Irish migrants into Scotland.[68]

In 1911 12,451 Scots-born made Belfast their home, a city that could claim to be the first town outside of Scotland to publish an edition of Burns, marked when the poet's son and namesake visited the town and enjoyed a supper in his, and his father's, honour.[69] Belfast peaked its interest in Burns for the 1859 centenary with 300 gathering to celebrate the occasion, but numbers lessened over the century, and it was left to the Belfast Benevolent St Andrew's Society to carry the associational identity of the Scots from 1867. The geographical closeness between Scotland and Ireland and the religious and political inter-play between them were reflected in the actions of the Scottish community in Belfast – as was the case with the Irish on Scotland's west coast. The Belfast Scottish Unionist Club, formed in 1893, was one such response to the home rule debate.[70] Importantly also, Belfast offered opportunities for Scottish middle-class capitalists and industrialists. Examples include Charles E. Allan of the shipbuilders Workman, Clark & Co. and David Duncan Leitch, founder of the linen and flax merchants that took his name. Scots businessmen rose to the political office of mayor as well as holding influential administrative posts within the Chambers of Commerce and the Harbour Commissioners.[71] There was sufficient wealth amongst the Scottish community to support the Belfast Benevolent Society of St Andrews (founded in 1867) – helping community formation as well as the relief of poverty.

The personal connection has remained an important reason for moving to the near diaspora as to other parts of the globe. In 1911 three quarters of the Scots in England and Wales were located in and around London and the counties closest to the Scottish border, a pattern of propinquity nearly identical to the pre-modern distribution.[72] One study suggests that the relatively longer range of movement required by Scots to get to the labour markets of England, as opposed to movement internal to England, leads to greater upward mobility in the period 1750–1920 and also during the 1920–94 span.[73] With Scots starting from a low base, this was always likely. A head of family's income, even in reward for skilled work, provided no more than between 44 per cent and 57 per cent of all income brought into the family.[74] The 1906 wages census showed 40 per cent of men in the cotton industry and 31 per cent of men in the metal and shipbuilding industries earned less than 25s weekly.[75] The Board of Trade survey in 1908 found that disposable incomes in urban Scotland were still around 10 per cent lower than in England due to the combination of lower wages and higher costs of comparable foodstuffs. An Aberdeen brick-layer earned £36 compared to £38 in Dundee and £44 in London; and the differentials for an engineering labourer were £21, £23 and £29 for the same cities.[76] These investigations confirmed Scotland as a low-wage economy: cotton workers earned £28 instead of £36 earned in England; builders earned £62 rather than £66, and shipyard workers earned £70 whereas in England the figure was £76. Some industries recorded no marked differences between the two nations, while work in the blast furnaces and in mining rewarded their workers on average £1 more per year in Scotland. To Scots' benefit skilled jobs within the heavy industries around the Clyde were paying more than the UK average in 1906 although unskilled work was still at a disadvantage, with parts of the Borders and Tayside paying their workers below average wages.[77]

E CONCLUSION

The balance of structure and action was as valid for movements within Britain and Ireland as it was for migration overseas. Important for many, though, was a prior connection to facilitate the decision. Even in the age of the telephone, telegram and the Pathé News, personal and ethnic connections were called upon to make the migration a successful one, as these memories from 1945 reveal:

> I came against a lot of Scots obviously when I first came south. A lot of them came and spoke to me. Again family histories or someone knows something else and word soon gets round that there's someone new in the locality who's come from Scotland so you've obviously got a meeting point to begin with and I was welcomed by many Scottish families.[78]

There were some advantages to leaving one labour market for another, but not for all workers. The usual fluidity of pull and push factors played out differently over the period, and if there was an already established network of family, friends or business associates in England, then migration grew as an option. But of course these same factors shaped the decision to emigrate as we have already seen in some of the thematic chapters.

NOTES

1. Daunton and Halpern, 'Introduction', p. 4.
2. Caudle, 'James Boswell (*H. Scoticus Londoniensis*)', pp. 109 and 115.
3. Wrigley, 'A simple model of London's importance in changing English society and economy'.
4. Weber, *The Growth of Cities in the Nineteenth Century*, pp. 59–60.
5. Pooley and Turnbull, *Migration and Mobility in Britain since the Eighteenth Century*, p. 3.
6. Nenadic, *The Scots in London*; Colley, *Britons*.
7. Morton, *Ourselves and Others*, pp. 194–6 and 279–80.

8. Anderson and D. J. Morse, 'The people', pp. 8–11.
9. Langford, 'South Britons' reception of North Britons', p. 144.
10. Ball and Sunderland, *An Economic History of London*, pp. 49–50.
11. White, 'Not just rugby clubs', p. 212.
12. See http://www.ons.gov.uk/ons/rel/mro/news-release/census-2-1----london/census-gives-insights-into-characteristics-of-london-s-populati on.html (accessed 3 February 2013).
13. Flinn et al., *Scottish Population History*, p. 442 (Table 6.1.2); Harper, *Scotland No More?*, p. 19.
14. The inter-censal figures are derived by comparing the rise of Scots enumerated in other parts of the UK while allowing for mortality rates.
15. Ibid, p. 179.
16. Harper, *Scotland No More?*, p. 26.
17. Marsh, *The Changing Social Structure of England and Wales*, p. 92.
18. Online Historical Population Reports, http://www.histpop.org (accessed 10 February 2013).
19. Baines, *Migration in a Mature Economy*, pp. 209–306.
20. Langford, 'South Britons' reception of North Britons', p. 143.
21. McCrone, 'Who do you say you are?'.
22. Morton and Morris, 'Civil society, governance and nation', p. 359; Langford, 'South Britons' reception of North Britons, 1707–1820', p. 153.
23. Harper, *Scotland No More?*, pp. 24–5.
24. Ibid., p. 39.
25. Morton, *Ourselves and Others*, pp. 4–5 and 187–200.
26. Ibid, pp. 275–280; Harper, *Scotland No More?*, pp. 48–9.
27. Jung, '"Staging" an Anglo-Scottish identity', pp. 73, 79–80, 88.
28. Colley, *Britons*, p. 111; Devine, 'Scottish elites and the Indian Empire', p. 214.
29. Ibid, p. 35.
30. Morton, *Unionist Nationalism*, pp. 14–15.
31. Colley, *Britons*, pp. 112–15, 121.
32. 'Diary of Queen Victoria, September, 1852' in *Leaves from the Journal of Our Life in the Highlands*, ed. Helps, p. 315.
33. *Mr Punch in the Highlands*, various authors, ed. Charles Keen.
34. Morse, *High Victorian Culture*, pp. 47–8.
35. Harper, *Scotland No More?*, p. 36.
36. Macaulay, 'Minute on education', pp. 107–17.
37. Arnold, *On the Study of Celtic Literature*, p. 12.
38. Hutchison, 'Anglo-Scottish political relations in the nineteenth century', p. 247.
39. Ashton, 'The Carlyles in London', p. 234; Morton, 'Scotland is Britain'.

40. Nenadic, 'Military men, business men, and the "business" of patronage', pp. 230, 241–3 and 246–7.
41. Morton, 'Returning Scotland, returning nation', pp. 114–17.
42. Redford, *Labour Migration to England*, p. 135; Langford, 'South Britons' reception of North Britons', p. 155; Harper, *Scotland No More?*, p. 20.
43. Cage, 'The Scots in England', p. 32.
44. Ibid., pp. 29, 31, 33.
45. Redford, *Labour Migration to England*, p. 135–6.
46. Cage, 'The Scots in England', p. 30.
47. Schmiechen, *Sweated Industries and Sweated Labor*, p. 90.
48. Smout, 'Centre and periphery in history'.
49. Weber, *The Growth of Cities*, p. 203.
50. Harper, *Scotland No More?*, pp. 20–4.
51. Croal, *A Book About Travelling*, p. 556.
52. Harper, *Scotland No More?*, pp. 27–9.
53. Ibid, p. 32.
54. Redford, *Labour Migration to England*, p. 138.
55. Belchem, 'Hub and diaspora, p. 21.
56. Hepburn and Douglas, *The Chronicles of the Caledonian Society of London*, p. 2.
57. Harper, *Scotland No More?*, p. 43.
58. Ibid, p. 42.
59. Langford, 'South Britons' reception of North Britons', pp. 155–6.
60. McCarthy, 'The Scots Society of St Andrew, Hull', pp. 205 and 239; *Harper, Scotland No More?*, p. 42.
61. Ibid., p. 39.
62. Burnett, '"Hail brither Scots o' coaly Tyne"', pp. 1–2.
63. Ibid., pp. 3 and 5.
64. Burnett, '"Department of Help for Skint Scotchmen!"', p. 224.
65. Ibid, pp. 6–7.
66. Burnett, '"Department of Help for Skint Scotchmen!"', pp. 222–3.
67. McCarthy, 'The Scots Society of St Andrew, Hull', pp. 237–8.
68. Brock, *The Mobile Scot*, p. 25.
69. Hughes, '"Scots stand firm and our Empire is safe"', p. 205.
70. Ibid., pp. 205–6.
71. Ibid., pp. 203–4.
72. Harper, *Scotland No More?*, p. 19; Cage, 'The Scots in England', p. 30.
73. Pooley and Turnbull, *Migration and Mobility*, pp. 165–6.
74. Ibid, p. 78.
75. Rose, *Limited Livelihoods*, p. 79.
76. British Parliamentary Papers (1908). Board of Trade Report of an enquiry by the Board of Trade into working class rents, housing and retail prices

and rates of wages in certain occupations in the industrial towns of the United Kingdom. CD 6864.

77. Smout, 'Scotland 1850–1950', pp. 218–21.
78. Quoted in McCarthy, 'National identities and twentieth-century Scottish migrants in England', p. 175.

CHAPTER 10

The United States

When Samuel Johnson made his famous journey through the Highlands with James Boswell in 1773, he referred to the 'epidemical fury of emigration.'[1] According to his account, America dominated this 'desire of wandering' which had spread 'contagiously from valley to valley'.[2] Boswell made similar observations about 'the present rage for emigration',[3] recounting a conversation with a Mrs M'Kinnon who described the departure of an America-bound emigrant ship from Skye the previous year. There was great distress among those who watched the ship leave, yet a year later when another ship set sail, the scene was very different, there being a belief among those left behind that they would soon follow. While on Skye, Boswell described a dance called 'America', inspired by the volume of emigration taking place. 'Each of the couples', according to Boswell, 'after the common involutions and evolutions, successively whirls round in a circle, till all are in motion; and the dance seems intended to show how emigration catches, till a whole neighbourhood is set afloat.'[4]

A SETTLEMENT IN THE THIRTEEN COLONIES

Although America would go on to become the most popular destination among emigrant Scots, the long tradition of Scottish emigration to Europe, where better opportunities existed, meant that its appeal was relatively slow in taking hold. Before 1640 there were as few as 200 Scots settled on English plantations, while attempts at establishing Scottish colonies before 1707 were either short-lived or, at best, modest in size.[5] One endeavour in 1669 ended when a ship carrying passengers bound for New York was wrecked before it even made it off the Scottish coast,[6] while a settlement of banished and persecuted Covenanting Presbyterians in South Carolina, named Stuart's Town, was completely destroyed by Spaniards only two years after its establishment in 1684.[7] More successful was the attempt to establish a Scottish colony in East Jersey, which, between 1683 and 1685, received four major shipments of immigrants. But even here, by the end of the decade, Scottish emigration, as was the case elsewhere in America, was in decline.[8] While the seeds that would transform Scottish emigration in the long run had perhaps been sown, the total number of Scots residing in America by the end of the seventeenth century was modest.

Movement continued to be slow into the eighteenth century. In spite of the opportunities brought about by the 1707 Act of Union's removal of restrictions on trade and settlement with English (now British) colonies, the total number of Scots who arrived in North America between 1700 and 1760 is estimated at only 30,000.[9] Of those who went, most were attracted by the availability of land, although the admission of 798 new members to the Scots Charitable Society of Boston between 1707 and 1763 is an important reminder of the urban dimension of Scottish emigration.[10] In the 1730s there were three attempts at establishing Scottish settlements, and while the number of initial recruits can be measured in hundreds, their long-term impact on future settlement patterns was significant.

The first settlement was initiated by James Oglethorpe and his fellow Trustees for Establishing the Colony of Georgia in America. Because of its border position with Spanish Florida, the Trustees wished to recruit those who would not only cultivate the land but also protect it. When the initial settlers, mostly made up of impoverished Englishmen, proved wanting in both these areas, Oglethorpe turned to the Scottish Highlands for more suitable recruits.[11] In 1735 the *Prince of Wales* sailed from Inverness with 163 immigrants bound for the southernmost frontier of Britain's American colonies, where they established the town of Darien – named after the failed Scottish colony on the isthmus of Panama as a gesture of defiance against the Spanish they now bordered. A further sixty highlanders – deemed necessary to bolster defences along the Spanish border – arrived in 1737. Unfortunately, when war broke out between Spain and Britain in 1739, fifty-one of the sixty-seven Darien highlanders who had joined an assault on the Spanish were either killed or captured at the Battle of Fort Mosa. The defeat was disastrous for the Darien settlement, which, by 1740, had a decimated population of only fifty-three. To save the ailing settlement a further recruitment mission was made to Scotland. The settlement survived and in 1742 soldiers from Darien were able to avenge those who had fallen at Fort Mosa by helping fend off a Spanish invasion into the colony.

As well as their reputation for fighting qualities, the settlers of the Darien settlement also gained notoriety for producing one of the first anti-slavery petitions in American history, in which they claimed 'it is shocking to human nature, that any Race of Mankind and their Posterity should be sentenc'd to perpetual Slavery.'[12] Although the petition was used by the colony's Trustees as justification for rejecting proposals to introduce the practice, we should not be too quick in praising these Scots for their moral ideals. Not only is there evidence that some of the signers were threatened into doing so, but in return for the petition, which was being advocated by Oglethorpe, the townspeople demanded the establishment of a store and a loan to buy cattle. Furthermore, after Georgia became a royal colony in 1748, slavery was introduced, and despite their apparent former opposition, on the eve of the American Revolution, many of the largest local land- and slaveowners came from the ranks of Darien Scots, providing further evidence of the extent to which Scots, even if more indirectly than other groups, benefitted from slavery.[13]

The other two Scottish settlements that had their beginnings in the 1730s were in New York and North Carolina. The former followed an advertisement by the Royal Governor regarding the availability of 100,000 acres of land for willing settlers. After visiting New York, Lachlan Campbell, a British half-pay officer from Islay, made arrangements to bring over 423 fellow islanders in several shiploads between 1738 and 1740. After their arrival, however, the New York government officials refused to fulfil the grant under the promised scheme, leaving the immigrants to either apply separately for land grants, which would not be located together, or relocate elsewhere. Not until 1764, and only because of the persistence shown by Lachlan Campbell's son, Donald, were 47,000 acres granted to the original settlers and their descendants.[14] In contrast, the authorities in North Carolina were considerably more helpful. Keen to encourage settlement in the underdeveloped Cape Fear Valley, North Carolina's Scottish Governor, Gabriel Johnston, helped secure several thousand acres of land and a ten-year exemption from taxes for 350 immigrants who arrived from Argyllshire in 1739. The settlement they established would go on to become the largest highland settlement in America. Whilst there are references to subsequent arrivals in 1742, the scale of the settlement remained small at this time. Indeed its growth, as with the other settlements and Scottish emigration to America generally, did not really accelerate until the conclusion of the French and Indian War in 1763.[15] From that point until the outbreak of the American Revolution in 1775 it is estimated that 25,000 Scots settled in America.[16]

Part of this growth was on account of the placement of discharged soldiers from the 77th Regiment (Montgomery Highlanders), the 42nd Regiment (Black Watch) and the 78th Regiment (Fraser's Highlanders) each of which took part in the conflict. These were the first highland regiments to serve in North America and included many of the first highlanders to join the British army following the failed Jacobite rising of 1745, and the subsequent efforts by the British authorities to destroy the clan system.[17] The decision to recruit highlanders, and their willingness to serve, may seem strange, but there were advantages in doing so for both. For the British the removal of men from the Highlands further reduced the threat of a Jacobite recurrence, while the highlanders themselves, as servants of the King, could wear highland dress and carry arms – practices which had been outlawed as part of the attack on clanship. Perhaps more importantly, service offered them a way back from that defeat. Those who joined included a scattering of former Jacobites, and, ironically, several of the battalions that operated alongside highland regiments in America included officers and men who had fought against highlanders in the '45 Rebellion.[18] Yet by the end of the North American conflict not only had a total of 4,200 highlanders become involved, the military prowess which they demonstrated helped establish the reputation that was to gain highland regiments a permanent place within the structure of the British army.[19]

At the end of the war those who wished to remain in America were offered land. Most settled in areas they had become familiar with during the conflict, such as the soldiers from the Montgomery Highlanders, who joined the recently resolved Scottish settlement in New York. British victory also removed most French support for Native American resistance to the expansion of British settlement. Highlanders were quickly targeted by land speculators, and, in part due to returning Scottish soldiers and those who wrote to friends and family at home in favourable terms about the desirability of land in America, they proved to be a rich source of new settlers.

The Highlands were, however, not the only place from where Scottish emigrants came. While details of most of those who arrived between 1763 and 1775 are not known, a Register of Emigrants, which was supposed to record every person who left Britain for America from December 1773 to March 1776, does give valuable insights. Bernard Bailyn acknowledges that it is incomplete, but details of 3,589 Scots destined for the thirteen colonies were recorded.[20] While more than half of those with known residences were from highland regions, all of Scotland was engaged in emigration.[21] The next biggest contributor to Scottish emigration was the Western Lowlands from where came 477. This was a period of high unemployment in the weaving industries, with many emigrants arriving as indentured servants. Indeed, according to the Register of Emigrants, one in five Scots arrived under terms of indenture, where, in exchange for the cost of transportation to America, they had to work in full-time service for a specified period. Upon the completion of their contract, which could range from three to seven years, they were free of all obligations. While the attraction of indentured servitude was obvious, servants could be employed in any work their purchasers wished to assign them, illustrating that the costs could also be high. As a correspondent with Edinburgh's *Weekly Magazine* noted, indentured workers were treated with 'the greatest humanity and discretion'. But as with most aspects of emigration, the experience could vary considerably, with some being treated fortunately, but many others less well.[22] A large number (166) of the indentured servants were textile workers, but the largest occupational group were servants, most of whom were women.[23] Those who did not arrive as indentured servants were most likely to be farmers, although there were significant numbers of textile workers, construction workers and labourers.

Regardless of whether or not they came as indentured servants, most were destined for the same places. In contrast to English emigrants, who were primarily drawn to Pennsylvania, Maryland and Virginia, more than 70 per cent of Scots were bound for New York and North Carolina, two of the colonies in which Scottish settlement initiated in the 1730s. Furthermore, although the proportion of Scots destined for Georgia was relatively small, two-thirds of those who migrated directly to that colony from Britain were born in Scotland.[24] While the specific destinations of the emigrants were not recorded, Bailyn's argument that, by 1776, the highland population of the Cape Fear region was potentially greater than 12,000, would suggest that these initial areas of settlement greatly impacted on the direction of subsequent Scottish emigration.[25]

Yet, as was previously mentioned, the emigrant list is incomplete. Where this is particularly evident is with regards to Scottish emigration to Virginia and Maryland. According to the Register, only seventy-five Scots were destined for these two colonies, which in light of the Scottish tobacco trade with them seems too small.[26] From 1707 the Chesapeake-Clyde tobacco trade had experienced considerable growth. From an annual import rate average of 1,450,000 lbs shortly after the Union, the rate had reached 8 million lbs by 1741. A good decade later, it had increased dramatically, to 24 million lbs, before reaching an all-time high of 47 million lbs in 1771.[27] Glasgow's rise to prominence in the tobacco trade was largely on account of its adoption of the direct purchase system, whereby firms established chains of stores in the colonies which offered goods, money or credit to planter customers in exchange for tobacco. Such a system stood in contrast to other major importers who were commission merchants, taking crops on consignment and disposing of them in domestic and European markets for a commission on sales.[28] The 'store system' as carried out by the Glasgow merchants had significant advantages over the consignment, none less than the fact that they could undersell their competitors, who, depending upon commission, held out for the highest price possible. Although the bulk of the tobacco was destined for continental Europe, because it was coming from America it had to be imported via a British port before being re-exported. For their return voyages, the ships carried European goods to America, which were often made in Scotland. As Devine has argued, the tobacco commerce, though not a decisive force in Scottish economic development, was nonetheless a powerful influence on the rise of industry, banking, agrarian improvement and new commercial structures in the western Lowlands, particularly in Glasgow itself where most of the merchant houses which dominated tobacco importation had their headquarters.[29]

The Glasgow tobacco trade is an important illustration of how Scots in America impacted on both the old and the new homeland. The direct purchase system enabled small planters in Maryland and Virginia to flourish. Although work on tobacco plantations was usually carried out by slaves, Scots were recruited as factors, store keepers and store assistants. Towns around the Chesapeake soon contained substantial populations, and although there is no evidence of large-scale settlement, there was a steady expansion of the Scottish population in Virginia and Maryland.[30] And whilst the American Revolution heralded the end for the Glasgow tobacco trade, bringing a virtual halt to tobacco imports for the duration of the Revolution, and afterwards, by no longer requiring tobacco destined for Europe to go via a British port, its lasting impact on both sides of the Atlantic was significant.

B   THE SCOTTISH ENLIGHTENMENT AND AMERICA

The extent of ill will generated by Scots during the American Revolution is evident from an early draft of the Declaration of Independence in which the phrase 'Scotch and foreign mercenaries' was used in reference to the tyranny perpetuated by George III and the armies he was sending 'to complete the Work of Death, Desolation and Tyranny.'[31] William Jefferson's language may have reflected Scottish unpopularity at the time, but their singling out did cause offence to some members of the Continental Congress, which dropped the reference from the final version. Two members of the Congress were born in Scotland – John Witherspoon and James Wilson – and there is some evidence that it was Witherspoon in particular who objected to the castigation of his countrymen.[32] Yet there were others among America's founding fathers who, owing a debt to Scotland, may have supported its removal.

Scotland's contribution to America is well documented, and while much of what has been written falls into the 'Burns Supper school of Scottish historians', in which bias and tenuity are commonplace, since 1954, when a special issue of *The William and Mary Quarterly* was devoted to Scotland and America, there has been a serious attempt at assessing cultural exchanges between the two countries.[33] Particular attention has been given to the contribution of the Scottish Enlightenment; amongst those whom its ideas influenced were the signers of the Declaration. That both Witherspoon and Wilson experienced the Enlightenment first-hand can be seen in their respective careers upon coming to America: Witherspoon as President of the College of New Jersey (now Princeton University), and Wilson as a lawyer, in his contributions to the United States Constitution and as one of six original justices appointed to the Supreme Court.[34] Another contributor to the Constitution, as well as author of the Bill of Rights and the United States' fourth president, was James Madison, who was deeply influenced by the ideas of David Hume.[35] Adam Smith is known to have been widely read by America's founding fathers, and his views influenced the structure of American government.[36] Perhaps the grandest and most controversial assertion is that Thomas Jefferson based the Declaration of Independence on the ideas of Scottish moral philosophers (in particular Francis Hutchison), rather than the widely accepted view that it was those of Englishman John Locke. While much of the evidence offered by its proponent, Gary Wills, in *Inventing America* has since been discredited, recent work, while claiming that Wills overstated the case against Locke, suggests that Jefferson may still have been deeply influenced by Hutcheson's moral sense doctrine.[37]

Such analysis is obviously somewhat speculative, but what is clear is that no single Scottish philosopher or idea dominated among the founding fathers. This is consistent with the Scottish Enlightenment whose contributors often disagreed with each other, and from which emerged multi-faceted views. As one scholar has put it: '[t]he Scots spread a rich intellectual table from which the Americans could pick and choose and feast'.[38] Yet while it is impossible to speak of 'the' Scottish impact on America, the Enlightenment is acknowledged to have influenced American literature, science, theology, social thought and, most of all, American higher education.[39]

As early as 1693, with the appointment of James Blair as first President of the College of William and Mary, Scots commanded prominent positions in American higher education, although it was not until after 1750 that the influence of the Scottish Enlightenment can be seen.[40] Pivotal in this process were two individuals. The first, William Smith, was born and educated in Aberdeen, and came to America to be a tutor for the sons of a rich New York family. Inspired by reforms taking place at King's and Marischal Colleges in Aberdeen, he published an outline of his ideas for an educational institution in America entitled *A General Idea of the College of Mirania* in 1753. Benjamin Franklin, impressed by Smith's ideas, invited him to join the faculty at Philadelphia Academy as a professor of logic, rhetoric and moral and natural philosophy. Two years later, when the Academy developed into the College of Philadelphia (now the University of Pennsylvania), Smith was appointed as its first provost, implementing a new curriculum closely resembling the proposals he had previously set out.[41]

The second person who must be singled out is John Witherspoon. Appointed as President of the College of New Jersey in 1768, he too introduced a curriculum that closely reflected the Scottish model. He added to the faculty a professor of mathematics and natural philosophy, and himself taught moral philosophy, divinity, rhetoric, history and French.[42] In doing so, Witherspoon channelled the ideas of the Enlightenment into the minds of his pupils, who, under his stewardship, included six delegates to the Continental Congress, twenty senators, twenty-three members of the House of Representatives, three justices of the Supreme Court, one vice-president, and one president of the United States.[43]

Philadelphia and New Jersey may have been the first American colleges to reveal the influence of the Scottish Enlightenment, but others were to follow. Dickenson College appointed the Scottish minister Charles Nisbet as its first president in 1785; he taught moral philosophy, mental philosophy, *belle lettres*, and logic – subjects that were core to the interests of the school of Scottish common-sense philosophy. Increasingly, such subjects were adopted into curricula elsewhere, with Scottish philosophers becoming standard reading. Works by Francis Hutchinson, Thomas Reid and William Duncan were typically used in such courses, while Hugh Blair's *Lectures on Rhetoric and Belles Lettres* went through no fewer than three dozen American editions, and was exposed to large numbers of college-educated Americans, including those at Yale, where it was introduced in 1785, and Harvard, where it was introduced in 1788.[44]

More impressive still was the Scottish influence upon the development of American medicine. Over 100 Scottish doctors are known to have migrated to the American colonies during the eighteenth century, with considerably more Americans coming to Scotland to gain a medical education.[45] Although some were attracted to Glasgow, which had opened its medical faculty in 1748, it was Edinburgh's, established in 1726, that by the second half of the century had gained a reputation as the leading medical school in Europe. It was during his time at Edinburgh that John Morgan began drawing up plans to establish a medical school at the College of Philadelphia.[46] Opened in 1765, not only was its curriculum and organisation based on Edinburgh, ten of the school's first twelve professors had attended Edinburgh medical school.[47] Two years later a second medical school was opened in America, at King's College, New York; two Edinburgh graduates and Scotsman Peter Middleton were instrumental in its establishment. Unlike Philadelphia, however, which survived the Revolution, King's College was disrupted, only to be re-established in 1792.[48]

The impact of medical study in Edinburgh on America extended beyond the inspiration to create medical schools. The study of medicine fostered specialisations in chemistry, botany, palaeontology and geology, and in general led to the academic institutionalisation of science.[49] A prime example of this was

Benjamin Rush who, after studying medicine at Edinburgh in 1766–8 where he became a disciple and friend of William Cullen, returned to the colonies to become Professor of chemistry in the College of Philadelphia's medical department; a year later he published the first American textbook on chemistry. In 1776 Rush represented Pennsylvania in the Continental Congress and, as the only signatory of the Declaration of Independence with a medical degree, was another founding father with a debt to Scotland.

C MOVING WEST

Scottish emigration to the United States after the Revolution was relatively slow in returning to pre-1775 levels. War between Britain and France from 1793 to 1815 interrupted outward movement, but even among those who did leave, Canada was the preferred destination.[50] By 1825, when the first reliable emigration statistics are available, the number of Scots entering the US was still in the low hundreds, less than half those bound for Canada.[51] Emigration levels between Scotland and the United States increased slowly, but it was not until the late 1840s that the annual figures exceeded 10,000 for the first time, and the US overtook Canada as the preferred emigrant destination among Scots.

As its popularity as an emigrant destination continued to grow, new passenger companies and sea routes developed to meet the demand. The Anchor and Allan Lines both began sailing between Glasgow and New York in 1856, and, in time, included routes to Baltimore, Philadelphia and New Orleans. In 1879, Donaldson Line also entered the fray, initially with sailings to Portland, Maine, and then also to Baltimore.[52] By the 1880s the number of Scots entering the US was consistently over 10,000 a year, and on occasion exceeded 20,000 – a pattern which continued into the next century, with a total of 171,149 Scots arriving in its first decade. Thirty-four ships sailed from the Clyde to the US in 1921 and thirty-seven the following year,[53] although Scottish movement into the States peaked in 1923 at 46,343, when, for the first time, the number exceeded that of England. This was something of an anomaly, brought about by the impending introduction of stricter quotas by the United States, limiting the number of foreign-born entrants to 2 per cent of the number of people from that country already living in the States. Concerns about its impact appear to have prompted many to make the move the year before its implementation, a move vindicated by the havoc wreaked on sailing arrangements in 1924.[54] In spite of the new legislation, migration afterwards continued to exceed 10,000 annually, and only with the onset of the Great Depression in the 1930s, when the numbers dropped dramatically, did Scotland cease making substantial additions to the US.

Until this point the total number of Scots living in the States had been steadily increasing: when place of birth was recorded for the first time in the 1850 census, there were 70,500 Scots or people of Scottish descent.[55] The American Civil War contributed to a decrease in the number of emigrants crossing the Atlantic, but it also provided an opportunity for many Scots to make their mark in the New World society in which they had settled. One of these Scots was Glasgow-born Allan Pinkerton, who made his way to the United States in 1842, initially settling in Dundee, Illinois, about 50 miles outside of Chicago. By 1844 Pinkerton, who had been a Chartist when still in Scotland, was a committed supporter of the abolition of slavery, with his home in Illinois being part of the network of safe houses known as the 'Underground Railroad' which stretched to the provinces of Canada where slavery was illegal. In 1849, Pinkerton became the first detective in Chicago, and was later involved in the formation of the North-Western Police Agency, a detective agency that became chiefly responsible for solving train robberies along the Illinois Central Railroad. It was in the context of this work that Pinkerton first met Abraham Lincoln. After the outbreak of the Civil War Pinkerton served in the Union Army, developing surveillance and undercover techniques. Between 1861 and 1862 Pinkerton was head of the Union Intelligence Service, a predecessor of the Secret Service, and, in that role, was responsible for guarding Abraham Lincoln (Figure 10.1), averting at least one assassination attempt.[56]

By 1900 the number of Scots or those of Scottish descent resident in the United States had climbed to 233,500, before peaking in 1930 at 354,500.[57] Most lived in the north-east, with the neighbouring states of Connecticut, Massachusetts, New Jersey, New York, Ohio and Pennsylvania containing the greatest concentrations. Amongst these, New York was consistently the most popular, and, by 1930, it was home to almost double the number of Scots of any other state.[58] North Carolina and Georgia, both of which had been among the most popular destinations before the Revolution, ceased to have as much importance. Not only did they fail to attract many new arrivals, but several of the original settlers uprooted with their families to Alabama, Mississippi, Tennessee and Texas.[59] Many soon joined the westward movement and, by 1850, several thousand Scots lived beyond the Mississippi River, with even more in between. The Midwestern state of Illinois alone was home to around 5,000 Scots, and was littered with communities such as Argyle, Bannockburn, Dundee and Midlothian.[60] Scots are also recognised as making an important contribution to the early development of the state's largest city, Chicago, which, by 1870, had a Scottish population that exceeded 4,000.[61] Elsewhere, place names such as Scotland County in Missouri, Inverness in California, and Montrose in Colorado reveal the widespread penetration of Scots across America, although, with fewer Scots emigrating in large groups, such naming practices were not necessarily a reflection of high densities of Scottish

Figure 10.1 Allan Pinkerton with Abraham Lincoln, c. 1861 [source: SCRAN; Resource Rights Holder: Hulton Getty; SCRAN ID: 000-000-202-999-C]

population. One of the last attempts at a planned settlement involving Scots in the US came in 1873 under the stewardship of George Grant, who, after carrying out an extensive publicity campaign in Scotland, was able to entice several families to his western Kansas settlement. Grant is also credited with introducing Aberdeen Angus cattle into the United States, but while they were able to thrive, drought, an invasion of grasshoppers, and Grant's premature death in 1878 led to the settlement's abandonment before it had become fully established.[62] When the Scottish population was at its largest in 1930, the north-east remained the most densely populated part of the country, although there were significant concentrations in the upper Midwest, and also along the West Coast in both California and Washington state. By 1930 it was also a predominantly urban population. Compared to 1850, when 75 per cent of Scots were classified as living in rural areas, by this time, it was 84 per cent urban.[63]

Another change that occurred over this period was the ratio between male and female Scottish migrants. Compared to the English, where men outnumbered women more than four to one in the years immediately prior to the American Revolution, the ratio among Scots was six to four.[64] This was still the case in 1850, although the gap had almost completely narrowed by the early twentieth century. The reason Scots had a higher proportion of women than the English was primarily due to the family nature of Scottish emigration to the States, although as is evident from later census data there were also many who arrived as single women.[65] As with the wider working female population, most female Scots were employed as domestic servants. While some of these may have performed their duties in farmhouses, unlike non-Scots comparatively few worked as farmers or farm labourers, instead being disproportionately represented in industrial pursuits, such as weaving or as other industrial operatives.

The pattern was similar among the Scottish male workforce. Although farming accounted for around 30 per cent of working Scotsmen in 1850, this was considerably less than the 50 per cent of non-Scots who were employed in agricultural pursuits. Half a century later, only 15 per cent of Scots were employed in agriculture, compared with 40 per cent of non-Scots. Overall, the Scottish male workforce was extremely diverse, with a mixture of manual and non-manual occupations, requiring varying degrees of skill and education. Yet there were certain occupations in which Scots were disproportionately represented.

One of these was mining. In 1900 it was the second most common occupation among Scottish men, accounting for 9 per cent of workers, compared with 2 per cent of non-Scots. Enticed by the discovery of precious metals, for years Scots had been coming to Colorado, Nevada, Wyoming and California to work in the mines.[66] By the turn of the century, however, Illinois could boast the highest number of Scottish miners. The state was home to several mining communities, one of which was named after James Braidwood, a Scotsman who sank the community's first mining shaft, where during a visit in 1867, Scottish mining leader Alexander McDonald claimed to have been greeted by 500 miners, most of whom were Scottish.[67] While the Scot to have most impact on the industry was John Stewart MacArthur, a Glaswegian chemist whose process of gold extraction dramatically increased gold production, the experience brought by ordinary miners who had learned the trade in Scotland was equally vital in the industry's development.[68]

Scottish experience was also influential to the Untied State's textile industry. Having played such a prominent role in the industrial revolution in Scotland, ideas were often replicated to help do the same in the US. While visiting Britain between 1810 and 1812 Francis Cabot Lowell closely studied the textile industries in Lancashire and Scotland. Upon his return he established the Boston Manufacturing Company, the first 'integrated' textile mill in the US which could convert raw cotton to finished cloth in one building. Not only did Lowell implement manufacturing techniques he had seen during his overseas visit, but working conditions and the provision of worker housing, schools and boarding houses were almost certainly inspired by those at Robert Owen's New Lanark.[69] Ideas were copied, and personnel were often recruited in Scotland. In 1853 an agent for the Hadley Falls mills in Massachusetts secured eighty-two female weavers and, in 1865, 200 women were recruited for the Holyoke mills, also in Massachusetts.[70] While recruitment of mill workers in Scotland had ceased by the end of the century, it is revealing that 10 per cent of the female Scottish workforce were employed as weavers in 1900, compared to 2 per cent of non-Scots.

In other aspects of the textile industry, Scottish companies were directly involved. By 1890, thread-making had become one of the most important segments of the American cotton textile industry, the leading company in which was J. & P. Coats of Paisley. Up until 1869 Coats had exported to the US, but the introduction of prohibitive tariffs and the strengthened position of its Paisley rival Clark & Co. in the States after securing a manufacturing subsidiary in New Jersey, led it to do likewise by acquiring the Conant Thread Company in Pawtucket, Rhode Island. J. & P. Coats soon surpassed Clark & Co. and, in 1896, the Company's strength was such that it was able to acquire its three main British rivals, including Clark & Co., as well as two of its manufacturing subsidiaries in the US. The company's eventual dominance in the American cotton thread industry has been attributed to its careful investment and its managerial structure, which, as well as having an American Department at its Paisley headquarters, had a board of directors responsible for routine operational procedures within each of its subsidiaries.[71] Several of these board members were members of the Coats family and although an analysis of the J. & P. Coats US workforce remains to be done, it would seem likely that, as with the textile workforce elsewhere, many, including its machine operators, mechanics, clerks and managers, were Scottish.

From the late eighteenth century until the first decades of the twentieth century, Scots penetrated all parts of the United States. Even in the Great

Plains, where they did not make a great numerical impact, Scottish capital played an important part in the region's development. In 1880 three-quarters of all foreign investment in the US originated in Scotland, with finances being primarily concentrated in railways, utilities, land mortgages and cattle ranches.[72] In particular, as obscure as it may seem, Scots came to dominate the ranch enterprises across the Midwest, there being eleven Scots-owned companies. These included the Swan Land and Cattle Company which had control of 600,000 acres in Nebraska and Wyoming, the Espuela Cattle Company, which controlled 500,000 acres across Texas, the XIT Ranch, with 3 million acres also in Texas, and the best known, the Dundee-based Matador Land and Cattle Company, which at the time of its purchase in 1882 had 40,000 heads of cattle and privileges on 1.5 million acres.[73] Under Scottish ownership the Matador Company invested in its property, changed pasturing practices and improved breeding techniques and in the process made considerable profits. A crude analysis of its workforce shows that just less than a quarter (385) of its cowboys had Scottish surnames. More significantly, it was at managerial level that Scots dominated.[74] Most of the company's ranch managers were Scottish immigrants, the longest serving of whom was Murdo Mackenzie, who held the position for forty-six years. Under his guidance, the company excelled, earning top prizes in cattle competitions and gaining international recognition.[75] Mackenzie was a friend of Theodore Roosevelt, who referred to him as 'the most influential of American cattlemen'.[76] Scots were also present as assistant managers, bookkeepers and foremen. Harsh winters and economic depression towards the end of the nineteenth century turned most Scottish investors away, although the Matador Land and Cattle Company did continue to operate until 1951, when it was sold for $20 million.[77] Like J. & P. Coats, the longevity and success of the Matador Land and Cattle Company has been attributed to good management.

D CONCLUSION

Dancing 'till the whole neighbourhood was afloat'; all ready to go to America. The transformation in Scotland's migration history – from its origins in the markets and professional armies of Eastern Europe, and early preference for the trading opportunities of Asia – to settlements of families and the development of cultural and economic exchange, at all levels of society, is epitomised by the migrant flows to America. Slow to capture the Scots' migratory attention, a pre-1760s trickle to the thirteen Colonies became a flood as the nineteenth century unfolded. From soldier settlement in Georgia to family settlement in New York, North Carolina and Chicago, the Scots flocked to America.

Land was not just economic and social freedom for migrants, it was an opportunity for Scots investors at home and within the host nation. The Scottish cowboy is a narrative that can be added to the Enlightenment power-houses of David Hume, Adam Ferguson and Adam Smith – even accounting for their influence on the likes of James Witherspoon and John Wilson – for the impact the 'Cowboy and the Indian' had on Scottish culture. 'A dance called America' returned as Sheriff Lobey Dosser, connecting the twa lands.

NOTES

1. Johnson, *A Journey to the Western Islands of Scotland*, p. 87.
2. Ibid., p. 147.
3. Boswell, *The Journal of a Tour to the Hebrides*, p. 145.
4. Ibid., p. 262.
5. Dobson, *Scottish Emigration to Colonial America*, p. 33.
6. Ibid., p. 45.
7. Murdoch, *Scotland and America*, p. 24.
8. Landsman, *Scotland and Its First American Colony*, p. 134.
9. Smout, Landsman and Devine, 'Scottish emigration in the seventeenth and eighteenth centuries', p. 98.
10. Dobson, *Scottish Emigration*, p. 81.
11. Parker, *Scottish Highlanders in Colonial Georgia*, p. 1.
12. The full text of the petition is reproduced in Parker, *Scottish Highlanders*, Appendix C, pp. 126 and 127.
13. See also Chapter 13 in this book.
14. McLean, *An Historical Account of the Settlements of Scotch Highlanders in America Prior to the Peace of 1783*, p. 182.
15. Meyer, *The Highland Scots of North Carolina*, p. 68.
16. Donaldson, 'Scots', p. 910.
17. Dobson, *Scottish Emigration*, p. 96.
18. Brumwell, *Redcoats*, p. 270.
19. Ibid., p. 266; see also Chapter 12 for details on the involvement of Scottish soldiers in Africa.
20. Bailyn, *Voyagers to the West*.
21. Calculations based on Bailyn's figures, ibid., p. 111.
22. Ibid., p. 173.
23. Ibid., p. 169.
24. Ibid., p. 205.
25. Ibid., p. 503.
26. Ibid., p. 206.
27. Price, 'The rise of Glasgow in the Chesapeake tobacco trade', p. 180.

28. Devine, 'The golden age of tobacco', p. 146.
29. Devine (ed.), *A Scottish Firm in Virginia*, p. x.
30. Dobson, *Scottish Emigration*, p. 103.
31. Fetter, 'Who were the foreign mercenaries of the Declaration of Independence?', p. 509.
32. Ibid.
33. Reference to the 'Burns Supper school of historians' was made by Shepperson in 'Writings in Scottish-American history', the introductory article in the *William and Mary Quarterly* special issue, vol. 11, no. 2 (April 1954). Two recent examples which fall into this category are: Herman, *How the Scots Invented the Modern World*; and Fry, *How the Scots Made America*.
34. Sher, 'Introduction: Scottish-American Cultural Studies, past and present', p. 20.
35. McCoy, *The Elusive Republic*.
36. Fleischacker, 'Adam Smith's reception among the American Founders', pp. 897–924.
37. Wills, *Inventing America*; Fleischacker, 'The impact on America', p. 324.
38. Walker Howe, 'Why the Scottish Enlightenment was useful to the framers of the American Constitution', p. 580.
39. Sloan, *The Scottish Enlightenment and the American College Ideal*, p. 1.
40. Brock, *Scotus Americanus*, p. 90.
41. Ibid., p. 111; Hook, 'Philadelphia, Edinburgh and the Scottish Enlightenment', p. 234; Sloan, *The Scottish Enlightenment*, p. 84.
42. Diamond, 'Witherspoon, William Smith and the Scottish philosophy in Revolutionary America', p. 128.
43. Fry, *The Scottish Empire*, p. 60.
44. Daiches, 'Style periodique and style coupe', p. 210.
45. Brock, *Scotus Americanus*, p. 118.
46. Brunton, 'The transfer of medical education', p. 244.
47. Ibid., p. 247.
48. Brock, *Scotus Americanus*, p. 119.
49. Sloan, *The Scottish Enlightenment*, p. 231.
50. Donaldson, 'Scots', p. 910.
51. Carrier and Jeffrey, *External Migration*.
52. Aspinwall, 'The Scots in the United States', p. 84.
53. Harper, *Emigration From Scotland, 1918–1939*, p. 29.
54. Ibid., p. 31.
55. US Census Aggregates, http://www.census.gov/prod/www/abs/decennial/ (accessed 15 February 2013).
56. For details on Pinkerton, see Morn, '*The Eye that Never Sleeps*'.
57. Ibid.

58. Data extracted from the National Historical Geographic Information System, http://www.nhgis.org (accessed 22 February 2013).

59. Ray, 'Scottish immigration and ethnic organization in the United States', p. 52.

60. Rethford and Skinner Sawyers, *The Scots of Chicago: Quiet Immigrants and Their New Society*, p. 147.

61. Noble, 'The Chicago Scots', p. 139; Rethford and Sawyers, *The Scots of Chicago*, p. 25.

62. Szasz, *Scots in the North American West*, pp. 83 and 84. See also Szasz, *Abraham Lincoln and Robert Burns*.

63. Data extracted from the National Historical Geographic Information System, http://www.nhgis.org (accessed 22 February 2013).

64. Bailyn, *Voyagers to the West*, p. 131.

65. Ibid., p. 140.

66. Szasz, *Scots in the North American West*, p. 85.

67. Aspinwall, 'The Scots in the United States,' p. 101.

68. Szasz, *Scots in the North American West*, p. 86.

69. Rosenberg, *The Life and Times of Francis Cabot Lowell*, p. 296.

70. Aspinwall, 'The Scots in the United States,' pp. 96 and 97.

71. All Coates references in Dong-Woon, 'The British multinational enterprise in the United States before 1914', pp. 523–51.

72. Campbell, *Scotland since 1707*, p. 66.

73. Swan, *Scottish Cowboys and the Dundee Investors*, p. 27.

74. Ibid., p. 52.

75. Ibid., p. 54.

76. Gibson, *Plaids and Bandanas*, p. 125.

77. Szesz, *Scots in the North American West*, p. 94.

CHAPTER 11

Canada

An article that appeared in the *Scottish Canadian* in 1890 uses an analogy in which the Scotsman is compared to a piece of cork. Regardless of where it is sunk, it always rises to the surface: 'It is so with a Scot. Plant him where you may, leave him only liberty of action, and he will make his presence felt; he will work his way to the surface of society.'[1] Beyond such contemporary observations, or the recent spate of popular histories claiming that the Scots 'invented' Canada, the impression created by several academics is that the Scots did enjoy a disproportionate influence in Canadian affairs. In *The National Dream: The Great Railway 1871–1881*, Pierre Berton states, the 'Irish outnumbered them, as they did the English, but the Scots ran the country. Though they formed only one-fifteenth of the population they controlled the fur trade, the great banking and financial houses, the major educational institutions, and, to a considerable degree, the government.'[2] Exemplified by the likes of George Simpson, one of the most influential individuals in the history of the Hudson's Bay Company, John A. Macdonald, a father of Canadian Confederation and the country's first prime minister, James McGill, a merchant and founder of McGill University in Montreal, and Donald A. Smith, who was pivotal in the building of the Canadian Pacific Railway, the *Dictionary of Canadian Biography* is strewn with high achieving Scots.[3] According to a study of Canadian business in the 1880s, in spite of only making up 3 per cent of the general population, Scots accounted for 20 per cent of the industrial elite, higher than any other non-Canadian ethnic group, and based on father's birthplace, 28 per cent were from Scotland, also higher than all ethnic groups, including those born in Canada.[4] Author of the study T. W. Acheson writes,

> The most characteristic Canadian success stories were those of the large group of young sons of Scottish farmers who, armed with little more than a traditional craftsman's training, descended upon the Canadas

in the 1840s and '50's and by dint of industry and frugal living rose in middle age to the proprietorships of substantial manufacturing establishments.[5]

Yet while the story of enterprising Scots remains one of the central narratives of Canadian history, it has recently been suggested that this greatly simplifies the actual process by which Canadian business and Canadian society developed. While a substantial number of Scots were involved in business circles, of the business community as a whole, their total numbers were fairly modest. As Canadian historian Douglas McCalla states, '"Scot" and "businessman" were not synonyms, and most Scots, like most other people in Canada, were not members of the leading business circles.'[6] Furthermore examination of Scots living in one of Canada's largest cities, Toronto, in the late nineteenth and early twentieth centuries, shows that Scots were more likely to be unskilled labourers than high-level businessmen or professionals.[7] This does not diminish the contribution of Scots in Canada, but rather serves as a reminder that the experiences of these immigrants were not one shared by the majority of migrants Scots. Additionally, reducing the account of Scots in Canada to that of a few individual contributions ignores many other important aspects of the narrative.

A SCOTS IN THE FUR TRADE

As the first transcontinental business enterprise, from the early sixteenth century indigenous people were exchanging furs and meats with Europeans who in return could offer tools, weapons, blankets and trinkets. While the Scots can claim little involvement in its early activities, when they did enter its fray a century later, it heralded the beginning of a long and far-reaching association. The extent to which Scots became involved in the trade, which played such a fundamental role in the creation of Canada, was so intrinsic that it arguably represents their greatest contribution to Canadian history.

In 1670 Charles II granted a charter to the Hudson's Bay Company for exclusive rights to all trade and natural resources in the territory drained by waters flowing into the Hudson Strait, a vast area encompassing about 15 per cent of the North American continent. The Company established trading-posts at the mouths of the major rivers leading into the Bay, where Native trappers would bring furs to trade. In particular there was a large demand for beaver pelts, used to make wide-brimmed felt hats which were highly fashionable in Europe at the time. The trading-posts were manned by workers who were initially recruited from the surrounding environs of the HBC's London headquarters, although dissatisfaction at their poor work habits prompted it to look further afield for more suitable candidates. In 1682 John Nixon, appointed the second governor to the Bay, suggested that Scotland should be considered as a source of labour,

> for that countrie is a hard country to live in, and poore-mens wages is cheap, they are hardy people both to endure hunger, and could, and are subject to obedience, and I am sure that they will serve for 6 pound pr. Year, and be better content, with their dyet than Englishmen.[8]

Although some Scots found their way into the Company's employment, it was not until the eighteenth century that the Company realised that its labour needs could be met at the same place as the HBC ships made their final stop before embarking on their Atlantic journey towards the Hudson's Bay.

The Orkney Islands met Nixon's demands for men who were used to a harsh environment, and with repeated crop failures, there was an ample supply of workers who could be enticed by £6 a year. Stromness, therefore, became the ideal place for picking up both provisions and men. So successful was this strategy that, by the 1730s, over half of HBC recruits came from the Orkneys – a number that rose to an even more significant 80 per cent by the turn of the nineteenth century.[9] Most served contracts of eight years or less, being employed in various tasks that included building and maintaining the trading posts, making and repairing trade goods, and transporting supplies and furs.[10] In spite of their perceived hardiness, there is no evidence that Scots or Orcadians in particular bore the extreme climate, scarcity, disease and other hazards faced in the Canadian wilderness better than any other ethnicity.[11] Although few Orcadians rose up the fur trade hierarchy, employment with the Company for a limited period enabled them to save enough money to purchase a farm when they returned home. The arrangement worked out for both parties until about the middle of the nineteenth century, when the HBC changed its trading policy and began moving its posts into the Canadian interior. Orcadians were reluctant to expose themselves to the discomforts of inland service and the Company was forced to start looking elsewhere for employees, although it continued to recruit some Orkney natives right up until 1891, when its ships ceased calling at Stromness.[12]

That the HBC had to change its ways of trade was largely a response to rival traders who were willing to push inland to carry out trade. Of greatest competition was the North West Company, an amalgamation of mostly Scottish traders based in Montreal which began coming together in 1783. Its key architect was Simon McTavish, an emigrant Scot who arrived in the American colonies in 1764 at the age of thirteen. Described as Canada's leading businessman of the second half of the nineteenth century, McTavish successfully built a business empire across the Canadian North-west, which,

Figure 11.1 Settlers in Western Canada [source: SCRAN; Resource Rights Holder: North Ronaldsay Heritage Trust; SCRAN ID: 000-000-584-515-C]

at its peak, operated almost 100 posts and employed up to 1,500 men.[13] Key in expanding the Company's business were two Scottish explorers, both of whom led several daring expeditions deep into the Canadian interior. Having helped to establish a trading fort on the Athabasca River, Alexander Mackenzie embarked on an expedition to find the Northwest Passage to the Pacific Ocean in 1789. Although unsuccessful, instead reaching the Arctic, he remained undeterred, setting out on a second expedition during which he made it to the Pacific, becoming the first European to cross North America north of Mexico. Also in search of a route which would allow overland transportation to the Pacific was Simon Fraser, a Scot who, in 1801 at the age of twenty-five, became one of the North West Company's youngest partners. Tasked with expanding the Company's operations west of the Rocky Mountains, Fraser led one of Canada's most daring explorations during which he discovered the river that would take his name. He established the first European settlements and a series of fur trading posts in a territory largely conterminous with what is now British Columbia, but which he named New Caledonia.

Many other Scots penetrated the ranks of the North West Company, and of its 128 senior figures from 1760 to 1800, seventy-seven had a Scottish background.[14] Although few were as adventurous as Mackenzie and Fraser, in 1785 the Beaver Club was formed in Montreal, with an exclusive membership limited to those fur traders who had spent at least one winter in the interior. Not all members were Scottish, but meetings appear to have represented something of a blend in highland and fur trading culture. Meals were piped in and plenty of whisky, along with other alcoholic beverages, was consumed. As one attendee of a meeting observed:

> In those days we dined at four o'clock, and after taking a satisfactory
> quantity of wine, perhaps a bottle each, the married men . . . retired,
> leaving about a dozen to drink to their health. We now began in right
> earnest and true highland style, and by four in the morning, the whole
> of us had arrived at such a state of perfection, that we could all give the
> war-whoop as well as Mackenzie and McGillivray, we could all sing
> admirably, we could all drink like fishes, and we all thought we could
> dance on the table without disturbing a single decanter, glass or place
> . . . We discovered that it was a complete delusion . . . and we broke all
> the plates, glass bottles, and the table also . . .[15]

The climax of the evening was 'The Grand Voyage' where members and guests sat on the floor in a row as if in a great canoe. With fire tongs, walking sticks or other props for paddles, they dipped and swung as they sang voyageur songs.

Competition between the two companies grew fierce and at times violent until their eventual merger in 1821, when the North West Company was essentially absorbed by the Hudson's Bay Company. Although the reasons behind the union were manifold, the crisis that brought the violent rivalry to a head and precipitated the merger involved the slaughter of twenty HBC men at the massacre of Seven Oaks in 1816. In 1811 the Hudson's Bay Company granted one of its major shareholders, Thomas Douglas, Earl of Selkirk, 116,000 square miles of land for the fee of 10 shillings. Selkirk advocated emigration as a solution to the problems of the Highlands and had previously established settlements of highlanders in Prince Edward Island and Upper Canada. He intended to set up a new colony at Red River, near present-day Winnipeg, for which in return he would supply the HBC with 200 workers each year and allow its officers to retire there. The North West Company was bitterly opposed to the colony, which its managers believed would affect their production of pemmican (dried buffalo meat in fat) which formed the core diet of their interior traders. When the colony's governor, Miles Macdonell, forbade the export of pemmican from the settlement, it confirmed the Nor' Westers' belief that the colony was a threat to their trade, sparking a course of intimidation which ended in the Seven Oaks massacre. The settlement was, however, beset with other problems, including a series of natural disasters. Yet while it thus could never be considered a success, it is significant in marking the beginning of the process that would extend Canada far beyond its hitherto commercial heartlands along the St Lawrence River.[16]

When the HBC and North West Company merged, it did little to alter the predominance of Scots. The major authority in the new regime was George Simpson who became the new Governor of the Northern Department and soon rose to be Governor of all of Rupert's Land (as all the HBC territories were called). His nickname Little Emperor reflected both his dislikeable personality and his success at building up the HBC empire. From 1821 to 1870, the year when the Company's territories became part of the Dominion of Canada, 171 out of 263 commissioned officers were of Scottish origin.[17] As well as favouring Scottish officers, the Company continued to employ Scots as clerks, skilled tradesmen and labourers. In 1870 it recruited twenty-eight men from the Orkneys, thirteen from Stornoway, and ten from the Shetlands, but unlike a century earlier the majority of Hudson's Bay Company employees were now native-born.

B PRE-CONFEDERATION PATTERNS OF SETTLEMENT

While the fur trade may account for the first significant presence of Scots in Canada, the earliest parties of Scottish emigrants with the intention of permanent settlement did not begin arriving until 1770. In that year a group of indentured servants made its way to St John's Island (renamed Prince Edward Island in 1799). In return for free passage and land, these settlers had to work for four years on a flax plantation that was being established on the island.[18] They were soon followed by a second group of settlers from Argyle, and then, in 1772, by 200 Roman Catholic highlanders, some of whom were escaping religious persecution. Although the Thirteen Colonies remained the preferred North American destination of Scottish emigrants at this time, the Maritimes continued to attract a small flow of Scottish settlers. In 1773 100 further settlers arrived when the *Hector* landed on the north coast of Nova Scotia in what is often depicted as the birth of 'New Scotland'.[19] An advertisement for settlers had appeared in Scottish newspapers in September 1772, offering land and passage for £7 5s per adult. For those who paid the sum, it was a gruesome experience. The *Hector* was old and according to one account 'so rotten that the passengers could pick the wood out of her sides with their fingers.'[20] Poor weather slowed the journey, creating a scarcity of provisions, while smallpox and dysentery also took their toll, claiming the lives of eighteen infants. When the ship did eventually reach land, the passengers were shocked to be faced with dense forest as far as the eye could see. The prospect of what lay ahead drove many to tears and, according to accounts, the first few years were filled with many horrors and hardships. That said, within a year, wheat, rye, peas, barley, oats and flax were all being successfully grown, and the settlement was in possession of herds of oxen, cows, cattle, sheep and a pig.[21] The settlement had also started producing timber, which would soon become a major source of income. In spite of the initial hardships, within several years, the worst had been overcome and the settlement was able to welcome other Scottish emigrants to their fold. Many more would follow but by the outbreak of the American Revolution in 1775, the Maritime colonies were home to little more than a 1,000 emigrant Scots.[22]

As discussed in Chapter 10, the American Revolution led to the recruitment of thousands of highlanders for the purpose of serving in the conflict, as well as causing considerable disruption among the Scottish communities in Georgia, the Carolinas and New York. Upon the cessation of hostilities in 1783, a significant number of settlers were not keen on living in the emergent Republic, seeking refuge instead in what became known as British North America. These so-called Loyalists, approximately 50,000 in total, included an estimated 10,000 Scots.[23] As a result of their migration, many new settlements and towns were established in the Maritimes, with the greatest concentration of Scots locating to St John's Island, where land was granted to former officers, and around Pictou in Nova Scotia, where much of the area was given to men of the 84th Regiment (The Royal Highland Emigrants).[24]

As well as reinforcing the Scottish presence in the Maritimes, a proportion of Scottish Loyalists were settled on what, in 1791, would become Upper

Canada (and later Ontario). These included one of Canada's most enduring highland communities, comprising emigrants originally from western
Invernessshire, who, in 1773, had settled in New York and were subsequently
relocated to Upper Canada's Glengarry County. The original settlers were followed by others who arrived directly from the Highlands and, after a series of
nine migrations between 1785 and 1815, around 2,500 Scots were settled in the
area.[25] Over 90 per cent of the migrants travelled with family members, and
often as part of a larger community group, enabling the rebuilding of almost
whole western Invernessshire communities and ensuring a remarkable degree
of cultural transfer and continuity.[26]

Elsewhere Gaelic communities also flourished. Emigrants, both Loyalist
and pre-American Revolution arrivals living in highland enclaves, maintained
links with families and friends who had remained in Scotland. Similar to
the Glengarry settlement, these continued connections facilitated migration
streams which added to the strength of these communities. Between 1776
and 1815, a total of 13,000 Scots, most of whom were highlanders, emigrated
to British North America.[27] Although considerably greater than the numbers
previously coming to these parts of the North American continent, they
were still considerably less than the earlier rates among Scots headed to the
Thirteen Colonies. In part, this was a direct result of warfare in North America
and Europe disrupting migration routes, but also of the growing hostility in
Britain towards emigration. The authorities in Prince Edward Island, Cape
Breton and Nova Scotia each received warnings in the late eighteenth century
about encouraging emigration to their territories from the British government,
which at home demonstrated its antipathy towards emigration by putting
the cost of passage beyond the means of most prospective emigrants with
the passing of the Passenger Vessel Act of 1803 (see Chapter 5).[28] Yet, there
were developments in the transatlantic shipping trade that ensured passage
costs did not get out of hand. Whereas ships carrying emigrants had formerly
returned virtually cargo-free, demand for timber, which was in great supply
in British North America, soon ensured that both directions of the voyage
could be profitable. The vessels used in the trade could be crudely adapted for
carrying passengers, who, as well as providing a paying cargo, supplemented
the timber-cutting workforce, of which highlanders proved to be quite adept.
In this way the timber trade was vital in sustaining Scottish immigration to
British North America when it had few other proponents.[29]

It would be misleading, however, to suggest that emigration had no influential supporters. While the government and most highland landlords were
strongly opposed, the previously encountered Earl of Selkirk was convinced
that colonising North American lands could help uprooted highlanders and be
of benefit to the colonies. To demonstrate this, he purchased land on Prince
Edward Island for which he recruited 800 highlanders. Having arrived and

settled successfully in 1803, the following year he was granted 1,200 acres on Lake St Clair on a site he named Baldoon, where he established another highland settlement. Unfortunately, due to natural problems with the site and managerial difficulties, the settlement became an expensive failure. While this may have curbed Selkirk's enthusiasm for some time, a decade later he embarked on his grandest foray into colonisation with the establishment of Red River. As we have already seen, this settlement was also beset with problems and by the time of his death in 1820, Selkirk was virtually bankrupt from trying to save it. Yet in spite of uncertainty surrounding Red River's future, the arguments that had driven him to embark on these schemes, which he set out forcefully in *Observations of the Present State of the Highlands* published in 1805, had gained much acceptance and, by 1815, a new era of emigration was looming.

Following the Napoleonic Wars the British government offered demobilised military personnel and civilians who could provide a certificate of character, in return for a £16 deposit, free passage, plots of 100 acres in new settlements along the Ottawa Valley and supplies for six months after their arrival.[30] Although the government's primary intent was to create a line of protection against invasion from the United States, the scheme demonstrates a changed attitude towards emigration. One of the first movements included 700 Scots who set sail from Glasgow in August 1815. They settled in Lanark County, which, by the following year, had grown to 1,500 strong. Spiralling costs and dispute over the merits of assisted emigration led to the scheme's abandonment, but as economic conditions in Scotland continued to decline, the government was forced to step in to help unemployed textile workers in Glasgow and Paisley emigrate to Upper Canada. A total of 2,700 people emigrated in 1820 and 1821 as part of this government scheme.

The government was not, however, alone in offering assistance to emigrants. The scheme agreed to by officials for the textile workers did not include the cost of passage which in theory had to be paid by the emigrants themselves. In reality, though, much was raised by private donation, with individuals and groups increasingly stepping in to assist emigrants to Canada. As the economic situation in the Highlands further deteriorated, more and more landlords also provided support for their tenants in making the transatlantic move. One of the most active was John Gordon of Cluny who dispatched 3,200 tenants to Canada.[31]

Most emigrants, attracted by the opportunity to possess their own land, however, paid their own way. Yet in spite of vast areas of uncultivated land, obtaining holdings was often more difficult than emigrants had been led to believe. By 1826 land companies controlled large parts of British North American on which they undertook clearing operations, built roads and buildings, and then sold plots to occupying settlers. The largest and most successful was the Canada Company, whose first superintendent in Canada was Scottish writer John Galt; within a decade it had sold 100,000 acres to settlers. According to one account

> The land here is good and well-watered, the terms of the Upper Canada Land Company are liberal, requiring the settler only to pay a fifth of the purchase money when the land is applied for, and the remainder in five yearly instalments with interest at six per cent . . . There are grist mills and saw mills within a few miles of us east and west, also a store where goods of all kinds are sold. This settlement is mostly Scotch, almost wholly so where we are settled, and the utmost goodwill and unanimity prevails. We enjoy, though obtained at present by hard labour and perseverance, all the necessary worldly comforts and with the prospect, if we and our families are spared, of seeing them and us all independent and comfortable farmers, farming our own land.[32]

In pursuing its activities, the Company carried out an aggressive marketing campaign involving the placement of agents at key British ports and distribution of printed material. One pamphlet published in 1841 summarising the benefits of emigrating to Canada, stated that the Scots were the most successful settlers.[33]

Scots were unlikely to be any more or less successful than other emigrants arriving in Canada at this time, but with more than 150,000 Scots emigrating to British North America between 1815 and Canadian Confederation in 1867, they did so at considerably higher rates than before the Napoleonic Wars.[34] As well as an increase in numbers, the pattern of migration also underwent some changes. According to a study of 7,478 Scots who emigrated to British North America between 1770 and 1870 (about 4 per cent of Scots in early Canada), not only did the origins of emigrants change, but so did their settlement patterns. Highlanders continued to outnumber lowlanders throughout the period, although their dominance was in steady decline. The Maritimes, which had long been the favoured destination of Scots and dominated the period pre-1815, saw Scottish emigration fall behind Ontario, even among highlanders who continued to move in kin groups, in well-defined migration streams. Availability of land accounts for the movement west, where migrants could, to a large extent, reproduce the demographic, cultural, linguistic and religious characteristics of their old highland communities.[35]

In contrast, lowlander emigration tended to comprise individuals or small family groups. Lowlanders are often seen as assimilating more easily into their surroundings and leaving less trace of their Scottish heritage.[36] Yet the extent to which this is true is questionable. While they may not have emigrated in community groups at a level similar to that of highlanders, there are examples.

In 1835, for instance, twenty emigrants from Aberdeen established a settlement called Bon Accord, named after the motto on their home city's coat of arms. These settlers were augmented by secondary waves of emigrants from Aberdeenshire, many of whom were family, neighbours and business associates who had followed in the wake of favourable reports.[37] Even those lowland Scots who did not settle in the vicinity of each other could maintain ties. Emigrant letters reveal informal networks of Scots stretching across vast areas amongst which advice is exchanged, temporary shelter for emigrants arranged and even loans provided. These geographically dispersed communities of lowland Scots point to the durability and flexibility of their Scottish ties and identity.[38]

C   PATTERNS OF SETTLEMENT POST-CONFEDERATION

In 1867 the British North American Act brought about a union of colonies to form the Dominion of Canada. Originally made up of Ontario, Quebec, Nova Scotia and New Brunswick, it soon expanded to include Manitoba and British Colombia, creating an expansive territory that stretched across the North American continent. Confederation was expected to boost immigration and, in particular, the opening of the prairies to large-scale agricultural colonisation. The building of the Canadian Pacific Railway (CPR) was fundamental in that it was hoped to transform Canada into a major immigrant destination. Yet in spite of the establishment of new international emigration offices and a massive propaganda effort to attract immigrants by the CPR, during the three decades that followed Confederation, Canada actually lost more of its population through emigration to the United States than it was able to gain from immigration. The unwillingness of the profit-driven CPR to allow land prices to fall too low, combined with poor farming conditions, meant that for at least the time being the United States offered better economic prospects for Canadians and prospective immigrants alike.

The turning point in Canadian immigration came in 1896 with the coming of the Liberals to government. Although largely the consequence of improving world economic conditions, Clifford Sifton, the minister in charge of immigration between 1896 and 1905, played a crucial role by encouraging the solicitation of immigrants beyond the British Isles and instigating a more business-like approach to the immigration process. Central to this was the role of immigration agents employed by the Canadian government to promote Canada as a destination to potential migrants. As many as five agents worked in Scotland at any one time, attending markets, cattle shows and fares, carrying out lecture tours, corresponding with and often meeting interested parties, and ensuring that Canada maintained a positive and prominent presence in the print media. In 1899 alone, 1,000 letters were received and replied to regarding emigration, 50,000 pamphlets were distributed, and fifty lectures were held by agents throughout the country.[39] These efforts were supplemented by emigration agents from the older provinces who worked to ensure that areas of Canada other than the prairies were promoted, and by steamship agents whose importance was well recognised by government agents who met with them regularly and kept them well supplied with the latest Canadian promotional literature.[40]

As well as being enticed by increasingly sophisticated promotional techniques, at various points between 1867 and 1914 Scots could take advantage of a limited number of assisted emigration schemes to Canada. In an effort to attract greater numbers of agricultural workers and female domestic servants, between 1872 and 1888 the Canadian government offered subsidised fares to both these classes of immigrants. Free land was another form of enticement. In 1872 the New Brunswick provincial government granted 50,000 acres for the establishment of a 'Scotch Colony' which was named New Kincardineshire after the area of Scotland from which most of its settlers were recruited.[41] The first contingent was made up of 750 settlers who had taken advantage of land grants up to 200 acres in size. The scheme was an experiment in community emigration and a further demonstration that such types of movement were not exclusive to highland communities. A later subsidised scheme, this time financed by the British government, involved the settlement of crofter families from the Outer Hebrides to Killarney, Manitoba in 1888, and a similar scheme the following year to Saltcoats (in what is now Saskatchewan).

Charitable and religious organisations also played their part in bringing emigrants to Canada. The Salvation Army, for example, became the largest single emigration agency in the British Empire, helping tens of thousands of working-class men, women and children to make their way to the colonies, with the majority destined for Canada.[42] Other smaller-scale operations worked specifically in Scotland, usually with a more narrow focus. Between 1883 and 1914 the Aberdeen Ladies' Union oversaw the emigration of 330 women, primarily to Canada, while others, such as Aberlour Orphanage, Whinewell Home and various local authority institutions, were responsible for the emigration of children.[43] As we have already seen in Chapter 5, the largest promoter of children's emigration was Quarrier's Orphan Homes of Scotland, which sent almost 7,000 children overseas, with the majority moving to Canada. In some years these children accounted for more than 10 per cent of the total number of emigrants departing Scotland.[44]

Most immigrants arriving from Scotland, however, made their own way, without government or charitable assistance. It is even questionable how much influence the activities of emigration agents had on the flow of migrants to Canada. In spite of the upsurge in agent activity after 1896, it was not until 1903 that Scottish emigration to Canada began to accelerate strongly. Although there had been an increase between 1900 and 1902, from 1,733 to 3,811, the following year numbers exceeded 10,000, and had doubled again by 1906. Scottish emigration to Canada peaked in 1911 at 41,218, to then level off until the outbreak of war, which brought the numbers crashing down again. Favourable economic conditions in Canada combined with uncertainty in Scotland were ultimately responsible for the dramatic rise in Scots leaving for Canada, although this pattern broadly replicated that of Canadian immigration as a whole, suggesting that Scottish emigration to Canada was part of a wider phenomenon and migratory cycles of which diverse ethnic groups were part.

As was intended by Canadian policy-makers, many Scottish settlers were attracted to the west as agricultural settlers. The opportunity to own land in 'the last best west', as the prairies were marketed, was a strong enticement to Scots who had little hope of doing so if they remained at home. Yet for other Scots, owning land does not appear to have been a priority. In spite of Canada's explicit discouragement of urban immigrants, many Scots (along with other ethnic groups) made their way to Canadian cities. Although they became widely dispersed, giving the impression of widespread assimilation, urban Scots maintained their strong ethnic identity through the Presbyterian Church and a thriving associational culture. The best known of these organisations was the St Andrew's Society whose membership was usually comprised of the business and social elite, but more representative of the Scottish community were in fact skilled manual and non-manual workers such as carpenters and blacksmiths, or clerks and salesmen.[45]

Not surprisingly the First World War brought about considerable disruption to immigration, and although it did not halt it completely, emigration from Scotland to Canada reached its lowest post-Confederation levels. While not returning to their pre-war high, Scots re-established their interest in Canada after the First World War, with the numbers moving to the country in the 1920s always exceeding an annual rate of 10,000.[46] For its part Canada was becoming increasingly reticent about accepting immigrants in such large numbers, and certain measures were introduced to restrict immigration. Although not aimed at immigrants from the British Isles, when the British government passed the Empire Settlement Act – an act designed to facilitate the emigration of British people to Empire destinations as well as a means to siphon off Britain's surplus population – Canada was a reluctant partner at best.[47] Canadian authorities were concerned that Canada would become a dumping ground for Britain's unemployed and undesirable population. Those Canada was willing to assist were, therefore, limited to agricultural workers, household workers and children, each class of which had to adhere to numerous additional conditions. Improved economic circumstances and growing public pressure led to the establishment of the '3,000 Families Scheme' of which many Scottish farming families took advantage and, by 1926, the Canadian government had agreed to spend an amount equal to that of the British government to contribute to the cost of passage, on placement and after-care for farm workers and household workers. Approved voluntary organisations were also able to benefit from Empire Settlement, receiving matching funds from the British government for what they spent on assistance to emigrants. George Cossar, a Scottish physician, established a training farm for boys near Glasgow where they spent three months before being sent to Australia or Canada, where they would take up work with a farming family. In total, 688 boys emigrated to Canada having passed through Dr Cossar's farms, and there were plenty more who emigrated under the auspices of other charitable organisations who similarly received funding under the Empire Settlement Act.

Of the 100,000 immigrants assisted through its various schemes, it is difficult to know how many were Scottish. In some cases the response was overwhelming. In 1928, when the 10,000 unemployed workers were sought for the Canadian harvest, 5,000 applications were received from Scots in the space of less than a week. Of the 8,449 who actually went out, over one third were Scots.[48] Unfortunately the experiment of using unemployed coal miners to harvest fields did not pay off, and 6,000 of the men returned to the UK. Others were more successful, including those who had taken advantage of the 3,000 Families Scheme and the approximately 500 Hebrideans who formed the Clandonald settlement organised by the Scottish Immigration Aid Society.[49] The effects of the Act must also be kept in perspective. Of the 15,473 Scots who emigrated to Canada in 1927, only 2,000 did so with the intention of taking up agricultural work. This would suggest that in spite of the Canadian government's best efforts, at least amongst Scottish emigrants, town and cities were the primary destination. Empire settlement was essentially brought to an end in 1930 when the Canadian government suspended immigration from Europe. While not completely cutting the flow of Scottish emigrants bound for Canada, the Great Depression reduced it to a very slow pace, from which it would never fully rebound.

D CONCLUSION

The Orcadians' predominance in the Hudson's Bay Company and the highlanders' infiltration of the North West Company have been a lasting narrative indicative of the Scots' engagement with Canada. Alongside fur, it was timber that underpinned transatlantic trade; commonly it was the migrant ship's cargo on the eastern leg of its voyage to pick up more Scots preparing for their new lives. For good reason 'Homecoming' – as organised by the Scottish

Government in 2009 and again in 2014 – had its origins in the 1999 homecoming of Canadians of Orcadian descent.

Canada was a place for Scots migrants in business, for Scots to do business with, and Canada was a place for settlement – for soldiers, individuals, families, communities and clans. Chain migration to the Maritime provinces stood alongside more scattered migration to the urban settlements of Upper Canada – with arrivals later travelling to Manitoba, Saskatchewan and British Columbia as those Provinces' policies of boosterism encouraged immigration facilitated by improvements in transportation.

Imagining a new start within British conditions, Quarrier's first orphans came in 1872, and a steady flow of children was to follow. The Quarrier Home in Brockville, Ontario, established in 1898, acted as a 'distribution centre' for orphaned and abandoned Scots boys and girls. Their successful migration was never less than precarious, with much dependent on the hiring or (it was hoped) adopting family. That these vulnerable children were sent in the first place – pictured on board smiling with their newly gifted dolls and teddy bears in hand – shows a marked confidence in a Canadian future.

NOTES

1. *The Scottish Canadian*, 4 December 1890.
2. Berton, *The National Dream: The Great Railway*, p. 319.
3. *Dictionary of Canadian Biography Online*, http://www.biographi.ca/index-e.html (accessed 22 February 2013).
4. Acheson, 'The social origins of the Canadian industrial elite', pp. 144–74.
5. Ibid., p. 152.
6. McCalla, 'Sojourners in the snow?', p. 82.
7. Hinson, 'Migrant Scots in a British city'.
8. Burley, *Servants of the Honourable Company*, p. 64.
9. Hicks, 'Orkneymen in the HBC', p. 119.
10. Burley, *Servants of the Honourable Company*, p. 1.
11. Rigg, *Men of Spirit and Enterprise*, p. 90.
12. Ibid.
13. Simon McTavish entry in *Dictionary of Canadian Biography Online*, http://www.biographi.ca/index-e.html (accessed 11 February 2013).
14. Pannekoek, *The Fur Trade and Western Canadian Society*, p. 12.
15. Ibid., p. 12.
16. Marshall, 'British North America', p. 392.
17. Mitchell, 'The Scot in the fur trade', p. 42.
18. Campey, *An Unstoppable Force*, p. 68.
19. Vance, 'Powerful pathos', p. 158.

20. Bumsted, *The People's Clearance*, p. 62.
21. Ibid., p. 64.
22. Bumsted, 'Scots'.
23. Devine, *Scotland's Empire*, p. 210.
24. Bumsted, 'Scottish emigration to the Maritimes', p. 74.
25. McLean, 'Peopling Glengarry County: The Scottish origins of a Canadian community', p. 157.
26. McLean, *The People of Glengarry*, p. 5.
27. Bumsted, 'Scottish emigration to the Maritimes', p. 67.
28. Devine, *Scotland's Empire*, p. 209.
29. Campey, *An Unstoppable Force*, p. 41.
30. Harper, *Adventurers and Exiles*, p. 37.
31. Ibid., p. 53.
32. Peter McNaughton to Revd D. Duff, 24 October 1835, quoted in Campey, *An Unstoppable Force*, p. 92.
33. Harper, *Emigration From North-East Scotland*, Volume 1, p. 199.
34. Carrier and Jeffrey, *External Migration*.
35. Hornsby, 'Patterns of Scottish emigration to Canada', p. 412.
36. Gray, 'The course of Scottish emigration', p. 19.
37. Harper, *Emigration From North-East Scotland*, vol. 1, p. 223.
38. Gibson, '"In quest of a better hame"', p. 128.
39. Sessional Papers of the Dominion of Canada, 1900.
40. Ibid., 1888.
41. Harper, *Adventurers and Exiles*, p. 156.
42. Magee and Thompson, *Empire and Globalisation*, p. 94.
43. Harper, *Adventurers and Exiles*, p. 276.
44. Abrams, *The Orphan Country*, p. 125.
45. McNabb, 'Butcher, baker, cabinetmaker?', pp. 242–262; Hinson, 'Migrant Scots in a British city'.
46. Carrier and Jeffrey, *External Migration*, p. 96.
47. Schultz, '"Leaven for the lump"', p. 150.
48. *Glasgow Herald*, 6–14 August 1928.
49. Parliamentary Papers, Report by the Earl of Clarendon and Mr T. C. MacNaughten on their visit to Canada in connection with British Settlement, HMSO (2760).

CHAPTER 12

Africa

By the time journalist and explorer Henry Morton Stanley had located Scottish missionary David Livingstone on the shores of Lake Tanganyika in what is now Tanzania in late 1871, allegedly greeting him with the words 'Dr Livingstone, I presume',[1] Livingstone's accounts of his work and explorations in Africa had long since found a captive audience around the world.[2] It was through Livingstone, and explorers such as Mungo Park, that Africa was placed firmly on the Scottish diaspora map.[3] Their charting of unknown lands and missionary activity was substantial throughout the African continent, though the most enduring links between Scotland and Africa were forged in southern Africa. Yet while the role of missionaries was very important for the Scottish connection with the continent, a Scottish influence can be traced in several spheres of life, including that of the military. It was in the late nineteenth century that Scottish regiments cemented their role as empire-builders, fighting at many fronts throughout the British Empire. Africa was a key battleground, especially at the turn of the century when the Anglo-Boer War waged in southern Africa, impacting significantly upon the region and the very fabric of the British Empire. Elsewhere, Scots left notable imprints in the mining industry. In the Rand they were engaged in the growing number of gold and diamond mines – not only as workers, but also as organisers of mining trades unions. Yet while born out of a socialist ideal brought from the Clyde in the late nineteenth century, the Scottish involvement in trades unions in southern Africa de facto contributed to wider social developments that eventually fed into the segregation of blacks and whites. By the 1920s, in fact, trade unionism in southern Africa was deeply racialised, and the slogan had become one not of miners' rights, but of white miners' superiority. With this in mind, the connections of Scots with southern Africa also permit consideration of the important issues of race and racial interactions at the African frontier. Some of the roots of these interactions, however, can be found in the Scots' involvement in the slave trade. The question, therefore, must not only be whether slavery helped make Scotland great,[4] but also how the involvement of Scots in the slave trade impacted upon Africa itself, being the earliest example of Scottish influence on the continent prior to any of the connections that subsequently developed through missionary activity, the military, business or cultural ties. It is to the slave trade, therefore, that this chapter first turns its attention.

A   THE SLAVE TRADE AND THE SCOTS IN AFRICA

As Devine has recently emphasised, the role of Scots in the slave trade has largely been ignored in traditional scholarship – a result too of the fact that prominent eighteenth-century Scots, including some of the leading think-ers of the Enlightenment, were opposed to it. For David Hume, slavery was 'more cruel and oppressive than any civil subjection whatsoever',[5] while Adam Smith wrote about the destructive effects of slavery in his *The Wealth of Nations*. Another reason for the neglect of the Scots' participation in the slave trade lies in the relative unimportance of Scottish ports in the trade: the circular slave trade was concentrated in the ports of Bristol, Liverpool and London – ports already well established in the trade with Africa that could, therefore, easily specialise in the slave trade. As a result, there was little of a market for Scottish ports to enter, providing one reason why the number of ships trading in slaves leaving Scottish ports was low, with an estimated total of 4,500 slaves embarked.[6] The opposition to slavery in Scotland was also a key factor, with much of the existing scholarship being focused, in fact, on the role Scots played in slavery's abolition.[7] This role was important indeed. When the American Colonization Society held a public meeting in Aberdeen's East Church, for example, the purpose was to gain support for their efforts in Liberia to develop an independent African settlement there to aid the Christianising of Africa and the abolition of the slave trade. The cause was one of 'liberty, humanity, and religion' to bring an end to slavery in the British colonies.[8] Yet despite this opposition, and while the Scots were not involved in the direct trading of slaves at a significant level in Scotland itself, they nonetheless played an important role in the trade, with many Scots amiable to the benefits slave labour could have for their business ventures. Among them were Scotland's eighteenth-century west-coast merchants whose prosper-ity blossomed greatly in the 1760s and 1770s, and rested in no small part on the availability of a cheap workforce. The tobacco plantations, like the sugar plantations in the Caribbean and the tea and rubber plantations in India and South America, were dependent on slave labour for their operations. For all his musings on egalitarianism, Robert Burns was busily settling his affairs and readying himself for a more profitable life as a Caribbean slaveowner before the success of the Kilmarnock edition of his poems precipitated the decision to forsake the diaspora. While Burns's idea to become a slaveowner 'may have been a sign of personal desperation; it is still shocking, and contradicts the ideology implicit and explicit in much of his poetry.' As Crawford thus rightly concludes, '[t]hat Scotland's bard should have been so ready to become part of the system of slavery is one of the most striking indications of how complicit Scotland was in the slave trade.'[9]

Further south, Scottish merchants and agents based at English ports were also heavily involved in the trade, with as many as one in ten traders in London who traded with Africa in the mid-eighteenth century being Scottish.[10] In Bristol too there was a contingent of Scottish merchants, including Richard Holden,[11] while at least five Scots were responsible for the management of Liverpool slaving firms.[12] Moreover, Scots acted as managers of the Company of Merchants Trading to Africa, and private traders also left their mark, embarking on their own slaving expeditions. One of these private traders was Robert Gordon from Moray who, between 1745 and 1769, sent out twelve ships on eighteen different expeditions from Bristol to Africa, concentrating primarily on Cape Coast Castle, Annamaboe and Angola.[13] Apart from such slaving expeditions, Scots were also working at Company forts on the west African coast, especially as overseers and surgeons: ethnic networks and patronage played an important role in bringing out these Scots to slave trading posts.[14]

Alongside the influence of Scots channelled through the Company of Merchants Trading to Africa, Scottish trading consortia were active in Africa itself, shaping the trade and trading practices directly. In the mid-eighteenth century, one such consortium was formed between five Scots – namely Richard Oswald, Augustus Boyd and his son John Boyd, Alexander Grant, and John Mill; an Englishman, John Sargent, was also brought on board. Together they bought a slave trading 'castle' or factory on the Windward Coast near the mouth of the Sierra Leone River – an area abundant in natural resources and slaves. The timing of the purchase was crucial, with the consortium buying the fort at a point in the mid-eighteenth century when the demand for sugar was outstripping supply. As a result, new plantations were set up in the West Indies at an increasing rate, and these required slave labour in larger numbers than ever before.[15] The consortium capitalised on this demand, successfully developing, first, the castle's military defences, and then its commercial facilities. Blocks of houses were built to give space to visiting traders wishing to display their merchandise, and rooms for factory agents meeting African chiefs were constructed, as were facilities in which those taken captive could be held before the so-called Middle Passage.[16] With the demand for slaves ever-increasing, however, even these extended facilities were not sufficient. Hence the proprietors of the fort pushed even further inland, and decided to establish out-factories there; further expansion of the main fort took place under the management of John Aird, another Scot and the principal agent of the factory. Nine out of the thirteen agents of the factory were of Scottish descent.[17]

Beyond the immediate impact structural improvements made at the fort, particularly with respect to the number of slaves processed, the fort's importance lies in the introduction of a new type of slaving practice that it facilitated. Rather than the accustomed ship trade, under which the selling of slaves took place aboard ships, the Scottish proprietors of the fort shifted to trading at the fort itself: those taken captive by African middlemen were brought 'to fort employees, who paid for the slaves and sold them to European or Afro-European shippers.'[18] This meant that a premium could be charged because this process decreased the time ships had to spend at the coast. Another noteworthy characteristic of the trade at the fort was that it focused on attracting Africans through barter rather than capture or the kidnapping of slaves – the proprietors were keen for their employees not to become involved in tribal warfare in the interior. In fact, in mid- to late eighteenth-century British West Africa, the slave trade was 'largely structured by the Africans';[19] this practice contributed significantly to the overall profitability of the trade, and also the outflow of slaves.[20]

The example of this partnership of Scots trading in slaves highlights the ways in which Scots were engaged in the slave trade in Africa itself, actively contributing to the alteration of the human landscape in Africa, as well as influencing slave trading practices. These Scots, like merchants and agents from other countries, benefitted from the demand for slaves, making good business. But there is also another side to the Scots' involvement in slavery in Africa: that of those actively seeking its abolition. While many early missionaries, including David Livingstone, strove to end slavery – Livingstone sought to do so partly by promoting his ideal of commerce and Christianity – the Scottish contribution to its abolition continued for much of the nineteenth century and beyond. Among the abolitionists was one of the Scottish pioneers of East Africa, Sir John Kirk. Born in Barry, a small village just east of Dundee, in 1832, Kirk trained as a physician at Edinburgh University before joining the medical service in the Crimea during the war. When Kirk returned from his service in 1857, David Livingstone had just received money from the British Parliament in support of his Zambezi expedition, and was looking for a surgeon to accompany it. Between 1858 and 1863 Kirk thus traversed the African jungle with Livingstone, acting as his chief assistant and seeking to promote 'commerce, Christianity and civilization'. It was in his role as British Vice-Consul of Zanzibar, however, that Kirk left the most notable imprint on African life, helping to end the slave trade in that country in the late nineteenth century. While the Atlantic slave trade had already come to an end at that point in time, the east African trade was still growing strongly. Carried out chiefly by Arabs, the Zambezi was the key thoroughfare for the eastern slave trade.[21] In 1872, Kirk wrote to the Foreign Office that 'never, since coming to Zanzibar, have I seen so many large dhows come in, crowded with slaves, and seldom have the slaves imported been landed in a worse state.'[22] Appalled by the situation and the inhumane conditions, Kirk continued to work towards ending slavery, negotiating with the Sultan of Zanzibar, Seyyid Barghash-bin-Said, who eventually signed the *Treaty between Great Britain and Zanzibar for the Suppression of the Slave Trade* in 1873. The signing of the Treaty was a great victory for Kirk, who 'received acclamations from all over Europe and America for his role in the negotiations.'[23]

B   SCOTTISH MISSIONARY ACTIVITY IN AFRICA

In March 1913 the Livingstone Centenary was celebrated in London and all throughout the United Kingdom. An assemblage of notables from church and civic life had gathered around Livingstone's grave at Westminster Abbey for a special memorial service, and a great meeting was held later on in the evening at the Royal Albert Hall. Among those present at the meeting was the Archbishop of Canterbury, who delivered one of the speeches of the evening. He praised Livingstone's life and work, recognising that he left behind

> in the most literal sense, footprints on the sands of time . . . The records of his heroism had made the very fibres of the nation's life to tingle, and when they contrast the Africa of Livingstone's time with the Africa to-day they realized how much was due to his life and pioneer work.[24]

Scottish missions in Africa formed part of a wider imperial network of Scottish missionary activity that extended from Scotland to the far-flung corners of the world. Yet while the foreign mission movement was formalised in Scotland at about the same time as in England, with the Scottish Missionary Society and the Glasgow Missionary Society being set up in the mid-1790s, there was only limited interest in Scotland in the late eighteenth and early nineteenth centuries to directly send missions overseas. The General Assembly of the Church of Scotland 'was for the most part hostile to foreign missions.'[25] As a results, those Scots keen on going overseas in this period, were better off joining one of the English mission societies to make their way overseas.[26]

David Livingstone too went abroad through the London Missionary Society, initially planning on going to China. After meeting southern African pioneer missionary and fellow Scott Robert Moffat, however, Livingstone changed his mind, heading to Africa instead, where he arrived in Cape Town in 1841.[27] Livingstone's ventures in Africa, including his expedition across Africa during 1853–6, did much to publicise the endeavours of Scottish missionaries, thus consolidating the important contribution the Scots made to the expansion of the British Empire. The Scots' involvement in overseas missions powerfully legitimised their role as a 'race of Empire builders'.[28] Moreover, their work also attracted the attention of European powers. Livingstone's accounts of the natural resources available in the African interior, for instance, were part of the reason for the shifting imperial policies of several European countries towards Africa. Livingstone presented Africa not as a barren wasteland but 'as a land suitable for cultivation' – a vision that 'helped drive the so-called "Scramble for Africa"' in the late nineteenth century.[29]

While a significant number of Scots went to Africa with the London Missionary Society prior to the mid-nineteenth century, it was then that a notable change took place. This was triggered by the Disruption of the Church of Scotland in 1843. After its formation, the Free Church began to keenly promote foreign missions. This had the effect that the Established Church, perhaps sensing an air of competition, followed suit quickly, also increasing its missionary activities overseas. As Esther Breitenbach has noted, the Disruption 'released an evangelical energy reflected in the growth of the foreign mission movement'.[30] In South Africa, and by the mid-1800s, the Free Church alone had thirteen missions in Kaffraria, fourteen missions in the Transkei, and five missions in Natal, with a total of 144 Scottish missionaries. There was a substantial number of native staff, and hundreds of schools, catering for well over 15,000 pupils, had also been set up.[31] Yet while this proliferation is remarkable, when measured in proportion to the Scottish population, the overall number of Scottish missionaries was small. This holds true in particular when compared with the number of Scottish soldiers or administrators engaged in the British imperial venture – although the wives of Scottish missionaries and women missionary organisations supplied an additional workforce that is hidden from view in these numbers.[32] Despite the relatively low numerical relevance then, it was the Scots missionaries' reputation and public profile that cemented their lead role: well educated and qualified as a result of their education in Scotland, Scottish mission recruits were of a high calibre.

The provision of education was a central staple of Scottish missionary activity in Africa. As Taylor observes, '[t]he establishment and development of European-type schooling in what was to become Anglophone Africa resulted more from the work of Christian missionaries than from any other group'. While England 'minimised state provision and maximised parental responsibility in regard to the schooling of children', Scots '[in] their overseas missionary educational activity . . . encouraged as many children as possible to attend school'.[33] At the Free Church of Scotland's Calabar mission schools in south-east Nigeria, Scottish Presbyterians, though small in number, left a notable imprint through their educational endeavours. Among the Scottish missionaries working in Calabar was Hugh Goldie. Born in Kilwinning in Ayrshire, Goldie had originally been appointed, in 1840, a lay missionary to Jamaica. Subsequently ordained by the Jamaica Missionary Presbytery for service in Africa, Goldie arrived in Nigeria in 1847 to commence with his work at Calabar. He was very interested in the local Efik people and, after working with them extensively, Goldie published an Efik translation of the New Testament in 1862; he also went on to write an Efik-English dictionary.[34] Calabar is perhaps best known, however, because of Mary Slessor – her portrait widely circulated thanks to it being used on the Scottish £10 note issued by the Clydesdale Bank on its 'Famous Scots' banknote series. As MacKenzie has observed, Slessor is 'often depicted as one of the principal heroines of missionary endeavour in Africa'.[35] She was one of a significant number of female missionaries actively engaged overseas, many of whom were supported by societies such as the Greenock Ladies' Overseas Missionary Association or the Glasgow Ladies' Association for the Advancement of Female Education in India (Figure 12.1). Slessor stood out partly because of the esteem in which she was held in Africa. When Slessor died at her station in Africa, 'her body was transported down the Cross River to Duke Town for the colonial equivalent of a state funeral.'[36]

Further south, in the Eastern Cape, William Govan left a similarly important mark as first Principal of the Lovedale Institution, a school established by the Glasgow Missionary Society in 1841. Govan, who had studied at the University of Glasgow, firmly believed in the Scottish ethos of education for all, developing the school as a non-racial institution. Govan's central objective was to train a Christian academic elite, but he also introduced practical classes, such as printing and carpentry. Problematic was Govan's belief that the school should focus on training an elite – a conviction not shared by all. When fellow Scot and missionary James Stewart arrived at Lovedale in the late 1860s, he argued that the school should 'provide the widest possible spread of primary education'.[37] Authorities in Scotland decided to back Stewart rather than Govan, leading to Govan's resignation as Principal. Despite such differing opinions and the complications that arose as a result, Bengt Sundkler and Christopher Steed stress that 'the college for training teachers at Lovedale provided one of the most significant opportunities for African Christians', both blacks and whites, until the officially sanctioned separation of races at schools was introduced.[38]

One of the first pupils of the school, in 1841, was Jan Beck Balfour, Xhosa Christian and son of Robert Balfour, 'a first-generation convert'[39] and native assistant at Lovedale. As Natasha Erlank has noted, father and son were important in that they 'acted as colonial translators, able to speak in at least two moral codes . . . as they mediated and negotiated among Xhosa and Scottish

Figure 12.1 Mary Slessor and Mrs J MacGregor at the Church of Scotland Foreign Mission, Calabar [source: SCRAN; Resource Rights Holder: The Scotsman Publications Ltd; SCRAN ID: 000-000-060-259]

Presbyterian meanings and intentions'.[40] The Scots first arrived in Xhosaland under the banner of the Glasgow Missionary Society in the early 1820s,[41] though pioneer missionary John Brownlee had initially made his way to the frontier on the orders of the London Missionary Society, establishing Chumie Station, which eventually became the first Glasgow Missionary Society station. Several Scottish families followed suit, setting up further stations in the area, soon finding that they had arrived in 'one of the most troubled sections of the Cape colonial frontier' – the result of an eastward expansion of Dutch and British settlers that coincided with the Xhosa's move west.[42] What the Scots' position in Xhosaland also highlights is that Scottish missionaries were not confined in their activities to the traditional remits of the evangelising mission. As MacKenzie has noted for southern Africa, missionary and military frontiers were intertwined, not least because 'Scottish missionaries, in various societies, positioned themselves on this frontier and became embroiled in the processes of frontier closure'[43] – a process through which colonial borders pushed through the frontier zone and eventually closed it.

Elsewhere, in parts of central and eastern Africa, Scottish missionaries influenced British imperial 'frontier politics' in even more direct ways. One of the most notable examples relates to the history of modern-day Malawi, where both the Free and the Established Church of Scotland sent missions in the late nineteenth century. The Free Church founded Livingstonia in 1875, while Blantyre was set up by the Established Church a year later.[44] Livingstonia was to 'construct a community of African Christians who could replace the immoral economy of slavery', blending 'Christian evangelism and the drive towards economic progress'.[45] While this already highlights the degree to which Scottish missionary activity in the region shaped social life, even more significant in this respect was the missionaries' involvement in a campaign designed to avert Portuguese occupation of parts of Malawi in the late 1880s. The strong connections that existed between local churches in Scotland and foreign missions overseas played an important role here:[46] with missionaries alerting church authorities in Scotland to the problematic situation, a large-scale campaign was mounted that united political and religious opinions in Scotland, seeking 'to declare the area of land roughly equivalent to modern Malawi a British sphere of influence.'[47] The then British prime minister, Lord Salisbury, dismissed the request in the first instance, but the campaign continued, reaching its climax in the summer of 1889. As was reported in *The Times*,

> Lord Salisbury received at the Foreign Office the representatives of
> the joint committee of the Presbyterian churches in Scotland, who
> presented a memorial signed by 11,000 ministers and elders expressing
> a very widely-spread feeling in Scotland that the interests of Great
> Britain were most material in Nyassaland [sic], and that they ought not
> to be abandoned to Portugal.[48]

With Parliament unwilling to finance a British intervention, little happened until the point when Cecil Rhodes offered to administer a Protectorate in the area of modern Malawi free of charge for three years. Salisbury accepted this offer, and the Portuguese withdrew their claim; the British Central African Protectorate was established as a result, with its borders being agreed through treaties and conventions with different European powers that also included the Germans. While the immediate goal of hindering the Portuguese from laying claim to Malawi had been achieved, the newly established Protectorate remained a concern for many of the local Scottish missionaries. Dr David Clement Scott, based at the Blantyre Mission, was worried about Rhodes's involvement, of whom he was very critical. Scott assumed that Malawi 'might still become part of Cecil Rhodes's empire', and made it clear that he, therefore, did not want to see Malawi handed over to Rhodes's British South African Company.[49] Born in Edinburgh in 1853, Scott was ordained in 1881 and then sent to Blantyre to head the Church of Scotland mission there. Genuinely interested in African people and culture, Scott produced the *Cyclopaedic Dictionary of the Mang'anja Language* in 1892, and, not surprisingly, continued his opposition to Rhodes and the local imperial officer in Malawi, H. H. Johnston, until his departure from Blantyre in 1898.

The case of Malawi provides a formidable example of active missionary intervention, in this case in imperial politics, underscoring the missionaries' wider influence: though welcoming imperial government, they 'had little desire to see it act in an imperial manner'. Missionaries like Dr James Stewart were in favour of indirect rule, 'preventing other powers moving into the Malawi regions, but leaving the existing political situation largely undisturbed.'[50] Such immediate engagement and intervention was not confined to the political sphere, especially given that many missionaries, like Livingstone, were also explorers, land surveyors or botanists. Dr John Croumbie Brown, for example, played an important role in this respect. As Richard Grove has noted, '[t]he adaptation for state purposes of the environmental evangelism of Brown and his missionary predecessor, Robert Moffat, far outlasted their own lifetimes.'[51] On a more negative note, however, it must also be said that many of the positive advances brought by Scottish missionaries were undermined in the twentieth century, especially in the educational sector. While radical approaches promoting the mixed education of whites and blacks had been a key characteristic in the nineteenth century, congregations became exclusive. In South Africa the black missions were specifically excluded when the Presbyterian Church of South Africa was established in 1924, and mission schools, such as Lovedale, had to offer separate education from the mid-1950s.[52]

C SOLDIERS, MINERS AND RADICALS

As soldiers of the British imperial armies Scots were visible on many African battlegrounds, including in West Africa, Egypt and, most notably, in South Africa. Scottish regiments were conspicuous, earning 'accolades as empire-builders'.[53] Or, as Richard Finlay has observed, '[u]ndoubtedly, the military contribution of the Scottish regiments was the most important factor in the propagation of a distinctive Scottish input into British imperial activity.'[54] This input, though relatively small in numerical terms given that the number of Scottish soldiers was low relative to Scotland's wider emigrant population, was perceived as enduring and powerful. This was the case too because the Scots 'were everywhere in the visual record.'[55] Clad in highland kilts and with tartan trews becoming a mainstay even for lowland regiments, an iconography emerged around the Scottish soldier that was as recognisable as it was powerful in cementing the image of the Scottish soldier as the builder and defender of Empire. As nationalist P. E. Dove of the National Association for the Vindication of Scottish Rights argued in a pamphlet in 1853, Scottish soldiers were 'seen foremost in every hard-won field'.[56] In the visual record was reflected one of the central ways in which Scots could play out their national identity on an imperial stage – and one in which Africa played a key role.[57] Royal patronage from Queen Victoria, dispensed in recognition of the Scottish soldiers' service and valour, further consolidated this image.[58]

In southern Africa, where there were intermittent frontier wars over the course of a century, from about 1770 to 1870, Scottish soldiers were among the earliest arrivals, providing security for the Cape Colony. Thus was established the foundation of what became not only a long, but also a complex relationship between South Africa and Scottish military culture.[59] While these foundations in South Africa were important, however, it was only with the Asante War of 1873–4, that a Scottish regiment was engaged in frontline fighting in Africa.[60] The war had been triggered by the Asante invading the Gold Coast in West Africa, a British protectorate, and it came down to the 42nd Highlanders (1st Battalion, the Black Watch) to do much of the fighting on the ground – valiantly for crown and Empire. Other engagements, for instance in Egypt and the Sudan, were of significance in the late nineteenth century and brought about many an easy victory because the opposing armies 'lacked modern weaponry and organisation.'[61]

This all changed, however, during the most notable war on African soil, the Anglo-Boer War (1899–1902).[62] A result of the ongoing disputes between the two independent Boer republics and the British government over the settlement and status of the Transvaal and the Orange Free State, the war broke out in October 1899 when Britain failed, after an ultimatum had been issued, to withdraw its troops from the borders of the two states. Boer forces were much better prepared and had better equipment compared to other African forces. They were also well versed in making use of modern tactics. The new conditions of warfare in South Africa, combined with the fact that many of the Scottish soldiers fighting in that particular war were relatively new to combat,[63] took its toll, with losses increasing significantly. Of particular note is the Battle of Magersfontein in December 1899, where the Highland Brigade eventually had to retreat – though even this retreat could not undermine the 'legend of martial invincibility',[64] as this had, by that stage, become deeply engrained in Scottish popular perception. This sense of Scottishness, one underpinned by a long-standing military tradition, was intrinsically bound to Britishness: 'Scottish military activity in South Africa [was] part of the successful British project of overrunning the territories of Africans and Afrikaners.'[65]

What makes the Anglo-Boer War so important is that it involved every Scottish infantry regiment, as well as Scottish auxiliary forces, with around 5,000 Scottish volunteers serving during the Boer Wars.[66] The contribution

Figure 12.2 Grantown-on-Spey soldiers enlisted to fight in the Anglo–Boer War [source: SCRAN; Resource Rights Holder: Grantown Museum and Heritage Trust; SCRAN ID: 000–000–599–531–C]

of these citizen soldiers provided an immediate connection between Scotland and South Africa, and contributed to Scots feeling 'intensely proud of the men from their own localities who had volunteered to serve in the war.'[67] This also explains why Scottish units who fought in the Anglo–Boer War were held especially high in public regard – a fact reflected too in their 'specific memorialization' at the Scottish National War Memorial in Edinburgh.[68] Scots were engaged disproportionately by the navy and land forces of the British army, with the gun and the bayonet sustaining the Empire against indigenes and rival imperial powers alike.

While British territorial expansion in Africa was a key reason for the commencement of the South Africa War, a movement spearheaded by English-born Cecil Rhodes, so too was the question of who would control the lucrative gold mines in the Rand. Scots had been connected with southern Africa even before the British first took over the Cape Colony in 1797, for instance through their involvement in the Dutch East India Company.[69] There never was, however, a large-scale migration from Scotland to South Africa. Overall numbers are difficult to establish given the lack of succinct records, but census statistics provide a useful yardstick. By the mid-1870s, a little over 200,000 whites resided in the Cape Colony, with perhaps 11 per cent claiming British Isles descent; the percentage of Scots among them was lowest at a little over 1 per cent. These figures rose in the 1880s, but the most significant increase can be found in the late nineteenth and early twentieth centuries. While the Anglo-Boer War temporarily halted the migratory flow, it then picked up again, and, by 1904, the Scots made up nearly 3 per cent of the colonial population at the Cape. By 1911 that percentage had risen even further to a significant 14.3 per cent – a shift in pattern that was the immediate result of the opening of gold mines in the Rand in conjunction with the late nineteenth-century economic downturns in the traditional settler colonies of Canada, Australia and New Zealand.[70]

The discovery of precious metal has long since been one of the key 'pull factors' for migrants in terms of destination choice for their emigration. Hence the fact that the period that witnessed the most significant Scottish migration to South Africa commenced in the late 1880s, coinciding with the mineral revolution in the Rand, comes as no surprise. The scale of Scottish migration to South Africa was certainly affected by the establishment of gold mines and is reflected in early twentieth-century migrant numbers. In 1911 a little over 20 per cent of the population of what had become the Union of South Africa were white migrants; in terms of those hailing from the British and Irish Isles, who made up the bulk, the composition based on the 1911 census is 48.6 per cent English, 14.3 per cent Scots, 5.6 per cent Irish, and 1.4 per cent Welsh.[71] The importance of mining work is also clearly evident in the provincial settlement distributions, with nearly 50 per cent of Scots settling in the Transvaal, where the largest mines could be found, followed by 26 per cent in the Cape Colony, 19 per cent in Natal, and 7 per cent in the Orange Free State. As in other areas where mineral rushes had taken place, for instance on the gold fields of New Zealand, the majority of Scottish arrivals were male.[72]

Apart from their arrival in substantial numbers in that period, which were disproportionate to their population share in the UK itself, the Scots were also an important group among the migrants because they brought with them techniques crucial to the mining of gold in the Transvaal, where gold was often locked within other sulfide minerals, making its mining much more complicated. Scottish brothers Robert and William Forrest, together with fellow Scot John Stewart MacArthur, developed a method of gold recovery using potassium cyanide as a gold solvent. The method was patented in Britain and the Transvaal, 'with patent rights vested in the Cassel company of Glasgow'.[73]

Even more importantly, Scots also brought with them to the mines their ideas of trade unionism and the organisation of labour, and were thus heavily involved in both the South African labour movement, and the syndicalist movement. The most notable syndicalist was James Thompson Bain. Born in Dundee in 1860, Bain had joined the British Army at an early age and was sent to Pretoria in the late 1870s, fighting alongside Boer soldiers against the Zulus. Bain went on to serve in India in the early 1880s, before returning to Scotland to hone his socialist credentials in the 1880s, being engaged in the short-lived Scottish Land and Labour League, but also as a member of the Amalgamated Society of Engineers (ASE). Despite these beginnings in Scotland, it was in South Africa, to which Bain had emigrated in 1890, where his socialist ethos would leave its most lasting imprint.[74] After his arrival in the Rand in 1890, he was involved, for instance, in setting up the Witwatersrand Mine Employees' and Mechanics' Union, and later also in founding the Rand branch of the ASE. His sympathies lay firmly with his new homeland, the Boer republic – a fact best exemplified by Bain's service as soldier for the republic during the Boer War. Bain was among those welcoming Keir Hardie to the Rand in 1908, and was deported shortly before the First World War for fear of his acting as agitator and leader of a miners' strike. Hence he was, '[w]ith eight other trade unionists (at least three of them Scots) . . . forcibly placed on board the SS Umgeni and sent back to Britain',[75] where, to his surprise, he was welcomed by various Labour lead figures, being celebrated a working-class hero. Bain eventually returned to South Africa in 1914, 'a prophet outcast' as Hyslop has noted.[76] Yet while Bain was fighting for workers' rights, he was never concerned with the rights of black labour: 'for him black labour was a threatening force rather than a brotherhood of the oppressed',[77] documenting that the history of Scots in Africa is closely 'entwined with the history of racial domination in Empire.'[78] Working-class Scots developed a form of 'white labourism' that based its criticism of capitalism and the exploitation of labour, at least in part, on racist arguments.[79] The powerful ideology of white labourism, however, tends to hide that there was also an active non-racialist movement, and one that was influenced disproportionately by Scots.[80] Among them was Alexander Seaton Raitt. He was born in Renfrew in 1867, becoming an apprentice to a Blairgowrie engineering firm before making his way to South Africa in 1890 to work on mines in the Rand. As MacKenzie notes, '[h]e became an important figure in the ASE in the Transvaal and served in the Anglo-Boer War on the imperial side.'[81] Raitt served on the municipal council of Johannesburg and the Transvaal legislative council in the early twentieth century; while Raitt was opposed to the enfranchisement of non-whites, the welfare of black workers was a major concern for him – and one triggered, for instance, by their high mortality rates.

D   CONCLUSION

The Scottish diaspora in Africa is not as straightforward to characterise as that of other countries and regions explored in this book. This is the case, first, because it is very diverse and cannot be subsumed under a broad explanatory banner – it was neither primarily the destination of sojourners like Asia (Chapter 13), nor was it, as a whole, a principal settler destination. This does not surprise given the sheer size of Africa, and the diverse ways in which Scots came into contact with different places and peoples throughout the continent. The earliest connection between Scotland and Africa was channelled through trade, chiefly the engagement of Scots in the slave trade. This contact, therefore, does resemble some of the characteristics we have identified for sojourners (Chapter 2 and Chapter 13), with those engaged in the trade eventually making their way back to Scotland. Similar patterns are evident for some of the later nineteenth- and early twentieth-century movements of Scots to South Africa. A key point is that among the earliest Scottish traders who ventured to Africa, contact with Africans was limited; this was the case even in the slave trade because African middlemen tended to carry out most of the work in the interior, and because the slave trade was largely confined to coastal regions. More substantial contact, therefore, really only began to develop through the Scottish missionary endeavours of the late eighteenth and nineteenth centuries. These span the African continent more broadly and had long-lasting impacts on diverse African societies, for instance in education.

A second important characteristic of the Scottish diaspora in Africa is that it was consistently framed around an indigenous 'other'. While, as we have seen with respect to developments on the 'frontier zone', tensions were higher in some areas than in others, it was generally the case that migrants from outside of Africa defined their own status largely in terms of 'us' and 'them', with the latter referring to indigenous peoples. In South Africa the situation was complicated even further given that there was also a 'European other' in the form of the Dutch. This is an important point as the existence of a prominent 'other' – be it European or non-European – tends to shape the ways in which ethnic groups define their own boundaries. While perhaps less strong than in Africa, the 'other' also played a part in the Scots' connection with Asia, which is the focus of the next chapter.

NOTES

1. Pettitt, *Dr Livingston, I Presume?*; see also Mackenzie, 'David Livingstone: The construction of the myth'.
2. Livingstone, *Missionary Travels and Researches in South Africa*.
3. Shepperson, 'Mungo Park and the Scottish contribution to Africa'.
4. Cf. Devine, *To the Ends of the Earth*, chapter 2.
5. Hume, Essay XI: 'Of the populousness of ancient nations', p. 144.

6. Devine, *To the Ends of the Earth*, table 1, p. 35. Scotland later found its niche in the tobacco and sugar trade.

7. For a detailed study on the role of the Scots in the abolition of slavery, see Whyte, *Scotland and the Abolition of Black Slavery*; also Peterson (ed.), *Abolitionism and Imperialism in Britain, Africa, and the Atlantic*.

8. *The Aberdeen Journal*, 6 February 1833.

9. Crawford, *The Bard*, p. 223.

10. This number increased further as the trade progressed, Devine, *To the Ends of the Earth*, p. 36.

11. See Richard Holden Papers, National Library of Scotland, Acc.11272/4; also Robinson, *A Sailor Boy's Experience Aboard a Slave Ship*.

12. Hancock, 'Scots in the slave trade', p. 63.

13. Ibid.

14. Ibid., p. 64.

15. For a detailed study of the Scots' involvement in the plantation economy of the Caribbeans, see Hamilton, *Scotland, the Carribeans and the Atlantic World*.

16. The Middle Passage was an intrinsic part of the triangular slave trade, being the part of the journey that slaves were forced to undertake from Africa to the West Indies or America. For further details on the Middle Passage, see Klein, *The Middle Passage*, and Smallwood, *Saltwater Slavery*.

17. Hancock, 'Scots in the slave trade', p. 72.

18. Ibid., p. 73.

19. Ibid., p. 74.

20. For details on the slave exports from the fort, see Hancock, *Citizens of the World*, table 6.1, p. 205.

21. Liebowitz, *The Physician and the Slave Trade*; see also Papers of Sir John Kirk, National Library of Scotland, Acc.9942.

22. Dhow is the Arab word for a sailing vessel. Cited in Liebowitz, *The Physician and the Slave Trade*, p. 167.

23. Ibid., p. 178.

24. *The Times*, 20 March 1913.

25. Devine, *To the Ends of the Earth*, p. 194.

26. The London Missionary Society 'recruited missionaries disproportionately from Scotland' – not least, perhaps, because there had been several Scots among its founders. See Breitenbach, 'Scots churches and missions', p. 210.

27. Ross, *David Livingstone*, p. 27.

28. Devine, *The Scottish Nation*, p. 366.

29. Devine, *To the Ends of the Earth*, p. 201.

30. Breitenbach, *Empire and Scottish Society*, p. 4.

31. MacKenzie with Dalziel, *The Scots in South Africa*, p. 123.

32. Breitenbach, 'Scots churches and missions', pp. 211 and 214.

33. Taylor, *Mission to Educate*, p. 5.

34. Johnston, 'Goldie, Hugh', p. 248.

35. MacKenzie, 'Empire and national identities', p. 224.

36. Proctor, J. H., 'Serving God and the Empire', p. 45.

37. Ross, 'Govan, William', p. 253.

38. Sundkler and Steed, *A History of the Church in Africa*, p. 359.

39. Erlank, 'Sexual misconduct and Church power on Scottish mission stations', p. 70; see also Hodgson, 'A battle for sacred power'.

40. For details, see ibid., p. 71. Jan Beck later became embroiled in a case of sexual misconduct that also revealed some of the tensions between Xhosa and Church moral codes.

41. For details on the wider context of Scottish settlement on the eastern frontier, see MacKenzie with Dalziel, *Scots in South Africa*, pp. 48ff; also Keegan, *Colonial South Africa and the Origins of the Racial Order*.

42. Erlank, 'Re-examining initial encounters between Christian missionaries and the Xhosa', pp. 7–8; see also Erlank, 'Gender and Christianity among Africans attached to Scottish mission stations in Xhosaland'; for details on the settlement of British migrants among the Xhosa, see also Lester, *Imperial Networks*, chapter 3.

43. MacKenzie with Dalziel, *Scots in South Africa*, pp. 94–5.

44. See for instance Sindima, *The Legacy of Scottish Missionaries in Malawi*; also Thompson, *Christianity in Northern Malawi*; for a more detailed study of the Scottish influence on Malawi and the Scottish missionaries' attitudes to African culture and religion, see also Thompson, *Ngoni, Xhosa and Scot*.

45. Devine, *To the Ends of the Earth*, p. 203.

46. For details on these connections, see Breitenbach, *Empire and Scottish Society*.

47. Ross, *Colonialism to Cabinet Crisis*, p. 14.

48. *The Times*, 18 May 1889; see also McCracken, *Politics and Christianity in Malawi*, pp. 197ff.

49. Ross, *Colonialism to Cabinet Crisis*, p. 16.

50. McCracken, *Politics and Christianity*, p. 198.

51. Grove, 'Scottish missionaries, evangelical discourses and the origins of conservation thinking in Southern Africa', p. 164.

52. MacKenzie with Dalziel, *Scots in South Africa*, p. 124.

53. Spiers, *The Scottish Soldier and Empire*, p. 1.

54. Finlay, *A Partnership for Good?*, p. 27.

55. MacKenzie 'On Scotland and the Empire', p. 727.

56. Dove, *The National Association for the Vindication of Scottish Rights*, p. 1.

57. Forsyth, 'Empire and Union, p. 6.

58. Spiers, *The Scottish Soldier and Empire*, pp. 4ff; also Spiers, *The Victorian Soldier in Africa*.

59. See for instance Juta, *The History of the Transvaal Scottish*; Mitchell, *Tartan on the Veld*; and Orpen, *The Cape Town Highlanders*.

60. Spiers, *The Scottish Soldier and Empire*, p. 24.

61. Devine, 'Soldiers of Empire, p. 191.

62. For a perspective on how the war influenced political opinion in Scotland itself, see Brown, '"Echoes of Midlothian"', pp. 156–83.

63. Spiers, 'The Scottish soldier in the Boer War', p. 157.

64. Devine, 'Soldiers of Empire', p. 190.

65. Hyslop, 'Cape Town highlanders, Transvaal Scottish', p. 99.

66. Devine, 'Soldiers of Empire', p. 195.

67. Spiers, *The Scottish Soldier and Empire*, p. 182.

68. Hyslop, 'Cape Town Highlanders, Transvaal Scottish,' p. 96.

69. These connections were often the result of the close ties that had developed between Scottish merchants and the Netherlands in the early modern period. See MacKenzie with Dalziel, *Scots in South Africa*, p. 29; also Grosjean and Murdoch (eds), *Scottish Communities Abroad in the Early Modern Period*, especially section III.

70. MacKenzie with Dalziel, *Scots in South Africa*, pp. 65–6.

71. Ibid., p. 66.

72. Ibid., p. 161.

73. Brock, *William Crookes*, p. 414.

74. Hyslop, *The Notorious Syndicalist*.

75. MacKenzie with Dalziel, *Scots in South Africa*, p. 231.

76. Chapter title in Hyslop, *The Notorious Syndicalist*, p. 267.

77. MacKenzie with Dalziel, *Scots in South Africa*, p. 232.

78. Hyslop, 'Cape Town highlanders, Transvaal Scottish', p. 98.

79. Hyslop, 'The imperial working class makes itself "white"'.

80. See Kenefick, 'Confronting white labourism'.

81. MacKenzie with Dalziel, *Scots in South Africa*, p. 232.

CHAPTER 13

Asia

'No-one', noted a reporter in the *North China Herald* in 1896, 'would be audacious enough even to hint a doubt that Scotsmen are very enterprising and thorough, especially in the Far East'.[1] Befitting the festive occasion – Shanghai's annual Caledonian Ball held in honour of St Andrew's Day – the reporter's positive take on the enterprising Scot in Asia does not surprise. The comment nonetheless points to what was, by the late nineteenth century, a long-standing and deep connection between Scots and the Far East.

Scots first made their way to India after the the failure of the Company of Scotland and the country's own imperial venture at Darien, when the Union of 1707 gave them access to the British Empire. In this early period of imperial enterprise and trade in the Far East, the Scots primarily channelled and substantiated their connection with the Indian subcontinent through the East India Company (EIC), which continued to play a pivotal role for Scots in the Far East until it lost its trade monopoly in the early nineteenth century. The EIC employed a significant number of Scottish soldiers and merchants, including, for example, Alexander Hamilton and Sir Hector Munro. Yet while it was through the Company that the Scots first exerted influence, their impact was greatest after the Company's rule had come to an end. It was then that Scottish merchants and businessmen could expand their reach into the previously closed markets of China and beyond. What the EIC highlights is that the connection between Scots and Asia was one primarily defined in terms of trade: India and other settlements in the region that gradually became part of the formal and informal British Empire in the Far East can suitably be classed as 'business outposts' of the Scottish diaspora.

Another characteristic, and one already touched upon in Chapter 8, is important, namely that for the majority of the Scots who ventured to Asia, their stay in the Far East was not a permanent relocation, but rather a sojourn that often saw them move frequently between different Asian sites of settlement before the eventual return to Scotland. Hong Kong was one such settlement, becoming the temporary home for many a sojourning Scot, including Scottish businessmen such as William Jardine and James Matheson. The two left a lasting mark in the city, starting one of the original Hong Kong trading houses; one that eventually expanded well beyond the city's shores, trading with India, setting up business in Shanghai, Japan, and even establishing strong pan-Pacific links. For Jardine and Matheson, Asia was the principal hub for their trade, with the firm's trade connections criss-crossing the globe from there. Against the backdrop of such enterprises, this chapter will explore the Scottish 'trade diaspora' in Asia, assessing the role of Scottish businessmen and their economic ventures as a distinct aspect of Scottish migration overseas. In particular, the chapter will investigate how the Scots, as part of the more limited white populations of Asia which were primarily comprised of a narrow mix of elite, military, bureaucratic and commercial migrants, left a lasting mark in the Far East.

A VENTURING EAST: THE SCOTS IN INDIA

The loss of the original American colonies signalled the end of Britain's First Empire.[2] By the time of the Wars of Independence Britain had been an Atlantic power for a good two centuries, seeking to expand its hold over territories in the West.[3] While British North America, and, after Confederation in 1867, the Dominion of Canada, secured a continuous British presence on the North American continent, the future lay clearly in the East, which offered unprecedented commercial prospects. As was argued in a pamphlet published in the late eighteenth century,

> we must perceive, that the commerce of India will ever continue to be highly advantageous to Britain; and will also remain secure to her . . . but that the commerce of America will, so soon as she is freed from restraint, not only cease to be useful, but will even prove detrimental to Britain.[4]

It was this recognition that heralded a new phase in British imperial expansion, and one that saw India become the 'battering ram of empire'.[5] This new expansion was, however, not simply territorial, but rather an undertaking founded primarily on commercial interests, driving forward an economic expansion on an unprecedented scale. Importantly, and as Devine has noted, 'the old colonial system was shattered by this new globalization of British commerce.'[6] A key facilitator in this commercial expansion were the forces of industrialisation, which came early in Britain – and Scotland in particular – giving it an advantage over other countries looking to enter and profit from markets overseas.[7] Advances in communication and transportation systems were also crucial in facilitating British expansion in the Far East.

After the ill-fated Darien venture,[8] many Scots first began participating in eastern trade through European chartered companies, 'but for those Scots who remained at home the key to future succes lay in the establishment of a foothold within the East India Company itself.'[9] The Union of 1707, which gave Scots access to the British Empire, facilitated this to some extent. Even prior to the Union, however, the East India Company had attracted a number of Scots, including Captain Alexander Hamilton, who rose to prominence with his accounts of life in the British bases that had been established in Bombay, Madras and Calcutta.[10] Though generally dominated by Englishmen, there was also a clearly visible presence of Scots among Company directors in London, and Scottish capital, for instance from Lawrence Dundas, financed some of the Company activities.[11] In terms of numbers, however, the most significant involvement of Scots in India in the eighteenth century was in the East India Company's (or the king's) military forces. In Bengal, in the early 1770s, there were an estimated thirty Scottish civil servants, 280 Scots among the ordinary soldiers, and 250 Scots among the officers. The latter was a particularly strong contingent given that the overall number of officers stood at about 800.

In terms of the share of the European population in Bengal, Scots made up around 13 per cent.[12] Other estimates suggest that, between 1720 and 1780, a minimum of 2,000 Scots made their way to the Indian subcontinent in the military, as civil servants, aboard East Indiamen, as physicians and also as free merchants. The number of the latter group increased throughout the later eighteenth and early nineteenth centuries, with an estimated 300 Scottish free merchants trading in the East Indies by the 1830s. Overall, McGilvary suggests that around 3,500 Scots were present in the Indies between c. 1720 and 1833.[13] Among them was, for instance, Sir David Baird. Born in East Lothian in 1757, he was first sent to India in 1779 and, soon after his arrival, was taken prisoner at the battle of Pollilur. After four years in prison Baird was released and continued his military carreer, returning to Britain from 1787 to 1791, when he once again made his way to India. It was then that he rose to fame during the fourth Anglo-Mysore War, particularly as a result of the victory at Seringapatam and the discovery of the body of Sultan Tippoo Sahib in 1799 – a now iconic event thanks to the work of another Scot, painter Sir David Wilkie, who vividly captured it in a painting commissioned by Baird's wife after his death (Figure 13.1).[14]

Another notable Scottish officer in India under employment of the EIC was Sir Hector Munro of Novar. While he first made his way into the military in one of Loudoun's Highland regiments, Sir Hector was made famous through

Figure 13.1 General Sir David Baird discovering the body of Sultan Tippoo Sahib after having captured Seringapatam on the 4 May 1799 [source: SCRAN; Resource Rights Holder: National Gallery of Scotland, Edinburgh: NG 2430; SCRAN ID: 000-000-485-835-C]

his sojourn in India. As Linda Colley observes, he 'literally fought his way to notice', and his involvement in the battle of Baksar, where his Company army defeated the forces of emperor Shah Alam II and the Nawabs of Bengal, stands out in that it 'effectively ensured that Britain would annex Bengal'.[15]

Munro returned to Britain in the mid-1760s and was elected a Member of Parliament for the Inverness Burghs in 1768. He only remained in Britain for a decade, however, making his way back to India in 1778, where he soon became involved in the siege of Pondicherry, the central French base in India at the time. Victory there, with the French capitulating, gained Munro 'a public note of thanks from King George III and a Knighthood of the Bath.'[16] Munro's reputation, however, was almost completely forfeited when his campaign at Polillur in 1780 failed, being 'the worst defeat inflicted on British arms in India during the entire century.'[17] In light of these difficulties it is important to note the reason behind Munro's second venture to India. Though he returned a 'nabob'[18] after his first stint on the subcontinent, the collapse of the Ayr Bank had left Munro in a precarious financial position which he believed he could best resolve by returning to India, lured by the opportunity it could offer for making a profit. The willingness to consider this long-distance sojourn for a second time highlights how much it had become 'a readily accepted tactic for addressing a host of mundane domestic difficulties.'[19]

At the same time, however, and while the number of Scots involved in EIC military service in India was significant, and even higher for the royal regiments dispatched to India between 1754 and 1784, many of the Scots were actually reluctant to serve in India. As one royal Scottish officer remarked, '"I'd almost as soon live in Hell as in India"'. This is a sentiment that would probably have been shared by the men of the 78th Foot, who mutinied when they heard a rumour that, instead of being sent to America, they had been sold to the East India Company.[20] Such views were not uncommen among the lower military orders, being fuelled by the knowledge that many ordinary soldiers died in India, and that the adjustment to life in the Far East was by no means straightforwarward, marred significantly by the unfamiliar social practices, different climate and poor living conditions.

The higher ranks of Scottish society did not show that same reluctance, clamouring increasingly, in fact, 'for posts in the Company's civil line or its officer corps.'[21] As in the case of Sir Hector Munro, the incentive for these Scots lay in the belief that spending time in India would allow them to acquire a level of wealth they were unable to acquire in Scotland,[22] eventually return-ing home with prospects improved.[23] The reason why Scots were keen to be employed directly with the EIC was thus not so much a result of the salaries paid, which were quite small, but rather a result of the firm belief that working for the Company would allow them to establish private trade networks in India for their own benefit, maximising the profits they could make. Military service, especially in the lower ranks, was the least effective way to achive that goal, offering one further reason as to why there was a significant reluctance towards it. What this meant, however, was that many Scots in India focused on the quick acquision of wealth, becoming 'part of a small but remarkably aggressive cadre of political, commercial and military elites that wielded inordinate authority within India in order to accrue profits by any legal and, if necessary, dubious means.'[24] This route of acquiring wealth overseas was an attractive one for members of the lower gentry, as well as the sons of gentry families, especially because these tended to have a large number of offspring in the eighteenth century who, consequently, had only limited opportunities at home in Scotland.[25]

As a result of fierce competition for posts in the EIC, patronage systems played a key role in facilitating entry, particularly to civil positions.[26] The main reason for this was less the potential danger of military service, but the fact that the civil line provided better opportunities to establish one's own private trade. What this meant was that 'greater patronage power was required to become a civil servant than to secure a commission in the Company's army'.[27] While money was occasionally used to buy appointments, the common route was active lobbying through Scottish ethnic and kinship networks. Alexander Campbell of Ardchattan, for example, became a junior merchant at Madras as a result of family connections, and, in return, facilitated entry for a number of his relatives.[28] Political connections were also significant, and in this case any benefits reaped could potentially be reciprocal, as 'aspiring Scottish politicians who could command Indian patronage used it to bolster their electoral position and used their political connections to acquire patronage power in the Company.'[29] This type of patronage flow could also be especially effective because the EIC relied on the support of ministers and politicians in Britain to maintain its monopoly. As new studies highlight, this 'combination of financial contacts in London and political interests in the Scottish shires and burghs . . . expedited the placement of Scots [in the Company]', and did so 'from the mid-1720s' – hence earlier than traditional scholarship has suggested.[30]

Scots who did not have access to these patronage systems could attempt to make their way as free merchants in the local Indian trade, but even such activity often required EIC connections until at least the late eighteenth century – the Company's grasp was all-embracing. More successful tended to be the establishment of trading partnerships that consisted essentially of business networks that ran throughout South-east Asia; this was a trend that facilitated the development of the agency house. William Fairlie, for example, had left Scotland in the early 1780s and then set up as a free merchant in Bengal together with John Fergusson.[31] Drawing in family members and wider kinship connections, Scottish trade oligarchies began to develop, ensuring the Scots' success as free merchants. As Parker has noted, 'the Scots agencies were almost entirely family concerns', and were strengthend because agencies became indispensable to the East India Company's system of trade.[32] What is more, it was the agency houses that rose to the fore when the EIC lost its trade monopoly in 1813.[33] Problems soon emerged in India, however, with several of the Calcutta houses collapsing in the early 1830s; so-called managing agents filled the gap.[34] Despite these somewhat unsteady beginnings, this period was crucial for the Scots in Asia as it saw the emergence of the roots of global trading companies, such as Jardine, Matheson & Co. With the EIC monopoly largely abolished, it was through these new trading companies that the Scottish sphere of influence could move further east, first to the Straits Settlement and then on to China, capitalising on the abundant trade opportunities there.

Scottish traders left a notable mark in a number of specific trades, including, for instance, in the tea trade. Born in Glasgow in 1848, Thomas Lipton's company had become the largest company trading in tea by the late nineteenth century. Tea was not the only commodity that forged enduring links between Scotland and India, however, with mill owners from Dundee playing a vital role in the establishment of the jute industry in Calcutta. The two cities thus became the major trading centres of jute, and, as Stewart notes, 'both cities and their hinterlands prospered by jute; both were blighted by jute.'[35]

While the EIC had lost much of its monopoly by the mid-nineteenth century, it still controlled most of the territorry on the Indian subcontinent and beyond, including parts of Pakistan and the Straits Settlements of Malacca, Dinding, Penang and Singapore. Frictions in India, however, were on the rise, culminating in the uprising of 1857, when sepoys of the East India Company army staged a mutiny. In the aftermath of the rebellion, the British government took full control from the EIC and wound up the Company, heralding the period known as the British Raj (1858–1947).[36] Scots were at the forefront yet again. James Ramsay, first marquess of Dalhousie, was Indian Governor-General at the time of the uprising, and Sir Colin Campbell was the leader of an army that was largely responsible for crushing the uprising. Later on in the nineteenth century, a number of Scots served as viceroys, including the seventh and eighth earls of Elgin, and the first Marquess of Dufferin and Ava; later on in the twentieth century, Lord Linlithgow acted as one of the last viceroys from 1936 to 1943. As was common throughout Scottish diaspora settlements, India also saw the arrival of Scottish doctors, with many already having come out to India in EIC service in the eighteenth century; Scots were also strongly represented among architects, surveyors and botanists. Of the latter group, Francis Buchanan made an important contribution. He arrived in India in 1794 under the auspices of the East India Company, and was employed to conduct a number of surveys, most notably of Mysore in 1800 and Bengal in 1807.[37] These explorations and the charting of the land, together with new trade connections, contributed to the arrival of a growing number of Scottish merchants. These were found, as Sir Charles Dilke observed in his *Greater Britain*, in larger numbers than Englishmen, especially among those merchants who had risen from 'small beginnings without external aid'.[38] This business community of Scots in India was united not only through its trade, but also a plethora of social activities that aided their community cohesion as Scots and as key players of the white colonial elite.[39] India was also the location for Scottish women's missionary interventions, where the spread of Presbyterianism abroad was an extension of vibrant religiosity at home. The Edinburgh Ladies' Association for the Advancement of Female Education in India (1837), for instance, was part of a significant conjunction of women's public activity and religious endeavour.

B EXPANDING THE DIASPORIC REACH IN THE EAST: THE SCOTS IN CHINA

Of great importance for the facilitation of trade and Scottish enterprise beyond the shores of the Indian subcontinent was the development of shipping interests. One name that stands out in this respect is that of Sir William Mackinnon. Born in Campbeltown, Argyll, in 1823, Mackinnon proceeded to work for a merchant in Glasgow who traded with the East before embarking to India himself in 1846. As Munro explains, Scots 'William Mackinnon and James Macalister Hall, it seems, were sent out to join Robert Mackenzie in India with a view to the development of a trade between Calcutta, Liverpool and the Clyde.'[40] Different trade partnerships were subsequently established, with Mackinnon Mackenzie & Co. in Calcutta proving to be the most successful. These partnerships, and others that followed, were founded not only on Scottish kinship ties, but more specifically on connections that had their origins in Campbeltown. Local roots in Scotland were important in many a Scottish network.[41] More notable than these smaller trading ventures, however, was Mackinnon's role in the shipping world: he owned five shipping companies that eventually formed the foundation for the Inchcape Group.[42] Mackinnon, who, according to some observers, could 'lay claim to being the greatest Scottish tycoon of all time',[43] had established 'the most extensive multi-regional business group ... of interlocked partnerships', with the original cluster of shipping companies at its centre.[44] Though particularly eminent, Mackinnon was not the only Scot involved in shipping. Thomas Sutherland, for instance, was fundamental in the establishment of P&O in the Far East and Australasia. Other shipping companies in which Scots were involved specialised in the transport of particular commodities, raw materials and products – tea in the case of the Glen Line for example.

What these shipping lines had in common was that they were all established, or at least largely aided, by the industrial ingenuity and technical advances developed on the Clyde. The knowledge and skills that had been taken overseas by the Scottish entrepreneurs and shipping magnates involved in these businesses was fundamental. With these innovations coming directly

from Scotland, Scottish shipping agents and merchants were in an exception-
ally good position to capitalise on new trading routes, including, for instance,
the Suez Canal, which was opened in 1869 and significantly reduced the travel
time to the Far East.[45] Together with existing Scottish networks in Asia, many
of which 'founded ultimately on the earlier growth of Scottish influence in
the eighteenth-century East India Company and the private trading houses
of Asia',[46] Scottish interests and connections in the ports of the East were
strengthened substantially, facilitating the further expansion of Scottish agencies and trading houses beyond India.

Numbers are impressive. In Singapore, twelve of the first seventeen trading
houses were Scottish, or at least predominantly Scottish, including, for
example, Guthrie and Co., which had been set up in 1821 – two years after
the foundation of Singapore – and traded in sugar, coffee and spices, before
moving into investment in the late nineteenth century, focusing on Malayan
rubber plantations.[47]

The most remarkable story, however, is that of Jardine, Matheson & Co.,
which brings us from the Straits Settlement to China.

> As [Dirk] Struan walked among the main deck, he glanced at the shore
> and excitement swarmed over him. The war with China had gone as
> he had planned. Victory was as he had forecast. The prize of victory
> – the island – was something he had coveted for twenty years . . . The
> island was Hong Kong. Thirty square miles of mountainous stone
> on the north lip of the huge Pearl River in south China. A thousand
> yards off the mainland. Inhospitable. Infertile. Uninhabited except for
> a tiny fishing village on the south side . . . But Hong Kong contained
> the greatest harbour on earth. And it was Struan's stepping-stone into
> China . . . He was Tai-Pan of the Noble House.[48]

Tai-Pan, a term first used for foreign merchants and other businessmen in
Hong Kong and mainland China in the early 1830s, translates as 'big shot' –
used here to describe Struan's leading role in the Noble House, the fictional
trading company at the heart of James Clavell's novel *Tai-Pan*. Modelled on
Jardine, Matheson & Co., and with Struan loosely based on William Jardine,
Tai-Pan explores the development of trading companies in Hong Kong in the
aftermath of the first Opium War. The real story of Jardine, Matheson & Co.
formally began earlier than that, in 1832, when William Jardine and James
Matheson formally founded their partnership. Its antecedents go back even
further, however, as it 'had evolved from an unbroken line of partnerships and
was the inheritor of extensive trading relationships'[49] that had their origins in
Calcutta and Bombay trading houses and, in part, the East India Company.
Pan-Asian networks, which were consolidated after William Jardine had

joined Magniac & Co. in 1825,[50] were vital for the later establishment of Jardine, Matheson & Co.

After its establishment, Jardine, Matheson & Co. began trading in a variety of goods, chiefly including tea, cotton, silk and opium. The last of these was a commodity that contributed to much of the Company's early growth and expansion along the coast of China. Set up as an agency house, however, Jardine, Matheson & Co. also engaged in shipping, insurance brokerage and banking. Importantly, Jardine, Matheson & Co. became the first trading house to export tea directly from China to Britain when, in 1834, the East India Company's remaining China monopoly was abolished. Even prior to the end of this monopoly, a private trade in opium from India to China was thriving in the early nineteenth century.[51] The heyday of the opium trade, however, only came in the 1830s, and Jardine, Matheson & Co. was at the forefront: dealing in opium was a much more successful and profitable part of the business than the tea or cotton trade.[52] The Chinese government, recognising the impact the opium trade had on the Chinese population,[53] officially banned the trade in 1836. With the opium trade thus prohibited, Jardine, Matheson & Co. continued its trade with the drug through private merchants, and utilised contraband trade to do so. The prohibition issued by the Chinese government thus had little to no effect. This was the case too because Jardine, Matheson & Co. was very effective in trading under the radar, hiding, for instance, 'behind "neutral" flags' – a strategy that also explains why 'James Matheson acted as the Danish consul in Canton and put several Jardine, Matheson ships under the Danish flag'.[54] The Chinese government was well aware of these methods and, in seeking to end the opium trade for good, eventually declared war in 1839. Thus commenced the first Opium War, a gunboat diplomacy where the British military was deployed to safeguard trading routes, actively defending and protecting the trade interests of British merchants and companies. This direct involvement of the British military had been made possible by years of effective lobbying in London, often through Scottish networks that existed in the business and political circles there. This lobbying, as Meyer explains, got 'the British government to take an aggressive posture to get the Chinese to remove trade restrictions'.[55] While China 'deployed a feudal military with simple weapons, and relied on primitive, slow logistical support for the troops . . . the British deployed heavily armed troops with advanced weapons and operated swift, mobile warships and logistical support vessels.'[56]

It is easily understandable why business interests lobbied in favour of this gunboat diplomacy. The level of opium smuggling channelled through Jardine, Matheson & Co. was substantial: while a total of 19,956 opium chests were shipped in 1830–1, this had more than doubled, to 40,200, by 1838–9.[57] One reason why Jardine, Matheson & Co. was so successful in the smuggling was that it built special opium ships – the so-called opium-clippers – which allowed it to complete up to three round-trips per season between Calcutta and Canton; a fleet of smaller schooners and brigs was then used to trade the opium along the Chinese coast.[58] It was these opium-clippers that gave Jardine, Matheson & Co. an advantage over many other trading companies as the clippers could sail very fast. Most famous of all was the *Red Rover*. Built in 1829, the clipper's voyages were described by one observer as 'quite astonishing and unparalleled, and until now considered perfectly incompatible from repeated failures of the finest men-of-war to make passage up the China sea against the monsoon.'[59] This also highlights the role of the opium trade in the expansion of Jardine, Matheson & Co. – a role that reflects more broadly on the importance of opium in the eastern trade, as well as in the expansion of British influence in the region.[60] The outcome of the Opium War was certainly far-reaching. Not only did the Chinese government not achieve its main objective – the ending of the opium trade – the Opium War also led to the secession of Hong Kong, as well as the establishment of several so-called treaty ports. Provided for by the Treaty of Nanking in 1842, these treaty ports, including Shanghai, Amoy and Foochow, were special administrative zones where Chinese law did not apply, opening these settlements to foreign trade for Scots and others.

The transfer of Hong Kong to the British encouraged many merchants

Figure 13.2 Hong Kong, wood engraving by Frederick Grosse, 1866 [source: State Library of Victoria, mp000989]

and trading houses to relocate their headquarters to the settlement, including Jardine, Matheson & Co., whose main office was moved there from Macao in 1844. It was from Hong Kong that the Company continued its opium trade – a trade that went on to flourish in the 1840s and 1850s. And it was this trade that cemented a web of connections between India and China, but also with London, through a strong network of companies that included Jardine Skinner & Co. of Calcutta, Matheson & Co. in London, and also P&O, 'which from the 1850s established a monopoly over the Bombay-China opium trade which lasted until the early twentieth century.'[61] What these connections highlight is the dominance of private family partnerships, and how these were underpinned by the recruitment of Scots – a characteristic Devine has aptly described as 'systematic nepotism'.[62] Kinship alone, however, did not necessarily suffice. Thus wrote William Jardine to a nephew who was hoping to work for the firm:

> impress this on the minds of your young cousins . . . [that] I can
> never consent to assist idle and dissipated characters however nearly
> connected with me, but am prepared to go to any reasonale extent in
> supporting such of my relatives as conduct themselves prudently and
> industriously.[63]

Through its trade in opium, as well as its engagement in other financial and insurance services, Jardine, Matheson & Co. grew to be the largest British trading company before the First World War.[64] This was a result not least of its diversification and expansion from the 1860s, when the Company estbalished branches all over China, and also in Japan and New York, thus 'combining a diversified services and manufacturing business in the Far East with a worldwide venture capital business.'[65]

The activities of Jardine, Matheson & Co., and the expansion of trade throughout China after the First Opium War, also tie in with the development of banks in support of the growing trade. The most notable example is the Hongkong and Shanghai Banking Corporation (HSBC), which was founded in Hong Kong in March 1865 as the 'Hongkong and Shanghai Banking Company Ltd' on the initiative of Thomas Sutherland. Born in Aberdeen in 1834, Sutherland, the first superintendent and later managing director for P&O in Hong Kong, was keen on promoting the development of a bank in Asia itself that would 'combine banking with the tremendous business opportunities in trade and shipping between Hong Kong and Shanghai',[66] also incorporating into the bank a strong Scottish ethos. The first branch manager of the Shanghai office, which was opened shortly after that in Hong Kong, was David MacLean, who managed the branch between 1865 and 1873. It was perhaps MacLean's friendship with Robert Hart, the Inspector-General of Shanghai

Imperial Maritime Customs, that influenced its decision to deposit its entire income in the Hongkong and Shanghai Banking Corporation. It was also this important connection that contributed to the Quing government's frequent borrowing from the bank – an example of it dealing with government loans as well as commercial ones.[67]

While Shanghai was a key port for the China trade, as well as a financial centre, it was also an important gateway that connected China with Japan. In nineteenth-century Japan Scots were at the vanguard of European arrivals. Trade attracted Scots to the country, and 'the first British diplomatic plenipotentiary sent to Japan was a Scot, the 8th Earl of Elgin',[68] who was brought there to try to open up trade opportunities. Developments of such opportunities were slow, however, due to the resistence of the Japanese government towards foreign interference. It was only with the establishment of the merchant communities in Nagasaki and Yokohama that the 'modern relations between Britain and Japan' began.[69] Among the earliest arrivals in Nagasaki was Thomas Blake Glover. Born in Fraserburgh, Aberdeenshire in 1838, Glover first made his way to Japan in 1859, arriving in Nagasaki from Shanghai. A prime example of the workings of Scottish trading networks spanning the Far East, Glover had made his way to Shanghai under the auspices of Jardine, Matheson & Co. in 1857, and initially worked for the firm after his arrival in Nagasaki, before setting up his own business, Glover Trading Co., in 1861. Through that company Glover sold arms, developed coal mines and, most importantly, was fundamental in establishing a ship-yard in Nagasaki that would later become the Mitsubishi Corporation of Japan, importing the required technology for the goods it was manufacturing directly from the Clyde. Glover was the purveyor of Japanese industrialisation,[70] but he was by no means the only Scot who played a role in the modernisation of Japan. In engineering in particular Scots had significant influence. Henry Dyer, for example, was recruited to establish the Imperial College of Engineering in Tokyo in 1872, developing an innovative curriculum that combined theory and practice. Elsewhere, Scottish lighthouse technology, manufactured by the Stevenson brothers, made it to Japan with the help of Richard Henry Brunton, who left Edinburgh for Japan in 1868, spending eight years there.[71] Of great significance too was Neil Gordon Munro, the director of Yokohama's General Hospital and one of the first Westerners to study the Ainu people of Hokkaido. Born in 1863, Munro graduated from the University of Edinburgh in the late 1880s. Munro fell ill, however, and was thus unable to receive his Master's degree in surgery, travelling to India instead. It was in India that he was hired as a ship's surgeon in 1891, thus making his way to Japan. Still stricken with sickness on his arrival, Munro became a patient of the Yokohama General Hospital – the very hospital he was to become the director of in 1893. Munro remained in Yokohama until

1930, when he moved to Hokkaido to devote the remainder of his life to studying the Ainu people and culture.[72]

C CONCLUSION

What unites most of the Scots who made it to the Far East in the period under investigation here is that they viewed Asia as a sojourn. In some places this was effectively the policy of the time: in India, for example, British settlers were not officially forbidden to settle permanently, but they were not encouraged to do so. As a result, and by the nature of the sojourning experience, the Scottish diaspora in Asia, to this day, is a different diaspora from that of the principal settlement destinations explored in this volume, including, for instance, the United States or Australia.

First, and because a sojourn is premised on the eventual return home from the outset, there was little actual settlement migration to Asia: the Scottish soldiers of the EIC, or merchants and bankers in Shanghai, did not seek to make their homes in the Far East. Their time there was intended as a spring-board for wealth and better opportunities at home rather than in the New World. Consequently, life throughout the Far East was much more transient, and therefore, not conducive to family life – a fact reflected in the lack of families who came out to Asia. This was the case too because a sojourn often meant frequent relocation within Asia. Banker Sir Charles Stewart Addis, for example, was posted to over ten different cities in Asia, ranging from Calcutta to Singapore and Bejing, between 1883 and 1905.

Secondly, and as a result of the high level of transience in the Far East, Scots located there had a strong orientation to the homeland; this was often expressed in a more pronounced sense of boundary maintenance – as part of limited white populations, the Scots who ventured out to Asia, especially Scottish merchants, could often be found in clusters, drawing extensively on ethnic and kinship networks to facilitate their moving forward, provide business opportunities, and act as a safety net if required. Scottish trading houses in particular maintained a strong 'Scottishness' through their recruitment patterns of fellow Scots. This behaviour documents that, for all the diversity of experience, the Scottish sojourn in Asia was underpinned by distinct diaspora actions that were specific to it, these being framed almost exclusively through the orientation to the homeland. This orientation still existed, too, for those Scots who made it to even more far-flung corners of the diaspora, including Australia and New Zealand.

NOTES

1. *North China Herald*, 4 December 1896.
2. Tucker and Hendrickson, *The Fall of the First British Empire*.
3. For details on the history of the British Atlantic world, see for example Armitage and Braddick (eds), *The British Atlantic World*; Mancke and Shammas (eds), *The Creation of the British Atlantic World*.
4. *The Importance of the British Dominion in India, Compared with that in America*, p. 11. For details on how this geographical shift impacted upon America after independence, see also Fichter, *So Great A Proffit*.
5. Gallagher, *The Decline, Revival and Fall of the British Empire*, p. 77.
6. Devine, *To the Ends of the Earth*, p. 57.
7. Whatley, *The Industrial Revolution in Scotland*.
8. See for example Prebble, *Darien*; or Armitage, 'The Scottish vision of empire'.
9. Parker, 'Scottish enterprise in India', p. 193.
10. Hamilton, *A New Account of the East Indies*; the account was first published in 1727.
11. McGilvary, *Guardian of the East India Company*, p. 162; see also table 4.7 in Bowen, *The Business of Empire*, which details the geographical distribution of East India stockholders between 1756 and 1830. The percentage of Scots, however, is not an accurate reflection of numbers as many London-based Scots who owned stock would not have been included for Scotland. See also Mackillop, 'Locality, nation, and empire', tables 3.2 and 3.3, p. 69.
12. The total European population is estimated at 4,250, see Bryant, 'Scots in India in the eighteenth century', p. 23.
13. McGilvary, 'Return of the Scottish nabob', p. 91.
14. The painting is on display in the National Gallery of Scotland.
15. Colley, *Britons*, p. 127.
16. Mackillop, 'The Highlands and the returning nabob', p. 240; see also by the same author 'Europeans, Britons and Scots'.
17. Mackillop, 'The Highlands and the returning nabob', p. 240.
18. See Chapter 8; also Nechtmann, *Nabobs*.
19. Ibid., p. 239.
20. Bryant, 'Scots in India in the eighteenth century', p. 25, quote on p. 27.
21. Ibid., p. 26.
22. Mackillop, 'The Highlands and the returning nabob', p. 235.
23. For details on these returning 'nabobs' as part of the return movement of Scots, see Chapter 8.
24. Mackillop, 'The Highlands and the returning nabob', p. 236.
25. Bryant, 'Scots in India in the eighteenth century', p. 29.

26. See McLaren, *British India and British Scotland*; also McGilvary, *East India Patronage and the British State*; Tomlinson, 'From Campsie to Kedgeree'.

27. Bryant, 'Scots in India in the eighteenth century', p. 30.

28. Ibid., p. 31.

29. Ibid., p. 32.

30. Mackillop, 'Locality, nation, and empire', p. 60.

31. Parker, 'Scottish enterprise in India', p. 199.

32. Ibid., p. 202.

33. For details on the Scottish contribution to the national campaign against the renewal of the Company's charter and in favour of free trade, see Kumagai, 'Kirkam Finlay and John Crawfurd'.

34. Parker, 'Scottish enterprise in India', pp. 205–7.

35. See for example Stewart, *Jute and Empire*, p. 1.

36. For details on the Raj, see Judd, *The Lion and the Tiger*.

37. Vicziany, 'Imperialism, botany and statistics in early nineteenth-century India'. See also Buchanan's *A Journey from Madras through the Countries of Mysore, Canada and Malabar*.

38. Dilke, *Greater Britain*, p. 511.

39. See for example Buettner, 'Haggis in the Raj'.

40. Munro, *Maritime Enterprise and Empire*, p. 21.

41. See also Bueltmann, *Scottish Ethnicity*.

42. For details on the Inchcape Group see Jones (ed.), *The United Nations Library on Transnational Corporations, Volume 2*.

43. Cited in Devine, *To the Ends of the Earth*, p. 76.

44. Jones, *Merchants to Multinationals*, p. 55; see also Munro, 'Scottish overseas enterprise and the lure of London', p. 75.

45. It is also worth noting that, trade aside, emigration itself became a main business strand for many shipping lines. See for instance Harper and Constantine, *Migration and Empire*.

46. Devine, *To the Ends of the Earth*, p. 78.

47. Ibid.

48. Clavell, *Tai-Pan*; the book was first published in 1966 and is part of a series of novels set in Asia, including *Shogun* and *Noble House*.

49. Matheson Connell, *A Business in Risk*, p. 4; see also figure 1.2 on p. 7 for details about the evolution of Jardine, Matheson & Co. from earlier trade ventures that encompass Calcutta-based Matheson & Co. (which Matheson had established in 1827), Jardine's activities in Bombay, and joint connections then made via Magniac & Co. in Canton.

50. For details on Magniac & Co., see for instance Farooqui, *Smuggling as Subversion*, p. 212.

51. Jones, *Merchants to Multinationals*, p. 32.

52. Cheong, *Mandarins and Merchants*, p. 263; other Scottish merchants were also heavily involved in the opium trade, including for instance David Scott, a friend of Henry Dundas. Scott, Director of the East India Company from 1788, utilised his extensive patronage networks in Asia, accumulating substantial sums through the trade. See McGilvary, 'Return of the Scottish nabob', p. 97.
53. For details, see Le Pichon, *China Trade and Empire*, pp. 36ff; also Yangwen, *The Social Life of Opium in China*.
54. Jones, *Merchants to Multinationals*, 32.
55. Meyer, *Hong Kong as a Global Metropolis*, p. 48.
56. Ibid., p. 49.
57. Numbers established by Michael Greenberg, cited in Yangwen, *The Social Life of Opium*, p. 93.
58. Meyer, *Hong Kong as a Global Metropolis*, p. 44.
59. From the *Bengal Courier* (1831), cited in Janin, *The India-China Opium Trade in the Nineteenth Century*, p. 85.
60. This approach is even more obvious in connection with the Second Opium War (1856–60), which was essentially engineered by Britain (and also France) for the purpose of opening up even more parts of China for free trade, as the concessions received through the Treaty of Nanking were deemed insufficient. For details see Scott, *China and the International System*, pp. 35ff.
61. Jones, *Merchants to Multinationals*, p. 33.
62. Devine, *To the Ends of the Earth*, p. 83. See also Le Pichon, *China Trade and Empire*, which highlights some of the connections through Jardine and Matheson's correspondence.
63. Parker, 'Scottish enterprise in India', p. 201.
64. Table 3.1, Jones, *Merchants to Multinationals*, p. 54.
65. Jones, *Merchants to Multinationals*, p. 61, also p. 57.
66. Ji, *A History of Modern Shanghai Banking*, p. 45.
67. Ibid., p. 48.
68. Checkland, 'The Scots in Meiji Japan, 1868–1912', p. 255.
69. Ibid., p. 256.
70. For further details, see McKay, *Scottish Samurai*; also Pedlar, *The Imported Pioneers*, chapter 31, 'Thomas Glover and the early foreign traders'. For a detailed study of the industrial connections between Japan and Scotland, see Mairi Hamilton Arbuckle Araki, 'Japanese engineering and Scotland'.
71. Pedlar, *The Imported Pioneers*, pp. 154ff; also Brunton, *Schoolmaster to an Empire*.
72. Refsing, 'Introduction', pp. 70ff.

CHAPTER 14

The Antipodes

Alexander McMaster, born in Stranraer in 1822, immigrated to Australia in the early 1840s, pursuing a diverse range of careers.[1] Australia, however, was not to be McMaster's final destination as he decided to move on to New Zealand, making his way to Oamaru, a small settlement a good 70 miles north of Dunedin in the South Island, in the mid-1850s. Shortly after his arrival in New Zealand, McMaster went into a partnership with John Borton, with the two jointly purchasing a number of runs in the vicinity of Oamaru to breed cattle. Evidence suggests that McMaster and Borton had probably already met in Australia in the early 1850s, when Borton made his way down under. Australia continued to play an important role in McMaster's life in any case as he returned there in the late 1850s to convince his friend James Gardiner, whom he had first met aboard the ship that was taking him from Scotland to Australia, to join him and Borton as station manager in New Zealand. Disposed favourably towards such a move, Gardiner accepted the offer and worked for Borton and McMaster until his death in 1867.[2] A testament to the strength of Scottish ethnic and business networks at 'world's end', McMaster's story is also indicative of how Australia and New Zealand were connected through trans-Tasman migration.

Overall, between 1861 and 1945, the Scots accounted for a steady 15 per cent of Australia's UK-born migrants, and made up nearly a quarter of all UK-born migrants to New Zealand. This makes them the third largest migrant group, after the English and Irish, in Australia, and the second largest, after the English, in New Zealand. These numbers become even more remarkable when considered in relation to the Scots' population share in the UK, which had decreased from around 15 per cent in the eighteenth century to 12 per cent in 1901, and then continued to decline further (see Chapter 3, Table 3.3).[3] The Scots were thus over-represented in the Antipodes in terms of their population share within the British Isles, and especially markedly so in New Zealand.

Despite their numerical significance, however, the Scots were largely ignored before the 1960s in Antipodean historical scholarship, and the general histories that then followed, including Manning Clark's *A History of Australia* or Kevin Sinclair's *History of New Zealand*, essentially continued that tradition. Early scholarship that does exist on the Scots in Australia and New Zealand tends to investigate more specific aspects of their migration. David Macmillan's *Scotland and Australia 1788–1850*, for instance, explores the Scots within the context of Australian economic history.[4] By and large, knowledge has remained hidden in regional histories, or was of a more popular nature.[5]

In Australia, academic currents began to change in the 1980s with the publication of Malcolm Prentis's *The Scots in Australia*,[6] which provided the first in-depth study, focusing on New South Wales, Victoria and Queensland. It was to take almost another two decades for a more substantial interest in the Scots to develop in New Zealand, with Donald Harman Akenson's ground-breaking study on the Irish serving as the initial catalyst.[7] A problem in both countries has been the perception that Scottish migrants blended in well. While this has not made them invisible it contributed to ignorance towards them, especially when compared to migrant groups who struggled with their relocation abroad, such as the Catholic Irish.[8] Moreover, the research that has been carried out in the latter half of the twentieth century has tended to concentrate on narrow themes, for instance particular settlements.[9] The broader patterns of Scottish migration and immigrant community life have only recently been brought to the fore.[10]

Within this wider historiographical context, this chapter focuses on exploring the types of Scots who made it to Australia and New Zealand respectively, investigating the timing and flow of their migration. By investigating capital and entrepreneurial links established by Scots, and the role Scots played in Antipodean colonial life, the chapter will also discuss how these migrants shaped their southern hemisphere host cultures in distinct ways.

A CONVICTS, TRADERS AND EARLY SCOTTISH SETTLEMENT

Scottish settlement in the Antipodes was, in general terms, more sporadic than that to North America, and on a smaller scale.[11] While the migration of Scots to Australia commenced earlier than that to New Zealand, there was only a small trickle of Scottish migrants prior to the 1820s.[12] Moreover, it is important to recognise that Australia was first put on the Scottish diaspora map not as a migrant destination of choice, but as a convict settlement. The overall number of convict Scots was, however, low. Of the estimated total of nearly 155,000 convicts sent to the Australian mainland and Van Diemen's land, only about

8,200 were Scots. A slightly larger proportion of Scots, possibly up to 700, were among the nearly 10,000 male convicts sent to Western Australia between 1850 and 1868.[13] But even these numbers pale compared to those of convicts who arrived from England. As Prentis explains, 'the Scottish transportation rate was consistently about 20 to 25 per cent' of that of England.[14] The reason for the relatively small number of Scottish convicts can be found in Scotland's legal system. Preserved in its own right as an integral pillar of Scottish civil society after the Union of 1707, the Scottish legal system was more moderate than the English one in terms of the penalties for what one might call 'smaller crimes'. In Scotland a sentence for transportation was a punishment almost exclusively reserved for more serious crimes and repeat offenders. As much was noted by a mid-nineteenth century observer, A. Majoribanks, in 1847:

> Both in New South Wales and Van Diemen's Land, Scotch convicts are considered the worst, and English the best. This seems to arise not so much from the laws of the two countries being so essentially different, as their being differently administered; the punishment for minor crimes in particular, being infinitely more severe in England than in Scotland. Hence, hundreds are transported annually from England for offences which, in Scotland, would be punished by sixty days confinement in jail at Bridewell . . . In Scotland . . . they are mostly old offenders before they are transported.[15]

Yet while there were fewer Scottish convicts when measured in absolute numbers, what this meant was that the Scots who were transported were among the worst offenders in terms of the crime committed, with women convicts allegedly even worse than their male counterparts.

The proportion of Scottish women convicts was actually higher than that of their male Scottish counterparts, particularly among the post-1840 convicts sent to Van Diemen's Land. Of these, nearly 14 per cent were Scottish women.[16] Among the arrivals in Van Diemen's Land in 1846 were Jean Watson, Catherine Hill and Christine Nish, all three of whom arrived on the *Emma Eugenia* together with another 167 women, with at least 20 per cent of them being Scottish.[17] Jean Watson had been found guilty of theft in October 1845 by the Perth Court of Justiciary – a verdict also reached for her accomplice, Isabella Watson. While the relationship between the two women is not entirely clear, they committed the robbery together and both were sentenced to seven years' transportation.[18] As was reported in the *Dundee Courier* in August 1845, the pair 'were charged with carrying off a quantity of wearing apparel from a house in Scouringburn, the latter [Jean Watson] having been twice previously convicted of theft.'[19] Prior conviction also played its part in the ten-year sentence given to Catherine Hill. While she was also convicted for theft, the crime was 'aggravated by being a habit'.[20] Convict Transportation Registers reveal that the majority of sentences for the women convicts on the *Emma Eugenia* was seven years, making Christine Nish stand out: she had been sentenced to a term of life on 23 September 1842 by the Glasgow Court of Justiciary.

The Scottish convicts' poor reputation that preceded them was soon outweighed, however, by the virtues of the free Scottish immigrant.[21] It is also worth noting that more recent scholarship has stressed that while Scottish convicts may not have compared well with the free immigrants, 'when compared with convicts of other nationalities, they were far from worthless.'[22] Moreover, early Australia was not entirely comprised of convicts: the Scottish military, as in other settlements in the British Empire, played an important role in providing security in the early colony.[23] Other professions, notably civil servants, also saw a large proportion of Scots take up roles. Many of the early colonial administrators were Scots[24] for instance, and among them in Australia was Lachlan Macquarie, Governor of New South Wales from 1810 to 1821. Born on the island of Ulva in the Inner Hebrides in 1762, Macquarie volunteered for the army in 1776 and became an ensign in the Royal Highland Emigrants a year later. This was a position that first brought him to North America and then to the West Indies, from where he decided to move east. He eventually made it to India in 1788, having been posted to Bombay; he spent the next two decades on the subcontinent and in other imperial arenas, pursuing his military career. It was somewhat by chance, and perhaps in part due to his boldness, that Macquarie became Governor of New South Wales, following in the footsteps of deposed governor William Bligh – commanding the *Bounty* when its crew mutinied. In his new role, Macquarie was paramount to Australia's transition from a penal colony to a free settlement, focusing on the promotion of trade, agriculture, public works and the reintegration of ex-convicts into society proper.[25] It was also during his time in office that the number of Scottish civil officials increased significantly: it 'became markedly disproportionate',[26] patronage networks being heavily utilised as elsewhere in the Scottish diaspora.

Across the Tasman Sea another Scot, James Busby, was of key importance in developing New Zealand as a British colony. Initially settled in Australia to pursue viticulture, Busby made his name writing reports on the state of New Zealand, thereby gaining his appointment as the first official British Resident there in 1833. Although tasked with protecting settlers and traders, as well as protecting Maori from Europeans, Busby was not given real authority to enforce these tasks. He was 'reluctantly paid for by the Colony of New South Wales',[27] as New Zealand was still under the jurisdiction of New South Wales at the time. As a civilian, there was also no way for Busby to receive troops in support, so his mission always stood on feeble grounds. Yet despite the many setbacks and lack of financial, administrative and military support, Busby successfully established more formalised contact with Maori, and drafted the Declaration of Independence of New Zealand to prevent Baron de Thierry from declaring French sovereignty over New Zealand in 1835. Signed by thirty-five chiefs, the United Tribes of New Zealand, the Declaration 'deemed New Zealand an independent state under British protection.'[28] Most notably, it was James Busby and William Hobson (who later was to become the first Governor of New Zealand) who drafted the Treaty of Waitangi in 1840. The treaty marks a key caesura in New Zealand history, officially asserting British sovereignty over the country.[29]

Of great importance too in the early days of both Australia and New Zealand were the many Scottish explorers, surveyors and pastoral pioneers. Among the group of surveyors, Sir Thomas Livingstone Mitchell stands out in his role as Surveyor General in Australia between 1828 and 1855.[30] Of similar importance in New Zealand was James Hector, the director of the Geological Survey of Otago and founder of the Geological Survey of New Zealand.[31] These Scots, together with many others, were fundamental to the charting of the two colonies.

The majority of Scottish arrivals in Australia prior to 1830 were farmers, 'men of substance . . . [who] could not afford either the high cost of capitalisation or the high rents of Scottish agriculture'.[32] In fact, a disproportionate number of applications for land grants in the 1820s came from Scots. This migration was that of the middle and upper classes, with many of the settlers bringing with them substantial captial of £2,000 or more.[33] It was Scottish merchants, however, who left a more visible imprint in this early settlement period. Concerned about the economic problems Scotland was facing in the 1820s, many looked abroad for opportunities to develop their businesses. Prior to the emergence of Australia as a primary settler dominion in the nineteenth century, Scottish trade ventures served an important role in facilitating the transition of Australia to a free settler colony, involving some of the Asian trade networks explored in detail in Chapter 13. This was a development spearheaded by Robert Campbell. Born in Greenock in April 1769, Campbell moved to India aged twenty-seven to join his older brother, a partner in the Calcutta agency house of Campbell, Clarke & Co. With the Clarkes leaving the partnership a few years later, the firm became Campbell & Co. in 1799, continuing its trade with New South Wales which had first commenced in 1796. Robert was keen to establish further connections, thus making his way to Australia in 1798, building a warehouse and a private wharf. Campbell & Co. quickly rose to dominate trade 'having £50,000 worth of goods in its Sydney warehouses in 1804.'[34] More importantly, Campbell had introduced 'Australia into the network of Asian trade', and was central to identifying key early exports such as sealskins.[35]

It was another Campbell, though unrelated, who shaped early business and trade in New Zealand, namely John Logan Campbell. A trained surgeon, Campbell left Greenock for Australia in the summer of 1839, but moved on to New Zealand in early 1840. It was there that he was reunited with William Brown, a Scottish lawyer he had first met aboard the *Palmyra*, the ship that had brought him out to Australia. With both having made it across the Tasman Sea, the two embarked on a number of joint ventures, eventually setting up Auckland's first merchant firm in December 1840.[36] Logan Campbell's mercantile links with Asia served the business well. While he initially focused on supplying basic commodities, he 'soon became involved in land speculation, the promotion of the Bank of New Zealand and the New Zealand and South British Insurance Companies.'[37]

Yet while these prominent Scots in Australia and New Zealand were fundamental in shaping early colonial society, a focus on their activities does not necessarily reflect the wider experiences of Scottish migrants down under, and has, therefore, been criticised as a 'great man bias' by some.[38] To better understand the history of Scots in the Antipodes, therefore, it serves well to explore the strands of their migration to Australia and New Zealand from the point when they arrived in larger numbers.

B SCOTTISH MIGRATION STRANDS TO THE ANTIPODES

Moving beyond the early Scottish arrivals in Australia and New Zealand, different strands of Scottish migration can be established that tie in with the expansion of settlement in the two countries. In Australia first signs of this expansion appeared in the 1830s, when the number of immigrants arriving, their composition and also regional destination in Australia changed and diversified. As Prentis shows, it was then that Van Diemen's Land lost some of its appeal for Scots, 'as the Port Phillip district opened up.'[39] Of particular importance were the ideas of systematic colonisation promoted by Edward Gibbon Wakefield. Blossoming enterprise in Australia required an increasing amount of free labour, and planned settlements, as well as assisted emigration schemes, were designed to help provide it, serving as a key 'pull-factor' for migrants first in Australia and then in New Zealand. Settlement companies such as the South Australian Company were set up, organising migration.[40] In New Zealand systematic colonisation was specifically designed to facilitate the arrival of a better class of settlers, excluding, as Sinclair has observed, 'the lowest stratum.'[41] Viewed in conjunction with developments in Scotland in the 1830s and 1840s, when high unemployment was a real concern, the appeal of Antipodean emigration schemes is clear. Hence, while Canada was the main destination for Scots prior to 1847, between 1910 and 1914 and then again after the First World War, Australia and New Zealand were growing in importance as a migrant destination of choice from the 1830s.[42]

As a result of organised migration schemes, nearly 45 per cent of assisted immigrants in New South Wales in 1837 were of Scottish descent. While their number decreased quite significantly, Prentis suggests that, overall, 14.5 per cent of assissted immigrants were Scots.[43] Most of them came in kinship groups, and were from the Lowlands, chiefly from the Lothians and Glasgow, but also parts of Ayrshire and the north-east of Scotland.[44] Parallel to the arrival of poorer migrants through these assisted schemes, the 1830s and 1840s also saw a smaller group of wealthy Scots arrive in Australia who had enough capital to finance their migration to take advantage of the opportunities and land available. Seeking new markets to invest in, 'capital and enterprise from Scotland came to Australia in concentrated flows which flavoured specific sectors, most notably pastoralism and commerce.'[45]

In New Zealand larger-scale immigration only developed after the signing of the Treaty of Waitangi in 1840, but soon led to a significant influx of settlers from the British Isles. Some early New Zealand Company arrivals from Scotland settled in Wellington, but the majority of Scots bound for New Zealand in the 1840s and 1850s went to the province of Otago in the South Island. This migration is directly connected to developments in Scotland, with Dunedin, organised under the New Zealand Company's offshoot, the Otago Association, being established as a Free Church Settlement in 1848.[46] Here, and as a result of the Disruption of 1843, Scottish Presbyterian settlers were, for the first time, made 'a central element of a colonisation scheme.'[47] Among the first arrivals was the Revd Thomas Burns of Dumfriesshire, who had been offered the position of minister to the Otago-bound migrants in mid-1843 by the Colonial Committee of the Free Church of Scotland. A nephew of Scotland's national bard, Robert Burns, the Revd Thomas Burns made his name by his strict moral standards, seeking to uphold the Presbyterian faith in the 'new Edinburgh'.[48]

An even more important 'pull-factor' than the emigration schemes that had been running under the flag of systematic colonisation was the discovery of gold – first in Victoria, Australia, in the 1850s, and then in the interior of Otago and the West Coast in the South Island of New Zealand in the 1860s. Even assisted passengers followed this pull, the bulk of assisted Scots, 24 per cent, settling in Victoria in the mid-nineteenth century.[49] The migration triggered by the precious metal also brought a larger number of unassisted migrants, and influenced the gender balance, with the majority of gold-seekers being young single men. One of them was William Wilson of Aberdeenshire. Though he had originally emigrated to New Zealand for labouring work, he was soon attracted to the West Coast of New Zealand's South Island in a quest to make his fortune in gold.[50] A similar plan was pursued by Alexander McKay from Kirkcudbrightshire, who arrived in New Zealand in 1863 to try his luck on the gold fields of Otago.[51] An increasing number of migrants like Wilson and McKay, many of whom had mined the Victorian gold fields of Australia prior to moving on to New Zealand, had made their way across the Tasman Sea. Scots were significant among the new arrivals, coming in proportions markedly higher than their share of the British home population.[52]

The influx of these new migrants fundamentally reshaped New Zealand's ethnic character. Moreover, with the arrival of larger numbers of immigrants as a result of the gold rushes, more diverse settlement patterns developed in both Australia and New Zealand. While the majority of early Scots in New Zealand had gone to Otago and Southland in the South Island, Scots began settling all over the country, making up 'at least 15 per cent in almost all provinces in the censuses up to the First World War.'[53] Clusters of Scottish settlement were less obvious in Australia, but records relating to the early assisted immigrants show that they preferred New South Wales (which, in the 1830s included Victoria and Queensland) over other areas, with almost 11 per cent settling there.[54] In the course of the nineteenth century, however, there was a preference for Victoria over New South Wales once the two had become separate states, with 65 per cent of Scots living in Victoria in 1861, and still a significant 35 per cent in 1901; New South Wales, however, had taken over by 1911.[55]

State-assisted schemes by provincial governments, initiated in the 1870s, were a second key pull-factor for New Zealand. These schemes offered a free passage to labourers and domestic servants, the migrants being sought to promote economic and infrastructural growth under Julius Vogel's 1870 Immigration and Public Works Act.[56] Low immigration, from the 1880s through to the early twentieth century, succeeded the peak years of the gold rushes and assisted immigration, and the economic downturn, combined with soaring unemployment, contributed to high levels of emigration from New Zealand.[57] Despite these developments, the number of Scots entering New Zealand between 1891 and 1915 remained relatively constant, with an estimated total of 117,000 Scottish-born migrants arriving in New Zealand between 1840 and 1939.[58]

While a detailed regional profile of the migrants' origins has not yet been established for Australia, it is clear that the majority came from the Lowlands. This also holds true for New Zealand, where the most recent demographic study of Scottish migration and settlement there demonstrates the degree to which the migrants represented a microcosm of Scotland in terms of their regional origins.[59] Establishing the exact number of Scottish arrivals in the Antipodes is not straightforward, however, and poses particular problems in the New Zealand context given that the original census returns have been

Table 14.1 Scots as a percentage of the total population and foreign-born population in New Zealand [source: adapted from McCarthy, 'Scottish migrant ethnic identities in the British Empire since the nineteenth century', p. 144]

Census year	Number	Per cent of total population	Per cent of foreign population
1861	15,534	15.7	21.8
1871	36,871	14.4	22.6
1881	52,753	10.8	19.8
1891	51,916	8.3	20.0
1901	47,858	6.2	18.6
1911	51,709	5.1	16.9
1921	51,654	4.2	16.5
1936	54,188	3.7	18.4
1951	44,049	2.3	16.5

Table 14.2 National composition of UK immigrants to New Zealand (percentages) [source: adapted from Table 1 in Phillips and Hearn, *Settlers*, p. 52]

	1800–39	1840–52	1853–90	1871–90	1891–1915	1916–45
English	62.1	64.3	46.6	54.6	65.0	60.1
Scottish	20.4	20.6	30.2	21.5	22.2	28.7
Irish	15.6	13.5	21.4	21.7	10.9	8.6

destroyed. The figures in Table 14.1 and Table 14.2 can be calculated on the basis of the *New Zealand Population Census*.

These general trends have recently been confirmed in Rebecca Lenihan's study of records collected by the New Zealand Society of Genealogists, Scottish Interest Group.[60] Despite the steady arrival of Scots in New Zealand, it is important to remember, however, that of the estimated 2 million emigrants who departed from Scotland between the mid-nineteenth and mid-twentieth centuries, a mere 10 per cent at most made it to New Zealand. The important point is that while this percentage is relatively unimportant to Scotland, it constituted a sizeable element of New Zealand's much smaller population. This is emphasised by the fact that the Scots were significantly over-represented as a migrant group in New Zealand in terms of their UK population share. These numbers are remarkable given that New Zealand was the British Empire's most distant colonial outpost. At the time when Scots and others began emigrating there in larger numbers, the voyage out could easily take up to five months, and was a notoriously strenuous journey, especially for steerage passengers.

No comparable data exists for Australia, but the broad patterns have also been established, revealing that the early 1860s, mid-1870s and 1880s saw the

Table 14.3 Estimated percentages of Scots in relation to the Australian population [source: adapted from Prentis, *Scots in Australia* (2008), p. 8]

	Per cent of Scots in relation to Australian population
1861	12.4
1891	13.5
1947	14.7

Table 14.4 Scots as a percentage of the total population and foreign-born population in Australia [source: adapted from McCarthy, 'Scottish migrant ethnic identities in the British Empire', p. 145]

Census year	Number	Per cent of total population	Per cent of foreign population
1891	123,818	3.9	12.3
1901	101,753	2.7	11.9
1911	93,083	2.1	12.3
1921	108,756	2.0	13.0
1933	132,489	2.0	14.7
1947	102,998	1.4	13.8

largest number of Scots arriving in Australia, whereas the 1890s Depression resulted in a significant cut in immigration numbers.[61]

C HIGHLAND MIGRATION TO THE ANTIPODES

Highland migration down under was generally sporadic, 'the product of specific, short-lived schemes',[62] but they were schemes that nonetheless resulted in a 'concentrated movement which brought these people [highland emigrants] into disproportionate significance.'[63] The appointment of government emigration agents in Scotland, a general feature of Scottish emigration as we have already seen, facilitated the emigration of highlanders. The Highlands, in fact, became a key area for the recruitment of immigrants to Australia in the late 1830s and early 1840s – a time when labour was needed in Australia, while evictions in the Highlands, famine and land congestion were a major concern in Scotland. Departures directly from the Highlands facilitated the move down under, eliminating the journey to ports in the south of Scotland or even England,[64] and emigration agents canvassing the Highlands also played a central role. As was reported in the *Caledonian Mercury* in 1838,

Dr Boyter, the Government Emigration Agent for Australia, arrived
at Fort William on Friday the 18th ultimo, and intimated his intention
of meeting with intending emigrants on Monday the 21st. The news of
his arrival, like the fiery cross of old, soon spread through every glen of
the district; and at an early hour on Monday, thousands of enterprising
Gaels might be seen ranked around the Caledonian Hotel, anxious to
quit the land of their forefathers, and to go and possess the unbounded
pastures of Australia. Dr Boyter enrolled upwards of 300, who are to
embark from Oban in the month of July.[65]

Boyter was, as Richards notes, particularly successful in encouraging highlanders to emigrate.[66] While neither Australia nor New Zealand were the
main destination for displaced highland emigrants, as these had mostly been
'shipped to Canada by their landlords',[67] there were, nonetheless, distinct
migrant streams from the Highlands to the Antipodes, with an estimated
20,000 highlanders being settled in Australia by 1857.[68] Specific migration
schemes and special settlements facilitated this migration. The Highland and
Island Emigration Society, for instance, was set up for the express purpose of
matching 'the population crisis in the Highlands with the needs of the colonies
. . . [and] transmitted 5,000 in the mid 1850s, many of whom arrived in the
poorest physical and mental condition, often to meet a mixed if not hostile
reception.'[69] The migration channelled through the Society focused on migration in kinship groups, had specific age restrictions, and was looking for people
of 'good character'. The scheme found support from all quarters of society;
Alexander Ewing, the Scottish Episcopal bishop of Argyle and the Isles, for
instance, utilised his sermons to promote the Society's emigration scheme.[70]
In 1852 the first year of the Society's operations, Ewing thus 'spoke of the
virtues of the Celts as the leaders of a new colonial race'.[71] However, not all
were convinced that the Society's work was useful. As Edward Grimes, the
immigration agent in Victoria, outlined in his 1852 annual report, most of the
highland emigrants

are in a most deplorable state of ignorance, and quite unacquainted with
the English language . . . However desirable the system may be as a
means of charitable relief, I scarcely look upon this class of immigrants
as one that should be brought out at the expense of the colony; very few
of them are acquainted with agricultural or pastoral employment, and
from their indolent habits, I do not think they are likely to prove a very
great acquisition to our labour market.[72]

While Grimes's view is replete with stereotypes of the highland savage
similar to those expressed by painter John Wilkes in the eighteenth century,[73]

there were genuine problems with migration from the Highlands, some of which are exemplified well in the migration of thirty-six St Kildans to Australia in October 1852. While St Kilda, as with other parts of mainland Scotland, was faced with the effects of a succession of potato crop failures, there was a shortage of agricultural labourers in the Port Phillip area because many earlier settlers had relocated to the gold fields of south-east Australia. These new migrants were ill prepared, and, though emigrating in kinship groups, which is generally viewed as a safer option than individual migration, even that support network did not help meet a series of other problems, including the St Kildan emigrants' lack of immunity to diseases. While St Kildans constituted only 12 per cent of the passengers on board the *Priscilla*, the ship that brought them to Australia, they made up 45 per cent of the fatalities.[74] Their isolated island life had made them especially vulnerable. The arrival in Australia did not halt the migrants' plight, with their ninety-eight-day journey ending in quarantine. Furthermore, by the time the St Kildans arrived in Port Phillip that port had grown to be the point of entry for well over 90,000 immigrants a year. There was congestion, the supply of food was a problem, and so was overcrowding in the temporary accommodation made available. The arrival of 'another shipload of Gaelic-speaking Highlanders and Islanders, some of them penniless and sick',[75] was not viewed in a positive light by Australian officials. Stereotypes about the highlanders' background and attitude to work were consolidated, and the volatile economic state contributed further problems.

In New Zealand, highland emigration too caused a number of problems, specifically in the context of some of the so-called special settlements that had been conceived as part of Julius Vogel's Public Works scheme in the 1870s to facilitate infrastructural growth and the settlement of remoter parts of New Zealand. What is especially interesting about these settlements is that a significant number of Shetland Island settlers were recruited for the schemes. The first group of Shetlanders thus settled, in mid-1873, in the Port William settlement on Stewart Island. This scheme was backed by influential politician Robert Stout (a Shetlander himself), and the Superintendent of Otago, James Macandrew. The argument brought forward in favour of the settlement of Shetland Islanders on this southernmost outpost of New Zealand was that they were ideal settlers for Stewart Island, being 'inured to the hardships of a rigorous climate', and with inherited 'maritime instincts' that would ensure their successful acclimatisation and settlement at the southern end of New Zealand.[76] The settlement, however, had been ill conceived from the start, and the harsh conditions in Foveaux Strait posed significant problems, with the migrants being unfamiliar with many of the ways of life and labour they would have needed to make a good living there.[77] Karamea, located on the West Coast of New Zealand's South Island, was another special settlement established under Vogel's scheme that attracted a large group of Shetlanders.

Figure 14.1 Scottish immigrants bound for the Group Settlement Scheme, 1926 [source: State Library of Western Australia, Izzy Orloff collection ; BA1059/1693]

Unfortunately, the settlement, though generally in a more favourable location, was also plagued with problems and largely failed – as did many of the other special settlements that were set up.[78]

Later schemes, developed as a result of the Empire Settlement Act in the 1920s, were somewhat more successful in settling highlanders in the Antipodes. The so-called Group Settlement Scheme, for example, was specifically developed for the purpose of attracting labourers to Australia. As with earlier schemes, passages were funded by the government, which provided a major incentive for intending migrants. Among those who took up the Western Australian Group Settlement Scheme were a significant number of Hebrideans, who had been encouraged by a visit to Lewis from William C. Stillman, chief clerk of the Commonwealth Government's Migration and Settlement Office in London, to emigrate under the scheme. As a result partly of his propaganda, nearly 10 per cent of the passengers aboard the *Bendigo*, which left London for Australia in late August 1923, were from Lewis. Even the usually sceptical local press viewed the idea of this group emigration in a favourable light.[79] While, as we have seen from previous examples, group schemes were by no means always successful, they could still, similarly to chain migration, provide a strong safety net.

D SCOTTISH CULTURE AND ANTIPODEAN
SOCIAL LIFE

Scots were, as some of our explorations in this chapter have already indicated, important players in colonial politics, business life, agriculture, and a number of other professions in the Antipodes. Their influence, however, went even further than that, extending deep into wider social life and the cultural sphere. While 'migrants did not inevitably fall back into prescribed cultural continuities'[80] in the New World, the Scots were very adept at utilising Scottish traditions not only within their own community bounds, but also at integrating them into, what were at the time, emerging societies.

In Antipodean holiday culture the Scots left a significant legacy, and one connected to two very Scottish traditions: Highland Games and Hogmanay. The Games were organised chiefly, as we have seen in Chapter 7, by Caledonian societies, but were by no means serving an exclusively Scottish purpose. An intrinsic element of the annual events calendar in both Australia and New Zealand, Highland Games successfully promoted leisure activities, institutionalising them at a time when organised sports were still in their infancy. While the events included traditional Scottish contests such as caber tossing, the focus on wider sporting activities – cycling was particularly popular in New Zealand for example – not only guaranteed the Games' survival over a long period of time, but also their role for the wider community. This was the case too because the Games provided an annual meeting place for colonials, Scots and non-Scots alike, thereby aiding social cohesion in settlements large and small.[81]

Given the reversal of the seasons in the southern hemisphere, there was a preference for the Games to be held over the Christmas and New Year holiday period, with New Year's Day being especially popular in New Zealand. This link contributed to giving the New Year holidays pre-eminence over Christmas in some areas.[82] This highlights that many Scottish activities 'came to reflect a wider and deeper Scottish contribution to the development of New Zealand society ... Scottish culture was normalised, becoming integral to New Zealand culture.'[83]

Other examples can be found in education, including the use of the Scottish four-year honours system at New Zealand universities, and the pioneering role of Scottish women like Learmonth White Dalrymple in the promotion of education for girls. In Australia, similar patterns are evident. A strong Scottish influence can also be traced, for instance, in literature. As Prentis notes, 'Australian poetry has a very strong Celtic colouring'.[84] What is more, Scottish writers did not necessarily seek to impose Scottish traditions or themes, but rather 'because some of the themes of Scottish literature were compatible ... helped turn Australian literature towards Australian themes.'[85]

E CONCLUSION

While we do not wish to overstate the case, the impact of the Scots in the Antipodes has been remarkable given not only their numbers, which made them the second- and third-largest immigrant groups in New Zealand and Australia respectively, but also their early arrival in the two colonies: Scots were at the forefront of settlement. In combination, and through their subsequent prominence in leading positions that span political, social and cultural life, this contributed to the Scots being disproportionately responsible for the development of colonial society in the Antipodes, and in New Zealand in particular.

With this in mind, the exploration of the Scots in the Antipodes provides an opportune moment for one final consideration of the Scottish diaspora that this book has sought to capture: that determined by the actions of its agents. In societies where Scots were a prominent migrant group, they were particularly adept at utilising diasporic actions to fit the circumstances they encountered in their respective new home. The important point is this: the Scots' diasporic actions, although clearly informed by an orientation to the homeland and the wish to maintain ethnic boundaries, often transcended both. In societies like New Zealand the Scots thus became 'interlocked ethnics'[86] because both ethnic boundaries and the boundary between 'the ethnic' and 'the civic' were fluid. Consequently, many Scots were able to utilise their ethnicity for wider civic purposes – even if on a small scale and only in their local community – and could do so to such a degree that it became integral to the making of colonial society.

NOTES

1. McAloon, *No Idle Rich*, p. 36.
2. Obituaries for Gardiner and McMaster: *North Otago Times*, 21 May 1864 and 14 September 1885; see also McMaster Family, Tokarahi Station records, 1869–73, Hocken Library, Dunedin, New Zealand, MS-1011–05.
3. See table 2.1 in Bryant, *The Nations of Britain*, p. 40; also Harper, 'A century of Scottish emigration to New Zealand', p. 221.
4. Macmillan was the first scholar to explore sources in both Scotland and Australia, focusing in particular on trade and the organisational aspects of Scottish investment in Australia and the emigration of Scots. He did not, however, investigate the Scots' actual settlement experiences. See Macmillan, *Scotland and Australia*.
5. For instance Pearce, *The Scots of New Zealand*.

6. Prentis, *The Scots in Australia* (1983); also the updated Prentis, *The Scots in Australia* (2008).

7. Akenson, *Half the World from Home*; the first serious work on the Scots in New Zealand is a collection of essays: Brooking and Coleman (eds), *The Heather and the Fern*.

8. See for instance O'Farrell, *The Irish in Australia*; and Fraser, *To Tara via Holyhead*.

9. Waipu in New Zealand provides one example. See Molloy, *Those Who Speak to the Heart*.

10. Including Bueltmann, *Scottish Ethnicity*; and Lenihan, 'From Alba to Aotearoa'.

11. Marjory Harper, 'A century of Scottish emigration', p. 221.

12. Cage, 'Scots – early migration', p. 646.

13. Prentis, *Scots in Australia* (2008), p. 37.

14. Ibid., 39. See also Donnachie, 'Scottish criminals and transportation to Australia', and Donnachie, 'The convicts of 1830'.

15. Cited in Richards, 'Australia and the Scottish connection', p. 115.

16. Prentis, *Scots in Australia* (2008), p. 43.

17. This calculation is based on the records of convicts on this voyage available through the State Library of Queensland Convict Transportation Registers Database, http://www.slq.qld.gov.au/info/fh/convicts (accessed 7 March 2012).

18. *Dundee Courier*, 14 October 1845.

19. *Dundee Courier*, 12 August 1845.

20. *Dundee Courier*, 14 October 1845.

21. Eric Richards, 'Australia and the Scottish connection', p. 116.

22. See Prentis, '"It's a long way to the bottom"', p. 205.

23. Eric Richards, 'Australia and the Scottish connection', p. 117.

24. Prentis, 'Scots – Scottish recruitment to Australian elites', p. 661.

25. McLachlan, 'Macquarie, Lachlan', *Australian Dictionary of Biography*, http://adb.anu.edu.au/biography/macquarie-lachlan-2419/text3211 (accessed 12 March 2012); see also Ritchie, *Lachlan Macquarie*; and Ellis, *Lachlan Macquarie*.

26. Prentis, 'Scots – Lowland Scottish immigration until 1860', p. 647.

27. Mein Smith, *A Concise History of New Zealand*, p. 41.

28. Ibid., p. 42.

29. See Orange, *The Treaty of Waitangi* for details on the treaty, how it came about and its implications.

30. MacKenzie, 'Scots and the environment of empire', p. 163.

31. Nathan, *The Amazing World of James Hector*.

32. Cage, 'Scots – early migration', p. 646.

33. Prentis, 'Scots – lowland Scottish immigration until 1860', pp. 647–8.

34. Steven, 'Campbell, Robert (1769–1846)', *Australian Dictionary of Biography*, http://adb.anu.edu.au/biography/campbell-robert-1876/text2197 (accessed 12 March 2012); see also Newman, *The Spirit of Wharf House*.
35. Richards, 'Australia and the Scottish connection', pp. 117–18.
36. Stone, 'Campbell, John Logan – Biography', *DNZB*, http://www.TeAra.govt.nz/en/biographies/1c3/1 (accessed 12 March 2012).
37. Brooking, '"Tam McCanny and Kitty Clydeside"', p. 179.
38. See Prentis, '"It's a long way to the bottom"', p. 197.
39. Prentis, 'Scots – lowland Scottish immigration until 1860', p. 648.
40. See Denoon and Mein Smith with Wyndham, *A History of Australia, New Zealand and the Pacific*, p. 166; also Salesa, *Racial Crossings*, pp. 28ff.
41. Sinclair, *A History of New Zealand*, p. 60.
42. McCarthy, 'Scottish migrant ethnic identities in the British Empire since the nineteenth century', p. 120.
43. Prentis, *Scots in Australia* (2008), p. 58.
44. Prentis, 'Scots – lowland Scottish immigration until 1860', p. 648.
45. Richards, 'Australia and the Scottish connection, 1788–1914', p. 114.
46. McLintock, *The History of Otago*.
47. Carey, *God's Empire*, p. 346.
48. See McClean, 'Scottish piety'.
49. Prentis, *Scots in Australia* (2008), p. 65.
50. Cf. William Wilson letters, Alexander Turnbull Library, Wellington, New Zealand, MS-Papers-3957.
51. Alexander McKay Papers, 1909, Alexander Turnbull Library, Wellington, New Zealand, MS-Papers-4409-1.
52. See table 1 in Hearn, 'Scots miners in the goldfields', p. 73.
53. Bueltmann, *Scottish Ethnicity*, p. 39.
54. Prentis, 'Scots – lowland Scottish immigration until 1860', p. 648.
55. Lucas, 'Scots – Scottish immigration 1891–1945', p. 666.
56. See also Morris, 'The assisted immigrants to New Zealand'.
57. Gandar, 'New Zealand net migration in the latter part of the nineteenth century'.
58. Brooking, 'Sharing out the haggis', p. 49.
59. Lenihan, 'From Alba to Aotearoa'.
60. Lenihan, 'From Alba to Aotearoa'.
61. Prentis, *Scots in Australia* (2008), 67.
62. Harper, *Adventurers and Exiles*, p. 51.
63. Richards, 'Scots – highland and Gaelic immigrants', p. 650.
64. Richards, 'Australia and the Scottish connection', p. 122.
65. *Caledonian Mercury*, 7 June 1838.
66. Richards, 'Scots – highland and Gaelic immigrants', pp. 651–2.

67. Harper, 'A century of Scottish emigration to New Zealand', p. 222.

68. Richards, 'Scottish networks and voices in colonial Australia', p. 164.

69. Richards, 'Australia and the Scottish connection, 1788–1914', p. 135; see also Macmillan, 'Sir Charles Trevelyan and the Highland and Island Emigration Society'; and Richards, 'Highland emigrants to South Australia in the 1850s'.

70. Ewing, *Sermon on Emigration from the Highlands and Islands of Scotland to Australia*.

71. Carey, *God's Empire*, pp. 333–4.

72. House of Commons Parliamentary Papers, 1854 (436) (436–I) Emigration (Australia), Return to an address of the Honourable the House of Commons, dated 5 May 1854; – for, 'copies or extracts of any despatches relative to emigration to the Australian colonies (in continuation of papers presented to this House in April 1853).' Part I. New South Wales and Victoria, p. 169.

73. For example in Colley, *Britons*, p. 114.

74. Richards, *From Hirta to Port Phillip*, p. 17.

75. Ibid., p. 21.

76. Riverton correspondent, *Otago Witness*, 17 June 1871.

77. Hargreaves and Hearn, 'Special settlements of the South Island New Zealand'.

78. For details on Highland migration and special settlements, see Lenihan, 'From Alba to Aotearoa', especially chapters 2 and 6.

79. Harper, *Emigration from Scotland between the Wars*, pp. 94–5.

80. Bueltmann, *Scottish Ethnicity*, p. 1.

81. Bueltmann, *Scottish Ethnicity*, p. 206.

82. See also Clarke, *Holiday Seasons*.

83. Bueltmann, *Scottish Ethnicity*, p. 207.

84. Prentis, *Scots in Australia*, p. 227.

85. Ibid., p. 232.

86. Bueltmann, *Scottish Ethnicity*, p. 210.

Epilogue

'Ladies and Gentlemen, it is my great pleasure to propose to you *the* toast of the evening: "The Immortal Memory of Robert Burns".

You'll be pleased to hear a Scottish accent, of course. I've been here these ten years, and still I sound as broad as the day I left dear auld Scotia. And good to hear so many words from hame. I was just talking to a young man over there – by the bar of all places – telling tales from Dundee, and how many words he knows for rain. Aye, if it's no drizzling, then it's mizzling, or it's coming down in sheets, or it's p. . . well, you get the idea. Anyway, this young whatshisname here is looking for work. What wi' the jute industry all happening in far away Calcutta now, he's come to join us – his family – for a new adventure. Welcome, son of Scotland!

Burns, of course, had a good few words of his own for rain. He had a good few words for most things, especially if it involved the description of a pretty lass, and if it took a wee dram or two to complete the picture. And we're here because we're Scots ourselves, or descended from Scots, or married to Scots, or hold a candle, an affinity if ye like, with the land o' mountain and flood. We sit here, in the windy city of Chicago, and look back home, to Glasgow, or that other city in the east, or some wee village west of Wick (where did you say?) or to those fun folk up there at "Aiberdeen" (or whatever they say with that accent of theirs). I came from the thread-making toun of Paisley; my mate Chick over there (Hi Chick), he's frae Kirkcaldy – the lang toun no less ("haud yer nose, big yin, ye've just reached Kinghorn"). Na, but we're here now. And you are all here wi us, sitting in this great Home established by our forebears. The guid folk of the St Andrew's Society of Illinois. What great Scots they've been, helping the poor of this proud city down the years, especially after the fire. Aye, it still pains me to remember the stories I've heard.

We look after our brither Scots in this land, especially if they're in need of help, and we would have looked after Burns too, if he had come out to us, and if it stayed alive a bit longer to reach a *mature* age like me (because none of us greyhieds are old, right?). Well, Robert Burns was born on the 25 January in 1759. Born in the Ayrshire village of Alloway. We should sing "Happy Birthday" – the world's most popular song, but our final song tonight, "Auld Lang Syne", is probably the second most popular. Although where the Chinese national anthem fits in, I'm no so sure?; but we know Willie Jardine and Jimmy Matheson were likely involved in writing it! My old dad worked for them; a bit of a trader he was out in Hong Kong before wee stopovers in New York and London, and then he headed back to Paisley to marry my mother, who waited for him – what a romantic, she was! But my goodness, those brigands were no bad at making a bob or two. Biggest British trading country in Asia before the Great War. Maybe we should forget about the opium bit of the story; we certainly have to miss out a few dodgy bits when we talk about Burns – but, hey, what profits those guys made for our Scots sojourners (now that's a phrase that's hard to say even when ye're sober!)

That was us Scots going out to Asia to make some money. But most of us just wanted a home for our families, a job and maybe a bit o' land. That's why our ancestors left Scotland on those rickety old boats, with the rain coming in the port holes and flimsy decks strung across the cargo holds. I've got four of my own, children that is, and that's a big enough family for my wages to stretch. Aye, stretching as far as my pants are tonight after that meal (and let's thank the chef everyone for that genuine auld Scottish fare!). Burns came from a big family. The eldest of seven children, he was the son of a poor, tenant-farmer. Though held back by his family's poverty, he got himself a good education and was an avid reader. Burns got a bit o' teaching, had read his Shakespeare, Dryden and Milton, whilst also picking up a bit o' French and Latin. He was pushed in all this by his father, and his mother told him folk songs, legends, and some of the great Scottish proverbs. What a mixture, but that's us Scots – we like a bit o' education, like. Princeton, no less, that was us. And few of those graduates in New Zealand and in Canada (them up tae the north o' us, in the cauld bit) – they can thank us Scots for their studies.

I've got my skills from my old dad and from the Mechanics' Institute – then I got a guid job wi Coats – I was time served, like – when I came oot to the New World – or what you silly buggers call Amerikay. I came wi' skills and got a good job in another one of Coats' factories. Burns, of course, had a lot of talents, but maybe industry wasn't one of them. As a teenager and young man attempting to make his way as a farmer, he grew some of the passions that shaped his life. Aye, these were formative years, showing us how the poet saw himself and the world around him. By the age of fifteen, his interest in the fairer sex had started him writing his poetry:

- *O, Once I Lov'd A Bonnie Lass* (inspired by Nelly Kilpatrick)
- *Now Westlin' Winds* and *I Dream'd I Lay* (inspired by Peggy Thomson)
- *Tam O' Shanter* (prompted by an angry women, any of them!)

With the passing of his father in 1784, Robert along with his brother made a pretty ham-fisted attempt at farming. The tenancy had passed to the young lads; they should have then been in a position to settle down and marry, to stay fixed upon the land. There were plenty of lassies to choose from, with all the lads having emigrated, like. They should have been able to settle on the farm, although many beside them had left for Paisley, or Greenock like my Uncle Bill and his wife Jeannie; and others had already left for Canada. It's amazing how many Ayrshire farmers, and a few folk from up, up and away in Orkney and the like went off to New Zealand to look after the sheep. Did they no have enough of these furry so-and-sos in Sutherland? You'd have thought so! Anyway, Robert was more interested in poetry and lassies than farm labour, and, having had some misadventures with the lassies he planned to escape to the safer, sunnier climes of the West Indies – to Jamaica to become a slave driver, no less. Not once, but twice he was on the verge of leaving Scotland. Amazing really, but that was his poverty overcoming his principles on slavery. Like us all, though, we would stay if we could, but you have to follow the silver shilling.

But Burns, ye ken, he was special. He stayed. Amidst such personal troubles, his poetry would launch him into eighteenth-century stardom (just like ma jokes, nothing but the best of the best of course). In 1786, with the intention of raising money for a second go at Jamaica, he published the *Kilmarnock edition* of his poems. Aye, he talked a lot about the Scotland around him in these verses. His life as a farmer's son – in *The Cottars' Saturday Night* and *To a Mouse*. In these we're treated to the land we've all left behind, to our homeland, our community, the place we think about on nights like these, and in the quiet moments by the fire, looking forward tae meeting the Scottish family again in God's kingdom.

Burns's poetry also tells us more about the Scotland we left behind. The Scots Kirk was awfy powerful in those days, particularly when it came to morality. We know that round here, of course, the meenister (hello Reverend!) is always an important part of our lives. Did I mention my Mary got married last year? You remember her, the wee lass who replied to the lads at the last Supper? Well, Revd Macdonald did her a great service – even if she was marrying an Anglian (joke, joke!). Unlike me of course, being a good upstanding Mason, Burns's womanising and choice of friends brought him into conflict wi' the Kirk. Aye, his love of drink and of women are evident in *Holy Willie's Prayer*:

> Besides, I farther maun avow –
> Wi' Leezie's lass, three times, I trow –
> But, Lord, that Friday I was fou,
> When I cam near her,
> Or else, Thou kens, Thy servant true
> Wad never steer her.

His brother tells us that "he saw a goddess in every girl" – and that wasn't just the drink talking! Yet amidst such whimsy, we see he could be serious, too, in particular his disdain for hypocrisy. *Holy Willie's Prayer* forms a critique of the Kirk – sorry Reverend! – largely reserved for the double standards of some of its leading members.

> O Lord, my God! that glib-tongu'd Aiken,
> My vera heart and flesh are quakin
> To think how we stood sweatin, shakin,
> An pish'd wi' dread,
> While he, wi' hingin lip an' snakin,
> Held up his head.

The entire print-run of 612 copies sold out within a month. He left Ayrshire to spend the winters of 1787 and 1788 in Edinburgh receiving the acclaim of his admirers. While making the most of the big city social life, he also embarked upon several tours around Scotland absorbing the local culture of folklore and song. Like mauny Scots, he never stayed in one place for long, always travelling around looking for work (or lassies!). Still, he eventually settled into farm life at Ellisland, Dumfriesshire with Jean Armour, whom he married in 1788. Two years later he wrote his masterpiece *Tam O' Shanter*, telling the story of a man who stays too long at the pub and witnesses a disturbing vision on the way home. I remember an old Canadian-Scots Reverend who wouldn't have been too impressed – William Bell was his name – the miserable auld bugger was even known down here for his opposition to the drink. But then he didnae like our Highland friends very much, or our fellow migrants from the Emerald Isle; but he did like our Native folk. He has some kind of respect for their uncivilised ways right enough.

In 1791 our man Burns, for so much of his life an ordinary farmer, took up rather ordinary work as an Excise officer at Dumfries. Like maist country folk, he needed that bit of extra work to get by. A bit of learning work, it was too. Always handy if you ever needed an Empire job. After the outbreak of the French Revolution, Robert had become an outspoken champion of the Republican cause. Writing *A Man's A Man and A' That* he showed his support for some of that political radicalism finding favour in British society; the kind of stuff we like here in the land of the free – from Burns to Lincoln, it's a straight line, ye ken.

Then let us pray that come it may
(As come it will for a' that)
That sense and worth o'er a'the earth
Shall bear the gree for a' that
For a' that and a' that
It's comin' yet for a' that
That man to man the world o'er
Shall brithers be for a' that.

You know, I want to tell you a wonderful story from the Great War – and praise be to George our King that it has ended. I heard of a young man called Winston Churchill, serving with the 6th Royal Scots Fusiliers on the Western Front as a Lieutenant-Colonel. He asked his wife to send him a volume of Burns' poetry for his troops. He quite wisely thought: "I will soothe and cheer their spirits by quotations from it", and, more wisely still for an Englishman, he paused: "I shall have to be careful not to drop into a mimicry of their accent!". Aye, he knew what was good for them and *him* alright!

In his end, Burns succumbed to a poet's body. A night sleeping by the roadside after an evening on the drink led to a fever. In delirium, in poverty, chased for debt, he slipped away on the 21st of July 1796. Yet even as he did, his desire for so much life was witnessed by the birth of his last child; born while Rabbie lay on his death-bed. On the day of his burial more than 10,000 people came to watch and pay their respects. His popularity, though, was nothing compared to the heights it has reached since. Not only are we here this evening to celebrate the man himself, but also the ideas and images of Scotland conjured through his poetry.

Burns never did make it out to join us in the colonies (as we used to be known). But his family did. His oldest son wi' Jean, Colonel Robert, was a regular visitor to Belfast. Robbie's nephew, a meenister funnily enough!, Revd Thomas Burns, took a group of Scots with him to Otago in New Zealand. It was good for them to have someone they could trust to break open the Word o' the Lord, transplanting their home lives anew at the bottom of the world. And his great-granddaughter, Isabella Ferguson Brown, who sadly died at the tender age of ten, is buried in a wee Scottish town called Guelph in Canada, founded by another writer from Scotia's west coast by the name of John Galt.

Wherever ye go, there's a bit o' Burns; of that there's nae doubt. You all heard our Society President start off tonight's festivities with greetings from the Burns clubs of New York, New Jersey, Montreal and London, and from far away Cape Town and Shanghai We even got a telegram from the

Sunderland Burns Club: "Hail Brither Scots O' Coaly Tyne, We meet again for Auld Lang Syne" they sent us. Well, the telegraph is all well and good, but they could have picked up the telephone – we invented it after all!

Everyone, everywhere, loves Burns. There is something for everybody in Burns. Back in '88 we organised our plans to celebrate the poet with a statue – and fourteen years ago, in 1906, we got the man cast in bronze to remind us what all the fuss was about. An American hero so he is, and popular too wherever Scots have been, from Australia to Russia and all places in-between.

His memory is just like us, universal. All over the world are to be found Scots trying to make a difference, trying to make an honest living, simply trying to get on with our lives. We didnae want to leave, no, although some of us did, of course. But Burns's immortal memory is like us, everywhere in God's bountiful world. And we took the good Lord at his deed: "The LORD shall cause thee to be smitten before thine enemies: thou shalt go out one way against them, and flee seven ways before them: and shalt be removed into all the kingdoms of the earth'. Our enemy was poverty, our sword was our muscle, our intellect and our skills. Aye, I'm getting a little misty eyed. It's no always been easy, no for all of us, that's for sure. But like Burns, we do best when we're a little modest; aye, when we have a heart even for the mouse; for every wayfarer in the journey of life who needs a little charity. His journey has been our journey – the journey of the ordinary Scot.

Ladies and Gentlemen. I ask you to raise your glasses in a toast to "The Immortal Memory of Robert Burns".'

Bibliography

MANUSCRIPT SOURCES

Baxter Letters, Hocken Library: Dunedin, Misc-MS-0878.

Chisholm Diary, 10 July 1892, Hocken Library: Dunedin, 96–188.

Good Family Letters, University of Guelph Archive, XS1 MS A200.

Grant Letters, 1885–1918, no date, Alexander Turnbull Library: Wellington, MS-Papers-0339.

Thomson Letters, Alexander Turnbull Library, Wellington, New Zealand, MS-Papers-5174.

GOVERNMENT RECORDS AND OFFICIAL REPORTS

'Eleventh Report of Her Majesty's Commissioners Appointed to Carry Out a Scheme of Colonization in the Dominion of Canada of Crofters and Cottars From the Western Highlands and Islands of Scotland' (HMSO, 1901).

'Extracts from reports of the Highland Society of Scotland, 12 January 1802, appendix to First Report from the Committee on the Survey of the Coasts, &c. Of Scotland (Emigration)'.

Parliamentary Papers, 'Report by the Earl of Clarendon, chairman, and Mr T. C. MacNaghten, vice chairman, of the Overseas settlement committee on their visit to Canada in connection with British settlement' (HMSO (2760)).

Sessional Papers of the Dominion of Canada.

PRINTED PRIMARY SOURCES

Anon, *The Importance of the British Dominion in India, Compared with that in America* (London: printed for J. Almon, 1770).

Bell, George, *Day and Night in the Wynds of Edinburgh* (Edinburgh: Johnstone and Hunter, 1849).

Bell, William, *Hints to Emigrants in a Series of Letters from Upper Canada* (Edinburgh: Waugh & Innes, 1824).

Buchanan, Francis, *A Journey from Madras through the Countries of Mysore, Canara and Malabar . . . for the Express Purpose of Investigating the State of Agriculture, Arts and Commerce, the Religion, Manners, and Customs, the History and Natural and Civil Antiquities, in the Dominions of the Rajah of Mysore, and the Countries Acquired by the Honourable East India Company, in the Late and Former Wars, from Tippoo Sultaun* (2nd edn, Madras; originally published London: East India Company, London, 1807).

Brunton, Richard Henry, *Schoolmaster to an Empire: Richard Henry Brunton in Meiji Japan, 1868–1876*, ed. Edward R. Beauchamp (New York: Praeger, 1991).

Caitlin, George, *Adventures of the Ojibbeway and Ioway Indians in England, France and Belgium*, 2 vols, 3rd edn (London: Indian Collection, 1852).

Carrier, N. H. and J. R. Jeffrey, *External Migration: A Study of the Available Statistics, 1815–1950* (London: HMSO, 1953).

Cist, Charles, *Cincinnati in 1841: Its Early Annals and Future Prospects* (Cincinnati: E. Morgan & Co., 1841).

Croal, T. A., *A Book About Travelling: Past and Present* (Edinburgh: WP Nimmo, 1877).

Dilke, Charles W., *Greater Britain: A Record of Travel in English-speaking Countries during 1866 and 1867* (London: Macmillan & Co., 1869).

Dixon, John H., *Gairloch in North-West Ross-shire* (Edinburgh: Co-operative Printing Co., 1886).

Dove, P. E., *The National Association for the Vindication of Scottish Rights: Address to the People of Scotland and Statement of Grievances* (Edinburgh: Johnstone & Hunter, 1853).

Ewing, Alexander, *Sermon on Emigration from the Highlands and Islands of Scotland to Australia by the Bishop of Argyle and the Isles* (London: Francis & John Rivington, 1852).

Hamilton, Alexander, *A New Account of the East Indies*, ed. W. Foster (London: Argonaut Press, 1930).

Handbook for Travellers in Scotland, 6th edn (London: John Murray, 1894).

Hepburn, D. and J. Douglas, *The Chronicles of the Caledonian Society of London, 1837–1905* (London: Waterlow & Sons, 1890).

Howison, John, *Sketches of Upper Canada, domestic, local, and characteristic to which are added practical details for the information of emigrants of every class, and some recollections of the United States of America* (Edinburgh: Oliver & Boyd, 1821).

Hume, David, Essay XI: 'Of the populousness of ancient nations', in *Essays and Treatises on Several Subjects*, vol. II (Basil: J. J. Tourneisen, 1793).

Johnson, Samuel, *A Journey to the Western Islands of Scotland* (Glasgow: Stanhope Press, 1817).

Kelly, John Liddell, *Heather and Fern: Songs of Scotland and Maoriland* (Wellington, 1902).

Lawson, R., *The Famous Places of Scotland* (Paisley: Parlane, 1893).

Levi, Leone, 'On the economic condition of the Highlands and Islands of Scotland', *Journal of the Statistical Society of London*, 28, 3 (September, 1865).

Livingstone, David, *Missionary Travels and Researches in South Africa; Including a Sketch of Sixteen Years' Residence in the Interior of Africa, and a Journey from the Cape of Good Hope to Loanda on the West Coast; Thence Across the Continent, Down the River Zambesi, to the Eastern Ocean* (London: Murray, 1857).

Macaulay, T. B., 'Minute on education' [2 Feb. 1835], *Selections from Educational Records, Part I (1781–1839)*, ed. H. Sharp (Delhi: National Archives of India, 1965).

MacDonald, James S. (ed.), *Annals of the North British Society of Halifax, Nova Scotia for One Hundred and Twenty-Five Years* (Halifax, NS: John Bowes, 1894).

Malthus, Thomas R., *An Essay on the Principle of Population, As It Affects The Future Improvement of Society* (London: Joseph Johnson, 1798).

McCallum, Robert, *Home Rule for Scotland* (Fitzroy, Victoria: W. & J. Barr, 1925).

McHutcheson, William, *The New Zealander Abroad in England, America and the Highlands of Scotland, in Madeira, Capetown and the Sandwich Islands: Being Notes of a Six Months Holiday Tour round the World* (Glasgow: Hamilton, 1888).

Mr Punch in the Highlands, various authors, ed. Charles Keen et al. (np, The Educational Book Co. Ltd, nd).

Robinson, Samuel, *A Sailor Boy's Experience Aboard a Slave Ship* (Hamilton, 1867).

The Cyclopedia of New Zealand: Industrial, Descriptive, Historical, Biographical Facts, Figures, Illustrations, Volume 4, Otago and Southland Provincial Districts (Wellington: Cyclopedia Co., 1905).

Trollope, Anthony, *Australia and New Zealand, vol. 3* (Leipzig: Bernhard Tauchnitz, 1873).

Victoria, Queen of Great Britian, *Leaves from the Journal of Our Life in the Highlands, from 1848–1861*, ed. Arthur Helps (London, England: Smith, Elder & Co., 1868).

THESES

Araki, Mairi Hamilton Arbuckle, 'Japanese engineering and Scotland: Ryugakusei and Oyatoi between 1865 and 1900', unpublished PhD thesis, University of Edinburgh, 2007.

Erlank, Natasha, 'Gender and Christianity among Africans attached to Scottish mission stations in Xhosaland in the nineteenth century', unpublished PhD thesis, University of Cambridge, 1998.

Harland, Jill, 'The Orcadian odyssey: The migration of Orkney Islanders to New Zealand 1848–1914. With particular reference to the South Island', unpublished PhD thesis, University of Otago, 2013.

Hinson, Andrew, 'Migrant Scots in a British city: Toronto's Scottish community, 1881–1911', unpublished PhD thesis, University of Guelph, 2010.

Lenihan, Rebecca, 'From Alba to Aotearoa: Profiling New Zealand's Scots migrants, 1840–1920', unpublished PhD thesis, Victoria University of Wellington, 2010.

Morris, John, 'The assisted immigrants to New Zealand, 1871–79: A statistical study', unpublished MA thesis, University of Auckland, 1973.

BOOKS AND ARTICLES

Abrams, Lynn, *The Orphan Country, Children of Scotland's Broken Homes From 1845 to the Present Day* (Edinburgh: John Donald, 1998).

Acheson, T. W., 'The social origins of the Canadian industrial elite, 1880–1885', in David S. Macmillan (ed.), *Canadian Business History: Selected Studies, 1497–1971* (Toronto: McClelland and Stewart, 1972).

Akenson, Donald Harman, *Half the World from Home: Perspectives on the Irish in New Zealand, 1860–1950* (Wellington: Victoria University Press, 1990).

Akenson, Donald Harman, 'The Great European migration and indigenous populations', in Graeme Morton and David A. Wilson (eds), *Irish and Scottish Encounters with Indigenous Peoples: Canada, the United States, New Zealand, and Australia* (Montreal and Kingston: McGill-Queen's University Press, 2013).

Akenson, Donald Harman, 'The historiography of English-speaking Canada and the concept of diaspora: A sceptical appreciation', *Canadian Historical Review*, 76, 3 (1995), pp. 377–409.

Anderson, Benedict, *Imagined Communities* (London: Verso, 1983).

Anderson, M., 'Fertility decline in Scotland, England and Wales, and Ireland: Comparisons from the 1911 Census of Fertility', *Population Studies*, 52, 1 (1998), pp. 1–20.

Anderson, M., 'The demographic regime', in R. Mitchison and T. M Devine (eds), *People and Society, 1760–1830, Vol. I* (Edinburgh: John Donald, 1988).

Anderson, M. and D. J. Morse, 'High fertility, high emigration, low nuptiality: Adjustment processes in Scotland's demographic experience, 1861–1914, Part I', *Population Studies*, 47 (1993), pp. 319–43.

Anderson, M. and D. J. Morse, 'The people', in W. H. Fraser and R. J. Morris, *People and Society in Scotland, vol. II, 1830–1914* (Edinburgh: John Donald, 1990).

Armitage, David, 'The Scottish vision of empire: Intellectual origins of the Darien Venture', in John Robertson (ed.), *Political Thought and the British Union of 1707* (Cambridge: Cambridge University Press, 1995).

Armitage, David and Michael J. Braddick (eds), *The British Atlantic World, 1500–1800*, 2nd edn (Basingstoke: Palgrave Macmillan, 2009).

Armstrong, John, 'Mobilized and proletarian diasporas', *American Political Science Review*, 70, 2 (1976), pp. 393–408.

Arnold, Matthew, *On the Study of Celtic Literature* (London: Smith Elder & Co., 1967).

Ashton, Rosemary, 'The Carlyles in London', in T. C. Smout (ed.), *Anglo-Scottish Relations from 1603 to 1900* (Oxford: Oxford University Press, 2005).

Aspinwall, Bernard, 'The Scots in the United States', in R. A. Cage (ed.), *The Scots Abroad: Labour, Capital, Enterprise, 1750–1914* (London: Croom Helm, 1985).

Ball, Michael and David Sunderland, *An Economic History of London, 1800–1914* (London and New York: Routledge, 2001).

Bailyn, Bernard, *Voyagers to the West: A Passage in the Peopling of America on the Eve of the Revolution* (New York: Alfred A. Knopf, 1986).

Baines, Dudley, *Migration in a Mature Economy: Emigration and Internal Migration in England and Wales, 1861–1900* (Cambridge: Cambridge University Press: 1985).

Bajer, Peter Paul, *Scots in the Polish-Lithuanian Commonwealth, 16th–18th Centuries: The Formation and Disappearance of an Ethnic Group* (Leiden: Brill, 2012).

Basu, Paul, *Highland Homecomings: Genealogy and Heritage Tourism in the Scottish Diaspora* (Abingdon, 2007).

Basu, Paul, 'Macpherson Country: Genealogical identities, spatial histories and the Scottish diasporic clanscape', *Cultural Geographies*, 12 (2005), pp. 123–50.

Baumann, M., 'Diaspora: Genealogies of semantics and transcultural comparison', *Numen*, 47, 3 (2000), pp. 313–37.

Barber, Marilyn, 'In search of a better life: A Scottish domestic in rural Ontario', *Polyphony*, 8, 1–2 (1986), pp. 13–16.

Bayly, C. A., 'The British and indigenous peoples, 1760–1860: Power, perception and identity', in Martin Daunton and Rick Halpern (eds), *Empire and Others: British Encounters with Indigenous Peoples, 1600–1850* (Philadelphia: University of Pennsylvania Press, 1999).

Beath, Robert B., *Historical Catalogue of the St Andrew's Society of Philadelphia, Volume II, 1749–1913* (Philadelphia: St Andrew's Society of Philadelphia, 1913).

Belchem, John, 'Hub and diaspora: Liverpool and transnational labour', *Labour History Review*, 75, 1 (2010), pp. 20–9.

Bennett, Margaret, *Oatmeal and the Catechism: Scottish Gaelic Settlers in Quebec* (Montreal and Kingston: McGill-Queen's University Press, 2004).

Berton, Pierre, *The National Dream: The Great Railway, 1871–1881* (Toronto: McClelland and Stewart, 1970).

Blaikie, Andrew, 'Rituals, transitions and life courses in an era of social transformation', in Trevor Griffiths and Graeme Morton (eds), *A History of Everyday Life in Scotland, 1800 to 1900* (Edinburgh: Edinburgh University Press, 2010).

Bowen, H. V., *The Business of Empire: The East India Company and Imperial Britain, 1756–1833* (Cambridge: Cambridge University Press, 2006).

Boyle, Mark, 'Towards a (re)theorization of the historical geography of nationalism in diasporas: The Irish diaspora as an exemplar', *International Journal of Population Geography*, 7 (2001), pp. 429–46.

Braziel, Janna Evans and Anita Mannur, 'Nation, migration, globalization: Points of connection in diaspora studies', in Janna Evans Braziel and Anita Mannur (eds), *Theorizing Diaspora* (Oxford: Blackwell Publishing, 2003).

Breitenbach, Esther, *Empire and Scottish Society: The Impact of Foreign Missions at Home, c. 1790–1914* (Edinburgh: Edinburgh University Press, 2009).

Breitenbach, Esther, 'Scots churches and missions', in John M. MacKenzie and T. M. Devine (eds), *Scotland and the British Empire* (Oxford: Oxford University Press, 2011).

Brock, J. M., *The Mobile Scot: Emigration and Migration, 1861–1911* (Edinburgh: John Donald, 1999).

Brock, William H., *William Crookes (1832–1919) and the Commercialization of Science* (Aldershot: Ashgate, 2008).

Brock, William R., *Scotus Americanus: A Survey of the Sources for Links between Scotland and America in the Eighteenth Century* (Edinburgh: Edinburgh University Press, 1982).

Brooking, Tom, *Lands for the People? The Highland Clearances and the Colonisation of New Zealand: A Biography of John McKenzie* (Dunedin: Otago University Press, 1996).

Brooking, Tom, 'Sharing out the haggis: The special Scottish contribution to New Zealand history', in Tom Brooking and Jennie Coleman (eds), *The Heather and the Fern: Scottish Migration and New Zealand Settlement* (Dunedin: Otago University Press, 2003).

Brooking, Tom, '"Tam McCanny and Kitty Clydeside" – The Scots in New Zealand', in R. A. Cage (ed.), *The Scots Abroad: Labour, Capital, Enterprise, 1750–1914* (London: Croom Helm, 1985).

Brooking, Tom and Jennie Coleman (eds), *The Heather and the Fern: Scottish Migration and New Zealand Settlement* (Dunedin: Otago University Press, 2003).

Brown, Jennifer S. H., 'Partial truths. A closer look at fur trade marriage', in Theodore Binnema, Gerhard J. Ens and R. C. Macleod (eds), *From Rupert's Land to Canada* (Edmonton: University of Alberta Press).

Brown, Stewart J., '"Echoes of Midlothian": Scottish liberalism and the Anglo-Boer War, 1899–1902', *Scottish Historical Review*, LXXI, 1: 2 (1992), pp. 156–83.

Brubaker, Rogers, 'The "diaspora" diaspora', *Ethnic and Racial Studies*, 28, 1 (2005), pp. 1–19.

Brumwell, Stephen, *Redcoats: The British Soldier and the War of the Americas, 1755–1763* (Cambridge: Cambridge University Press, 2002).

Brunton, Deborah C., 'The transfer of medical education: Teaching at the Edinburgh and Philadelphia medical schools', in Richard B. Sher and Jeffrey R. Smitten (eds), *Scotland and America in the Age of Enlightenment* (Edinburgh: Edinburgh University Press, 1990).

Bryan, Tom, *Twa Tribes. Scots Among Native Americans* (Edinburgh: National Museum of Scotland Enterprises, 2003)

Bryant, Christopher G. A., *The Nations of Britain* (Oxford: Oxford University Press, 2006).

Bryant, G. J., 'Scots in India in the eighteenth century', *Scottish Historical Review*, LXIV, 1:177 (1985), pp. 22–41.

Bueltmann, Tanja, 'Ethnic identity, sporting Caledonia and respectability: Scottish associational life in New Zealand to 1910', in Tanja Bueltmann, Andrew Hinson and Graeme Morton (eds), *Ties of Bluid, Kin and Countrie: Scottish Associational Culture in the Diaspora* (Guelph: Guelph Series in Scottish Studies, 2009).

Bueltmann, Tanja, '"Gentlemen, I'm going to the Old Country": Scottish roots-tourists in the late nineteenth and early twentieth centuries', in Mario Varricchio (ed.), *Back to Caledonia: Scottish Homecomings from the Seventeenth Century to the Present* (Edinburgh: John Donald, 2012).

Bueltmann, Tanja, 'Manly games, athletic sports and the commodification of Scottish identity: Caledonian gatherings in New Zealand to 1915', *Scottish Historical Review*, LXXXIX, 2, 228 (2010), pp. 224–47.

Bueltmann, Tanja, *Scottish Ethnicity and the Making of New Zealand Society, 1850 to 1930* (Edinburgh: Edinburgh University Press, 2011).

Bueltmann, Tanja, '"The image of Scotland which we cherish in our hearts": Burns anniversary celebrations in colonial Otago', *Immigrants & Minorities*, 30: 1 (2012), pp. 78–97.

Bueltmann, Tanja, '"Where the measureless Ocean between us will Roar": Scottish emigration to New Zealand, personal correspondence and epistolary practices, c. 1850–1920', *Immigrants & Minorities* 26, 3 (2008), 242–65.

Bueltmann, Tanja, David Gleeson and Donald M. MacRaild, 'Locating the English diaspora: Problems, perspectives and approaches', in Tanja Bueltmann, David Gleeson and Donald M. MacRaild, *Locating the English Diaspora, 1500–2010* (Liverpool: Liverpool University Press, 2012).

Bueltmann, Tanja and Donald M. MacRaild, 'Globalizing St George: English associations in the Anglo-world to the 1930s', *Journal of Global History*, 7, 1 (2012), pp. 79–105.

Buettner, Elizabeth, 'Haggis in the Raj: Private and public celebrations of Scottishness in late Imperial India', *Scottish Historical Review*, 81, 2 (2002), pp. 212–39

Bumsted, J. M., 'Scots', in Paul Magocsi (ed.), *Encyclopedia of Canada's Peoples* (Toronto: Multicultural Society of Ontario, 1999).

Bumsted, J. M., 'Scottish emigration to the Maritimes 1770–1815: A new look at an old theme', *Acadiensis*, 10, 2 (1981), pp. 65–85.

Bumsted, J. M., *The People's Clearance: Highland Emigration to British North America, 1770–1815* (Winnipeg: University of Manitoba Press, 1982).

Burley, Edith I., *Servants of the Honourable Company: Work, Discipline, and Conflict in the Hudson's Bay Company, 1770–1879* (Toronto: Oxford University Press, 1997).

Burnett, John A., '"Department of Help for Skint Scotchmen!"; associationalism among Scots migrants in the north-east of England, ca. 1859–1939', in Tanja Bueltmann, Andrew Hinson and Graeme Morton (eds), *Ties of Bluid, Kin and Countrie: Scottish Associational Culture in the Diaspora* (Guelph: Guelph Series in Scottish Studies, 2009).

Burnett, John A., '"Hail brither Scots o' coaly Tyne": Networking and identity among Scottish migrants in the north-east of England, ca. 1860–2000', *Immigrants and Minorities*, 25, 1 (March, 2007), pp. 1–21.

Butler, Kim D., 'Defining diaspora, refining a discourse', *Diaspora: A Journal of Transnational Studies*, 10, 2 (2001), pp. 189–219.

Cage, R. A., 'Scots – early migration', in James Jupp (ed.), *The Australian People: An Encyclopedia of the Nation, Its People and their Origins* (Cambridge: Cambridge University Press, 2001).

Cage, R. A., 'The Scots in England', in R. A. Cage (ed.), *The Scots Abroad: Labour, Capital, Enterprise, 1750–1914* (London: Croom Helm, 1985).

Calloway, Colin, *White People, Indians and Highlanders: Tribal Peoples and Colonial Encounters in Scotland and America* (Oxford: Oxford University Press, 2008).

Campbell, R. H., 'Scotland', in R. A. Cage (ed.) *The Scots Abroad: Labour, Capital, Enterprise, 1750–1914* (London: Croom Helm, 1985).

Campbell, R. H., *Scotland Since 1707: The Rise of an Industrial Society* (Edinburgh: John Donald, 1985).

Campey, Lucille, *An Unstoppable Force: The Scottish Exodus to Canada* (Toronto: Natural Heritage Books, 2008).

Campey, Lucille, *'Fast sailing and copper-bottomed': Aberdeen Sailing Ships and the Emigrant Scots They Carried to Canada, 1774–1855* (Toronto: Natural Heritage Books, 2002).

Carey, Hilary M., *God's Empire: Religion and Colonialism in the British World, 1801–1908* (Cambridge: Cambridge University Press, 2011).

Caudle, James J., 'James Boswell (*H. Scoticus Londoniensis*)', in Stana Nenadic (ed.), *Scots in London in the Eighteenth Century* (Lewisburg: Bucknell University Press, 2010).

Checkland, Olive , 'The Scots in Meiji Japan, 1868–1912', in R. A. Cage (ed.), *The Scots Abroad: Labour, Capital, Enterprise, 1750–1914* (London: Croom Helm, 1985).

Cheong, W. E., *Mandarins and Merchants: Jardine, Matheson & Co., a China Agency of the Early Nineteenth Century* (London: Curzon Press, 1979).

Chilton, Lisa, *Agents of Empire: British Female Migration from Britain to Canada and Australia, 1860s–1930* (Toronto: University of Toronto Press, 2007).

Clarke, Alison, *Holiday Seasons: Christmas, New Year and Easter in Nineteenth Century New Zealand* (Auckland: Auckland University Press, 2007).

Clifford, James, 'Diasporas', *Cultural Anthropology*, 9, 3 (1994), pp. 302–38.

Cohen, Robin, *Global Diasporas: An Introduction* (London: UCL Press, 1997).

Colley, Linda, *Britons: Forging the Nation, 1707–1837* (London: Pimlico, 2003).

Cookson, J. E., 'Early nineteenth-century Scottish military pensioners as homecoming soldiers', *Historical Journal*, 52, 2 (2009), pp. 319–41.

Corrins, Robert D., 'The Scottish business elite in the nineteenth century: The case of William Baird & Company', in A. J. G. Cummings & T. M. Devine (eds), *Industry, Business & Society in Scotland since 1700* (Edinburgh: John Donald Publishers, 1994).

Craig, Cairns, *Intending Scotland: Explorations in Scottish Culture since the Enlightenment* (Edinburgh: Edinburgh University Press, 2009).

Crawford, Robert, *The Bard: Robert Burns, A Biography* (Princeton: Princeton University Press, 2009).

Daiches, David, 'Style Periodique and Style Coupe: Hugh Blair and the Scottish Rhetoric of American Independence', in Richard B. Sher and Jeffrey R. Smitten (eds.), *Scotland and America in the Age of Enlightenment* (Edinburgh: Edinburgh University Press, 1990).

Dakin, Susan Bryant, *A Scotch Paisano in Old Los Angela: Hugo Reid's Life in California, 1832–52 Derived from his Correspondence* (Berkeley: University of California Press, 1939).

Dalgleish, George R., 'Aspects of Scottish-Canadian material culture: Heart brooches and Scottish pottery', in Peter E. Rider and Heather McNabb (eds), *A Kingdom of the Mind: How the Scots Helped Make Canada* (Montreal and Kingston: McGill-Queen's University Press, 2006).

Daunton, Martin and Rick Halpern, 'Introduction', in Martin Daunton and Rick Halpern (eds), *Empire and Others: British Encounters with Indigenous Peoples, 1600–1850* (Philadelphia: University of Pennsylvania Press, 1999).

Denoon, Donald and Philippa Mein Smith with Marivic Wyndham, *A History of Australia, New Zealand and the Pacific* (Malden, MA: Wiley, 2000).

Devine, T. M. (ed.), *A Scottish Firm in Virginia, 1667–1777, W. Cuninghame and Co.* (Edinburgh: Scottish History Society, 1984).

Devine, T. M., 'Industrialization' in T. M. Devine, C. H. Lee and G. C. Peden (eds), *The Transformation of Scotland: The Economy Since 1700* (Edinburgh: Edinburgh University Press, 2005).

Devine, T. M., *Scotland's Empire and the Shaping of the Americas, 1600–1815* (Washington, DC: Smithsonian Books, 2004).

Devine, T. M., 'Scottish elites and the Indian empire', in T. C. Smout (ed.), *Anglo-Scottish Relations from 1603 to 1900* (Oxford: Oxford University Press, 2005).

Devine, T. M., 'Soldiers of empire, 1750–1950', in John M. MacKenzie and T. M. Devine (eds), *Scotland and the British Empire* (Oxford: Oxford University Press, 2011).

Devine, T. M., 'The golden age of tobacco', in T. M. Devine and Gordon Jackson (eds), *Glasgow Volume 1: Beginnings to 1830* (Manchester: Manchester University Press, 1995).

Devine, T. M., *The Great Highland Famine: Hunger, Emigration and the Scottish Highlands in the Nineteenth Century* (Edinburgh: John Donald, 1988).

Devine, T. M., 'The Highland Clearances', in T. M. Devine (ed.), *Exploring the Scottish Past: Themes in the History of Scottish Society* (East Linton: Tuckwell Press, 1995).

Devine, T. M., *The Scottish Nation 1700–2000* (London: Penguin, 2000).

Devine, T. M. (ed.), *The Tobacco Lords: A Study of the Tobacco Merchants of Glasgow and their Trading Activities, c. 1740–90* (Edinburgh: John Donald, 1975).

Devine, T. M., *To the Ends of the Earth: Scotland's Global Diaspora, 1750–2010* (London: Allen Lane, 2011).

DeVries, Jan, *European Urbanization: 1500–1800* (London: Methuen, 1984).

Diamond, Peter J., 'Witherspoon, William Smith and the Scottish philosophy', in Richard B. Sher and Jeffrey R. Smitten (eds), *Scotland and America in the Age of Enlightenment* (Edinburgh: Edinburgh University Press, 1990).

Dobson, David, *Scottish Emigration to Colonial America, 1607–1785* (Athens, Georgia: University of Georgia Press, 1994).

Dodgshon, Robert A., 'Everyday structures, rhythms and spaces of the Scottish countryside, 1600–1800', in Elizabeth Foyster and Christopher A. Whatley (eds), *A History of Everyday Life in Scotland, vol. II, 1600–1800* (Edinburgh: Edinburgh University Press, 2010).

Donaldson, Emily Ann, *The Scottish Highland Games in America* (Gretna, Louisiana: Pelican, 1986).

Donaldson, Gordon, 'Scots', in Stephan Thernstrom (ed.), *The Encyclopedia of American Ethnic Groups* (Cambridge, MA: Harvard University Press, 1980), pp. 908–16.

Dong-Woon, Kim, 'The British multinational enterprise in the United States before 1914: The case of J. & P. Coats', *Business History Review*, 72, 4 (1998) pp. 523–51.

Donnachie, I., 'The convicts of 1830: Scottish criminals transported to New South Wales', *Scottish Historical Review*, LXV, 1 (1986), pp. 34–47.

Donnachie, I., 'Scottish criminals and transportation to Australia, 1786–1852', *Scottish Social and Economic History*, 4 (1984), pp. 21–38.

Durie, A. J., *Scotland for the Holidays: Tourism in Scotland c1780–1939* (East Linton: Tuckwell Press, 2003).

Easterby, J. H., *History of the St Andrew's Society of Charleston South Carolina, 1729–1929* (Charleston, SC: St Andrew's Society of Charleston South Carolina, 1929).

Ellis, M. H., *Lachlan Macquarie: His Life, Adventures and Times* (Sydney: Harper Collins, 1965).

Erickson, Charlotte, *Invisible Immigrants: The Adaption of English and Scottish Immigrants in Nineteenth-Century America* (London: Weidenfeld and Nicolson, 1972).

Erlank, Natasha, 'Re-examining initial encounters between Christian missionaries and the Xhosa, 1820–1850: The Scottish case', *Kleio*, 31, 1 (1999), pp. 6–32.

Erlank, Natasha, 'Sexual misconduct and church power on Scottish mission stations in Xhosaland, South Africa, in the 1840s', *Gender & History*, 15, 1 (2003), pp. 69–84.

Farooqui, Amar, *Smuggling as Subversion: Colonialism, Indian Merchants, and the Politics of Opium, 1790–1843* (Oxford: Lexington Books, 2005).

Fedorowich, Kent, 'The assisted emigration of British ex-servicemen to the Dominions, 1914–1922', in Stephen Constantine (ed.), *Emigrants and Empire: British Settlement in the Dominions between the Wars* (Manchester: Manchester University Press, 1990).

Fernandez, Manuel A., 'The Scots in Latin America: A survey', in R. A. Cage (ed.), *The Scots Abroad: Labour, Capital, Enterprise, 1750–1914* (London: Croom Helm, 1985).

Fetter, Frank Whitson, 'Who were the foreign mercenaries of the Declaration of Independence?', *The Pennsylvania Magazine of History and Biography*, 104, 4 (October 1980), pp. 508–13.

Fleischacker, Samuel, 'Adam Smith's reception among the American Founders, 1776–1790', *The William and Mary Quarterly*, 58, 4 (2002), pp. 897–924.

Fleischacker, Samuel, 'The impact on America', in Alexander Broadie (ed.), *The Cambridge Companion to the Scottish Enlightenment* (Cambridge: Cambridge University Press, 2003).

Fichter, James R., *So Great A Proffit: How the East Indies Trade Transformed Anglo-American Capitalism* (Cambridge, MA: Harvard University Press, 2010).

Finlay, Richard J., *A Partnership for Good? Scottish Politics and the Union since 1880* (Edinburgh: John Donald, 1997).

Flinn, M. (ed.), *Scottish Population History: From the 17th Century to the 1930s* (Cambridge: Cambridge University Press, 1977).

Forsyth, David, 'Empire and Union: Imperial and national identity in nineteenth-century Scotland', *Scottish Geographical Magazine*, 113, 1 (1997), pp. 6–12.

Francis, Daniel, *The Imaginary Indian: The Image of the Indian in Canadian Culture* (Vancouver: Arsenal Pulp Press 1992, 2004).

Fraser, Lyndon, *To Tara via Holyhead: Irish Catholic Immigrants in Nineteenth-Century Christchurch* (Auckland: Auckland University Press, 1997).

Fry, Michael, *How the Scots Made America* (New York: Thomas Dunne Books, 2004).

Fry, Michael, *The Scottish Empire* (East Linton: Tuckwell; Edinburgh: Birlinn, 2002).

Gallagher, John, *The Decline, Revival and Fall of the British Empire* (Cambridge: Cambridge University Press, 1982).

Gandar, John M., 'New Zealand net migration in the latter part of the nineteenth century', *Australian Economic History Review*, 19, 2 (1979), pp. 151–68.

Gibson, A. and T. C. Smout, 'Scottish food and Scottish history, 1500–1800', in R. A. Houston and I. D. Whyte (eds), *Scottish Society, 1500–1800* (Cambridge: Cambridge University Press).

Gibson, Rob, *Plaids and Bandanas: From Highland Drover to Wild West Cowboy* (Edinburgh: Luath Press, 2003).

Gibson, Sarah Katherine, '"In quest of a better hame": A Transatlantic lowland Scottish network in Lower Canada, 1800–1850', in Angela McCarthy (ed.), *A Global Clan: Scottish Migrant Networks and Identities Since the Eighteenth Century* (London: Tauris Academic Studies, 2006).

Gillespie, Greg, 'Roderick McLennan, professionalism, and the emergence of the athlete in Caledonian Games', *Sports History Review*, 31, 1 (2000), pp. 43–63.

Gray, Malcolm, 'The course of Scottish emigration, 1750–1914: Enduring influences and changing circumstances', in T. M. Devine (ed.), *Scottish Emigration and Society* (Edinburgh: John Donald, 1992).

Griffiths, Trevor, *The Cinema and Cinema Going in Scotland, 1896–1950* (Edinburgh: Edinburgh University Press, 2012).

Grigg, D. B., 'E. G. Ravenstein and the "laws of migration"', *Journal of Historical Geography*, 3, 1 (1977), pp. 41–54.

Grosjean, Alexia, 'Returning to Belhelvie, 1593–1875: The impact of return migration on an Aberdeenshire parish', in Marjory Harper (ed.), *Emigrant Homecomings: The Return Movement of Emigrants, 1600–2000* (Manchester: Manchester University Press, 2005).

Grosjean, Alexia and Steve Murdoch (eds), *Scottish Communities Abroad in the Early Modern Period* (Leiden: Brill, 2005).

Grove, Richard, 'Scottish missionaries, evangelical discourses and the origins of conservation thinking in Southern Africa 1820–1900', *Journal of Southern African Studies*, 15, 2 (1989), pp. 163–87.

Hall, Stuart, 'The question of cultural identity', in Stuart Hall, David Held and Anthony McGrew (eds), *Modernity and its Futures* (Cambridge: Polity Press, 1992).

Hamilton, Douglas J., *Scotland, the Carribeans and the Atlantic World, 1750–1820* (Manchester: Manchester University Press, 2005).

Hancock, David, 'Scots in the Slave Trade', in Ned C. Landsman (ed.), *Nation and Province in the First British Empire* (Cranbury, NJ: Bucknell University Press, 2001).

Hancock, David, *Citizens of the World: London Merchants and the Integration of the British Atlantic Community, 1735–1785* (Cambridge: Cambridge University Press, 1995).

Hargreaves, R. P. and T. Hearn, 'Special settlements of the South Island New Zealand', *New Zealand Geographer*, 37, 2 (1981), pp. 67–72.

Harland, Jill, 'Island heritage and identity in the Antipodes: Orkney and Shetland Societies in New Zealand', in Tanja Bueltmann, Andrew Hinson and

Graeme Morton (eds), *Ties of Bluid, Kin and Countrie: Scottish Associational Culture in the Diaspora* (Guelph: Guelph Series in Scottish Studies, 2009).

Harper, Marjory, 'A century of Scottish emigration to New Zealand', *Immigrants & Minorities*, 29, 2 (2011), pp. 220–39.

Harper, Marjory, *Adventurers and Exiles: The Great Scottish Exodus* (London: Profile Books, 2003).

Harper, Marjory, *Emigration from North-East Scotland*, vols 1 and 2 (Aberdeen: Aberdeen University Press, 1988).

Harper, Marjory, *Emigration from Scotland, 1918–1939: Opportunity or Exile* (Manchester: Manchester University Press, 1998).

Harper, Marjory, *Emigration from Scotland between the Wars* (Manchester: Manchester University Press, 1998).

Harper, Marjory, 'Exiles or entrepreneurs? Snapshots of the Scots in Canada', in Peter E. Rider and Heather McNabb (eds), *A Kingdom of the Mind: How the Scots Helped Make Canada* (Montreal and Kingston: McGill-Queen's University Press, 2006).

Harper, Marjory, 'Probing the pioneer questionnaires: British settlement in Saskatchewan, 1887–1914', *Saskatchewan History*, 52, 2 (2000) pp. 28–46.

Harper, Marjory, *Scotland No More? The Scots Who Left Scotland in the Twentieth Century* (Edinburgh: Luath Press, 2012).

Harper, Marjory, 'Transplanted identities: Remembering and reinventing Scotland across the diaspora', in Tanja Bueltmann, Andrew Hinson and Graeme Morton (eds), *Ties of Bluid, Kin and Countrie: Scottish Associational Culture in the Diaspora* (Guelph: Guelph Series in Scottish Studies, 2009).

Harper, Marjory and Stephen Constantine, *Migration and Empire* (Oxford: Oxford University Press, 2010).

Harper, Marjory and Michael E. Vance (eds), *Myth, Migration and the Making of Memory: Scotia and Nova Scotia, c. 1700–1900* (Halifax, NS: Fernwood, 1999).

Harrison, Phyllis, *The Home Children: Their Personal Stories* (Winnipeg: Watson & Dwyer, 1979).

Hart, John Fraser, 'The changing distribution of sheep in Britain', *Economic Geography*, 32, 3 (1956), pp. 260–74.

Hassam, Andrew, *Sailing to Australia: Shipboard Diaries by Nineteenth-Century British Immigrants* (Manchester: Manchester University Press, 1994).

Hearn, Terry, 'Scots miners in the goldfields, 1861–1870', in Tom Brooking and Jennie Coleman (eds), *The Heather and the Fern: Scottish Migration and New Zealand Settlement* (Dunedin: Otago University Press, 2003).

Herman, Arthur, *How the Scots Invented the Modern World: The True Story of How Western Europe's Poorest Nation Created the World and Everything in It* (New York: Crown Publishers, 2001).

Hesse, David, 'Finding Neverland: Homecoming Scotland and the "affinity Scots"', in Mario Varricchio (ed.), *Back to Caledonian: Scottish Homecomings from the Seventeenth Century to the Present* (Edinburgh: John Donald, 2012).

Hicks, John, 'Orkneymen in the HBC, 1780–1821', in *Old Trails and New Directions: Papers of the Third North American Fur Trade Conference*, ed. Carol M. Judd and Arthur J. Ray (Toronto: University of Toronto Press, 1980).

Hinson, Andrew and Graeme Morton, 'Observations of a Scottish moralist: Indigenous peoples and the nationalities of Canada', in Graeme Morton and David A. Wilson (eds), *Irish and Scottish Encounters with Indigenous Peoples: Canada, the United States, New Zealand, and Australia* (Montreal and Kingston: McGill-Queen's University Press, 2013).

Hodgson, Janet, 'A battle for sacred power: Christian beginnings amongst the Xhosa', in Richard Elphick and Rodney Davenport (eds), *Christianity in South Africa: A Political, Social and Cultural History* (Oxford: James Currey and David Phillip, 1997).

Hook, Andrew, 'Philadelphia, Edinburgh and the Scottish Enlightenment', in Richard B. Sher and Jeffrey R. Smitten (eds), *Scotland and America in the Age of Enlightenment* (Edinburgh: Edinburgh University Press, 1990).

Hooper-Greenhill, Eileen, *Museums and the Interpretation of Visual Culture* (London: Routledge, 2000).

Hornsby, Stephen J., 'Patterns of Scottish emigration to Canada, 1750–1870', *Journal of Historical Geography*, 18, 4 (1992), pp. 397–416.

Howe, Daniel Walker, 'Why the Scottish Enlightenment was useful to the framers of the American Constitution', *Comparative Studies in Society and History*, 31, 3 (July 1989), pp. 572–87.

Hughes, Kyle, '"Scots stand firm and our Empire is safe": The politicization of Scottish clubs and societies in Belfast during the Home Rule era, c1885–1914', in Tanja Bueltmann, Andrew Hinson and Graeme Morton (eds), *Ties of Bluid, Kin and Countrie: Scottish Associational Culture in the Diaspora* (Guelph: Guelph Series in Scottish Studies, 2009).

Hulme, Peter, 'Introduction: The cannibal scene', in Francis Barker, Peter Hulme and Margaret Iversen (eds), *Cannibalism and the Colonial World* (Cambridge: Cambridge University Press, 1998).

Hutchings, Kevin, '"Teller of tales": John Buchan, First Baron Tweedsmuir of Elsfield, and Canada's Aboriginal peoples', in Graeme Morton and David A. Wilson (eds), *Irish and Scottish Encounters with Indigenous Peoples: Canada, the United States, New Zealand, and Australia* (Montreal and Kingston: McGill-Queen's University Press, 2013).

Hutchison, I. G. C., 'Anglo-Scottish political relations in the nineteenth century, c. 1815–1914', in T. C. Smout (ed.), *Anglo-Scottish Relations from 1603 to 1900* (Oxford: Oxford University Press, 2005).

Hyslop, Jonathan, 'Cape Town highlanders, Transvaal Scottish: Military "Scottishness" and social power in nineteenth and twentieth century South Africa', *South African Historical Journal*, 47 (2002), pp. 96–114.

Hyslop, Jonathan, 'The Imperial working class makes itself "white": White labourism in Britain, Australia, and South Africa before the First World War', *Journal of Historical Sociology*, 12, 4 (1999), pp. 398–421.

Hyslop, Jonathan, *The Notorious Syndicalist: J. T. Bain: A Scottish Rebel in Colonial South Africa* (Johannesburg: Jacana, 2004).

Innes, Robert Alexander, 'Multicultural bands on the Northern Plains and the notion of "tribal" histories', in Robin Jarvis Brownlie and Valerie J. Korinek (eds), *Finding a Way to the Heart. Feminist Writings on Aboriginal and Women's History in Canada* (Winnipeg: University of Manitoba Press 2012).

Jack, Allen, *History of the St Andrew's Society of St John N. B. Canada, 1798 to 1903* (St John, NB: J. A. MacMillan, 1903).

Janin, Hunt, *The India-China Opium Trade in the Nineteenth Century* (Jefferson, NC: McFarland, 1999).

Ji, Zhaojin, *A History of Modern Shanghai Banking: The Rise and Decline of China's Finance Capitalism* (Armonk, NY: M. E. Sharpe, 2003).

Johnston, Geoffrey, 'Goldie, Hugh', in Gerald H. Anderson (ed.), *Biographical Dictionary of Christian Missions* (New York: Macmillan, 1998).

Jones, Geoffrey, *Merchants to Multinationals: British Trading Companies in the Nineteenth and Twentieth Centuries* (Oxford: Oxford University Press, 2000).

Jones, Geoffrey (ed.), *The United Nations Library on Transnational Corporations, Volume 2: Transnational Corporations – A Historical Perspective* (London and New York: Routledge, 1993).

Judd, Dennis, *The Lion and the Tiger: The Rise and Fall of the British Raj* (Oxford: Oxford University Press, 2005).

Jung, Sandro, '"Staging" an Anglo-Scottish identity: The early career of David Mallet, poet and playwright in London', in Stana Nenadic (ed.), *Scots in London in the Eighteenth Century* (Cranbury: Bucknell University Press, 2010).

Juta, H. C., *The History of the Transvaal Scottish 1902–1932* (Johannesburg: Hortors, 1933).

Karras, Alan L., *Sojourners in the Sun: Scottish Migrants in Jamaica and the Chesapeake, 1740–1800* (Ithaca: Cornell University Press, 1992).

Keegan, Timothy, *Colonial South Africa and the Origins of the Racial Order* (London: Leicester University Press, 1996).

Kehoe, S. Karly, 'Catholic identity in the diaspora: Nineteenth-century

Ontario', in Tanja Bueltmann, Andrew Hinson and Graeme Morton (eds), *Ties of Bluid, Kin and Countrie: Scottish Associational Culture in the Diaspora* (Guelph: Guelph Series in Scottish Studies, 2009).

Kenefick, William , 'Confronting white labourism: Socialism, syndicalism, and the role of the Scottish radical left in South Africa before 1914', *International Review of Social History*, 55, 1 (2010), pp. 29–62.

Klein, Herbert S., *The Middle Passage: Comparative Studies on the Atlantic Slave Trade* (Princeton: Princeton University Press, 1978).

Kumagai, Yukihisa, 'Kirkam Finlay and John Crawfurd: Two Scots in the campaign for the Glasgow East India Association for the opening of the China trade, 1829–1833', *Journal of Scottish Historical Studies*, 30, 2 (2010), pp. 175–99.

Landsman, Ned, *Scotland and Its First American Colony, 1683–1764* (Princeton: Princeton University Press, 1985).

Langford, Paul, 'South Britons' reception of North Britons, 1707–1820', in T. C. Smout (ed.), *Anglo-Scottish Relations from 1603 to 1900* (Oxford: Oxford University Press, 2005).

Le Pichon, Alain, *China Trade and Empire: Jardine, Matheson & Co. and the Origins of British Rule in Hong Kong, 1827–1843* (Oxford and New York: Oxford University Press, 2007).

Lee, C. H., 'Scotland, 1860–1939', in Roderick Floud and Deirdre McCloskey (eds), *The Economic History of Britain, Vol. II, Economic Maturity, 1860–1939*, 2nd edn (Cambridge: Cambridge University Press, 2004).

Lee, C. H., *Scotland and the United Kingdom: The Economy and the Union in the Twentieth Century* (Manchester: Manchester University Press, 1995).

Lenihan, Rebecca, '"Counting" migrants: New Zealand Scots 1840–1920, a case study', in Rosalind McClean, Brad Patterson and David Swain (eds), *Counting Stories, Moving Ethnicities: Studies from Aotearoa New Zealand* (Hamilton: University of Waikato, 2012).

Lester, Alan, *Imperial Networks: Creating Identities in Nineteenth-Century South Africa and Britain* (London: Routledge, 2001).

Liebowitz, Daniel, *The Physician and the Slave Trade: John Kirk, the Livingstone Expeditions and the Crusade against Slavery in East Africa* (New York: Freeman, 1999).

Lucas, D., 'Scots – Scottish immigration 1891–1945', in James Jupp (ed.), *The Australian People: An Encyclopedia of the Nation, Its People and their Origins* (Cambridge: Cambridge University Press, 2001).

Lucassen, Jan and Leo Lucassen, 'Migration, migration history, history: Old paradigms and new perspectives', in Jan Lucassen and Leo Lucassen (eds), *Migration, Migration History, History: Old Paradigms and New Perspectives* (Bern: Peter Lang 1997).

MacDonagh, Oliver, *A Pattern of Government Growth, 1800–60: The Passenger Acts and their Enforcement* (London: MacGibbon & Kee, 1961).

MacDonnell, Margaret, *The Emigrant Experience: Songs of Highland Emigrants in North America* (Toronto: University of Toronto Press, 1980).

MacKenzie, John M., 'A Scottish empire? The Scottish diaspora and interactive identities', in Tom Brooking and Jennie Coleman, *The Heather and the Fern: Scottish Migration and New Zealand Settlement* (Dunedin: University of Otago Press, 2003).

MacKenzie, John M., 'David Livingstone: The construction of the myth', in Graham Walker and Tom Gallagher (eds), *Sermons and Battle Hymns: Protestant Popular Culture in Modern Scotland* (Edinburgh: Edinburgh University Press, 1990).

MacKenzie, John M., 'Empire and national identities: The case of Scotland', *Transactions of the Royal Historical Society*, 6, 8 (1998), pp. 215–31.

MacKenzie, John M., '"Making black Scotsman and Scotswomen?" Scottish missionaries and the Eastern Cape Colony in the nineteenth century', in Hilary M. Carey (ed.), *Empires of Religion* (Basingstoke: Palgrave Macmillan, 2008).

MacKenzie, John M., 'On Scotland and the Empire', *International History Review*, 15 (1993), pp. 714–39.

MacKenzie, John M., 'Scots and the environment of Empire', in John M. MacKenzie and T. M. Devine (eds), *Scotland and the British Empire* (Oxford: Oxford University Press, 2011).

MacKenzie, John M. with Nigel R. Dalziel, *The Scots in South Africa: Ethnicity, Identity, Gender and Race, 1772–1914* (Manchester: Manchester University Press, 2007).

Mackillop, Andrew, 'Europeans, Britons and Scots: Scottish sojourning networks and identities in India, c. 1700–1815', in Angela McCarthy (ed.), *A Global Clan: Scottish Migrant Networks and Identities since the Eighteenth Century* (London: Tauris, 2006).

Mackillop, Andrew, 'Locality, nation, and Empire: Scots and the Empire in Asia, c. 1696–c. 1813', in John M. MacKenzie and T. M. Devine (eds), *Scotland and the British Empire* (Oxford: Oxford University Press, 2011).

Mackillop, Andrew, 'The Highlands and the returning nabob: Sir Hector Munro of Novar, 1760–1807', in Marjory Harper (ed.), *Emigrant Homecomings: The Return Movement of Emigrants, 1600–2000* (Manchester: Manchester University Press, 2005).

Macmillan, David, *Scotland and Australia 1788–1850: Emigration, Commerce and Investment* (Oxford: Clarendon Press, 1967).

Macmillan, David, 'Sir Charles Trevelyan and the Highland and Island Emigration Society', *Journal of the Royal Australian Historical Society*, 49, 3 (1963), pp. 161–88.

Magee, Gary B. and Andrew S. Thompson, *Empire and Globalisation: Networks of People, Goods and Capital in the British World, c. 1850–1914* (Cambridge: Cambridge University Press, 2010).

Mancke, Elizabeth and Carole Shammas (eds), *The Creation of the British Atlantic World* (Baltimore: Johns Hopkins University Press, 2005).

Marsh, David C., *The Changing Social Structure of England and Wales, 1871–1961* (London: Routledge, 2002 [1958]).

Marshall, Peter, 'British North America, 1760–1815', in P. J. Marshall (ed.), *The Oxford History of the British Empire: The Eighteenth Century* (Oxford: Oxford University Press, 2009).

Matheson Connell, Carol, *A Business in Risk: Jardine Matheson and the Hong Kong Trading Industry* (Westport, CT: Praeger, 2004).

McAloon, Jim, *No Idle Rich: The Wealthy in Canterbury and Otago, 1840–1914* (Dunedin: Otago University Press, 2002).

McCalla, Douglas, 'Sojourners in the snow? The Scots in business in nineteenth-century Canada', in Peter E. Rider and Heather McNabb (eds), *A Kingdom of the Mind: How the Scots Helped Make Canada* (Montreal and Kingston: McGill-Queen's University Press, 2006).

McCarthy, Angela, 'Exploring ethnicity and ethnic identity in New Zealand asylums, before 1910', in Rosalind McClean, Brad Patterson and David Swain (eds), *Counting Stories, Moving Ethnicities: Studies from Aotearoa New Zealand* (Hamilton: University of Waikato, 2012).

McCarthy, Angela, '"For spirit and adventure": Personal accounts of emigration to New Zealand, 1921–1961', in Tom Brooking and Jennie Coleman (eds), *The Heather and the Fern: Scottish Migration and New Zealand Settlement* (Dunedin: Otago University Press, 2003).

McCarthy, Angela, 'National identities and twentieth-century Scottish migrants in England', in W. L. Miller (ed.), *Anglo-Scottish Relations from 1900 to Devolution and Beyond* (Oxford: Oxford University Press, 2005).

McCarthy, Angela, 'Scottish migrant ethnic identities in the British Empire since the nineteenth century', in John M. MacKenzie and T. M. Devine (eds), *Scotland and the British Empire* (Oxford: Oxford University Press, 2011).

McCarthy, Angela, 'The Scots Society of St Andrew, Hull, 1910–2001. Immigrant, ethnic, and transnational association', in Tanja Bueltmann, Andrew Hinson and Graeme Morton (eds), *Ties of Bluid, Kin and Countrie: Scottish Associational Culture in the Diaspora* (Guelph: Guelph Series in Scottish Studies, 2009).

McCleod, John, *Beginning Postcolonialism* (Manchester: Manchester University Press, 2000).

McCormack, Patricia A., 'Transatlantic rhythms: To the far nor'wast and back again', in Graeme Morton and David A. Wilson (eds), *Irish and Scottish*

Encounters with Indigenous Peoples: Canada, the United States, New Zealand, and Australia (Montreal and Kingston: McGill-Queen's University Press, 2013).

McCoy, Drew, *The Elusive Republic: Political Economy in Jeffersonian America* (Chapel Hill, NC: University of North Carolina Press, 1980).

McCracken, John, *Politics and Christianity in Malawi 1875–1940: The Impact of the Livingstonia Mission in the Northern Province* (Zomba: Kachere Series, 2000).

McCrone, David, 'Who do you say you are? Making sense of national identities in Modern Britain', *Ethnicities*, 2, 3 (2002), pp. 301–20.

McGilvary, George, *East India Patronage and the British State: The Scottish Elite and Politics in the Eighteenth Century* (London: Tauris, 2008).

McGilvary, George, *Guardian of the East India Company: The Life of Laurence Sulivan* (London: Tauris, 2006).

McGilvary, George, 'Return of the Scottish nabob, 1725–1833', in Mario Varricchio (ed.), *Back to Caledonian: Scottish Homecomings from the Seventeenth Century to the Present* (Edinburgh: John Donald, 2012).

McKay, Alexander, *Scottish Samurai: Thomas Blake Glover 1838–1911* (Edinburgh: Canongate, 1993).

McLaren, Martha, *British India and British Scotland, 1780–1830: Career Building, Empire Building, and a Scottish School of Thought on Indian Governance* (Akron, OH: University of Akron Press, 2001).

McLean, J. P., *An Historical Account of the Settlements of Scotch Highlanders in America Prior to the Peace of 1783* (Baltimore: Genealogical Publishing Co., 1968).

McLean, Marianne, 'Peopling Glengarry County: The Scottish origins of a Canadian community', Canadian Historical Association, *Historical Papers* (1982), pp. 156–71.

McLean, Marianne, *The People of Glengarry: Highlanders in Transition, 1745–1820* (Montreal: McGill-Queen's University Press, 1991).

McLean, Rosalind, 'Reluctant leavers? Scottish women and emigration in the mid-nineteenth century', in Tom Brooking and J. Coleman (eds), *The Heather and the Fern: Scottish Migration and New Zealand Settlement* (Dunedin: Otago University Press, 2003).

McLean, Rosalind, 'Scottish piety: The Free Church Settlement of Otago, 1848–1853', in J. Stenhouse and J. Thomson (eds), *Building God's Own Country: Historical Essays on Religions in New Zealand* (Dunedin: Otago University Press, 2004).

McLintock, A. H., *The History of Otago: The Origins and Growth of a Wakefield Class Settlement* (Dunedin: Otago Centennial Historical Publications, 1949).

McNabb, Heather, 'Butcher, baker, cabinetmaker? A view of Montreal's

Scottish immigrant community from 1835 to 1865', in Peter E. Rider and Heather McNabb (eds), *A Kingdom of the Mind: How the Scots Helped Make Canada* (Montreal & Kingston: McGill-Queen's University Press, 2006).

Mein Smith, Philippa, *A Concise History of New Zealand*, 2nd edn (Cambridge: Cambridge University Press, 2012).

Meyer, David R., *Hong Kong as a Global Metropolis* (Cambridge: Cambridge University Press, 2004).

Meyer, Duane, *The Highland Scots of North Carolina, 1732–1776* (Chapel Hill, North Carolina: The University of North Carolina Press, 1961).

Mitchell, B. R., *European Historical Statistics, 1750–1975* (London: Macmillan, 1975).

Mitchell, B. R. and P. Dean, *Abstract of British Historical Statistics* (Cambridge: Cambridge University Press, 1962).

Mitchell, Elaine Allan, 'The Scot in the fur trade', in Stanford Reid (ed.), *The Scottish Tradition in Canada* (Toronto: McClelland and Stewart, 1976).

Mitchell, J. H., *Tartan on the Veld: The Transvaal Scottish 1950–1993* (Johannesburg: Transvaal Scottish Regimental Council, 1994).

Molloy, M., *Those Who Speak to the Heart: The Nova Scotians at Waipu, 1854–1920* (Palmerston North: Dunmore, 1991).

Morgan, Philip D., 'Encounters between British and "indigenous" peoples, c 1500–c 1800', in Martin Daunton and Rick Halpern (eds), *Empire and Others: British Encounters with Indigenous Peoples, 1600–1850* (Philadelphia: University of Pennsylvania Press, 1999).

Morn, Frank, *'The Eye that Never Sleeps': A History of Pinkerton National Detective Agency* (Bloomington: Indiana University Press, 1982).

Morris, R. J., 'In search of twentieth-century Edinburgh', *Book of the Old Edinburgh Club*, New Series, 8 (2010), pp. 13–26.

Morris, R. J., 'The Enlightenment and the thistle: The Scottish contribution to associational culture in Canada', in Tanja Bueltmann, Andrew Hinson and Graeme Morton (eds), *Ties of Bluid, Kin and Countrie: Scottish Associational Culture in the Diaspora* (Guelph: Guelph Series in Scottish Studies, 2009).

Morris, R. J., 'Urban Ulster since 1600', in Liam Kennedy and Philip Ollerenshaw (eds), *Ulster Since 1600: Politics, Economy and Society* (Oxford: Oxford University Press, 2013).

Morse, David, *High Victorian Culture* (New York: New York University Press, 1993).

Morton, Graeme, 'Ethnic identity in the civic world of Scottish associational culture', in Tanja Bueltmann, Andrew Hinson and Graeme Morton (eds), *Ties of Bluid, Kin and Countrie: Scottish Associational Culture in the Diaspora* (Guelph: Guelph Series in Scottish Studies, 2009).

Morton, Graeme, 'Identity out of place', in Trevor Griffiths and Graeme

Morton (eds), *A History of Everyday Life in Scotland, 1800 to 1900* (Edinburgh: Edinburgh University Press, 2010).

Morton, Graeme, 'Identity within the Union State, 1800–1900', in *The Oxford Handbook of Modern Scottish History*, ed. T. M. Devine and Jenny Wormald (Oxford: Oxford University Press, 2012).

Morton, Graeme, *Ourselves and Others: Scotland, 1832–1914* (Edinburgh: Edinburgh University Press, 2012).

Morton, Graeme, 'Returning nationalists, returning Scotland': James Grant and Theodore Napier', in Mario Varricchio (ed.), *Back to Caledonian: Scottish Homecomings from the Seventeenth Century to the Present* (Edinburgh: John Donald, 2012).

Morton, Graeme, 'Scotland is Britain: The Union and Unionist-nationalism, 1807–1907', *Journal of Irish and Scottish Studies*, 1, 2, (2008), pp. 127–41.

Morton, Graeme, 'The social memory of Jane Porter and her *Scottish Chiefs*', *Scottish Historical Review*, vol. 91, 2: no. 232 (October 2012), pp. 311–35.

Morton, Graeme, *Unionist Nationalism: Governing Urban Scotland, 1830–1860* (East Linton: Tuckwell Press, 1999).

Morton, Graeme, and R. J. Morris, 'Civil society, governance and nation, 1832–1914', in R. A. Houston and W. W. J. Knox (eds), *The New Penguin History of Scotland* (London: Penguin, 2001),

Munro, J. Forbes, *Maritime Enterprise and Empire: Sir William Mackinnon and his Business Network, 1823–1893* (Woodbridge: Boydell Press, 2003).

Munro, J. Forbes, 'Scottish overseas enterprise and the lure of London: The Mackinnon Shipping Group, 1847–1893', *Scottish Economic and Social History*, 8 (1988), pp. 73–87.

Murdoch, Alexander, *Scotland and America, c. 1600–c. 1800* (Basingstoke, Hampshire: Palgrave Macmillan, 2010).

Murdoch, Steve, 'Children of the diaspora: The "homecoming" of the second-generation Scot in the seventeenth century', in Marjory Harper (ed.), *Emigrant Homecomings: The Return Movement of Emigrants, 1600–2000* (Manchester: Manchester University Press, 2005).

Murdoch, Steve, *Scotland and the Thirty Years' War, 1618–1648* (Leiden: Brill, 2001).

Murdoch, Steve, 'Scotland, Europe and the English "missing link"', *History Compass*, 5, 3 (2007), pp. 890–913.

Murdoch, Steve, and Esther Mijers, 'Migrant destinations, 1500–1750', in T. M. Devine and Jenny Wormald, *The Oxford Handbook of Modern Scottish History* (Oxford: Oxford University Press, 2012).

Murray, Jock, and Janet Murray, 'The seed, the soil and the climate: The Scottish influence on Canadian medical education and practice, 1775–1875', in Peter E. Rider and Heather McNabb (eds), *A Kingdom of the Mind: How the Scots Helped Make Canada* (Montreal and Kingston: McGill-Queen's University Press, 2006).

Nathan, Simon, *The Amazing World of James Hector* (Wellington: Awa Press, 2008).

Nechtman, Tillman W., *Nabobs: Empire and Identity in Eighteenth-Century Britain* (Cambridge: Cambridge University Press, 2010).

Nenadic, Stana, 'Military men, business men, and the "business" of patronage', in Stana Nenadic (ed.), *Scots in London in the Eighteenth Century* (Cranbury: Bucknell University Press, 2010).

Nenadic, Stana (ed.), *Scots in London in the Eighteenth Century* (Cranbury: Bucknell University Press, 2010).

Newman, C. E. T., *The Spirit of Wharf House* (Sydney: Angus & Robertson, 1961).

Newton, Michael, '"Going to the Land of the Yellow Man": The representation of indigenous Americans in Scottish Gaelic culture', in Graeme Morton and David A. Wilson (eds), *Irish and Scottish Encounters with Indigenous Peoples: Canada, the United States, New Zealand, and Australia* (Montreal and Kingston: McGill-Queen's University Press, 2013).

Noble, Gus, 'The Chicago Scots', in Tanja Bueltmann, Andrew Hinson and Graeme Morton (eds), *Ties of Bluid, Kin and Countrie: Scottish Associational Culture in the Diaspora* (Guelph: Guelph Series in Scottish Studies, 2009).

Oberholtzer, Cath, 'Thistles in the north: The direct and indirect Scottish influence on James Bay Cree material culture', in Peter E. Rider and Heather McNabb (eds), *A Kingdom of the Mind: How the Scots Helped Make Canada* (Montreal and Kingston: McGill-Queen's University Press, 2006).

O'Connor, Shannon, '"Nowhere in Canada is St Andrew's Day celebrated with greater loyalty and enthusiasm": Scottish Associational Culture in Toronto, c. 1836–1914', in Tanja Bueltmann, Andrew Hinson and Graeme Morton (eds), *Ties of Bluid, Kin and Countrie: Scottish Associational Culture in the Diaspora* (Guelph: Guelph Series in Scottish Studies, 2009).

O' Farrell, Patrick, *The Irish in Australia: 1788 to the Present* (Notre Dame, IN: University of Notre Dame Press, 2000).

Orange, Claudia, *The Treaty of Waitangi*, 2nd edn. (Wellington: Bridget Williams Books, 2011).

Orpen, Neil, *The Cape Town Highlanders 1885–1985* (Cape Town: Cape Town Highlanders History Committee, 1986).

Palmer, Colin, 'Defining and studying the modern African diaspora', *Perspectives*, 36, 6 (1998), pp. 22–5.

Pannekoek, Frits, *The Fur Trade and Western Canadian Society, 1670–1870* (Ottawa: The Canadian Historical Association, 1987).

Parker, Anthony W., *Scottish Highlanders in Colonial Georgia: The Recruitment,*

Emigration, and Settlement at Darien, 1735–1748 (Athens, Georgia and London: The University of Georgia Press, 1997).

Parker, James G., 'Scottish enterprise in India, 1750–1914', in R. A. Cage (ed.), *The Scots Abroad: Labour, Capital, Enterprise, 1750–1914* (London: Croom Helm, 1985).

Patterson, Brad, '"It is curious how keenly allied in character are the Scotch highlander and the Maori": Encounters in a New Zealand colonial settlement', in Graeme Morton and David A. Wilson (eds), *Irish and Scottish Encounters with Indigenous Peoples* (Montreal and Kingston: McGill-Queen's University Press, 2013).

Pearce, G. L., *The Scots of New Zealand* (Dundee: William Collins, 1976).

Pedlar, Neil, *The Imported Pioneers: Westerners Who Helped Build Modern Japan* (Folkestone: Japan Library Ltd, 1990).

Peterson, Derek R. (ed.), *Abolitionism and Imperialism in Britain, Africa, and the Atlantic* (Athens, OH: Ohio University Press, 2010).

Pettitt, Clare, *Dr Livingstone, I Presume? Missionaries, Journalists, Explorers and Empire* (London: Profile Books, 2007).

Phillips, Jock and Terry Hearn, *Settlers: New Zealand Immigrants from England, Ireland and Scotland* (Auckland: Auckland University Press, 2008).

Pocock, J. G. A., 'British history: A plea for a new subject', *New Zealand Journal of History*, 8, 1 (1974), pp. 3–21.

Pool, Ian , 'A "Caledonian" conundrum: Scottish reproductive regimes in the "Old Country" and the "Better Britain of the South Seas", 1876–1901', in Rosalind McClean, Brad Patterson and David Swain (eds), *Counting Stories, Moving Ethnicities: Studies from Aotearoa New Zealand* (Hamilton: University of Waikato, 2012).

Pooley, Colin G. and Jane Turnbull, *Migration and Mobility in Britain since the Eighteenth Century* (London: UCL Press, 1998).

Powell, J. M., 'The debt of honour: Soldier settlement in the Dominions, 1915–1940', *Journal of Australian Studies*, 5, 8 (1981), pp. 64–87.

Prebble, John, *Darien: The Scottish Dream of Empire* (London: Pimlico, 2002).

Prentis, Malcolm, '"It's a long way to the bottom": The insignificance of "the Scots" in Australia', *Immigrants & Minorities* 29, 2 (2011), pp. 195–219.

Prentis, Malcolm, 'Scots – lowland Scottish immigration until 1860', in James Jupp (ed.), *The Australian People: An Encyclopedia of the Nation, Its People and their Origins* (Cambridge: Cambridge University Press, 2001).

Prentis, Malcolm, 'Scots – Scottish recruitment to Australian elites', in James Jupp (ed.), *The Australian People: An Encyclopedia of the Nation, Its People and their Origins* (Cambridge: Cambridge University Press, 2001).

Prentis, Malcolm, *The Scots in Australia* (Sydney: University of New South Wales Press, 2008).

Prentis, Malcolm, *The Scots in Australia: A Study of New South Wales, Victoria and Queensland* (Sydney: University of Sydney Press, 1983).

Price, Jacob M., 'The rise of Glasgow in the Chesapeake tobacco trade, 1770–1775', *The William and Mary Quarterly*, 11, 2 (1954), pp. 179–99.

Proctor, J. H., 'Serving God and the Empire: Mary Slessor in South-eastern Nigeria, 1876–1915', *Journal of Religion in Africa*, 30 (2000), pp. 45–61.

Raudzens, George K., 'A successful military settlement: Earl Grey's enrolled pensioners of 1846 in Canada', *Canadian Historical Review*, 52 (1971), pp. 389–403.

Ravenstein, E. G., 'The laws of migration', *Journal of the Statistical Society of London*, 48, 2 (June, 1885), pp. 167–227.

Ravenstein, E. G., 'The laws of migration', *Journal of the Statistical Society of London*, 52 (June 1889), pp. 214–301.

Ravenstein, E. G., 'Census of the British Isles, 1871; birthplaces and migration', *Geographical Magazine* 3 (1876).

Ray, Celeste, 'Ancestral clanscapes and transatlantic tartaneers', in Mario Varricchio (ed.), *Back to Caledonian: Scottish Homecomings from the Seventeenth Century to the Present* (Edinburgh: John Donald, 2012).

Ray, Celeste, 'Scottish immigration and ethnic organization in the United States', in Celeste Ray (ed.), *Transatlantic Scots* (Tuscaloosa: The University of Alabama Press, 2005).

Redford, Arthur, *Labour Migration to England, 1800–1850*, rev. and ed. W. H. Chaloner (Manchester: Manchester University Press, 1976 [1926]).

Refsing, Kirsten, 'Introduction', in Kirsten Refsing (ed.), *Early European Writings on Ainu Culture: Religion and Folklore, Volume 1* (London: RoutledgeCurzon, 2002).

Rethford, Wayne and June Skinner Sawyers, *The Scots of Chicago: Quiet Immigrants and Their New Society* (Chicago: Kendall/Hunt Publishing Co., 1997).

Richards, Eric, *A History of the Highland Clearances: Vol. 2: Emigration, Protest, Reasons* (London: Croom Helm, 1985).

Richards, Eric, 'Australia and the Scottish connection, 1788–1914', in R. A. Cage (ed.), *The Scots Abroad: Labour, Capital, Enterprise, 1750–1914* (London: Croom Helm, 1985).

Richards, Eric, *From Hirta to Port Phillip: The Story of the Ill-fated Emigration from St Kilda to Australia in 1852* (South Lochs, Isle of Lewis: The Islands Book Trust, 2010).

Richards, Eric, 'Highland emigrants to South Australia in the 1850s', *Northern Scotland*, 5, 1 (1982), pp. 1–30.

Richards, Eric, 'Scots – highland and Gaelic immigrants', in James Jupp (ed.), *The Australian People: An Encyclopedia of the Nation, Its People and their Origins* (Cambridge: Cambridge University Press, 2001).

Richards, Eric, 'Scottish networks and voices in colonial Australia', in Angela McCarthy (ed.), *A Global Clan: Scottish Migrant Networks and Identities Since the Eighteenth Century* (London: Tauris, 2006).

Richards, Eric, *That Land of Exiles: Scots in Australia* (Edinburgh: HMSO, 1988).

Richards, Eric, 'The last of the clan and other highland emigrants', in Tom Brooking and Jennie Coleman (eds), *The Heather and the Fern: Scottish Migration and New Zealand Settlement* (Dunedin: Otago University Press, 2003).

Rigg, Elizabeth, *Men of Spirit and Enterprise: Scots and Orkneymen in the Hudson's Bay Company, 1780–1821* (Edinburgh: John Donald, 2011).

Ritchie, J. D., *Lachlan Macquarie: A Biography* (Melbourne: Melbourne University Press, 1986).

Rodger, Richard, *The Transformation of Edinburgh: Land, Property and Trust in the Nineteenth Century* (Cambridge: Cambridge University Press, 2001).

Rose, Sonya O., *Limited Livelihoods: Gender and Class in Nineteenth-Century England* (Berkeley: University of California Press, 1992).

Rosenberg, Chaim M. *The Life and Times of Francis Cabot Lowell, 1775–1817* (Plymouth: Lexington Books, 2011).

Ross, Andrew C., *Colonialism to Cabinet Crisis: A Political History of Malawi* (Zomba: Kachere Series, 2009).

Ross, Andrew C., *David Livingstone: Mission and Empire*, 3rd edn (London and New York: Hambledon, 2006).

Ross, Andrew C., 'Govan, William', in Gerald H. Anderson (ed.), *Biographical Dictionary of Christian Missions* (New York: Macmillan, 1998).

Safran, William, 'Diasporas in modern societies: Myths of homeland and return', *Diaspora* 1, 1 (1991), pp. 83–99.

Safran, William, 'The Jewish diaspora in a comparative and theoretical perspective', *Israel Studies*, 10, 1 (Spring 2005), pp. 36–60.

Salesa, Damon Ieremia, *Racial Crossings: Race, Intermarriage, and the Victorian British Empire* (Oxford: Oxford University Press, 2011).

Schmiechen, James A., *Sweated Industries and Sweated Labor: The London Clothing Trades, 1860–1914* (London: Croom Helm, 1984).

Schultz, John A., '"Leaven for the lump": Canada and Empire settlement, 1918–1939', in Stephen Constantine (ed.), *Emigrants and Empire: British Settlement in the Dominions Between the Wars* (Manchester: Manchester University Press, 1990).

Scott, David, *China and the International System, 1840–1949* (Albany, NY: State University of New York Press, 2008).

Shepperson, George, 'Mungo Park and the Scottish contribution to Africa', *African Affairs*, 70, 280 (1971), pp. 277–81.

Shepperson, W. S., *British Emigration to North America: Projects and opinion in the Early Victorian Period* (Oxford: Basil Blackwell, 1957).

Sher, Richard B., 'Introduction: Scottish-American cultural studies, past and present', in Richard B. Sher and Jeffrey R. Smitten (eds), *Scotland and America in the Age of Enlightenment* (Edinburgh: Edinburgh University Press, 1990).

Sinclair, Keith, *A History of New Zealand* (Auckland: Penguin, 1988).

Sindima, H. J., *The Legacy of Scottish Missionaries in Malawi* (Lewiston: Edwin Mellen Press, 1992).

Sloan, Douglas, *The Scottish Enlightenment and the American College Ideal* (New York: Teachers College, Columbia University, 1971).

Smallwood, Stephen E., *Saltwater Slavery: A Middle Passage from Africa to American Diaspora* (Cambridge, MA: Harvard University Press, 2008).

Smandych, Russell and Anne McGillivray, 'Images of Aboriginal children: Contested governance in the Canadian West to 1850', in Martin Daunton and Rick Halpern (eds), *Empire and Others: British Encounters with Indigenous Peoples, 1600–1850* (Philadelphia: University of Pennsylvania Press, 1999).

Smith, Susan, '"Bordering on identity"', *Scotlands*, 3, 1 (1996), pp. 18–31.

Smout, T. C., 'Centre and periphery in history; with some thoughts on Scotland as a case study', *Journal of Common Market Studies*, 18, 3 (1980), pp. 256–71.

Smout, T. C., 'Scotland 1850–1950', in F. M. L. Thompson (ed.), *The Cambridge Social History of Britain, 1750–1950: Regions and Communities* (Cambridge: Cambridge University Press, 1990).

Smout, T. C., N. C. Landsman and T. M. Devine, 'Scottish emigration in the seventeenth and eighteenth centuries' in Nicholas P. Canny (ed.), *Europeans on the Move: Studies in European Migration* (Oxford: Clarendon Press, 1994).

Spiers, E. M., *The Scottish Soldier and Empire, 1854–1902* (Edinburgh: Edinburgh University Press, 2006).

Spiers, E. M., 'The Scottish soldier in the Boer War', in John Gooch (ed.), *The Boer War: Direction, Experience and Image* (London: Frank Cass, 2000).

Spiers, E. M., *The Victorian Soldier in Africa* (Manchester: Manchester University Press, 2004).

Stewart, Gordon T., *Jute and Empire: The Calcutta Jute Wallahs and the Landscapes of Empire* (Manchester: Manchester University Press, 1998).

Stewart, Mairi and Fiona Watson, 'Land, the landscape and people', in Trevor Griffiths and Graeme Morton (eds), *A History of Everyday Life in Scotland, 1800 to 1900* (Edinburgh: Edinburgh University Press, 2010).

Strong, Lisa, 'American Indians and Scottish identity in Sir William Drummond Stewart's Collection', *Winterthur Portfolio*, 35, 2/3 (Summer–Autumn, 2000), pp. 127–55.

Stuart, Ken, 'The Scottish crofter colony, Saltcoats, 1889–1904', *Saskatchewan History*, 24, 2 (1971), pp. 41–50.

Sullivan, Kim, 'Scottish associational culture in early modern Victoria, Australia: An Antipodean reading of a global phenomenon', in Tanja Bueltmann, Andrew Hinson and Graeme Morton (eds), *Ties of Bluid, Kin and Countrie: Scottish Associational Culture in the Diaspora* (Guelph: Guelph Series in Scottish Studies, 2009).

Sundkler, Bengt and Christopher Steed, *A History of the Church in Africa* (Cambridge: Cambridge University Press, 2000).

Swan, Claire, *Scottish Cowboys and the Dundee Investors* (Dundee: Abertay Historical Society, 2004).

Szasz, Ferenc Morton, *Abraham Lincoln and Robert Burns: Connected Lives and Legends* (Carbondale: Southern Illinois University Press, 2008).

Szasz, Ferenc Morton, *Scots in the North American West: 1790–1917* (Norman: University of Oklahoma Press, 2000).

Szasz, Margaret, *Scottish Highlanders and Native Americans: Indigenous Education in the Eighteenth-Century Atlantic World* (Norman: University of Oklahoma Press 2007).

Taylor, Justine, *A Cup of Kindness: The History of the Royal Scottish Corporation, a London Charity, 1603–2003* (East Linton: Tuckwell Press, 2003).

Taylor, William H., *Mission to Educate: A History of the Educational Work of the Scottish Presbyterian Mission in East Nigeria 1846–1960* (Leiden: Brill, 1996).

Thompson, Jack, *Christianity in Northern Malawi: Donald Fraser's Missionary Methods and Ngoni Culture* (Leiden: Brill, 1995).

Thompson, Jack, *Ngoni, Xhosa and Scot* (Zomba: Kachere Series, 2007).

Tölölyan, Khachig, 'Diasporama', *Diaspora: A Journal of Transnational Studies*, 3, 2 (1994), p. 235.

Tölölyan, Khachig, 'Diasporama', *Diaspora: A Journal of Transnational Studies*, 9, 2 (2000), pp. 309–10.

Tomlinson, B. R., 'From Campsie to Kedgeree: Scottish enterprise, Asian trade and the company Raj', *Modern Asian Studies*, 36, 4 (2002), pp. 769–91.

Tranter, N., *Population since the Industrial Revolution: The Case of England and Wales* (London: Croom Helm, 1973).

Treble, J. H., 'The occupied male labour force', in W. H. Fraser and R. J. Morris (eds), *People and Society in Scotland, vol. II 1830–1914* (Edinburgh: John Donald, 1990).

Tsuda, Takeyuki, 'Why does the diaspora return home? The causes of ethnic return migration', in Takeyuki Tsuda (ed.), *Diasporic Homecomings: Ethnic Return Migration in Comparative Perspective* (Stanford: Stanford University Press, 2009).

Tucker, Robert W. and David C. Hendrickson, *The Fall of the First British*

Empire: Origins of the War of American Independence (Baltimore: Johns Hopkins University Press, 1982).

Vance, Michael E., *Imperial Immigrants: Scottish Settlers in the Ottawa Valley, 1815–1840* (Toronto: Dundurn, 2012).

Vance, Michael E., 'Powerful pathos: The triumph of Scottishness in Nova Scotia', in Celeste Ray (ed.), *Transatlantic Scots* (Tuscaloosa: University of Alabama Press, 2005).

Vicziany, Marika, 'Imperialism, botany and statistics in early nineteenth-century India: The surveys of Francis Buchanan (1762–1829)', *Modern Asian Studies*, 20, 4 (1986), pp. 625–60.

Waterston, Elizabeth and J. J. Talman, 'John Howison', in *Dictionary of Canadian Biography Online*, vol. VIII *1851–1860* (Toronto: University of Toronto Press, 1985).

Way, Peter, 'The cutting edge of culture: British soldiers encounter Native Americans in the French and Indian War', in Martin Daunton and Rick Halpern (eds), *Empire and Others: British Encounters with Indigenous Peoples, 1600–1850* (Philadelphia: University of Pennsylvania Press, 1999).

Ward, W. Peter, *Birth Weight and Economic Growth: Women's Living Standards in the Industrializing West* (Chicago: University of Chicago Press, 1993).

Weber, Adna Ferrin, *The Growth of Cities in the Nineteenth Century: A Study in Statistics* (New York: Columbia University Press, 1899).

Whatley, Christopher A., *Scottish Society, 1707–1830* (Manchester: Manchester University Press, 2000).

Whatley, Christopher A., *The Industrial Revolution in Scotland* (Cambridge: Cambridge University Press, 1997).

Whatley, Harlan Douglas, *Two Hundred Fifty Years, 1756–2006: The History of Saint Andrew's Society of The State of New York* (New York: St Andrew's Society of New York State, 2008).

White, Paul, 'Not just rugby clubs: Scottish- and Welsh-born migrants in London', *Scottish Geographical Journal*, 119, 3 (2003), pp. 209–27.

Whyte, Donald, *A Dictionary of Scottish Emigrants to Canada Before Confederation* (Toronto: Ontario Genealogical Society, 1986).

Whyte, Ian, *Scotland and the Abolition of Black Slavery, 1756–1838* (Edinburgh: Edinburgh University Press, 2006).

Wills, Gary, *Inventing America: Jefferson's Declaration of Independence* (New York: Doubleday, 1978).

Winegard, Timothy C., *Indigenous Peoples of the British Dominions and the First World War* (Cambridge: Cambridge University Press, 2012).

Winter, Jay, *Sites of Memory, Sites of Mourning: The Great War in European Cultural History* (Cambridge: Cambridge University Press, 1995).

Withers, Charles W. J., *Urban Highlanders: Highland-Lowland Culture and Urban Gaelic Culture, 1700–1900* (East Linton: Tuckwell Press, 1998).

Wright, Ian, 'The diaspora and its writers', in I. Brown et al (eds), *The Edinburgh History of Scottish Literature Volume Three: Modern Transformation: New Identities (from 1918)* (Edinburgh: Edinburgh University Press, 2007).

Wrigley, E. A., 'A simple model of London's importance in changing English society and economy, 1650–1750', *Past and Present*, 37, 1 (1967), pp. 44–70.

Yangwen, Zheng, *The Social Life of Opium in China* (Cambridge: Cambridge University Press, 2005).

Zarnowski, Frank, *All Around Men: Heroes of a Forgotten Sport* (Lanham, MD: Scarecrow Press, 2005).

Zarnowski, Frank, 'The amazing Donald Dinnie: The nineteenth century's greatest athlete', *Iron Game History*, 5, 1 (1998), pp. 3–11.

FICTIONAL WORKS

Clavell, James, *Tai-Pan* (London: Atheneum, 2006).

Munro, Alice, *The View from Castle Rock* (Toronto: McClelland & Stewart, 2006).

UNPUBLISHED PAPERS

Cranfield, John and Kris Inwood, 'Stayers and leavers, diggers and Canucks: The 1914–1918 war in comparative perspective', unpublished paper, February 2010.

WEBSITES (date of individual access recorded in the Notes)

'Agreement between the United Kingdom Government and the Scottish Government on a referendum on independence for Scotland', Edinburgh, 15 October 2012, http://www.scotland.gov.uk/About/Government/concordats/Referendum-on-independence

Australian Government, Department of Immigration and Citizenship, Fact Sheet 8: Abolition of the 'White Australia' Policy, http://www.immi.gov.au/media/fact-sheets/08abolition.htm

Australian Dictionary of Biography, National Centre of Biography, Australian National University, http://adb.anu.edu.au

Caledonian Society of Cincinnati, http://www.caledoniansociety.org/

Chicago Scots, http://www.chicagoscots.org

Dictionary of Canadian Biography Online, http://www.biographi.ca

Dictionary of New Zealand Biography, Te Ara – the Encyclopedia of New Zealand, http://www.TeAra.govt.nz/en/biographies

'Census gives insights into characteristics of London's population' http://www.ons.gov.uk/ons/rel/mro/news-release/census-2–1–london/census-gives-insights-into-characteristics-of-london-s-population.html

North American Immigrant Letters, Diaries, and Oral Histories, http://solomon.imld.alexanderstreet.com

Online Historical Population Reports, http://www.histpop.org

Oxford Dictionary of National Biography, http://www.oxforddnb.com

Scotland's Census, http://www.scotlandscensus.gov.uk

Shetland Hamefarin, http://www.shetlandhamefarin.com

State Library of Queensland Convict Transportation Registers Database, http://www.slq.qld.gov.au/info/fh/convicts

US Census Aggregates, http://www.census.gov/prod/www/abs/decennial/

Index

Aberdeen Ladies' Union, 88, 199
Adelaide Caledonian Society, 128
affinity Scots, 11, 26, 30, 257
Africa, 13, 16, 25, 57, 82, 100, 109, 204–18
  South Africa, 25, 30, 68, 109, 115, 121–2,
    125, 137
  West Africa, 88, 100
Akenson, D. H., 25, 96
Algonquin, 96
Allan Lines, 179
America, 12–13, 26, 57, 70, 73, 77, 78, 80,
    83–6, 100, 137, 143, 171–85, 192, 195,
    208, 223, 226, 240
  'A Dance Called America', 12, 171
  associational culture, 114–15, 117–18,
    121–2, 125, 127
  early migrations, 8, 159
  Gaelic speaking, 28, 99
  migration, 13, 62, 64, 68, 80, 106, 108,
    197, 242
  Native Americans, 102, 108
  philanthropic Scots, 11
  roots-tourism, 141
  soldiering, 139, 161
'Amerikay', 12, 258
Anchor Line, 179
Anglo-Boer War, 204, 214–16
Antipodes, 1, 11, 14, 78, 125, 239–53
  associational culture, 115
Armstrong, J., 22
Asia, 13, 124, 134 143, 184, 218, 222–35,
    243–4, 258
  associational culture, 5, 12, 87, 114–29,
    147, 200
Australia, 2–3, 18, 26, 82, 88, 98, 127, 137,
    144–5, 216, 235, 262

associational culture, 114–18, 121–3, 128
convicts, 13
height data, 73–4
identity, 27
indigenous peoples, 100, 104–9
migration, 13, 21, 30–1, 64, 68, 122, 201

Bailyn, Bernard, 174.
Baines, Dudley, 39, 54, 65, 67–9
Baltic, 62, 134
Barnardos, 30, 90, 92
Bathurst, Earl, 70
Baumann, M., 5, 19
Belfast Benevolent St Andrew's Society, 166
Bell, Dr George, 57
Bell, Revd William, 69–70, 96, 260
Bengal, 134, 224–5, 227–8
Black Peril, 109
Bon Accord, 198
Boswell, James, 154, 171
Boys' Brigade, 91
British North America, 195, 197, 202, 223
British North American Act, 198
Brooklyn Caledonian Club Games, 125
Brubaker, Rogers, 17
Bruce, King Robert I, 114, 123
Buchan, J., 103
Burns, Jean, 89
Burns, Revd T., 245
Burns, Robert, 11, 14, 114, 117, 166, 205–6,
    245, 257–62
Burns clubs, 115–17, 164–5
'Burns Supper school of Scottish historians',
    176
Burns suppers, 14, 38, 114, 124, 128
Busby, James, 242

Cage, R. A., 163
Caithness and Sutherland Association, 40, 118
Caitlin, George, 101
Calcutta, 13, 114, 134, 228–9, 230–3, 235, 243, 257
Caledonian Ball, 101, 222
Caledonian Games, 117, 122, 125–7
Caledonian societies, 115–17, 121–2, 125, 127, 144, 252
Caledonian Society of Adelaide, 128
Caledonian Society of Cape Town, 124
Caledonian Society of Chicago, 122
Caledonian Society of London, 117, 164
Caledonian Society of Melbourne, 116
Caledonian Society of Oamaru, 116
Caledonian Society of Otago, 116, 122
Caledonian Society of Perth, 125
Caledonian Society of Salmon Gums, 124
Caledonian Society of South Australia, 114
Caledonian Society of Tasmania, 123
Caledonian Society of Toronto, 128
Calloway, Colin, 97
Canada, 30, 37, 99, 100,180, 188–202, 216, 223, 249, 258
    '3,000 Families Scheme', 201
    associational culture, 115–19, 122
    education, 25; fur trade, 9, 189–93
    indigenous encounters, 100, 104–9
    legacies, 83, 114
    migration, 13, 64, 67–9, 135, 179, 244
    philanthropic migration, 3, 70, 77, 90–1
    seasonal migration, 4
    settlement, 51, 62, 70, 73, 84, 140, 193–201, 259, 261
Canada Company, 51, 104, 197
Canadian Pacific Railway (CPR), 198
Candlish, Revd Dr Robert, 28
cannibalism, 99
Cape Fear Valley, 28, 173
Carlyle, Thomas, 107, 159, 160
Cawnpore (Kanpur), 109
chain migration, 5, 6, 13, 30–1, 62, 69, 140, 202, 251
Charleston, 119, 120
Chesapeake, 136, 175–6
City of Glasgow Bank, 51
climate, 12, 47, 98, 104, 190, 226, 250
Coats, J. & P., 183–4
Cobbett, William, 158
Cody, William (Buffalo Bill), 11, 102–3
Cohen, Anthony, 24–6
Convict Transportation Registers, 242
convicts, 13, 240–2

Cook, Captain James, 99
Copway, G. (Ka-ge-ga-gah-Bowh), 102
Cossar, Dr G. C., 91, 201
Craig, Cairns, 17
Cree, 9, 99
Culloden, 5, 159
cultural assimilation, 31, 160
Curtin, John, 21

Darien, 1, 172–3, 222
Daunton, Martin, 95
Denmark, 6, 7, 58, 59
diaspora, concept, 1, 4–9, 16–31, 38–9, 63–4, 74, 128, 133, 146, 156
'"diaspora" diaspora', 17
Diasporama, 22
diasporic action, 1, 6, 18, 22, 29, 38, 73, 74, 129, 153, 156–7, 160, 253
Dinnie, Donald, 127
Dow, Neal, 82
Dundee, 38, 43, 52, 78, 101, 144, 166, 180, 184, 207, 216, 257
    jute, 10
Dundee (Illinois), 180, 228
Dunedin, 27, 116, 117, 122, 126, 143, 239, 245
Dutch Republic, 7, 8

East India Company (EIC), 30, 104, 109, 134, 136–7, 159, 215, 222, 224, 226–8, 230–1, 235, 239
Ellis Island, 86
emigrant guides, 45, 92, 104–7, 109
Empire, 24, 28, 29, 107, 159, 160–1, 199, 204, 209, 214–15, 217, 222–4, 242, 247
    diaspora, 4
    migration, 22, 24, 50, 88, 199, 200–1, 247
    slavery, 20–1
    soldiers, 140, 161, 214–15, 217, 242
    trade, 13, 48, 50, 134, 161, 190, 204, 213, 222, 260
Empire Settlement Act (1922), 20, 139, 200–1, 251
England, 1, 2, 5, 6, 8, 44, 46, 51, 57, 64, 73, 101–2, 107, 137, 153–67, 179, 208, 209
    migration, 10, 12, 18–19, 56, 58–61, 65, 68, 73–4, 137, 241, 248
    population, 41–2, 51–2, 57, 64, 66, 71
Enlightenment, 104, 110, 160, 176–9, 185, 205
'enterprising Scot', 13, 189, 222, 249
Espuela Cattle Company, 184
ethnic boundaries, 3, 10–11, 23, 38, 158, 164, 253

European migration, 7–10, 12, 20–2, 25, 44, 46, 50–3, 57–9, 61, 68, 70–1, 78, 95–6, 99, 104–10, 133, 142, 171, 175, 184, 189, 192, 195, 201, 207, 224, 234, 242

famine, 5, 44, 47–8, 62, 66, 135, 159, 164, 248
Farr, William, 59
Flying Scotsman, 142, 145, 163
'forced migration', 1, 5, 8–9, 18, 20, 24–5, 30, 47, 74, 108, 111, 133, 137
foster families, 91
France, 6–7, 22, 26, 43, 52, 57–9, 179
Francis, Daniel, 108
fur trade, 9, 13, 188, 189–93, 201

Gaelic, 3, 27–8, 83, 99–100, 106, 107, 116, 195, 250
Galt, John, 51, 104, 197, 261
gender, 16, 27–8, 61, 62, 69–71, 88, 106, 116, 245
Gibson, G. R., 132
Glasgow, 3, 5, 11–12, 31, 40, 43, 48, 51–2, 63, 79, 81, 96, 99–103, 106, 132, 138, 143–4, 154, 162, 175, 176–80, 196, 201, 216, 228, 229, 242, 245, 257
Glasgow Missionary Society, 208, 210–11
gold, 9, 11, 14, 30, 58, 68, 82, 87, 98, 101, 143, 183, 204, 215–16
Goldie, Hugh, 210
Good, James, 77, 81
Grant, James, 137–9, 161
Grant, John, 161
Great Yarmouth, 163
Greenock Ladies' Overseas Missionary Association, 210
Group Settlement Scheme, 251
Guelph, 261
gypsies, 21

haggis, 3, 114, 124, 125
Halpern, Rick, 95
'hamefarers', 145
Hardie, Keir, 217
Harper, Marjory, 84, 164
Hector, 194
Highland Society of Scotland, 79, 164
Hobson, William, 243
Hogarth, William, 159
homecoming, 2, 29, 144–5, 201
homeland, 2–5, 10, 17–21, 26, 29–31, 37–9, 47, 95, 108, 116, 125, 128, 132, 137, 140, 146, 153, 176, 217, 235, 253, 259
homesickness, 5, 18, 86
Hong Kong, 114, 124, 223, 230, 232–3, 258

Hongkong and Shanghai Banking Corporation (HSBC), 233
Hornsby, Stephen J., 68–9
Howison, John, 104–6
Hudson's Bay Company (HBC), 9, 11, 30, 69, 96, 108, 188–90, 193, 201

identity, 2–3, 26–8, 31, 124, 128, 145–7, 160–1, 198, 200, 214
illegal immigrants, 17, 180
Imaginary Indian, 108
imagined community, 22, 26, 38–9, 114
indentured migration, 4, 24, 30, 74, 89, 174–5, 194
India, 11–12, 21, 23, 30, 109, 115, 133–9, 140, 205, 210, 217, 222–35, 242–3
indigenous peoples, 9, 11, 25, 95–111, 189
Ireland, 1, 2, 8, 10, 12, 22, 41, 42, 52, 57, 58, 59, 62, 71, 73–4, 133, 137, 153–67
Iroquois, 99

Jacobites, 8–10, 173–4
Jamaica, 210, 259
Jardine, Matheson & Co., 13, 24, 134, 228, 230–4
Jardine, William, 134–5, 223, 231, 258
Jewish diaspora, 5, 20, 23, 26
Johnson, Samuel, 154, 158, 171

Kanpur, 109
Kat River rebellion, 109
Killarney (Canada), 85, 199
Kirkcaldy, 85, 257
Knox, Robert, 110

Lipton, Thomas, 228
Lithuania, 7, 8
Livingstone, David, 13, 204, 207–9, 213
Livingstone, Sir Thomas, 243
Livingstonia, 212
London (England), 5, 8, 12, 13, 26, 53, 63, 78, 101, 116–18, 123, 136–7, 142, 143, 153–7, 161–6, 205–6, 224 227, 231, 251, 258, 261
London Missionary Society, 208, 211
London Scottish Corporation, 123
Los Angeles Star, 98
Lowestoft, 163

McCalla, Douglas, 189
McCormack, Patricia, 100
McCrae, Col. John, 38
MacDonald, Alexander, 97–8
MacDonald, Donald, 96

MacDougall, Robert, 106–7
McGilvary, George, 137, 224
McHutcheson, William, 143
MacIntyre, Myrtle, 132
Mackenzie, Alexander, 96, 192
Mackenzie, Donald, 99
MacKenzie, John M., 210–11, 217
Mackenzie, Murdo, 184
Mackillop, Andrew, 136
McLean, Donald, 97
McLeod, Revd Norman, 31
Macquarie, Lachlan, 242
Magersfontein, battle of, 214
Malawi, 212–13
Malloch (Mallet), David, 158
Malthus, Revd Thomas, 10, 39–40, 44, 47, 80
Maori, 96–100, 108, 146, 242–3
Matador Land and Cattle Company, 184
Matheson, James, 134–5, 223
mechanics institute, 31, 129
Métis, 100–1, 108
Mill, James, 160
Mill, John Stuart, 39
Miller, Alfred Jacob, 100–1
Miller, Hugh, 158
missionary activity, 13, 88, 204, 229
Mississauga Indians, 96
Moffat, Robert, 208, 213
Mohawk, 99, 105
Morant Bay Rebellion, 109
Munro, Alice, 37
Munro, Neil Gordon, 100
Munro, Sir Hector, 135, 136, 222, 224, 226

nabobs, 12, 135, 137, 159, 226
Napier, Theodore, 137–9
National Association for the Vindication of Scottish Rights, 138, 214
Native Americans, 11, 99, 100–8, 110, 174
Netherlands, 8, 52, 58, 59
New Lanark, 183
New Settlers League, 144
New South Wales, 51, 240–3, 245–6
New York, 12, 28, 99–100, 114, 118, 125, 132, 171, 173–5, 177–80, 184, 194–5, 233, 258, 261
New York State St Andrew's Society, 118, 119, 120
New Zealand, 1, 3, 13, 20, 25–8, 30–1, 38, 62, 64, 68–9, 72–3, 78, 82–4, 86–7, 96–7, 104, 109, 115–17, 121–7, 137, 141–6, 216, 235, 239, 241–53
New Zealand Company, 245

New Zealand Society of Genealogists, Scottish Interest Group (NZSG), 72, 87, 247
Ngati Apa, 97
North America, 8, 10–11, 13, 20, 26, 28, 57, 70, 78, 99, 114–15, 117, 118, 121–2, 125, 127, 137, 139, 141, 143, 159, 161, 172, 173, 192, 196, 197, 240, 242
North Carolina, 8, 12, 79, 173, 175, 180, 184
North West Company, 99, 190, 192–3, 201
Northern Ireland, 2, 29, 42
Norway, 7, 8, 57, 58, 59
Norwich Scots Society, 162
Nova Scotia, 31, 69, 110, 194–5, 198

Oamaru Caledonian Society, 116
odyssey migrants, 30, 74
Ojibbeway, 11, 102
opium trade, 13, 134, 231–3, 258
Orange Free State, 214, 216
Orange Order, 31
Order of the Scottish Clans, 116, 122
Orkney, 9, 11, 25, 28, 31, 69, 99, 190, 201, 202
Otago, 14, 28, 62, 68, 72, 116–17, 122, 143, 150, 243, 245, 246, 250, 261

Paisley, 10, 77, 183, 196, 257
Park, Mungo, 13, 204
Passenger Acts, 64, 80, 195
pedlars, 6–8
Perth Caledonian Society, 125
Perth Library and Antiquarian Society, 99
philanthropic migration, 30
Pinkerton, Allan, 180–1
Pocock, J. G. A., 6
Poland, 7, 8, 26, 58, 62
Pooley, Colin, 61, 63
Port Phillip, 244, 250
Porter, Jane, 37, 159
Portneuf spongeware, 100
Princeton University, 12, 25, 177, 258
Prussia, 7
'pull' and 'push' factors, 9, 26, 28–9, 67, 68, 85, 139, 154, 167, 216, 244–6

Quarrier, William, 30, 89, 90, 92, 199, 202
Quebec, 22, 28, 69, 198

Rae, John, 9, 99
Ramsay, David, 98
Rand, the, 137, 204, 215, 216, 217
Ravenstein, E. G., 10, 58–64, 69
Red River, 193, 196

Register of Emigrants, 174
Reid, Hugo, 98
return migration, 12, 29, 63, 66, 74, 132–47
Rhodes, Cecil, 212, 213, 215
roots tourism, 12, 133, 141–7
Royal Scottish Corporation, 118, 164
Russia, 8, 58, 262

Safran, William, 25
St Andrew's Day, 114–15, 122–4, 128, 165, 222
St Andrew's societies, 11, 27, 115, 117–22, 125, 164
St Andrew's Society of St John, 121
St George's Day, 115
St Patrick's Day, 115
Saltcoats (Canada), 85, 199
Salvation Army, 91, 199
'Scotch Flats', 156
Scots and others, 96, 99, 110
Scots Charitable Society of Boston, 11, 118
Scott, Sir Walter, 37, 114, 154, 160, 208
Scottish American Trust, 51
Scottish Australian Company in New South Wales, 51
Scottish Canadian, 188
Scottish Government, 9, 29, 145
Scottish Missionary Society, 208
Scottishness, 2–3, 31, 125, 139, 214, 235
seasonal migration, 4, 18, 40, 43, 61
Selkirk, Earl of, 13, 30, 193, 195–6
Sellar, Patrick, 47
settler settlements, 30
sheep, 47, 82, 194, 259
'Sheriff Lobey Dosser', 103, 185
Shetland, 25, 145, 163, 193, 250
Singapore, 13, 114, 228, 230, 235
Sketches of Upper Canada, 104
Skottehandelen, 8
Skye, 30, 43, 48, 80, 171
slave trade, 12–13, 20, 82, 107, 172–3, 176, 180, 205–8, 212, 218, 259
Slessor, Mary, 13, 88, 210–11
sojourners, 4, 13, 29, 74, 132–3, 135–6, 146, 218, 258
soldiers, 6–8, 12–13, 30, 62, 82, 99, 103, 133, 139, 140–1, 147, 172–4, 184, 202
Sons of Scotland associations, 123, 128
South Africa, 30, 68, 109, 115, 121–2, 125–6, 137, 139, 141, 209, 213–18
South America, 25, 57, 206

Southland, 28, 68, 246
Spain, 7, 8, 57, 58, 59, 172
Stanley, Henry Morton, 204
steamships, 11, 25, 50, 63, 78–9, 80, 92, 101, 142, 199
step migration, 6, 60
Stewart, Sir William Drummond, 100–1
Sunderland Burns Club, 164–5, 262
Swan Land and Cattle Company, 184
Sweden, 7, 8, 58, 59
Szasz, Ferenc Morton, 97

tattooing, 98
temporary migrants, 5, 30, 40, 156
Thirty Years War, 7, 133
Tippoo Sahib, 224–5
tobacco, 48, 79, 96, 98, 106, 136, 175–6, 205
transnational, 6, 23, 26–7, 133, 141
transplanted communities, 31, 37, 129
trappers, 100, 104, 189
Treaty of Waitangi, 243, 245
Turnbull, Jane, 61, 63
'twa lands', 37–53, 55, 185

United Tribes of New Zealand, 243
Upper Canada, 31, 62, 70, 104, 140, 193, 196, 202

Van Diemen's land, 240, 241, 244
victim diaspora, 1, 5, 20, 24, 30
Victoria, Queen, 101, 102, 123, 142, 154, 159
Victorian Scottish Union, 118, 144
Vogel, Julius, 63, 246

wages, 44, 46, 49, 50, 53, 61, 85, 86, 153, 166–7, 190, 258
Waikato War, 109
Waipu, 31
Wales, 10, 12, 41, 42, 46, 52, 57–9, 64, 65, 68, 71, 74, 153–7, 166
Walking Rai, 101
Wallace, William, 114
Withers, Charles, 61, 293
Witherspoon, John, 12, 176–8, 185

Xhosa, 110, 210–11
Xhosaland, 211

Yarmouth, 158
Young, Douglas, 132